Fifth Edition

THE THEORY AND PRACTICE OF INTERNATIONAL RELATIONS

Edited by

Fred A. Sondermann
The Colorado College

David S. McLellan
Miami University

William C. Olson
Rockefeller Foundation

Prentice-Hall, Inc., Englewood Cliffs, N.J.   07632

Library of Congress Cataloging in Publication Data

SONDERMANN, FRED A   comp.
    The theory and practice of international relations.

    Includes bibliographical references.
    1. International relations—Addresses, essays,
lectures.   I. McLellan, David S.   II. Olson, William C.
III. Title.
JX1395.S623 1979   327   78-26774
ISBN 0-13-914507-9

© 1979, 1974, 1970, 1966, 1960 by Prentice-Hall, Inc., Englewood Cliffs, N.J. 07632

*All rights reserved. No part of this book
may be reproduced in any form or
by any means without permission in writing
from the publisher.*

Printed in the United States of America

10   9   8   7   6   5   4   3

Editorial/production supervision
and interior design by Joyce Turner
Cover design by Jorge Hernandez Porto
Manufacturing buyer: Harry P. Baisley

Prentice-Hall International, Inc., *London*
Prentice-Hall of Australia Pty. Limited, *Sydney*
Prentice-Hall of Canada, Ltd., *Toronto*
Prentice-Hall of India Private Limited, *New Delhi*
Prentice-Hall of Japan, Inc., *Tokyo*
Prentice-Hall of Southeast Asia Pte. Ltd., *Singapore*
Whitehall Books Limited, *Wellington, New Zealand*

We dedicate this book to our children:
Eric, Gary, and Judy Sondermann
Hilary, Michèle, Marjorie, and Eric McLellan
Jon, Peter, and Ann Olson
who grew up between the first and the fifth edition.

Contents

PART TWO:

DECISION-MAKING IN INTERNATIONAL RELATIONS

PART THREE:

TOOLS OF STATECRAFT IN INTERNATIONAL RELATIONS

PART FOUR:

ISSUES IN CONTEMPORARY INTERNATIONAL RELATIONS

PART V

PROSPECTS FOR WORLD ORDER IN THE 1980s

Preface

Like the earlier four editions, the present volume is designed primarily to meet the needs of the college or university student who is taking a first course in the field of international relations.

We are grateful for the favorable reception the previous four editions of this work have received. The reality of international relations, and the observer's understanding of that reality, change rapidly. Hence, each edition has been substantially different from prior ones, although certain common themes and approaches have endured. The present edition contains only nine articles that appeared in the preceding edition, and has twenty-nine new selections. In addition, the entire Part Four—Issues in Contemporary International Relations—is relatively new.

We have tried to be true to the promise of the title of the book by interweaving the theoretical with the practical aspects of international relations. At the same time, we have been careful not to make this a book on "current events" that, by definition, would only be current and would not recur in their precise form. In our judgment, it is essential to have a conceptual framework within which current events can be organized, viewed, and understood.

The book is an invitation to the thoughtful student to engage with us, and with the distinguished contributors to this volume, in an effort to organize the massive and complex raw material of international relations—the countless events, occurrences, and happenings that crowd our consciousness.

We express our gratitude to many colleagues across the country who have given us the benefit of their views on earlier editions, and who have suggested what to stress and what to avoid in this one. Our student's reactions have given us valuable clues as to what material is most useful to them. While we have tried to take into account many of these ideas and suggestions, the final responsibility for choice is, of course, ours.

Dr. Olson was unable, due to other commitments, to participate as actively in the preparation of the current volume as he had in that of prior editions. Still, his continued association with the volume is appreciated and is expressed by his listing as co-editor.

It is now nearly three decades since we, the co-authors and co-editors of this book, were graduate students at Yale University. Just as we are indebted to the teachers who introduced us to the subject matter, so we are indebted to the generation and more, of students we have taught at the Colorado College, the University of California at Riverside, Pomona College, and Miami University. They have stimulated our continuing efforts to master the intractable problems of this great and often tragic field of human activity.

Our colleague and co-editor, Fred Sondermann, passed away October 26, 1978 as this manuscript was in the process of publication. Fred continued to teach and work to the very end. He spent part of his last day correcting page proofs. This book bears the imprint of Fred's belief that the teaching of international relations must be grounded in theoretical knowledge made vital through its application to the issues of the times in which we live.

Part One

THE PARTICIPANTS
IN THE
INTERNATIONAL SYSTEM

I

Nationalism
and the
Nation-State

Despite spectacular shifts as well as routine adjustments in the configuration of world politics in recent years, the basic unit in international relations still remains the national state. Its designation as the most fundamental entity in contemporary world politics does not imply, however, that this is the only basic unit available to anyone seriously endeavoring to make sense out of the politically confusing global environment in which we live. One could, for example, decide instead to focus upon organizations within states, such as the most powerful political movements and interest groups, both within and outside the formal governmental structure, which comprise the political entity to which we attach the shorthand label "nation-state." Or one could even focus on individuals, some of whom (as the wave of international terrorism shows) exert considerable influence upon the course of events, both for good and for evil.

On the other hand, one might concentrate upon certain international, supranational or other-than-national bodies, such as world organizations (both public and private) which have made and continue to make an impact upon world affairs. Movements such as Zionism and institutions such as the

Catholic Church, international labor unions, multilateral corporations or professional organizations—and literally hundreds of others—all participate in and to some degree alter the character of international relations. The selection in this chapter by the late Arnold Wolfers takes many of these options into account. Concentrating upon one of them—the state and its government—does not render the others irrelevant, as the remainder of this book will make quite apparent. The state is the central entity simply because it is, at this stage of human history, where most power is centered. But it has been different in the past, and it is bound to be different again in the future.

To understand the nation-state, one must begin by making some important distinctions, the first of which is the difference between the two elements, "nation" and "state."

The term *"nation"* is essentially an ethnic one, based upon a common heritage, language, culture, and sense of identity among the people who make up a nation, whereas *"state"* is a legal and territorial expression involving a population politically organized under one government with sovereign rights. Sovereignty refers to the exclusive jurisdiction that a state possesses within its territory and to its freedom to act in international affairs without being subject to the legal control of another state. From a number of perspectives a state may encompass more or less than one nation, just as a nation may or may not possess statehood, but taken together nations and states form the units or bases of power whose interrelationships dominate the international system in which we live. It is the organization of man's activities and loyalties into national communities that gives international relations in our time its distinctive character. This may not have been so in the past, nor is it likely always to remain so, but for present purposes this is the heart of the matter.

A second distinction is between the *state* and the *government*, and can perhaps be explained most easily by observing that while governments come and go frequently, states come and go very infrequently. Normally, analysts of international affairs can depend upon the continued existence of a given state as a politically viable entity with infinitely more assurance than they can depend upon the continued existence of a given government or administration of that state. The old saying "The King is dead; long live the King" emphasized the idea of the continuity of the state, despite a change in its leader. In fact, today most monarchies are gone, but the states which they controlled (France, for example) still exist.

Third, it is most important to distinguish between states as they are organized for purposes of domestic government and internal politics, and states as they are organized for purposes of external relations or foreign policy. Among states, there are very nearly as many varieties of internal organization as there are states themselves. There are federal states and unitary ones, dynastic states and republican ones, democratic states and authoritarian states, totalitarian states and states in which the government performs only very limited functions. Yet it is the outward focus of a state, its ability to organize itself for purposes of conducting external relations, to formulate and pursue external goals, and to enter into engagements with other states that concern those who would understand world politics.

As Professors Enloe and Rejai as well as Professor Connor emphasize in their contributions to this chapter, the ethnic quality of the nation-state is a fundamental fact and one which is too often overlooked.

Many of the new states are artificial entities created in the last century by colonial governments in their rivalry to carve up Africa. They often contain within their boundaries as many as three, four, or more tribes or linguistic-cultural entities. Borders were drawn in such a way as to divide a people, putting part in one European country's colony and part in another's. In Asia, societies have been composed of several different ethnic or religious groups for many centuries (as, for example, in India or Indonesia); but as the central government attempts to exert its control, it makes ethnically and regionally different people conscious of each other as rivals, thereby stimulating severe tensions and even civil wars. Minority nationalism has led to the breakup of Pakistan (Bangladesh) and the attempted breakup of Nigeria (Biafra). The border wars that have broken out between India and Pakistan, between Ethiopia and Somalia, and between Cambodia and Vietnam are all examples of the unsettled relationship of nationalism to government in many countries of the Third World. These conditions contribute markedly to the tension and instability of the modern era, not only because of the breakdown of peace and order, but because the superpowers are often drawn into choosing sides in these contests, with dangerous and costly implications for world peace and security. As Walker Connor points out in his article in this chapter, it is one of the great dilemmas of the modern world that many governments still lack the means of establishing their authority peacefully, because they are not regarded as legitimate by some part of their population or because they cannot meet the economic needs fast enough to allay the fear and suspicion that different groups have for one another. But it would not do to say that minority nationalism exists only in the Third World; the examples of Quebec, Ulster, Scotland, and Wales all show that minority nationalism is a powerful force in developed countries as well.

Most students of the state, taken as the basic form of political organization, agree that there are some generally recognized attributes which characterize this particular form of human organization. First of all, a state must possess a territorial base. It must be somewhere on the map. The dimensions of that base are fairly irrelevant: Luxembourg is just as much a state as is the People's Republic of China. There are certain units, such as Lichtenstein, Andorra or the Maldive Islands, whose status remains somewhat uncertain and they are sometimes grouped under the label of "mini-states." This particular quality of a state implies that its territory is defined, that it is circumscribed, and that within it the government of the state has complete jurisdiction.

Another attribute of a state is that it must have a government—one that is capable of governing its people and to some degree meeting their basic needs, capable of entering into international commitments, and capable of abiding by the obligations that it has incurred. The specific form of the government is of less importance to the student of international relations than the effect that form may have on the functioning of the government in the conduct of its foreign relations. What is primarily important is that the government must have the loyalty and support of significant portions of the population, whether maintained by democratic or authoritarian means, in order to govern effectively.

A third characteristic of a state, obviously, is that it have a population. Again, as in the case of territory, there is no clearly defined lower (or upper) limit to a state's population. Populations range from a few thousand such as Tonga or Malta to nearly a billion in China.

A final aspect of statehood is sovereignty. To understand this complex concept, one must first note that the contemporary state system dates roughly from the end of the Thirty Year's War, which ended with the Peace of Westphalia in 1648. The temporal rulers of England, France, the German Reformation states, as well as the lesser princes and potentates of Europe, taking advantage of the anarchy produced by the religious wars, had assumed and kept authority within their respective territorial domains. Earlier they had not only been obliged to bow to the authority of the Pope in religious affairs and to the Emperor of the defunct Holy Roman Empire in secular matters, but they had had to put up with the challenge of powerful feudal lords within their own kingdoms. Now supreme authority (or sovereignty) came to be identified with the state, whose rights, independence, and power derived from what John Herz calls its "territoriality."[1]

Once established, sovereignty connoted the right of each state to utilize the strength of its people and its resources in whatever way it wished, without regard for any political superior, either inside or outside the national territory. This transformation created a world of sovereign, independent states theoretically equal but varying widely in real power. Each depended for its survival upon balancing its own resources and ingenuity with the constellation of forces existing outside its own boundaries.

From the middle of the seventeenth century on, then, individual security, diplomacy, international law, war, commerce, the development of culture and indeed of civilization itself would be influenced in their form and content by the nation-state, as the highest sovereign political entity.

[1]John Herz, "The Rise and Demise of the Territorial State," *World Politics*, 9 (1957), 473.

In its fundamentals that system of nation-states, now extended to the far corners of the earth, prevails right down to the present day. As Professor Connor points out, there are more than 130 such states on the world stage today,[2] a rapidly increasing number of them having emerged in the present century. Just before World War I, there were only about sixty-three independent countries in the world, and on the eve of World War II the number had increased to seventy. Subnational movements may produce even more states as large states break up, as in the case of Bangladesh's separation from Pakistan. At the same time, new states may result from the union of smaller ones, as in the case of the amalgamation of Tanganyika and Zanzibar into Tanzania. Over a hundred states lie completely in the Northern Hemisphere; eleven lie athwart the equator, and less than twenty lie completely in the Southern Hemisphere. Just under sixty countries lie completely in the tropics, while nearly fifty lie completely in temperate zones, the remainder straddling these geographic/climatic zones. About twenty states are insular. While almost thirty are landlocked, more than eighty face one or more bodies of water leading to the open ocean.

It would be a mistake, however, for the student of international relations to conclude from all this that the world is made up of completely independent political bodies, moving about, as it were, on the table of world action like so many billiard balls, changing direction as they bounce off each other but remaining internally unchanged. If there is a fundamental new trend in world politics it is that clear divisions between nation-states are breaking down, without so far destroying the integrity of the system.[3] There are two primary indicators of this breakdown; one is the increasing ability of groups and even individuals within states to influence and even change the policies of governments toward one another, often apparently against the will of those governments. The other is the fact that transnational forces (those which operate across national boundaries) are becoming more powerful, even though they do not as yet threaten the existence or continuation of the independent-state system. Connor, in his treatment of the building up and tearing down of nations, and Wolfers, in delineating the more actors in world politics, allude to these two phenomena.

During the long period in which the international system afforded at least the major powers an opportunity to develop in comparative peace and prosperity, the nation-state performed a timely and generally constructive function. With the coming of the twentieth century, however, certain trends which had already begun to undermine the principle of territorial impenetrability, which underlay the ability of each state to exist alongside similar

---

[2] In fact, by now the number is closer to 150 or 160.

[3] Hans Morgenthau, a leading authority on politics among nations, has argued that the nation-state is already obsolete, citing the absence of many of its characteristics in the new states which have emerged in the past half-century. See *Truth and Power, Essays of a Decade, 1960–70* (New York: Praeger Publishers, Inc., 1970), p. 274.

powers, became more pronounced, particularly after the Second World War. These trends reflect the difficulties inherent in the application of the principle of self-determination, in the intensified development of techniques and instruments of ideological-political interpretation, in growing economic interdependence, and in the accelerated development of weapons of mass destruction.

It remains to be seen whether these trends portend an end of the nation-state system as the world has known it in its various transmutations over the past three hundred or more years. For the moment, however, the system based upon the interrelationships of nation-states continues, in its often frightening way, to prevail if not to flourish.

1   The Actors in International Politics

Arnold Wolfers

The late Arnold Wolfers was for many years Sterling Professor of International Relations at Yale University.

Theorizing about almost any feature of international politics soon becomes entangled in a web of controversy. Even the identity of the "actors"—those who properly can be said to perform on the international stage—is a matter of dispute which raises not unimportant problems for the analyst, for the practitioner of foreign policy, and for the public. If the nation-states are seen as the sole actors, moving or moved like a set of chess figures in a highly abstract game, one may lose sight of the human beings for whom and by whom the game is supposed to be played. If, on the other hand, one sees only the mass of individual human beings of whom mankind is composed, the power game of states tends to appear as an inhuman interference with the lives of ordinary people. . . .

Until quite recently, the states-as-the-sole-actors approach to international politics was so firmly entrenched that it may be called the traditional approach. After the Napoleonic wars, nation-states, particularly the European "great powers," as they were called, replaced

This selection appeared first in Wm. T.R. Fox, ed., Theoretical Aspects of International Relations *(Notre Dame: University of Notre Dame Press, 1959). It is reprinted by permission of the publisher.*

the image of the princes or kings of former centuries as the sovereign, independent, single-minded actors, the movers of world events. To nation-states were ascribed the acts that accounted for changes in the distribution of power, for alignments and counter-alignments, for expansion and colonial conquest, for war and peace—the chief events in international affairs whenever a multitude of sovereigns have been in contact with one another. The concept of a multistate system composed of entities of strikingly similar character and behavior appeared realistic to observers and analysts.

Starting in the period between the two world wars and gaining momentum after World War II, a reaction set in against the traditional states-as-actors approach. This reaction has taken two distinct forms: one new theory has placed individual human beings in the center of the scene that had been reserved previously to the nation-states; the second theory emphasized the existence side by side with the state, of other corporate actors, especially international organizations. Both reactions have led to valuable new insights and deeper understanding of the dynamics of world politics, but they are in fact supplements to the traditional theory rather than substitutes for it.

I

The individuals-as-actors approach first appeared in the minds-of-men theory of international politics. It was soon to be followed by the decision-making approach which was a reaction against tradition from another angle. Both demanded that attention be focused on individual human beings as actors. Together, the new schools of thought represent a swing of the pendulum from an extreme "state" emphasis to an equally extreme emphasis on the men who act for states. These new approaches must be credited with humanizing international politics by attracting attention to the human element minimized in the traditional approach. It was the aim of the new theories to replace the abstract notion of the state with the living realities of human minds, wills, and hearts. But the result, on the whole, was to substitute one set of abstractions for another because, in politics, it is also an abstraction to examine the individual apart from the corporate bodies by means of which he acts politically. . . .

The new approach's criticism of the states-as-actors theory turns mainly on the distinction between genuine human needs and what appear to be the a-human interests of the state. There are those who claim that too great an emphasis on the role of states and their interests in power, prestige, territory, and the like, will divert political action from the satisfaction of the common man's real needs and desires to the service of the few who can parade their interests as those of the nation. Is it credible they ask, that Egyptian fellaheen and Pakistani peasants, desperately in need of food, shelter, and improved conditions of health, should, as their governments contend, yearn for the satisfaction of such "state interests" as the liquidation of Israel or the unification of

Kashmir under Pakistani rule, when the pursuit of such interests requires great sacrifices of the masses? Does the state not take on the character of an a-human monster to whom dignity is given gratuitously, if it is regarded as an actor in its own right, at liberty to place its interests above those of the human beings who compose it?

Still, one may question whether the quest for national security and power, for national independence, aggrandizement, or unification is any less "human"—and therefore necessarily less appealing to the masses —than the quest for food, shelter, comfort, and happiness. Actually, the minds-of-men theory and its humanization of international politics must be carried several steps further than its exponents have gone. Any analysis of the dynamics of international politics must take into account the fact that man is more than a private individual concerned only with his personal welfare or with the welfare of his family. Often enough he is ready to compromise his own well-being for the benefit of the groups and organizations with which he identifies himself. Psychologically, nothing is more striking today than the way in which men in almost every part of the globe have come to value those possessions upon which independent national statehood depends, with the result that men, in their public capacity as citizens of a state, are willing to make the most sweeping sacrifices of their own well-being as private individuals in the interest of their nation. Therefore, state interests are indeed human interests—in fact, the chief source of political motivation today.

One can argue that a nationalistic age has distorted men's pattern of values or that the manipulators of public opinion are chiefly responsible for this distortion. Nevertheless, the fact remains that a sufficient number of men identify themselves with their state or nation to justify and render possible governmental action in the name of state interests. . . .

One wonders today, for instance, whether the bulk of the population in countries facing the risks of nuclear war will long continue to regard as vital, and thus worthy of defense in war, all the state interests they were once ready to place in this category. Signs point to the likelihood that the masses, who have gained greater influence as behind-the-scenes actors, will push for greater restraints upon the pursuit of those state interests—such as national security or prestige—that are seen to conflict with private welfare needs. Such a development will indicate not that individuals are suddenly taking over the function formerly performed by states, but rather that larger bodies of individuals are sharing the role once reserved to the members of small elites who formerly decided what the "national interest" demanded or justified. It always would have been possible to interpret international politics through an examination of the individuals responsible for state action: the "humanizing" approach. But it must be recognized that in the course of the present century the number of these individuals has been greatly enlarged.

The failure to see man in his double capacity, as a private individual and as a political being, accounts for an illusion common among the more idealistic exponents of the minds-of-men approach. They assume that better understanding between peoples opens the safest path to peace, while Dunn has pointed out that peoples who know and understand each other perfectly may nevertheless become involved in war.[1] The explanation for this apparent paradox is not hard to find, provided one thinks in terms of the whole man rather than in terms solely of his private aims and desires. If one were in contact with the people of the Soviet Union today, one probably would find them preoccupied with the tasks of furthering their personal welfare, happiness, and social advancement in much the same way as any similar group of people in the United States. The discovery of such similarities of interest and aspiration tends to arouse a sense of sympathetic understanding; it certainly does not provoke fear or serve to justify policies based on the expectation of international conflict. As a result, people who think exclusively in terms of private individuals and who experience harmonious relationships with citizens of "hostile" countries are inclined to see nothing but unhappy misunderstanding, if not evil, in the way governments act toward one another.

Yet, the fact that Americans and Russians, in much the same fashion, pursue the same goals when acting as private individuals, gives no indication of their aims as citizens who are concerned with the national interests of their respective countries. Here there is far less chance that their aims will be found to be in harmony. Better understanding may in fact reveal the incompatibility of their respective objectives. . . .

It is therefore clear that an exclusive minds-of-men approach with its concentration on the motives and activities of individual actors is inadequate and misleading. It is undeniable that men alone, and not states, are capable of desires and intentions, preferences and feelings of friendship or hatred; men, not states, can be tempted or provoked, can overestimate or underestimate their own country's power relative to the power of other states, and can establish the goals of national policy and sacrifices consistent with national security. However, al-

[1] *War and the Minds of Men*, (New York: Harper & Row, 1950, p. 7.

though nothing can happen in the world arena unless something happens inside the minds and hearts of scores of men, psychological events are not the whole stuff out of which international politics is formed. If they were, the political scientist would have to leave the field to the psychologist.

The minds-of-men approach, while able to render important and indispensable services to a comprehensive theory of international politics, cannot do justice to all the essential events that fill the international arena. There can be no "state behavior" except as the term is used to describe the combined behavior of individual human beings organized into a state. Not only do men act differently when engaged in pursuing what they consider the goals of their "national selves," but they are able to act as they do only because of the power and influence generated by their nations organized as corporate bodies. Therefore, only when attention is focused on states, rather than on individuals, can light be thrown on the goals pursued and means employed in the name of nations and on the relationships of conflict or co-operation, of power competition or alignment that characterize international politics. . . .

The decision-making approach naturally appeals to the historian who is interested in identifying the unique aspects of past events, which necessitates consideration of all conceivable variables, including the personal traits of particular human actors. But it poses a serious problem for the theorist whose task is not to establish the uniqueness of events but rather to gain a generalized knowledge of behavior in international politics, which means knowledge on a relatively high level of abstraction. Should he not, therefore, abstract from the personal predispositions of those who are instrumental in the making of decisions? If his use of the deductive method, as described earlier, permits him to formulate expectations of probable state behavior that prove relatively accurate, why should he take a long, effort-consuming "detour" of the kind required by the decision-making approach and conduct an extensive empirical investigation into the motivations of Stimson or a Truman? Could it be that use of the A-bomb against Japan was predictable on the ground that "states tend to use their most powerful weapons," or American intervention in Korea by the proposition that "no great power, if it can help it, will permit its chief opponent to change the distribution of power by the unilateral use of military force"?

At first glance, it would seem as if the actual performance of a particular state could conform only by sheer coincidence with expectations based on extremely crude generalizations about the way states tend to act under given circumstances. Why should the particular individuals responsible for United States policy in 1945 or 1950, men differing from others by a multitude of psychological features—motivations, idiosyncrasies, preferences, temperament—reach decisions of the kind the states-as-actors theory deduces from its abstract model? Yet the correlation in many instances between the predictions of theory and actual behavior is not accidental. Such correlation may be expected if two assumptions on which the theory rests are justified by the circumstances prevailing in the real world.

There is, first, the assumption that all men acting for states share the same universal traits of human nature. Specifically, these men are expected to place exceedingly high value on the so-called possessions of the nation—above all, on national survival, national independence, and territorial integrity—and to react in fear against any threats to these possessions. It is also assumed that they share a strong inclination to profit from opportunities for acquisition or reacquisition of cherished national possessions, with national power as the chief means of preserving or acquiring national values. To the extent to which these traits are shared and have a decisive effect on the actions or reactions of statesmen and peoples, they create conformity as if by a kind of inner compulsion.

The second assumption concerns the environment in which governments are required to act. If it is true that the anarchical multistate system creates a condition of constant danger to national core possessions —specifically, to national survival—and, at the same time, provides frequent opportunity for new acquisitions, the actors can be said to act under external compulsion rather than in accordance with their preferences.

It is easy to see that both these sweep-ing assumptions are not the products of unrealistic fantasies. Attachment to posses-sions, fear, and ambition—although they vary in degree from man to man and from people to people—can properly be called "general traits of human nature," which are likely to operate with particular strength in men who hold positions of authority and national responsibility. That the condition of multiple sovereignty is one in which states "live dangerously" is also a matter of common experience and knowledge. The real question is whether internal and external pressures are strong enough everywhere and at all times to transform the actors into something like automatons lacking all freedom of choice. Certainly, to the degree that these com-pulsions exist in the real world, the psycho-logical peculiarities of the actors are deprived of the opportunity to express themselves and therefore can be discounted as irrelevant to an analysis of international politics.

2 Nation-States and State-Nations

Mostafa Rejai & Cynthia H. Enloe

Professor Rejai teaches at Miami University, Oxford, Ohio; Professor Enloe teaches at Clark University in Worcester, Massachusetts.

Nationalism takes a variety of forms and carries with it a variety of political consequences. A major variable distinguishing one pattern of nationalism from another has been the interplay between "nation" and "state." At bottom, this is a relationship between national identity and political autonomy, between national integration and political sovereignty.

In many of the developed countries of the post—World War II world the sense of national identity evolved prior to the crystallization of the structures of political authority. By contrast, in most of the currently underdeveloped, newly independent countries this sequence is reversed: authority and sovereignty have run ahead of self-conscious national identity and cultural integration. To this extent it can be said that Europe produced nation-states, whereas Asia and Africa have produced state-nations.

These two broad patterns of relationships have never been as clear-cut as has been traditionally supposed. Their implications are particularly pertinent for understanding the role of nationalism in political stabilization and economic modernization, as well as its possible role in reshaping the patterns of political control and consolidation. What is called for is an appreciation of the mobilization character of nationalism—specifically, nationalism as the embodiment

This excerpt from "Nation-States and State-Nations," by Mostafa Rejai and Cynthia Enloe reprinted from International Studies Quarterly, *Vol. 13, No. 2 (June 1969), 140–58, by permission of the publisher, Sage Publications, Inc. (Footnotes have been omitted.)*

of at least two types of mobilization that may outstrip one another.

We begin by defining our key terms and then proceed to an examination of the relationships between nation and state, relying on illustrative—and often conflicting—evidence from both the West and the non-West. We realize that any attempt to generalize at such an abstract level as we will be forced to do is fraught with risk and uncertainty. Exceptions and qualifications will be many. Our paper will have served its purpose if it succeeds in provoking further clarification of some of the distinctions among the various patterns of political development.

I

At the most general level, *nationalism* refers to an awareness of membership in a nation (potential or actual), together with a desire to achieve, maintain, and perpetuate the identity, integrity, and prosperity of that nation. At any point in time in a given society this awareness may be shared by a relatively large or a relatively small proportion of the total population. In the latter case there may be evidence of a nationalist movement but not of a "nation" (see below). . . .

For our purposes, we shall define a nation as a relatively large group of people who *feel* that they belong together by virtue of sharing one or more such traits as common language, religion or race, common history or tradition, common set of customs, and common destiny. As a matter of empirical observation, none of these traits may actually exist; the important point is that a people believe that they do. Although the variable of size is necessarily imprecise, it is intended to suggest that a nation is larger than a village, clan, or city-state. . . .

In approaching the subject of nationalism it is analytically useful to distinguish *nationalist ideology* and *nationalist movement*. The former refers to self-conscious attitudes and feelings toward the nation; the latter suggests social and political processes that seek to fulfill these attitudes and feelings. The nationalist movement signifies the action and organization component of nationalism: it refers to an actual historical process, energized and motivated by a set of ideals. Nationalism as an ideology refers to a "state of mind," a psychological condition in which one's highest loyalty is to the nation. It involves a belief in the intrinsic superiority of one's own nation over all other nations. It is worth reiterating that the attributes associated with a nation may or may not be real—the important point is the psychological condition of belief. In short, nationalism, as any other ideology, entails elements of myth.

The nationalist ideology and the nationalist movement may be directed toward creating a new nation, or toward increasing the power, prestige, and status of one that already exists. For convenience's sake, we shall designate the process of nation-building as "formative nationalism," and the process of nation-aggrandizing as "prestige nationalism." If the glorification of a nation spills over its own territorial boundaries, if it entails annexation of other lands or conquest of other countries, then we shall call it "expansive nationalism." Thus the peoples of many parts of Africa and Asia have been involved in a "formative" effort to throw off foreign rule and establish their own "nation"; contemporary nationalism in France is of the prestige variety, and the nationalism of Nazi Germany was motivated by an ambitious attempt to conquer and dominate other peoples. It is of course possible for one type of nationalism to be transformed into another. The German nationalism of the 20th century, for example, may be viewed as a transformation of the relatively more moderate nationalism of the 19th.

"Nation," it is clear, is not the same as "state." The latter refers to an independent and autonomous political structure over a specific territory, with a comprehensive legal system and a sufficient concentration of power to maintain law and order. "State," in other words, is primarily a political-legal concept, whereas "nation" is primarily psycho-cultural. Nation and state may exist independently of one another: a nation may exist without a state, a state may exist without a nation. When the two coincide, when the boundaries of the state are approximately coterminous with those of the nation, the result is a *nation-state*. A nation-state, in other words, is a nation that possesses political sovereignty. It is socially cohesive as well as politically organized and independent.

Nations and states, then, do not necessarily evolve simultaneously; nor is it possible to say, as an inflexible rule, which one comes first. . . .

A further distinction may be drawn between a state that from a chronological point of view merely precedes a nation (as in France) and a state that plays an active role in mobilizing and literally creating a nation (as in most of the developing countries today). In the former case, nationalism tends to be popularly based and cultivated upward toward certain goals; in the latter, it tends to be officially sponsored, cultivated at the top, and filtered downward. . . .

II

Nationalism is a distinctive phenomenon of the 19th century. The development of political thought from the Greek thinkers through Machiavelli, Grotius, Hobbes, and Rousseau is an intellectual prelude to the emergence of nationalism. The ideas of the secular state and political sovereignty had to be wedded to the concept of "mass politics" before nationalism could crystallize. It is the "mass" quality which distinguishes the French Revolution and which implies a pooling of energies and loyalties of an entire citizenry. Overnight, as it were, France—for long a monarchical state—became a nation; and the nation assumed responsibility for the destiny of its citizens, demanding loyalty and devotion in return.

The French Revolution spread the idea that the nation has a right and an identity of its own. Sovereignty was lodged squarely in the nation. The Declaration of the Rights of Man and Citizen (1789) boldly proclaimed that "sovereignty resides essentially in the nation; no body of men, no individual, can exercise authority that does not emanate expressly from it." With the French Revolution, nation and state merged.

The French Revolution idealized the masses at the expense of the clergy, monarchs, princes, and aristocrats. The people, having claimed the nation as their own, set out to abolish special privilege, dispossess the nobility, and confiscate church property. The glorification of the masses is systematically reflected in French nationalist intellectuals, including Jules Michelet, who dedicated his life to "People, Revolution, France." He interpreted the French Revolution as marking the beginning of a new civilization, and Rousseau's teachings as the inception of a new politics. The people, Michelet argued, constitute the motive forces of historical development; the Revolution is their work.

The rise of nationalism coincided with the growth of some democratic ideas and sentiments. "Liberty, Equality, Fraternity" were not accidental slogans of the French Revolution. The middle classes were demanding new rights, including the rights of representation and participation in public affairs. This in turn suggests a relationship between nationalism and industrialism: only industrialism could have produced the new classes which rose to assert their new powers and demand new rights. Indeed, without the advances in transportation, communication, trade, and commerce afforded by the Industrial Revolution, it would not have been possible for modern nations to come into being.

National honor, national self-determination, popular and national sovereignty were inescapable components of the doctrine of nationalism. A nation, it was felt, should choose its own form of government; it should decide for itself the course of action that it wishes to follow. Monarchy, tyranny, and absolutism no longer would be tolerated. Equally remarkable is the fact that all this was seen as a right, not only of France, but of all peoples and nations. Although nationalism would benefit every nation, however, the spreading and propagation of the new order was seen as a special mission of the French people. Michelet, for example, saw France as the center of universal history. The French people would bring enlightenment and freedom to all nations of the world: upon France depended the salvation of mankind. Inspired by the example of France, all peoples were to rise and overthrow privilege and dictatorship. If they refused "Liberty, Equality, Fraternity," the French would take it upon themselves to accomplish this task for them—by military force, if necessary. From early in its beginning, in short, nationalism became associated with messianism, militarism, and war. This war, however, was seen as a new type of conflict which put, not peoples against peoples, but peoples against tyrants and despots.

Militarism and expansionism encouraged the rise of military dictators: the emergence of Napoleon was not happenstance. Napoleonic armies, imbued with the stirring notes of the *Marseillaise,* launched an ambitious policy of conquest beyond the French borders. Nationalism and democracy collapsed into autocratic rule.

Inspired by the French example, the peoples of Europe began to look upon nationalism as a blessing to be enjoyed by all men. At the same time, frightened by French expansionism, they rallied around their respective rulers in armed attempts to curb the "excesses" of French nationalism. War and conquest by one nation intensified the need for national and political unity in other nations.

German nationalism of the 19th century —initially a response to Napoleonic expansionism—departed from its French counterpart. Long before 1789, there had existed among the German principalities a sense of social and cultural unity. The French Revolution intensified this.

Johann Gottfried von Herder (1744—1803) had expounded what in effect might be called a cultural nationalism. He had conceived of humanity as made up of a series of cultures each consisting of a group or a "folk" *(Volk)* with its own tradition, custom, literature, music, language, and even "soul" *(Volksgeist).* To Herder each culture represented natural and organic growth. He used a biological analogy in describing cultural groups as living organisms that are born, grow, and mature. He advocated a comparative "physiognomy" of the peoples of the world.

Herder did not call for the creation of nation-states. For him, nationalism was a romantic conception looking toward humanity rather than states; it was devoid of political imperatives. It was Georg Wilhelm Friedrich Hegel who succeeded in giving Herder's cultural nationalism a firm political grounding. What Hegel had done in theory and philosophy, Otto von Bismarck and Heinrich von Treitschke accomplished in practice.

At the hands of Hegel, the state was turned into a God-like creature capable of commanding the unquestioned loyalty of all Germans as a step toward final unification. The state was seen as the supreme repository of all moral and spiritual values, the supreme object of man's devotion.

Bismarck and Treitschke employed the teachings of Hegel to maximum advantage. Together, the two Prussians propagated the cult of the state as the embodiment of might and power.

The overriding and urgent task was still German unification, but now under Prussian leadership. Bismarck and Treitschke argued that Prussia should constitute the nucleus of a unified Germany, conquering and controlling the smaller principalities. The unification of Italy had preceded and inspired that of Germany. Bismarck and Treitschke watched developments in Italy with great interest and stressed the affinities of the Prussian and Sardinian regimes. They thought, in fact, that the two regimes should collaborate to break French predominance on the Continent.

Bismarck's successes in the war of 1866, in which Prussia fought Austria, Saxony, and most other German principalities, and in the war of 1870 against France, confirmed his (and Treitschke's) belief in Prussia's mission and destiny. The new German Reich, proclaimed by Bismarck on January 18, 1871, was in effect an expanded Prussia. It symbolized the union of militarism and nationalism.

This brief examination of French and German nationalism would seem to indicate that the relationship between "nation" and "state" is a complex one. In Germany, the nation preceded the state; in France, the state preceded the nation. It is of course true that although a united Germany had come into being, the problem of a fully effective nationalism remained unresolved, for the Germans lacked as firm a sense of national unity as the French. Moreover, the nationalism of Germany was state-sponsored and cultivated downward; that of France was popularly based and cultivated upward.

III

In the 20th century, nationalism spread rapidly throughout the non-Western world. The "new nationalism" took place, for the most part, in colonial areas; and it was, in large measure, a reaction against prior Western policies of imperialism and conquest.

Twentieth century non-Western nationalism differs in some respects from its Western counterpart. . . .

Non-Western nationalism is largely a consequence of the spread of Western civilization, that is to say, Western ideas, techniques, and institutions—even though non-Western countries have frequently taken a stance militantly resentful of Westernization. At the same time, the "paradox of colonialism" or "irony of imperialism" refers to the proposition that the colonial powers, by introducing these ideas and institutions, forged the instruments for their own destruction. The colonial peoples, in other words, seized upon these very instruments in their efforts to uproot imperialism. One of the processes running through most non-Western nationalism is an attempt to integrate foreign values and practices without

sacrificing the essential distinctiveness which justifies the practice of colonial peoples calling themselves "nations." Most Western nations did not suffer the traumas of this ordeal in their development. "Integration" has even more profound implications, therefore, in the non-Western nationalist experience.

Non-Western nationalism is, at least initially, a protest movement. The doctrinal and attitudinal content of non-Western nationalism is largely negative, signifying a reaction against foreign domination. Thus Coleman has defined nationalism in Nigeria, for example, as "sentiment and activity opposed to alien control."

A related feature of non-Western nationalism lies in the extremely important role played by the intellectual elite. This is not to suggest that the intellectuals have not played a critical role in all nationalism. But in the non-Western world in particular, nationalism has been almost exclusively the handiwork of the intellectuals. Non-Western intellectuals have in fact served as intermediaries between Western and non-Western cultures.

In the underdeveloped countries, where as a rule the state has preceded the nation, nationalism exerts two kinds of pressures on the political system, pressures not as apparent in the development of European nationalism. First, anticolonial nationalism poses a greater challenge to political legitimacy than did nationalism in the earlier-developing societies. Second, due to the fortunes of timing, nationalism in the postwar countries has been more visibly associated with growth, not just autonomy. The twin pressures of *legitimation* and *growth* have given nationalism in the underdeveloped world its distinctive character. More than was the case in Western Europe in its nationalist heyday, nationalism in 20th century Asia and Africa is being employed to sustain preexistent state authority and to accelerate state-directed modernization.

Throughout most of Africa and Asia the state, with its formal institutions, its explicit codes of law, its fixed territorial jurisdiction, was already in existence when nationalism emerged as a political force. It was colonialism, more than any other single factor, which determined this state-nation sequence: colonialism initially fashioned and entrenched the structures of political authority and then, later, provided the stimulus which provoked the nationalist movements. In other words, not only did the state precede the nation but it played a crucial role in creating and mobilizing it. . . .

The condition of the state in a postcolonial country is roughly analogous to a castle—a repository of rules and orders—which in the past had dominated a territory without actually resting upon it, held up instead by stilts representing coercive superiority, technological and organizational innovation, and indigenous deference. The end of colonial rule either weakened or cut through these supporting stilts, leaving the castle precariously hovering above the ground. The task of the castle's new occupants is to construct a first story or, better, a basement to the castle. Nationalism is the material most commonly employed in this post-independence construction.

This metaphor, if at all valid, implies that in the countries which have gained political autonomy since the mid-1940s nationalism will be cultivated at the top and filtered downward. This process is the reverse of that experienced in the 18th and 19th centuries in France, where nationalism developed from the bottom upward toward the formal institutions which it eventually transformed. . . .

A sense of nationhood which can bind the fragmented society together under the state's authority will have to be of a sort that does not depend heavily on linguistic and other cultural affinities. In addition, the nationalism prevalent in the postcolonial countries will be shaped by the perceived needs of the state. Thus it will be more self-consciously politicized. To be concise, whereas in most of the developed countries states have had cohesive nations corresponding to them, in the developing countries this has been rare.

The first question for the architects of the new nations is what integrative cement can serve as a substitute for cultural affinity. The very mixed success of national language acts (e.g., in India and Malaysia) and state religion establishments (e.g., in Burma) casts doubt on the ability of authorities to create cultural affinities by fiat. Therefore, the substitutes have been most frequently political and economic rather than cultural—even though the national language act may remain on the books for symbolic reasons. . . .

This reliance on economic bonds in lieu of cultural bonds makes modernization crucial to the realization of nationalism in the postcolonial countries. In Europe nationalism spurred modernization; in most of Africa and Asia modernization is looked to as a means of promoting nationalism. In the latter there has been a running parallel to the state-before-nation sequence: the precedence of the modernizing drive before nationhood. . . .

Nationalism is a species of mobilization. It involves the pooling of loyalties, interests, energies, and attentions at the level of community called the nation. Political elites in the new states have been more acutely aware of the mobilization character of nationalism than were their European counterparts. They have been preoccupied, consequently, with the relationship between organization and nationalism, since organization has proved one of the most effective tools for mobilization. Not surprisingly, organization is a downward-directed concept of relating individuals and groups. Thus we come full circle: the state precedes nationalism; nationalism is needed to legitimize the state's authority and to facilitate its expansion; given the disintegrative cultural attributes of the society, the state inclines toward a nationalism defined and promoted at the top; downward-directed nationalism relies on manipulable links which in turn require modernization; because modernization involves the pooling of resources, mobi-lization instruments are given top priority by the state authorities.

The result is that in the state-nations of Africa and Asia nationalism is translated into "nation-building." The prevalence of cultural heterogeneity and the pressures for modernization put a premium on organization and on authoritative guidance. In France the emergence of nationalism was analogous to a maturing personality; in Burma or Nigeria the more appropriate analogy is architectural construction. . . .

3   Nation-Building or Nation-Destroying?

Walker Connor

Walker Connor is Professor of Political Science at the State University of New York at Brockport.

Scholars associated with theories of "nation-building" have tended either to ignore the question of ethnic diversity or to treat the matter of ethnic identity superficially as merely one of a number of minor impediments to effective state-integration. To the degree that ethnic identity is given recognition, it is apt to be as a somewhat unimportant and ephemeral nuisance that will unquestionably give way to a common identity uniting all inhabitants of the state, regardless of ethnic heritage, as modern communication and transportation networks link the state's various parts more closely.

Reprinted from World Politics, *34, no. 3. Copyright © 1972 by Princeton University Press. Footnotes have been omitted. Reprinted by permission.*

Both tendencies are at sharp variance with the facts, and have contributed to the undue optimism that has characterized so much of the literature on "nation-building". . . .

The remarkable lack of coincidence that exists between ethnic and political borders is indicated by the following statistics. 12 (9.1 per cent) can be described as only 12 (9.1 per cent) can be described as essentially homogeneous from an ethnic viewpoint. An additional 25 states (18.9 per cent of the sample) contain an ethnic group accounting for more than 90 per cent of the state's total population, and in still another 25 states the largest element accounts for between 75 and 89 per cent of the population. But in 31 states (23.5 per cent of the total), the largest ethnic element represents only 50 to 74 per cent of the population, and in 39 cases (29.5 per cent of all states) the largest group fails to account for even half of the state's population. Moreover, this portrait of ethnic diversity becomes more vivid when the number of distinct ethnic groups within states is considered. In some instances, the number of groups within a state runs into the hundreds, and in 53 states (40.2 per cent of the total), the population is divided into more than *five* significant groups. Clearly, then, the problem of ethnic diversity is far too ubiquitous to be ignored by the serious scholar of "nation-building," unless he subscribes to the position that ethnic diversity is not a matter for serious concern.

The validity of this position apparently also rests upon one of two propositions. Either loyalty to the ethnic group is self-evidently compatible with loyalty to the state, or, as mentioned earlier, ethnic identification will prove to be of short duration, withering away as modernization progresses. More consideration will be later given to the matter of the two loyalties (i.e., to the ethnic group and to the state), but clearly the two are not naturally harmonious. One need only reflect on the ultimate political dissection of what was once known as the Habsburg Empire, or contemplate the single most important challenge to the political survival of Belgium, Canada, Cyprus, Guyana, Kenya, Nigeria, the Sudan, Yugoslavia, and a number of other multiethnic states. The theoretician of "nation-building" may well contemplate some proposal that he believes will reduce the matter of competing loyalties to manageable proportions (such as confederalism or cultural autonomy); but, if so, his proposal is an important element in his model and should occupy a prominent place in his writing.

As to the assumption that ethnic identity will wither away as the processes collectively known as modernization occur, it is probable that those who hold this premise have been influenced, directly or indirectly, by the writings of Karl Deutsch. It is debatable, however, whether such an opinion concerning the future of ethnic identity can be properly inferred from his works. His perception of the intereffects of what he calls "social mobilization" and of assimilation [i.e., "nation-building," so far as identity is concerned] . . . appears to have undergone significant fluctuations. . . . [His] most recent book provides no brief for those who assume that ethnicity will wane as modernization progresses. The opposite is the case. On the other hand, some of his earlier comments, and particularly those in which he propounded four stages of assimilative growth, could indeed be cited as supporting this school of thought. Regardless of the interpretation one places upon Deutsch, however, the doctrine that modernization dissolves ethnic loyalties can be challenged on purely empirical grounds.

If the processes that comprise modernization led to a lessening of ethnic consciousness in favor of identification with the state, then the number of states troubled by ethnic disharmony would be on the decrease. To the contrary, however, a global survey illustrates that ethnic consciousness is definitely in the ascendency as a political force, and that state borders, as presently delimited, are being increasingly challenged by this trend. And, what is of greater significance, multiethnic states at all levels of modernity have been afflicted. Particularly instructive in this regard is the large proportion of states within the technologically and economically advanced region of Western Europe that have recently been troubled by ethnic unrest. Examples include (1) the problems of Spain with the anti-Castilian activities of the

Basques, the Catalans, and on a lesser level, the Galicians; (2) the animosity indicated by the Swiss toward foreign migrant workers, and the demands of the French-speaking peoples of Berne for political separation from the German-speaking element; (3) the South Tyroleans' dissatisfaction with Italian rule, currently muffled by recent concessions on the part of the Italian Government; (4) evidence of Breton unhappiness with continued French rule; (5) the resurgence of Scottish and Welsh nationalism, the conflict in Northern Ireland, and the wide-scale popularity of anti-immigrant sentiments epitomized in the figure of Enoch Powell—all within the United Kingdom; and (6) the bitter rivalry of the Walloon and Flemish peoples within Belgium. Outside of Europe, the challenge to the concept of a single Canada represented by the Franco-Canadian movements, and the existence of black separatist movements within the United States also bear testimony that even the combination of a lengthy history as a state and a high degree of technological and economic integration does not guarantee immunity against ethnic particularism.

That social mobilization need not lead to a transfer of primary allegiance from the ethnic group to the state is therefore clear. Can we go beyond this to posit an inverse correlation between modernization and the level of ethnic dissonance within multiethnic states? Admittedly, there is a danger of countering the assumption that the processes of modernization lead to cultural assimilation with an opposing iron law of political disintegration which contends that modernization results, of necessity, in increasing demands for ethnic separation. We still do not have sufficient data to justify such an unequivocal contention. Nonetheless, the substantial body of data which is available supports the proposition that mate-

rial increases in . . . social communication and mobilization *tend* to increase cultural awareness and to exacerbate interethnic conflict. Again, the large and growing number of ethnic separatist movements can be cited for substantiation.

There are many statesmen and scholars, however, who would protest this macroanalytical approach because the data cited for support contain a number of former colonies. The inclusion of former dependencies in a list purporting to substantiate a correlation between modernization and ethnicity is improper, they would contend, because ethnic consciousness was deliberately kept alive and encouraged by the colonial overseers as an element in a policy of divide-and-rule. The prevalence of ethnic consciousness and antagonism in these territories is therefore held to be the product of the artificial stimuli of colonial policy. Otherwise, ethnicity would not constitute a serious problem for the new states.

The validity of such a conviction can be tested by contrasting the experience of former colonies with that of industrially retarded, multiethnic states that did not undergo a significant period as a colony. No important distinctions are discernible on this basis. Consider, for example, the cases of Ethiopia and Thailand, both of which have enjoyed very lengthy histories as independent states. Diverse ethnic elements were able to coexist for a lengthy period within each of these states because the states were poorly integrated, and the ethnic minorities therefore had little contact, with either their (mostly theoretic) state-governments or with each other. Until very recent times, then, the situation of the minorities was not unlike the situation of ethnic groups within colonies where the colonial power practiced that very common colonial policy of ruling through the leadership of the various ethnic groups. In all such cases, the conflict between alien rule and the ethnic group's determination to preserve its lifeways was minimized. The governments of these underdeveloped states may well have long desired to make their rule effective throughout their entire territory, but advances in communications and transportation were necessary before a governmental presence could become a pervasive reality in the remote territories of the minorities.

As a result of this new presence, resentment of foreign rule has become an important political force for the first time. In addition, quite aside from the question of who rules, there is the matter of cultural self-preservation. An unintegrated state poses no serious threat to the lifeways of the various ethnic groups. But improvements in the quality and quantity of communication and transportation media progressively curtail the cultural isolation in which an ethnic group could formerly cloak its cultural chasteness from the perverting influences of other cultures within the same state. The reaction to such curtailment is very apt to be one of xenophobic hostility.

Advances in communications and transportation tend also to increase the cultural awareness of the minorities by making their members more aware of the distinctions between themselves and others. The impact is twofold. Not only does the individual become more aware of alien ethnic groups; he also becomes more aware of those who share his identity. Thus, the transistor radio has not only made the formerly isolated, Lao-speaking villager of northeast Thailand aware of linguistic and other cultural distinctions between himself and the politically dominant Siamese-speaking element to the west; it has also made him much more aware of his cultural affinity with the Lao who live in other villages throughout northeast Thai-

land and across the Mekong River in western Laos. Intraethnic as well as interethnic communications thus play a major role in the creation of ethnic consciousness.

As an end result of these processes, Thailand is today faced with separatist movements on the part of the hill tribes in the north, the Lao in the northeast, and the Malays in the south. Similarly, as a result of growing cultural self-awareness by minorities and an increasing presence of the central government, the state of Ethiopia, despite its three-thousand-year history, is also currently faced with a number of ethnic separatist movements. Other underdeveloped, multiethnic states without a history of colonialism indicate a similar pattern. The colonial and noncolonial patterns are not significantly different. . . . Explaining the recent upsurge of militant ethnic consciousness in advanced as well as less advanced states involves not the nature or density of the communications media, but the message. Although the expression "self-determination of nations" can be traced to 1865, it did not receive great attention until its endorsement by a number of world-renowned statesmen during the World War I era. Moreover, by their failure, after the war, to apply this doctrine to the multiethnic empires of Belgium, Britain, France, the Netherlands, Portugal, and Spain, the statesmen indicated that they did not consider self-determination an axiom of universal validity. Not until after World War II was the doctrine officially endorsed by an organization aspiring to global jurisdiction. It is therefore of very recent vintage. But despite its short history, it has been widely publicized and elevated to the status of a self-evident truth. Today, lip service is paid to it by political leaders of the most diverse persuasions. Admittedly, the doctrine has often been misapplied, having been regularly invoked in support of all movements aimed at dissolving a political allegiance, regardless of the basis for secession. But in its pristine form, the doctrine makes ethnicity the ultimate measure of political legitimacy, by holding that any self-differentiating people, simply because it *is* a people, has the right, should it so desire, to rule itself. In recent years, with its wide acceptance as a universal truth, the doctrine has induced minorities in Europe and North America, as well as in Africa, Asia, and Latin America, to question the validity of present political borders. It has therefore been more than a justification for ethnic movements: it has been a catalyst for them. The spreading of effective communications has had an evident impact upon ethnic consciousness, but the full impact of the communications media did not precede the message of self-determination.

Still another element contributing to the upsurge in ethnic consciousness is the evident change in the global political environment, which makes it much more unlikely that a militarily weak polity will be annexed by a larger power. During the age of colonialism, the probability of that eventuality was sometimes so great as to encourage independent units to seek the status of a protectorate in order to be able to select rule by the lesser evil. By contrast, a number of relatively recent developments, including what is termed the nuclear stalemate, cause independence to appear as a more enduring prospect for even the weakest of units. Thus, a favorable environment, the generating and justifying principle of self-determination, an expanding list of successful precedents, and a growing awareness of all these factors because of increased communications, are all involved.

A summary of our findings thus far would consist of the following points. The preponderant number of states are multiethnic. Ethnic consciousness has been definitely increasing, not decreasing, in recent years. No particular classification of multiethnic states has proven immune to the fissiparous impact of ethnicity: authoritarian and democratic; federative and unitary; Asian, African, American, and European states have all been afflicted. Form of government and geography have clearly not been determinative. Nor has the level of economic development. But the accompaniments of economic development—increased social mobilization and communication—appear to have increased ethnic tensions and to be conducive to separatist demands. Despite all this, leading theoreticians of "nation-building" have tended to ignore or slight the problems associated with ethnicity.

II

Transnational Actors

The United Nations was established in the hope that in the area of peace-keeping it would serve as a form of supranational authority. By "supranational" we mean an authority which transcends that of the nation-state. Unfortunately the cold war and other developments have prevented it from performing any such function. Only the European Common Market has attained what might be called supranational authority, and at that, only in the realm of economic relations among its members.

With the growth of communication and technology, however, movements linking people and activities that go beyond the nation-state have been on the increase. We call these transnational movements and to the extent that they take an institutional form that has an impact upon the international system or upon states themselves we refer to them as transnational actors. The Catholic Church is a transnational actor of long standing. More recent examples are multinational corporations and the various terrorist organizations associated with the Palestine Liberation movement. The recent efforts both within and outside the United Nations to negotiate an agreement to condemn and punish acts of terrorism against airlines is a good example of the problems of emergent transnationalism.

In discussing transnational as well as supranational actors, we are focusing upon the total field of system level interactions. Because some scholars feel that the subject matter of this field is too diffuse, and unlikely to change the essential state-centered nature of the international system, its importance is open to controversy. Nevertheless, with the increase in communications and technology, new relations of dependence and interdependence are being created which statesmen can ignore only at their peril; and new forms of power are arising, such as the multinational corporation, which have the potential to challenge the nation-state. One need not go as far as to agree with Charles Kindleberger that the nation-state is just about through as an economic unit, nor need one accept Frank Tannenbaum's theory that the nation-state is becoming "functionless" and that the base for an alternative world order is already being formed by technicians, managers, and political elites who think in extranational terms. Nevertheless one could agree that new transnational forces are impinging upon the sovereignty of the state and forcing governments to adjust to a new level of activity.

The focus on transnational movements is also an aspect of the ongoing debate between the *federalists*, who favor a *supranational* organization at the regional or world level, and the *functionalists*, who have advocated the more *transnational* path to unification. The stunning rise of a striking number of new transnational movements and actors, whose actvities escape the control of states and force governments to negotiate functional agreements in order to regulate them, has given new life to the argument that it is through such transnational activities that states will be forced to knit an ever widening web of supranational authority.

Broadly speaking transnational actors may include such groups as the Catholic Church, the world Zionist movement, the guerrilla and terrorist movement associated with the Palestinian Liberation Front, as well as multinational corporations, worldwide labor movements, and any other associations that transcend national jurisdiction and have an economic or political impact upon the international system or upon the individual states, either directly or indirectly, by exerting pressure upon national governments through domestic affiliates or adherents.

However, the extraordinary number of forms which these relations have taken in the last three decades, and the confusion about what is an international organization (like the United Nations) and what is a transnational organization (like the Catholic Church or General Motors) has prompted Samuel Huntington to attempt a definition and clarification of the distinctions that exist. His article is reprinted in this chapter because it may help to clarify the confusions that exist about what is an international organization and what is a transnational organization. Do you feel that he is justified in arguing that the U.S. Air Force and the CIA are involved in transnational as well as national processes because they have operations and bases in foreign countries which give them a transnational stake in their maintenance?

In sheer numbers these groups have undergone an extraordinary proliferation. It is perhaps in keeping with the nature of the state system that the most marked proliferation has occurred in the areas of science, technology, economics, health, education, and religion, and less in the more sensitive areas of nation-state activity—politics, law, and ideology—although obviously this is less true of the European Common Market countries. On the face of it Werner Feld concludes, in his article reprinted below, that nongovernmental organizations (NGOs) do succeed in bringing about some changes in the international system, although their impact is undramatic, diffuse, slow, and suggests no single direction. (If one thinks of the Palestinian guerrilla organizations, radical youth movements, and multinational corporations, however, it can hardly be said that their impact has been undramatic, slow, or diffuse.)

Two questions are generally associated with the growth of transnational relations: (1) What impact does transnationalism have upon national sovereignty; does it presage the supercession of the nation-state in favor of some supranational political or economic organization? (2) What impact are transnational forces, particularly the multinational corporation, having upon the distribution of wealth and power among the different areas of the world?

In reference to the first question, Joseph Nye and Robert O. Keohane suggest five major effects of transnational interactions and organizations, "all with direct or indirect consequences for mutual sensitivity and thereby for interstate politics."[1] First and foremost, transnational interactions as a result of mass communications and exchanges may promote *attitude changes;* changes in the direction of creating new myths, symbols, and norms to conform to Western beliefs, life-styles or social practices are perhaps the most noticeable. A second effect of transnational relations, according to Nye and Keohane, is "the promotion of *international pluralism,*" by which they mean "the linking of national interest groups in transnational structures, usually involving transnational organizations for purposes of coordination."[2] A third effect is "the creation of *dependence and interdependence*" that is evident when certain policies which a government might otherwise follow become prohibitively costly because transnational relations have made its society too dependent on the function to be able to forego it. The need to observe international trade and monetary

[1]Joseph Nye, Jr. and Robert O. Keohane, *Transnational Relations and World Politics.* (Cambridge, Mass.: Harvard University Press, 1972), p. xvii.

[2]*Ibid.,* p. xviii.

relations provides an example. A fourth effect of transnational relations may be to give certain governments *new instruments for influence* over others. The use of terrorists, or exchange students as spies, or the cultivation of ethnic or religious groups in other states through transnational organizations, offer such examples. Finally the existence of transnational organizations as *autonomous institutions* in world politics may have an inhibiting effect on national politics. The Roman Catholic Church and multinational corporations stand out as examples.

While the consensus of most theorists is that states remain the most important actors in world affairs, the state-centered view of the universe does not give adequate weight to the importance of the role which transnational actors and processes are beginning to play in international relations. As transnational actors acquire resources and have the means of reaching important sectors of national populations (and even participate in political relations with governments), such actors can no longer be ignored. It is often hard for governments to negotiate arrangements in these areas until they have lost control over them; yet if government control over these areas is to be restored it has to be through agreements worked out with the transnational actors.

With reference to the second question regarding transnational relations, perhaps the most striking example of a transnational actor is the multinational corporation. Some of these corporate giants actually have holdings and annual budgets larger than all but the leading nations in the world (See the "Nations and Corporations" Table immediately following this selection.) There are those who see the multinational corporation as the precursor of an integrated supranational world. In the meantime, it is suggested, the "multinationals" are providing the world with the social benefits of an integrated world economy. Others decry the concentration of economic power and point out that what is actually happening is that the leading industrial powers are turning their multinational corporations loose on the rest of the world with no concern for economic and social consequences so long as their actions enhance profits and national power. Most analysts of the multinational corporation freely admit that such corporations exist to make profits and are not in business for extraneous political or social purposes. Nevertheless their enormous economic power and impact raises the question of accountability and whether they do not simply take advantage of the national system to evade responsibility. George Modelski argues that the giant companies with numerous subsidiaries have flourished precisely by

taking advantage of national frontiers as shelters within which to fashion markets in their own image. . . . national sovereignty is not really at bay at all, and the conflict of the multinational corporation with the [nation-] state is not really as great as it is made out to be.[3]

Far from being the precursor of a more manageable form of world order, the multinational corporation may merely be reinforcing the existing unequal distribution of economic wealth and contributing to the causes of international injustice and violence.

Finally the growth of transnational activities and of Nongovernment Organizations (NGOs) seem to be closely related to the phenomenon of growing functional interdependence of societies across national boundaries. Once upon a time the development of the national economy took place almost exclusively within the national territory and people looked to the national government to maintain economic stability and foster growth. But as industry, trade, banking, and investment have become globalized, the stability and growth of the domestic economy depends more and more on what happens to the demand for goods and services globally. Just when people expect their governments to do more to provide full employment and economic wellbeing their ability to do so is at the mercy of banks and businesses that operate on a global basis. National governments are also at the mercy of what other governments are willing to do to stimulate their economies or promote trade. We call this phenomenon interdependence and it is largely a byproduct of the increase of transnational economic activities. As a consequence governments today have to give as much attention to "low politics" (coordinating fiscal, monetary, trade, and investment policies with other governments) as to "high politics" (the traditional preoccupation of states with security, power, and prestige). This impact is discussed in the selection by Werner Feld.

[3]George Modelski, "Multinational Business: A Global Perspective," *International Studies Quarterly,* Vol. 16, No. 4 (December, 1972), 429.

**A COMPARISON OF GROSS ANNUAL SALES OF
CORPORATIONS WITH GROSS NATIONAL PRODUCTS
OF COUNTRIES, MEASURED IN BILLIONS OF DOLLARS.
FIGURES ARE AS OF 1970.**

1.	United States	974.10	36. Royal Dutch Shell	10.80
2.	Soviet Union	504.70	37. Philippines	10.23
3.	Japan	197.18	38. Finland	10.20
4.	West Germany	186.35	39. Iran	10.18
5.	France	147.53	40. Venezuela	9.58
6.	Britain	121.02	41. Greece	9.54
7.	Italy	93.19	42. Turkey	9.04
8.	China	82.50	43. General Electric	8.73
9.	Canada	80.38	44. South Korea	8.21
10.	India	52.92	45. IBM	7.50
11.	Poland	42.32	46. Chile	7.39
12.	East Germany	37.61	47. Mobil Oil	7.26
13.	Australia	36.10	48. Chrysler	7.00
14.	Brazil	34.60	49. Unilever	6.88
15.	Mexico	33.18	50. Colombia	6.61
16.	Sweden	32.58	51. Egypt	6.58
17.	Spain	32.26	52. Thailand	6.51
18.	Netherlands	31.25	53. ITT	6.36
19.	Czechoslovakia	28.84	54. Texaco	6.36
20.	Romania	28.01	55. Portugal	6.22
21.	Belgium	25.70	56. New Zealand	6.08
22.	Argentina	25.42	57. Peru	5.92
23.	General Motors	24.30	58. Western Electric	5.86
24.	Switzerland	20.48	59. Nigeria	5.80
25.	Pakistan	17.50	60. Taiwan	5.46
26.	South Africa	16.69	61. Gulf Oil	5.40
27.	Standard Oil N.J.	16.55	62. U.S. Steel	4.81
28.	Denmark	15.57	63. Cuba	4.80
29.	Ford Motor	14.98	64. Israel	4.39
30.	Austria	14.31	65. Volkswagenwerk	4.31
31.	Yugoslavia	14.02	66. Westinghouse Electric	4.31
32.	Indonesia	12.60	67. Standard Oil, Ca	4.19
33.	Bulgaria	11.82	68. Algeria	4.18
34.	Norway	11.39	69. Philips Electric	4.16
35.	Hungary	11.33	70. Ireland	4.10

71. British Petroleum	4.06	86. RCA	3.30
72. Malaysia	3.84	87. Goodyear Tire	3.20
73. Ling-Temco-Vought	3.77	88. Siemens	3.20
74. Standard Oil, Ind.	3.73	89. South Vietnam	3.20
75. Boeing	3.68	90. Lybia	3.14
76. Dupont	3.62	91. Saudi Arabia	3.14
77. Hong Kong	3.62	92. Swift	3.08
78. Shell Oil	3.59	93. Farbwerke Hoechst	3.03
79. Imperial Chemical	3.51	94. Union Carbide	3.03
80. British Steel	3.50	95. Daimler-Benz	3.02
81. North Korea	3.50	96. Proctr & Gamble	2.98
82. General Telephone	3.44	97. August Thyssen-Hutte	2.96
83. Nippon Steel	3.40	98. Bethlehem Steel	2.94
84. Morocco	3.34	99. BASF	2.87
85. Hitachi	3.33	100. Montecatini Edison	2.84

From Lester R. Brown, "The Multinationals and the Nation State," in *Vista* (now *Inter-Dependent*), June 1973. Reprinted by permission.

5 Transnational Organizations in World Politics

Samuel P. Huntington

The author is Professor of Political Science at Harvard University, presently on leave with the National Security Staff.

I

THE TRANSNATIONAL ORGANIZATIONAL REVOLUTION

Anaconda	Strategic Air Command
Intelsat	Unilever
Chase Manhattan	Ford Foundation
AID	Catholic Church
J. Walter Thompson	CIA
Air France	World Bank

These twelve organizations appear to have little in common. They are public and private, national and international, profit-making

Reprinted from WORLD POLITICS, 25, #3. Copyright 1973 by Princeton University Press. Some footnotes have been omitted. Reprinted by permission.

and charitable, religious and secular, civil and military, and, depending on one's perspective, benign and nefarious. Yet they do share three characteristics. First, each is a relatively large, hierarchically organized, centrally directed bureaucracy. Second, each performs a set of relatively limited, specialized, and, in some sense, technical functions: gathering intelligence, investing money, transmitting messages, promoting sales, producing copper, delivering bombs, saving souls. Third, each organization performs its functions across one or more international boundaries and, insofar as is possible, in relative disregard of those boundaries. They are, in short, *transnational organizations,* and the activities in which they engage are *transnational operations.* Such organizations have existed before in history. Armies and navies, churches and joint stock companies, as well as other types of organizations have been involved in transnational operations in the past. During the twenty-five years after World War. II, however, transnational organizations: (a) proliferated in number far beyond anything remotely existing in the past; (b) individually grew in size far beyond anything existing in the past; (c) performed functions which they never performed in the past; and (d) operated on a truly global scale such as was never possible in the past. The increase in the number, size, scope, and variety of transnational organizations after World War II makes it possible, useful, and sensible to speak of a *transnational organizational revolution* in world politics. The purpose of this essay is to analyze, in a preliminary way, the sources, nature, and dynamics of this revolution, and to speculate on its implications for politics at the national and international levels.

"Transnationalism" is a term which suffers from being "in" in social science. Many people now use it to mean many different things. It has achieved popularity at the price of precision. Consequently, it is important to emphasize that in this essay the expression transnationalism is used only to refer to the kinds of organizations and operations described in the preceding paragraph. This is, relatively speaking, a restricted use of the term. It differs from and is more limited than the broad sweep which Keohane and Nye give to the term in their pathbreaking study.[1] For them, transnationalism encompasses all interactions across state boundaries in which at least one of the

participants is not the agent of a government or an intergovernmental organization. Their emphasis is thus not on the scope of the operation, but on the public or private character of the participants in the operation. They direct their fire at what they describe as the "state-centric" view of world politics. In addition, transnational relations for them include all interactions, not just organizational ones; international trade and international travel, for instance, are included under their heading of "transnational processes." Their concern is principally with the activities in categories B, D, and F in Table I; our concern here is with those in categories A and B.

There is no point in debating definitions. But there is a need to insure that definitions clarify rather than obscure distinctions. By stressing the private-public character of the participants in an activity, Nye and Keohane direct attention to the tremendous increase in the number and significance of private international interactions in recent decades and the much larger and diverse number of private individuals and groups engaging in such interactions. They include but do not focus on the dramatic rise of relatively centralized, functionally specific, bureaucratic organizations which carry out their operations across state boundaries. This latter development is clearly related to "Nye-Keohane transnationalism" but is also clearly different from it, since it can involve public as well as private organizations.

General Motors and a Pugwash Conference are both non-governmental (and hence "transnational" in the Nye-Keohane sense), and yet they do not have any more in common than do the U.S. Air Force and the SALT Conference, both of which are governmental bodies. The similarities between SALT and Pugwash are, however, very great. So also are those between General

[1] Robert O. Keohane and Joseph S. Nye, Jr., eds., *Transnational Relations in World Politics* (Cambridge, Mass. 1972), *passim,* but esp. ix-xxii, 379-86.

Table I
DEFINING TRANSNATIONALISM

Type of Participant	Types of activity		
	Bureaucracy	Association	Transaction
Governmental	(A) AID	(C) UN General Assembly	(E) USA-USSR SALT Agreement
Non-Governmental	(B) Unilever	(D) Pugwash Conference	(F) Boeing-Air France Sales Agreement

Motors and the USAF, both transnational organizations operating on a global scale. In 1969, for instance, the USAF budget was approximately $27 billion; General Motors sales were a little over $24 billion. The Air Force had 54 major installations in 20 countries (apart from Vietnam) outside the United States; General Motors had 53 plants or facilities in 25 countries outside the United States. There were 862,000 men in the Air Force, one-third of them deployed overseas. There were 794,000 General Motors employees, slightly less than one-fifth of them abroad. Some foreign installations of both the military service and the private corporation were directly involved in the area where they were located, contributing planes to local defense or producing cars for local consumption. In other cases, the activities and products of the installation had relatively little connection with or impact on the area in which the latter was located; they were oriented to the defense of distant regions or to sales in a distant market. For both private corporation and military service, each installation, wherever located, was expected to fit into and to respond to the global needs of the overall organization as determined by the central leadership of that organization. In both cases, the establishment of an installation abroad was dependent

on the approval of a national host government which specified the terms and conditions of access to the national territory. The growth and multiplication of globally oriented bureaucratic organizations like GM and the USAF—public or private in character, nationally or internationally controlled— adds a critical new dimension to world politics.

The terms "international," "multinational," and "transnational" have been variously used to refer to the control of an organization, the composition of its staff, and the scope of its operations. Terminological confusion is further compounded because one word, "national," serves as the opposite of each of these three terms. To minimize ambiguity, at least on these pages, and to maintain some critical distinctions, each of these terms will in this essay be used to refer to only one of these organizational dimensions. An organization is "transnational" rather than "national" if it carries on significant centrally-directed operations in the territory of two or more nation-states. Similarly, an organization will be called "international" rather than "national" only if the control of the organization is explicitly shared among representatives of two or more nationalities. And an organization is "multinational" rather than "national" only if people from two or more nationalities participate significantly in its operations.

These distinctions are important, because almost any combination of internationalism, multinationalism, and transnationalism or their national opposites could exist in practice. The World Bank, for example, is formally international in control, highly multinational in personnel, and clearly transnational in its operations. The so-called "multinational" corporations, on the other hand, are often very transnational in their operations, reasonably multinational in personnel, but, with a few exceptions (Unilever, Royal Dutch Shell), almost wholly national in control.

For reasons which will be spelled out below, transnational operations and international control occur together only to a limited degree. Air Afrique, for instance, is an international airline in the sense that it is owned by twelve African governments plus some private French interests. It also engages in transnational air operations. Its transnational operations are, however, minuscule compared to those of Pan American, which is wholly owned by private American interests. Some international organizations may not engage in any transnational operations at all. The European Organization for Nuclear Research (CERN), for instance, is international in that it is sponsored by a dozen governments, and multinational because it employs people of several different nationalities. It was not, however, transnational so long as its operations all took place in a single laboratory in one locality and did not significantly cut across state boundaries.[2] Similarly, a Pugwash Conference, like the SALT talks, is international in control, multinational in personnel, but

[2]See Diana Crane, "Transnational Networks in Basic Science," *ibid.*, 245-46; Robert L. Thornton, "Governments and Airlines," *ibid.*, 193, 196.

not transnational in its operations. A Pugwash Conference derives its points from the fact that Soviet and American private citizens are sitting down together to talk about common problems even as Soviet and American governmental representatives do. The conference is successful to the extent that there is a meeting of the minds between the members of the two national groups. Such a conference cannot be indifferent to the fact of nationality. It is, instead, rooted in that fact.

Contrast this essentially international and multinational (albeit private) phenomenon with the operations of an organizatin like Royal Dutch Shell, which is engaged in the pursuit of particular objectives more or less on a global basis across national boundaries. It is, in theory, impossible for a Pugwash Conference to meet if only Americans are present. It is, in theory, possible for Royal Dutch Shell to operate with a staff which is 100 percent British, 100 percent Dutch, 50 percent each, or a motley mixture of diverse nationalities. As we shall see, the transnational operation may vary significantly. What makes Royal Dutch Shell a transnational phenomenon is the nature and scope of the operations it performs, not the nature of the people who perform those operations or the nature of the people who ultimately control those operations.

II. THE SIGNIFICANCE OF TRANSNATIONALISM

Nationalism, internationalism, and transnationalism have all been major factors on the contemporary world scene. At the end of World War II, observers of world politics expected nationalism to be a major force, and their expectations were not disappointed. The decline of Europe encouraged the blossoming forth of nationalist movements in Asia and Africa, and by the early 1960's colonialism in the classic familiar forms was virtually finished and scores of new nation-states had been formally recognized. The end of colonialism, however, did not mean the end of nationalism, in the sense of the behavioral and attitudinal manifestations by a people of their presumed ethnic or racial identity, nor the end of the political disruption of the newly independent nation-states. Colonialism led peoples of various ethnic or racial identities to suppress their antagonisms in order to win independence. The achievement of independence raised the question of *whose* independence had been achieved, and led to a re-awakening and, in some cases, a totally new awakening of communal antagonisms. Nationalism increasingly has meant "subnationalism," and has thus become identified with political fragmentation. Nationalism has remained a force in world politics, but a force which promises almost as much disruption in a world of independent states as it did in a world of colonial empires.

At the close of World War II, internationalism was also expected to be a wave of the future, and the United Nations was created to embody that hope and to make it reality. Nationalism has remained strong but its impact has changed. Internationalism, in contrast, has failed to gain the role and significance which it was expected to achieve. The great hopes for international organizations—that is, organizations whose activities involve the active cooperation of distinct national (private or public) delegations—have not been realized. In one form or another, internationalism involves agreement among nation-states. Interests have to be shared or to be traded for an international organization to work. This requirement puts an inherent limit on internationalism. The United Nations and other international organizations have remained relatively weak because they are inherently the arenas for national actors; the extent to which they can become independent actors themselves is dependent on agreement among national actors.

An international organization requires the identification and creation of a common interest among national groups. This common interest may be easy to identify, such as the exchange of mail. Or it may be the product of extensive and time-consuming negotiation among national units. A transnational organization, on the other hand, has its own interest which inheres in the organization and its functions, which may or may not be closely related to the interests of national groups. Nations participate in international organizations; transnational organizations operate within nations. International organizations are designed to facilitate the achievement of a common interest among many national units. Transnational organizations are designed to facilitate the pursuit of a single interest within many national units. The international organization requires *accord* among nations; the transnational organization requires *access* to nations. These two needs, accord and access, neatly summarize the differences between the two phenomena. The restraints on an international organization are largely internal, stemming from the need to produce consensus among its members. The restraints on a transnational organization are largely external, stemming from its needs to gain operating authority in different sovereign states. International organizations embody the principle of nationality; transnational organizations try to ignore it. In this sense the emergence of transnational organizations on the world scene involves a pattern of cross-cutting cleavages and associations over-laying those associated with the nation-state.

The emergence of transnational organizations on such a large scale was, in large part, unanticipated. Internationalism was supposed to furnish the threads tying the world together. In actuality, however, every international organization at some point finds itself limited by the very principle which gives it being. Much of the disappointment with the UN and its various agencies stems precisely from the failure to recognize this fact. While national representatives and delegations engage in endless debate at UN conferences and councils, however, the agents of the transnational organizations are busily deployed across the continents spinning the webs that link the world together. The contrast between the two forms of organization can be seen in the difference between the great bulk of UN bodies which are basically international in character and thus dependent for action on agreement among national delegations, and one organization that is formally international in control and related to the UN but in practice quite autonomous, which operates successfully in a transnational manner. Perhaps significantly, that organization, the World Bank, is headquartered in Washington, not in New York.

A similar contrast exists between private transnational organizations and international non-governmental organizations (or INGO's). Like transnational organizations, INGO's multiplied rapidly in numbers and functions in the decades after World War II. Of the INGO's in existence in 1966, 50 per cent were founded after 1950 and 25 per cent were founded in 1960 or later. During these same years, however, the average size of the INGO's did not increase and, if anything, decreased. In 1964 the mean INGO budget was $629,000 and the mean INGO staff

encompassed nine people.[3] INGO's simply did not have the resources, scope, or influence of nationally controlled, transnational, non-governmental organizations such as the Ford Foundation, IBM, or Exxon.

Transnational organizations thus may, in theory, be nationally or internationally, privately or governmentally controlled. The need to reach agreement among national units, however, restricts the purposes and activities of international bodies. Free of this internal constraint, nationally controlled organizations are much better able to formulate purposes, to mobilize resources, and to pursue their objectives across international boundaries. They may face greater political obstacles than international organizations in gaining access to national territories, but this disadvantage is more than compensated for by their relative freedom from internal political constraints. International organizations, even when their functions are relatively specialized and the participating governments have much in common, still confront great difficulties in developing their operations. The rather sparse activities of the European-controlled international organizations, for instance, contrast markedly with those of U.S.-controlled transnational corporations operating in Europe.[4]

A distinctive characteristic of the transnational organization is its broader-than-national perspective with respect to the pursuit of highly specialized objectives through a central optimizing strategy across national boundaries. The "essence" of a transnational corporation, as Behrman has argued, "is that it is attempting to treat

---

[3]Kjell Skjelsbaek, "The Growth of International Non-governmental Organization in the Twentieth Century," *ibid.*, 77.

[4]See, for instance, Crane (fn. 2), 245-46; Raymond Vernon, *Sovereignty at Bay* (New York 1971), 95-96.

the various national markets as though they were one—to the extent permitted by governments.''[5] In similar fashion, a transnational military organization treats the problems of defense of different national territories as if they were part of a single whole. For its specialized purpose, its arena assumes continental or global proportions and it thinks in continental or global terms. One of the early advantages of the American transnational corporation in Europe, for instance, as de Riencourt has argued, is that ''unlike most of its European competitors, it thinks 'European,' not local or national; it is mentally geared to tap the whole European market, not merely that of France, Britain, Germany, or Italy. Thinking in terms of a single continental market, with a sales network covering the whole continent and straddling dozens of nation-states, with a uniform accounting system, the American subsidiary is in truth more typically 'European' than any European firm rooted in one single country.''[6]

The transnational process developing today on a global scale is not unlike that which occurred within the United States during the nineteenth century. The struggle over the Constitution and much of the political controversy of the first part of the nineteenth century were essentially interstate in character. These issues were basically resolved by the Civil War. The actual integration of the United States as a national community, however, was accomplished not through agreements among the states but rather by the development of business cor-

porations, social organizations, and eventually national government bureaucracies which operated indiscriminately within states and across state boundaries. The emergence of these ''trans-state organizations'' was immensely stimulated by developments in transportation and communications, particularly the railroad, telegraph, rotary press, and telephone. It became dramatically evident when corporations legally domiciled in New Jersey or Delaware pursued their objectives of production and profit on a national basis, often with seeming disregard for the interests of individual states and localities.[7] The political controversies so generated plainly parallel those which currently concern the relations between so-called ''multinational'' or transnational corporations and national governments. Today's issues, arguments, and slogans neatly replicate those of a century ago between ''the trusts'' and the state governments. The feelings of powerlessness which the state legislatures in Illinois and Minnesota felt in their dealings with the New York Central and Great Northern railroads are duplicated today in the unease which national government leaders in Latin America, Asia, and even Europe feel in their dealings with IBM, Ford, or Unilever. Just as the railroad magnates then could make or break a community by deciding where to locate their terminals, so the transnational corporations of today can significantly influence the future of localities or regions in a number of countries by a decision as to

[5] Jack N. Behrman, *Some Patterns in the Rise of the Multinational Enterprise* (Chapel Hill, N.C.: University of North Carolina, Graduate School of Business Administration, Research Paper No. 18, 1969), 61.

[6] Ameury de Riencourt, *The American Empire* (New York 1970), 284.

[7] Just as states like New Jersey and Delaware provided tax and other advantages to companies which located their headquarters within the state, some European countries offer comparable concessions. American corporations thus set up Tax-Haven Companies in countries where ''after negotiations with the government, taxes are either greatly reduced for the company or completely eliminated.''. . .

where to place a new plant. The interaction between local interests and national organizations in the 1870's and 1880's gave rise to the Grangers and the Populists, who directed their fire at the monopolies, railroad titans, and eastern bankers who were exploiting them, even as Third-World nationalists

and populists level comparable charges at General Motors and Chase Manhattan. In both cases local groups attempted to use the local government to "nationalize" or assert control over the transcending organization.

6   Nongovernmental Entities and the International System

Werner Feld

The author is Professor of Political Science at Louisiana State University, New Orleans.

The purpose of this article is to examine the actual and potential impact of nongovernmental entities on the international system. . . .

The long-standing view that states are the exclusive actors in the international system has been questioned increasingly during the last twenty-five years. Not only have international organizations such as the United Nations or the European Economic Community been accepted as important actors in this sytem, but nongovernmental entities of varying kinds, including perhaps groups of guerrillas, have been recognized as acquiring international actor status when they engage in behavior that transcends national boundaries and play purposeful roles affecting the international arena. The traditional nongovernment organizations,

These excerpts from "Non-governmental Entities and the International System: A Preliminary Quantitative Overview" are reprinted, by permission, from ORBIS: A JOURNAL OF WORLD AFFAIRS, 15 (1971) 879-22. (Footnotes have been omitted).

usually called NGOs, are best known for activities that either aim at changes in the international system or have a bearing on it. Their diversity is staggering. Reaching into every aspect of human activity, they have even organized to advance the interests of manifold groups, professions and industries, to promote a cause or movement, or to carry out special undertakings such as administering relief. Still others engage in scientific research or simply confine their attention to disseminating information. Generally, traditional NGOs operate as nonprofit organizations although the objectives of some of them include the maximization of members' profits.

NGOs may have a universal character such as the International Confederation of Free Trade Unions (ICFTU) or may limit their activities to an international region as in the case of the Union of European Industries (UNICE). However, they may also be intranational: a group of educators or religious leaders may become international actors by privately or publicly appealing to their counterparts in another country to press for governmental adoption of a specific foreign policy position. . . .

A second major category of nongovernmental entities capable of affecting the international system is comprised of multinational corporations and transnational joint business ventures. Multinational corporations own property and operate in [several] countries, which enables them to escape the full control of the respective governments. They have special opportunities to influence the politics of these countries either directly or through international transactions and thus emerge as important international actors. Some multinational enterprises have a greater productive output and maintain larger bureaucracies than many small nation-states. (See p. 30, Nations and Corporations.)

Transnational joint business ventures involve the border-crossing collaboration of legally independent enterprises. This increasingly popular entrepreneurial arrangement enables the partners to exert coordinated influences in the countries where their companies are located which in turn may bring about changes in the inernational system. Examples of such ventures are the transnational collaborations of Fiat and Citroen in the European Common Market and similar undertakings between firms in developed and developing countries.

In addition, political parties can sometimes be regarded as nongovernmental organizations playing purposeful roles of more than national dimension.* Obviously, parties in totalitarian systems are part of the governmental machinery and therefore fall outside the scope of our study. Communist

parties in democratic countries, however, are "nongovernmental" and are known to have engaged in activities to influence the international system or its subsystems. A case in point is the continuing endeavor by the communist parties of France and Italy to prevent supranational progress in the European Community. Also, since the establishment of the European Coal and Steel Community in 1952, followed later by the EEC and Euratom, relationships among the Christian Democratic, Liberal and Socialist parties of the Six have suggested possible transnational efforts toward changes in the regional subsystem of Western Europe. Finally, we should note the attempts made during the last few years to create truly European parties dedicated specifically to the promotion of European unification—the *Europa Partei* and the *Parti Socialist Européen,* for example. These parties have not had much success, but they exist nevertheless.

Why is it that these nongovernmental entities can become actors on the international stage dominated by the governments of sovereign states from 1648 to the early part of the twentieth century? E. Raymond Platig argues that to the extent a government's power is less than total, individuals and groups within its territory can and do enter into independent transnational relations and activities, thus affording them the opportunity of becoming direct actors in the international system. While we accept this basic rationale, we should point out that national governments at times encourage and support the transnational activities of national and international nongovernmental entities, especially if these activities tend to buttress governmental objectives. . . . the practices of governments vary greatly as they attempt to encourage, monitor, restrict, manage or control the international transactions resulting from initiatives other than

*Editors' Footnote: A good example would be the financial aid the German Social Democratic Party gave to the Portugese Socialist Party in its struggle to win power against the Communist Party of Portugal in 1975-76.

their own. In this connection the kind of power individual nongovernmental actors possess is bound to be an important consideration. . . .

THE GROWTH OF NGOs

International NGOs . . . are assumed generally to date back to 1846 when the World's Evangelical Alliance was founded. Their dramatic growth from 1860 to 1968 is illustrated in Figure 1. Increases in the number founded are especially pronounced in the periods during which major wars (for example, the Russo-Japanese War and World Wars I and II) ended or those immediately following the end of hostilities, and they show decided dips during periods of rising international conflict and wars such as the time spans from 1911 to 1920 and 1931 to 1940. This suggests that strife and turmoil impede the establishment of international NGOs, while the settlement of devastating wars coupled with bitter memories of misery and deprivation seems to stimulate their formation, reflecting a revived spirit of border-crossing cooperation. A similar situation is noticeable in the growth pattern of intergovernmental organizations (IGOs) since 1860, also shown in Figure I. Expanded international cooperation after the two World Wars is clearly evidenced by sharp increases in IGO foundings between 1921 and 1930 and from 1941 to 1960. Equally visible is the distinct dip in increases during the 1931—1940 span. Overall increases in the number of both entities show a respectable correlation, with r being .61.

Table 1 provides a functional breakdown of international NGOs for selected years. Commerce and industry groups lead the field followed by health and scientific organizations. It is also noteworthy that those in the economic sector show a much higher growth rate from 1909—10 to 1968—69 than other groups. Besides the active NGOs listed, we find that according to the 1968—69 compilations a substantial number (674) were inactive or dead. While not all NGO disappearances may become a matter of record, the figures shown are suggestive. It may be a syndrome of our troubled times that in this category fall 103 international relations groups, almost as many as those in the active column (125). On a smaller scale, for organizations concerned with politics the inactive and active figures are nearly equal. The high percentage of inactive NGOs in these two fields and the much smaller percentage in all other fields may offer some indirect evidence for the argument that the dynamics of functionalism are more effective when pragmatic, "low politics" interests and objectives are pursued and less effective when the pursuit involves "high politics" and strongly opposed ideological commitments. . . .

NGO IMPACT ON THE INTERNATIONAL SYSTEM

The growing incidence of international NGOs, as demonstrated, throws no light on their activities with respect to the international system. Table 2 moves a small step in this direction by providing data over time regarding the number of NGOs which have consultative relations with different universal and regional organizations. It includes the note that not only international but also a few national NGOs have been admitted as consultants.

The remarkable increase of NGOs accorded some kind of consultative status suggests that access to the decision-making process of intergovernmental organizations

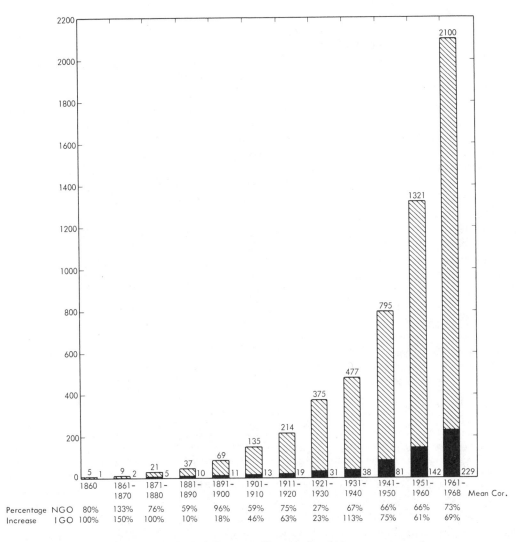

	1860	1861-1870	1871-1880	1881-1890	1891-1900	1901-1910	1911-1920	1921-1930	1931-1940	1941-1950	1951-1960	1961-1968 Mean Cor.
Percentage NGO Increase	80%	133%	76%	59%	96%	59%	75%	27%	67%	66%	66%	73%
IGO	100%	150%	100%	10%	18%	46%	63%	23%	113%	75%	61%	69%

FIGURE 1. Growth Pattern of International Nongovernmental Organizations Compared With Intergovernmental Organizations, 1860-1968

Key: Number of NGOs represented by entire bar

Number of IGOs represented by solid part of bar

Figures represent cumulative number of organizations founded by the end of each time period.

SOURCE: Adapted from Donald C. Blaisdell, *International Organization* (New York: Ronald Press, 1966), pp. 9, 11; and *Yearbook of International Organizations* (1968–1969, 12th edition), p. 13.

TABLE 1
FUNCTIONAL BREAKDOWN OF INTERNATIONAL NGOs

Category	1909–10	1956–57	1966–67	1968–69	Dead or Inactive 1966–67	Dead or Inactive 1968–69
Bibliography, press	19	26	58	69	28	29
Religion, ethics	21	70	93	103	60	61
Social sciences	10	57	80	90	34	35
International relations	12	61	111	125	101	103
Politics	3	13	15	21	21	21
Law, administration	13	28	48	54	31	32
Social welfare	10	52	76	88	50	52
Professions, employers	2	67	93	105	34	35
Trade unions	1	48	63	70	21	22
Economics, finance	3	15	35	40	15	15
Commerce, industry	5	123	211	233	31	34
Agriculture	5	27	76	83	24	24
Transport, travel	5	40	72	76	15	15
Technology	8	36	83	102	26	27
Science	21	69	137	152	49	53
Health, medicine	16	100	173	214	35	36
Education, youth	10	56	91	105	31	33
Arts, literature, radio	6	34	70	75	28	29
Sport, recreation	6	51	90	93	16	18
European Common Market and EFTA business and professional groups	—	—	245	273	—	—
National organizations in consultative status with UN	—	12	15	16	—	—
TOTAL NGOs	176	985	1,935	2,188	650	674

SOURCE: *Yearbook of International Organizations* (1st, 6th, 11th and 12th editions). The compilers of the 1909–10 edition defined "international" in a more restricted sense than is customary today. After discussions with the UN Economic and Social Council officials in 1950, the Union of International Associations adopted criteria allowing the inclusion of regional bodies (involving three countries or more) which had been excluded in 1909–10.

is valued highly and perceived as important by the NGOs in pursuit of their international objectives. . . .

The impression emerges that NGOs do succeed in bringing about some changes in the international system. However, their impact is undramatic, diffuse, slow, and suggests no single direction. The input into the international political system emanates from all functional and geographic segments of the environment as well as from national and international subsystems. Any hope that the spreading web of NGO activity might advance the integration of mankind and thereby contribute to prospects for international peace is sustained by little concrete evidence. One reason for the spotty and fragmentary NGO record of achievement may be that many of these groups lack sufficient organizational and financial resources. Such resources usually are found in multinational corporations and transnational joint business ventures. . . .

TABLE 2
NGOs ACCORDED CONSULTATIVE STATUS BY
INTERGOVERNMENTAL ORGANIZATIONS*

International Organization	1951–52	1958–59	1962–63	1966–67	1968–69	Growth based upon 1951–52 = 100
ECOSOC	212	302	332	360	379	178
ILO	5	47	58	81	87	1740
FAO	10	40	51	79	96	960
UNESCO	99	125	200	250	273	275
WHO	26	46	57	68	75	288
ICAO	17	26	27	28	28	164
ITU	18	23	28	30	26	144
WMO		11	11	15	15	136
IMCO			11	11	17	154
IAEA			19	19	19	100
UNICEF		57	70	75	76	133
IRO	9					
UNCTAD				17	17	100
COUNCIL OF EUROPE				76	76	100
OAS				48	48	100
TOTAL	396	677	864	1157	1232	

* Most of these NGOs are of the international kind, but a few national NGOs have also been granted consultative status: 12 in 1956–57, increased to 16 in 1968–69. They include some important American organizations, for example the Chamber of Commerce of the United States, the Committee for Economic Development, and the Carnegie Endowment for International Peace.

SOURCE: Adopted from the *Yearbook of International Organizations* for the years shown.

Part Two

DECISION MAKING IN INTERNATIONAL RELATIONS

III

Capability Analysis
and Its Limits

One of the most difficult but essential tasks for the student and practitioner of international relations is the determination of the capacity of given states to formulate and implement their policy objectives. This task is important because the analysis may help to clarify facets of relations among states which might otherwise remain incomprehensible. By comprehension is meant either an explanation, usually after the fact, or a prediction. Harold and Margaret Sprout, wrote a few years ago that:

> with reference to historical cases, the analysis is designed to answer the question: How was it possible for a given state to exert an influence or to play a role which it did in fact exert or play? With reference to the future, capabilities analysis is designed to yield a predictive estimate as to the influence which a state could exert or the international role that it could play, either in a specific postulated contingency or in a postulated overall configuration of political relationships in the Society of Nations.[1]

[1]*Foundations of International Politics* (Princeton, N.J.: D. Van Nostrand Co., Inc., 1962), p. 63.

Attention will be paid in chapters five and eight to the fact that force and the threat of force constitute the ultimate recourse regulating international relations; suffice it to note here that states can neither afford to neglect the elements which make up their respective force inventories, nor can they neglect to consider and compare these with those of other states. This is true even if items in the inventory are never utilized, and indeed for most states at the present time there is no intention of actually using them if the threat of their use, real or implied, is understood by neighboring states, or, in the case of the superpowers, anyone in the world. The deterrent function may in fact be more effective than forces and weapons in actual use or that have been used. The interrelationships between the "power inventory" and national strategy are discussed more fully in the article below by Professor Stephen Jones of Yale.

No discussion of a state's capabilities must be confined, as it all too often tends to be, to its ability to use physical coercion. The term *capability*, connotes many components. Such factors as natural resources, productive capacity, scientific inventiveness, technological know-how, diplomatic skill, governmental efficiency and stability, cohesiveness, confidence, ideological commitment, and morale are often more relevant to a state's effectiveness in foreign relations than the raw coercive power which it can bring to bear on other states. It is not just a matter of power, it is a matter of how decision makers use that power. In the relationship between capability and intention, the real question is: Will countries do whatever they are capable of doing? Or will they, under given circumstances, be content with doing less? The dominant tendency on the part of practitioners of international relations has been to equate the two, to assume that others (never oneself, always others!) will do the greatest damage they are capable of doing; will inflict the heaviest price they are capable of inflicting; will, in short, both bargain and act to the very limits of their capability. It is the assumption that the worst may happen which is one of the tragic hallmarks of international statecraft—tragic, yet apparently unavoidable, because which statesman, responsible for the lives and fortunes of vast numbers of people, would dare proceed on different assumptions? Thus far it seems to have defied human ingenuity to discover a way of escaping from this dilemma, and while the academic student of foreign policy may legitimately criticize the tendency to equate capability and intention and deplore the policies to which this tendency gives rise, he should also attempt to empathize with the policy maker who may at times conclude that he has little alternative but to act on this assumption.

In analyzing capability, one must exercise caution to avoid the temptation to think in deterministic categories. A country's geographic position, its economic potential, or its military capability, for example, will undoubtedly affect its policies, but the relationship is usually not a direct, automatic, causal one. Professor Sprout advocates the use of the term *political potential* instead of the term *power*, not only because of the coercive and military (and therefore restrictive) connotations of the term *power*, but also because the term *potential* draws attention to the fact that men in positions of influence and control can choose whether or not, and if so, in what ways and to what extent, to transform potentials into actualities.

With the advent of weapons systems of unprecedented destructive capacity we may well have reached a terminal point in traditional capability analysis, because the very power of these systems may render them useless in many kinds of situations in which coercive instruments were once quite useful indeed. This is a new fact in the study of international relations: in power calculations, provision must be made for those instruments of force which, because of their sheer magnitude and potency, are in practice unusable. Former Secretary of State Rogers, commenting on possible American responses to a North Korean attack, once put the matter succinctly when he said that "weak can be rash, but the powerful must be restrained." At first glance this may seem like upside-down logic, but on closer inspection the proposition appears entirely valid. Former Secretary of State Kissinger raised the question, "What can you *do* with nuclear superiority?" On the other hand, the excerpt from Dr. Cline's recent work, reprinted below, seems to indicate that there is continued utility in the consideration of the capability inventory.

It has been put in another way by a spokesman of a minor power, the foreign minister of Austria:

> . . . it is within the competence of even the smallest state to introduce conflict and unrest into the community of nations, thus provoking the great powers to take up a position. Often enough we have been witnesses of such escalations, which beginning as local quarrels, suddenly become world crises. On the other hand a small country can initiate the opposite effect and strive for calm relations, avoiding anything which could induce the great powers to take up a position. It thereby makes a positive contribution which, just as something negative produces continuing bad effects, gives rise by the power of example to something of lasting good. Indeed, when we justly criticise the fact that so little that is positive has happened in international life, we ought perhaps to take into account that much that was negative, but seemed the obvious thing to do, did not happen either.[2]

Thus the small power can be restrained too, and exercise some influence on the reactions of its larger neighbors. No mere computation of material power factors could lead one to such a conclusion, which again shows the limitations of capability analysis. At the same time, one can only understand the behavior of states if one has some comprehension of what they are able to do, so despite its evident limits this dimension of the analysis of international relations remains vitally important.

By way of summary, let us suggest that in attempting to measure

---

[2]Dr. Rudolf Kirschschläger, "An Austrian view of the future of All-European Cooperation and Security," *Wilton Park Journal,* 47 (1972), 5.

capability the serious student of power politics keep certain considerations clearly in mind.

1. The components of comparative analysis are multiple and the various ingredients interact with one another. Calculations of the capacity of a given society are almost never soundly based if they are based on but a single factor, be that factor geography, demography, economics, or even military capacity. What is needed is a "grand estimate," involving all the elements which may be relevant for the particular purpose under contemplation.

2. The ingredients which one must study are dynamic; they are always subject to change. Given the present levels of research and technological capabilities of some countries, such transformations may come about with extreme rapidity. This means that, once made, evaluations must constantly be renewed. Any change in any of the components affects the capability of one society vis-à-vis another. Countries rise and decline in their capacity to achieve objectives. The cause for either rise or decline may be internal or external, within or beyond the competence of a country to regulate or control. Note how Karl Deutsch has put it:

> The power to increase the probability of a specific positive outcome is the power of goal attainment and of control over one's environment. Like all goal attainment and control, it implies a high degree of self-control on the part of the actor. A charging elephant can smash down a large obstacle, but he cannot thread a needle. Indeed, he cannot make a right-angled turn within a three-foot radius.[3]

3. The various elements which constitute a country's capability arsenal should be studied on a comparative basis, comparing similar elements (or mixes of elements) in specific other countries. It is very tempting and relatively easy to compare a given country with itself at a previous time or stage, which is to be sure, a type of autocomparison not without value in that it may provide information about the direction and speed of trends *within* a society. But in international studies one is concerned with relations *between* societies and hence with comparisons between them, e.g., the margin of power between two countries is more important than the absolute power of either country. The more specific the comparisons the more useful the analysis will be and the easier it will become to discriminate carefully between a variety of possible situations. Country A may, for example, be deficient in one aspect of capability as compared with Country B, but it may make up for this deficiency in other ways. Furthermore, Country X may be militarily (or economically, or politically) weak compared with Country Y, but at the same time quite strong when compared with Country Z. (As viewed by Liechtenstein, Switzerland is a superpower,

[3]"On the Concepts of Politics and Powers," in John C. Farrell and Asa P. Smith, eds., *Journal of International Affairs,* 20 (1966), 56.

but as viewed by Russia it need not be taken too seriously.) Comparative analysis also involves coalitions, alliances, and other combinations of states, a task further complicated by the fact that, in addition to performing the necessary calculations for a number of countries, one must then also estimate the cohesiveness of the groupings involved.

4. Short cuts should be avoided. While short cuts may be useful, the conscientious student should not let himself be carried away by trying to resolve complex problems by overly simple means. Tidy, specific, and readily available comparisons of national income or steel production or gross national product, for example, are particularly tempting as short cuts. To be sure, they do reveal a great deal, and recent studies indicate that there is a high correlation between such factors and numerous other factors, so that knowledge of a limited number of ingredients in the capability inventory can provide a measure of confidence that other ingredients are present or absent as well. Still in the long run there seems to be no substitute for the "grand estimate." One of the reasons for this is that most short cuts tend to overlook what Stephen Jones refers to below as the "modifiers" of a power inventory—such factors as quantity, availability, change, sustaining capacity, substitution capacity and qualitative differences.

5. A determination should be made of the uses to which any given element or combination of elements of capability will be put. What if all this information were readily available (admittedly, an unrealistic assumption)? At that point another problem would arise—namely, what value should be assigned to the various ingredients. Since they are composed of different qualities and types, one cannot simply add them together. It is at this point that assumptions about possible uses of capabilities must enter the analysis. For example, does one assume relatively stable and peaceful relationships? Or does one posit the probability of coercive types of relationships? Does one envisage an active policy on a localized, on a broad regional, or even on a worldwide basis?

What all this adds up to is the fact that evaluations of power—grand estimates—cannot in the nature of things be precise. In view of the limitations upon the accurate measurement of national power, the evaluative process is best visualized as one in which the ingredients are always in flux both in relation to one another and in relation to those of other countries. All one can hope for is that the questions that are asked be defined as precisely as possible, that the data provided to answer these questions be as complete as possible, and that the assumptions which are made be as explicit as possible. Then if either questions, data, or assumptions are found to be deficient, the necessary corrections can be made.

7   The Power and National Strategy

Stephen B. Jones

Stephen B. Jones was Professor of Geography at Yale University.

. . . An estimate of national power has two aspects which are related, in a figurative way, like the two rays of a triangulation. Either ray gives direction, but it takes the two to give distance. A better analogy, perhaps, is that of two searchlight beams groping through the dark until they intersect on the target. One ray or beam is the conventional inventory of the elements or factors of power. It gives the power resources of a nation, using "resource" in a broad sense. The other ray is here called "national strategy. . . ."

DEFINITION OF TERMS

"Power" is here defined as "that which permits participation in the making of decisions,". . . This is perhaps not truly a definition; it tells not what power is, but what it makes possible. It has the virtues of including constructive uses and of saying that power is not solely material or possessed only by those who have a lot of it. Power, like radiant energy, can move in many directions at once. The interplay of British, American, and Russian power on Iran and the counter-radiation of Iranian power, through its ability to tantalize, frus-

From "The Power Inventory and National Strategy," by Stephen B. Jones, World Politics, *6, no. 4. Copyright © 1954 by Princeton University Press.*

trate, and play one great rival against another, show that even a state that comes near to being a vacuum, militarily, can exert a significant force.

"Strategy" . . . is defined here as "the art of using power for the attainment of goals in competition." . . .

We use the term "resources" in a very broad sense, . . . to mean anything a nation has, can obtain, or can conjure up to support its strategy. The items on an inventory of power resources are commonly called either "elements" or "factors." . . .

The concept we are endeavoring to establish is simply that inventories of power resources may contain items at several levels of organization. . . . The important point is that estimates of national power are made for comparative purposes and that valid comparisons are possible only if levels of organization are taken into account.

An inventory of power resources, or, briefly, a power inventory, could be a few lines or many pages in length. Taxonomists divide themselves into "lumpers" and "splitters" and the terms are appropriate here. An extreme lumper could compress the whole inventory into the familiar three factors of production of economics: land, labor, and capital. . . .

The splitter will immediately go to work on this basic group. Land includes two categories of resources. One might be called "area resources," including the size and the shape of the country and immobile resources like landforms, soils, and climates. The other is the mobile mineral and biological resources. Location, sometimes considered an attribute of land by economists, will be treated later in another manner.

The factor of labor is perhaps better called "human resources." There are likewise two parts. First is population, considered as to number, age structure, and so forth. Second is what might be called "mental resources," the social, political, economic, and military systems of a country and the stock of skills, leadership, and patriotism.

Capital is better called "equipment resources," since it includes not only economic capital goods but also military equipment and the material apparatus of government. An additional item is supplies or stockpiles of consumable materials and goods—foods, metals, merchandise, munitions, etc.—and the financial stockpile of precious metals and credit.

There is of course a high degree of relationship among the items mentioned. Equipment is produced by organized skill operating on mobile natural resources. In turn, it may be used to extract further natural resources. Whether an ore deposit of marginal tenor is usable or not depends on skill, organization, and equipment. Leadership and patriotism are like enzymes in metabolism. In the final analysis, without them there is no power.

The foregoing paragraphs list resources as tangible as soil, as intangible as leadership, as measurable as population, as difficult to measure as patriotism. There is no common unit and no statistical summation is possible. . . .

Even though one must give up the seductive hope that the power inventory can be summed up in dollars, kilowatt hours, or some other common unit, there remains the possibility that some key items may be used as rough indices of the probable total. The hope, of course, is to find measurable items that will so serve. Manpower of military age or the output of fuels, steel, or all heavy industry are some of the possibilities. Such data unquestionably are basic and under some conditions give a correct estimate of relative power. The longer a war lasts, the more likely are such data to be significant. They are particularly applicable when a country has limited access to external supplies. One could write a history of World War II in terms of supplies, with a measure of truth. But with far less than the whole truth: equally important is what was done with the supplies. Poverty of resources correlates with the weakness of Italy but does not explain the military failures against Greece or, for that matter, against the British at sea and in North Africa. Too little oil and too much intuition were long-run handicaps for Hitler, and it would be difficult to say which was the greater. Had his long-range strategy been sounder, he might have created a sufficient synthetic oil industry. Even in estimating potentials one must consider the strategic ray. To be sure, our analogy does not imply that the strategic ray is the more important, but only that *both* rays are important.

National income and its close relative, gross national product, have been considered possible indices of national power. They are operational in nature rather than being inventory items, but this would be no disadvantage if they measure what can be done with a given inventory. For one thing, they give an idea of the dislocations to be expected from the diversion of resources from civil to military purposes. Their chief value is as tools, not as indices, however. . . .

That quantifiable items like manpower or the output of heavy industry or economic aggregates like national income cannot serve as indices of national power does not, of course, mean that quantification is useless. Much of science consists of efforts to narrow the range of guessing. Since there is, inevitably, a large element of guesswork in an estimate of national power, quantitative information is highly desirable for all items for which it is obtainable. But, for the same reason, there is no use refining quantitative data to a high degree.

MODIFIERS OF THE POWER INVENTORY

If the power inventory is thus essentially a check-list, with some quantifiable items, it becomes desirable to run through the concepts that must be kept in mind when the check-list is used. If we take any item of the list of power resources, we find that a chapter or a book or possibly a shelf of books can be written about it. It can be qualified almost without limit. We might start with population, for example, and find ourselves many pages later discussing the rate of training of civil defense workers in the use of Geiger counters. Such thoroughness may be necessary and desirable for some purposes—for a detailed mobilization program, for example. For general thinking about power, more generic concepts are desirable. These generic concepts we shall call "modifiers" of the power inventory. Not all the modifiers are applicable to every item of the power inventory, though with some imagination most of them can be applied. It may seem absurd to apply "motivation" to petroleum, for instance, but the motivation of the investors, management, and workers determines whether oil is produced or not. To return to the earlier attempt to distinguish between an element and a factor,

motivation is essential to the petroleum industry as a factor of power.

One of the most obvious modifiers of the power inventory is quantity. In some commentaries on national power, quantity is the only modifier considered. That the United States produces three times as much steel as the Soviet Union closes the argument for some people. But quantity is a whole family of modifiers. Its principal genera are availability and change. Availability has two subdivisions, the space and time aspects. Spatial availability is summed up in the term "location.". . . Location has two subspecies, accessibility and mobility. To illustrate, Mackenzie River oil is highly inaccessible but highly mobile. The Canol pipeline (another non-combatant use of steel) did not improve the accessibility until after the need had passed. "Tonnage" ores like iron are less mobile than ores that can usefully be measured in pounds. Labrador iron ore probably could not have been made accessible during World War II even had the need arisen. Manpower is relatively mobile and with a man move his skills, but the mobility of manpower varies with culture. Aboriginal natives need fewer supplies than do more civilized troops and workers, but at the same time they may be more essential to the economy of their villages, which have no labor-replacing machinery.

The time aspect of availability appears in the familiar phrase "lead-time," which stands for the period required to convert plans into production.[1] Lead-time is a phase of the problem of potential power. That

[1] Lead-time has a range of meanings. An artillery man might think of it as the interval between placing an order and receiving the ammunition. An airman is more likely to think of the longer interval between conceiving a new airplane and the mass production of the final model. There is a different lead-time for each of the availability states discussed in this article, *infra*.

there is a difference between actual and potential power is obvious, but these two terms are too vague to be of much service. A geographer is likely to think of ore and fuel reserves when he hears the word "potential." An economist is likely to think of factories convertible to war production. A military man may think of the reserve corps or of mothballed ships. A fivefold classification of states of availability is here proposed: 1. power resources available immediately; 2. power resources available after activation; 3. power resources available after conversion; 4. power resources available after development; and 5. power resources available hypothetically. . . .

These availability states are of course not rigidly separated pigeonholes, but they do differ in kind as well as in degree. They should permit sharper thinking than do "actual" and "potential." A given power resource is not confined to one category. Many exist in all five states. Oil, for instance, may be immediately available in storage tanks. Idle wells and refineries may be activated. Non-essential use can be curtailed—this would be conversion. New wells may be drilled in proven fields—this is development—and favorable structures may be wildcatted on the hypothesis that oil exists in them. Intangibles like leadership can exist in all five states. How power resources are distributed through the availability series reflects the national strategy. The United States traditionally has left as much of its power as possible in the convertible and developable states. The trend is to push many items into higher states and to step up the pace of conversion and development. Not even the most spartan of nations could keep all its resources in a condition of immediate availability, but simple trust in "the power and potential of American mass production" goes the way of the faith that a

million Americans would spring to arms overnight if their country were attacked.

The term "potential" has another connotation than that of availability. It also implies the maximum sustainable rate of production, or, more precisely, for expenditure, of a given item of power. Maximum sustainable rates follow different rules, depending upon the nature of the resource, the time element, and national strategy. Where natural resources are ample and the rate of production depends largely upon capital and labor, long-continued increases are possible, though perhaps at the cost of diverting capital and labor from other items. American steel production, for example, is capable of much further growth, if low-grade and foreign ores are utilized. In other cases, the maximum sustainable rate may vary with the period of time involved. The expenditure of manpower, if in excess of natural replacement, is an obvious example. To estimate the maximum sustainable rates of power expenditure therefore requires knowledge of both resources and their probable strategic use.

The availability states discussed above are closely related to three aspects of the national economy discussed by Sherman Kent: fat, slack, and flexibility.[2] Kent defines these terms as follows:

> By *fat*, I mean such things as some of the things Britain had at the start of World War II: extensive external assets, a large merchant marine, access to necessary raw materials and the credits to buy them without going into current production, a large and up-to-date supply of capital equipment, a large inventory of finished goods, a national diet of three to four thousand calories

[2]Sherman Kent, *Strategic Intelligence for American World Policy* (Princeton, N.J.: Princeton University Press, 1949) p. 51.

per day, etc. Important elements of German fat may be said to have existed in the excess capacity of machine tools, a large amount of brand new plant and new housing. The Italians had practically no fat, indeed little enough lean.

By *slack*, I mean such things as the 40-hour week, twelve to sixteen years of education for youth, small proportion of women in the labor force, unemployment of both labor and capital, only partial utilization of equipment, etc.

By *flexibility*, I mean the capacity of the economy to beat plowshares and pruning hooks into swords, and that in jig time. I mean the ability of technicians to make typewriter factories over into machine gun factories, and put the manufacturers of dry breakfast food into the shell-fuse business. I mean the ability to make synthetics from scratch where the natural sources have dried up.

"Fat" and "slack" correspond to "resources available after activation." Steel production, for example, is expansible in several ways. Plants may be operating below capacity. To activate this unused capacity would be taking up slack. Or they may be operated temporarily above capacity by postponing repairs. This would be using up fat. "Flexibility" covers the two concepts of "conversion" and "development." The quotation from Kent illustrates both. Making war goods in typewriter and cereal factories is conversion. Making synthetics from scratch (if the basic processes are known and not hypothetical) is development. The difference is significant because the lead-time of change is likely to be greater for development than for conversion and the investment of money, manpower, and materials larger. The expansion of steel production by building new mills is development, and involves the temporary diversion of steel from other uses.

These terms can be applied to persons as well as to commodities or plants. The conversion of clerks into soldiers, of housewives into welders, is familiar. The longer process of producing physicians, physicists, or general officers is more appropriately called development. The population factor as a whole can be developed, as by the importation of labor, alliances, and public health measures. The long-term effect of pro-natalist policies on the birth rate is still somewhat hypothetical.

The importance of change in relation to quantity needs no emphasis. Change has two aspects, rate and range. Rates of production, mobilization, conversion, expansion, etc., need no discussion. Changes of rates, or accelerations and decelerations, are also important, and one may need to consider changes in the changes of rates. The higher derivatives of change are significant in demography, where one wishes to know not only the death rate, for instance, but whether it is rising or falling and how the rate of rise or fall is changing. Rates of resource accumulation or wastage are important. Secular changes of vast consequence may be taking place almost unperceived by untrained observers, such as soil erosion, climatic alteration, or the aging of the population. The range of change obviously applies to fluctuating quantities like temperatures or harvests. Better knowledge of the range of Russian winter temperatures would have aided Hitler in 1941–1942. Range may also apply to rates. There is an upper limit to the rate of oil production from a given field, for instance, beyond which recovery declines and salt water may intrude.

Rates and ranges of expansion are major considerations in estimating power. The expansion of American production during World War II surprised even optimists, though whether time will be available in a future conflict for similar expansion is debatable. Soviet recovery after World War II was also surprisingly rapid. Expansion has its converse, contraction. The ability to do without may be important in war. Many contractions are effected for the purpose of expanding or maintaining supply or effort in other lines or places. Rationing of gasoline to civilians permitted expanded military consumption. But expansion without concomitant contraction is of course possible, as in the activation of unused plants. Use of the electrolytic process of tinplating instead of the dipping process gave more plate from less tin, so that a reduced supply of a raw material was not reflected in an equivalent contraction of the product.

Substitution is another modifier of quantity. Substitution can be looked at from two sides. One can ask if an item in short supply can be replaced by a more abundant or a synthetic product, or one can ask if some item which is abundant may have other uses. We usually think of the former—glass for tinplate, synthetic for natural rubber—but the latter may be significant when weighing the power resources of other countries. An American thinks of potatoes as food, primarily, but they are an important source of industrial alcohol in the Soviet Union. Substitution of machines for men is a favorite American occupation. The high degree of automation possible in peace may be deceptive as to the possibilities in war, when destruction and disruption may make muscle-power indispensable. The reverse substitution of men for machines has its limitations also.

The doctrine of limiting factors in biology means, for example, that a plant needing nitrogen is not helped by an excess of phosphate. Man's ingenuity in finding substitutes makes this doctrine only loosely applicable to human affairs. Nevertheless, limiting factors do appear, particularly in war and under conditions of blockade and attri-

tion. Substitution very often requires time and imports, which may not be available. The limiting factors may be rates. For instance, there was no doubt that the United States could create a synthetic rubber industry adequate for its needs. The question was whether it could be created in time.

THE QUALITY MODIFIERS

Quality is a second family of modifiers. The two main branches of the quality family are the quality of materials and goods on the one hand, and of operation on the other. These terms are meant to apply very broadly. American schoolboys or African natives are materials in the present sense, having certain qualities in that condition. Trained as workers, soldiers, professional men, etc., they might be called goods, their qualities in that state depending not only on inherent vigor and intelligence and childhood environment but upon specific training. Operation is also used broadly, to include business management, military organization, and government.

Quality of course connotes the question, "How good?" For our study, the question really is, how well does something serve its strategic purpose? An example of the distinction is the use by the Communists in Korea of obsolete wooden-frame airplanes for night bombing, because these old planes give poor radar echoes.

Quality is often placed in opposition to quantity, the ideal of "the mostest of the bestest" being difficult to attain. It is not necessarily unattainable, however, and quality often has been improved while quantity was being increased. The *a priori* opposition of quality and quantity possibly dates from handicraft days. The Battle of Britain is often cited as a triumph of quality over quantity, British planes, pilots, and operations being considered superior to the German. Because of these qualitative superiorities and the fact that fighting took place over British soil, the Royal Air Force sometimes obtained local quantitative superiority. A different relationship of quality and quantity can be illustrated by a famine-struck area. The difference between high- and low-grade wheat would mean little. Quality would be negligible in comparison with quantity and availability.

Change of quality must also be considered. This has three aspects, durability, obsolescence, and variation. Durability and obsolescence might be lumped as life expectancy of materials or goods. The significance of durability needs little elaboration. The United States was able to get through four years of war with its initial stock of private automobiles, in part because the cars proved durable beyond customary expectation. (Gasoline and tire rationing of course lengthened car life by reducing use.) The durability of railroad equipment, machine tools, and the like was important. Materials and labor needed for maintenance and replacement of non-combatant equipment of course must be drawn from the supply available for military use. Durability can be obtained at excessive cost and can be offset by obsolescence. Military equipment, however, is subject to very hard usage, and expenditures to increase its durability usually are justified. Breakdowns are likely to occur at the worst possible time and place when the equipment is overworked during an emergency.

High durability and low rate of obsolescence are major criteria of materials and goods that are to be stock-piled or moth-balled. To judge when obsolescence has so reduced power value that goods should be scrapped requires something like clair-

voyance. Brodie argues cogently against prematurely scrapping obsolescent naval ships, on the grounds that quantity may offset a modern qualitative inferiority.[3] The destroyer-for-bases deal of 1940 is a supporting illustration. Whether the great stock of slow Liberty ships is a real or an illusory asset in event of war is a question currently debated. Rommel repeatedly refers to the gradual obsolescence of his tanks relative to those of the British.[4] Rommel's victories actually increased his problems, for the Germans came to think him a miracle worker who could win with any weapons, while the British were compelled to replace lost equipment and had fewer competing demands for their best tanks. There is perhaps more danger that obsolescent items will be rated too highly in terms of power than that they will be scrapped prematurely, but pruning the power tree of its fading branches does not strengthen it unless there is concomitant new growth. In the inorganic world of ships, tanks, and the like, new growth does not come spontaneously.

Variation in quality may involve the familiar phenomenon of "the weakest link." Ships in line of battle can steam no faster than the slowest vessel. One defective shell can jam a gun. All troops in combat may have to fall back of one unit gives way. In the first battle of El Alamein, Auchinleck directed major counter-attacks at Italian divisions, forcing the Germans to limit their own drives.[5] On the other hand, the phenomenon of "the strongest link" sometimes is encountered. Rommel's crack Afrika

[3]Bernard Brodie, *Sea Power in the Machine Age* (London: Oxford University Press, 1943), pp. 203, 334, 442–45.

[4]B. H. Liddell Hart, ed., *The Rommel Papers* (New York: Harcourt, Brace & World, 1953), p. 245 and elsewhere.

[5]*Ibid.*, pp. 252–54.

Korps saved many critical situations and kept the Italian army in battle long after it would otherwise have collapsed.

Variations in the quality of leadership —economic, political, military—are important modifiers of the power inventory and of course are difficult to assess. A change of leaders may change the power value of a military unit almost overnight. Even push-button warfare will require not only a man to push the button but, more important, a man to say when to push the button. This ineluctable individual factor may be overlooked in the power inventory because it cannot be treated statistically. It is apt to be neglected in the economist's or the geographer's approach to the study of power. Uncritical historians, on the other hand, may give too much attention to individuals. "The Gauls were not conquered by the Roman legions but by Caesar," said Napoleon, whose own history showed the potency of genius, but also that manpower, weather, and nationalism were not to be ignored.

OPERATION: FOCUS OF INVENTORY AND STRATEGY

When we speak of operation and of the quality of operation,we are at or near the common focus of the inventory and strategic beams of our opening analogy. We use "operation" in the broad sense of "the way things work."[6] How well things work is a major modifier of the power inventory. We

[6]"Operation" has the narrow military meaning of "a military action" and the broader one of any strategic, tactical, service, training, or administrative action. "Administration" was considered as a substitute for "operation" in the present paper, but was rejected because of its bureaucratic connotation and because, in military usage, it does not apply to strategic or tactical activities.

can apply this concept of working quality to items in wide variety—a squad of soldiers, a mine, a factory, an army, the whole of an economic or political system. This aspect of quality may be illustrated by Russian experience in the first five-year plan,when modern factories were built but sometimes nothing came off the assembly lines.

Operation has two main parts, motivation and organization. Motivation—involving reward, punishment, loyalty, leadership—is essential even for the most prosaic effort. To return to the example of petroleum as a factor of power, the motivation of the seamen on tankers may be a critical matter. Motivation for the long-haul usually demands pecuniary or other material rewards. But material motivation is not enough; it has proved insufficient for high quality of work even in purely economic activities. In this respect, however, states may go to the other extreme. As has been said, without patriotism there is no power, but one cannot expect patriotism to replace pay checks year after year. Americans seem particularly reluctant to admit that political and military operation really works from the top down, though checked and criticized (in both senses of criticism) from below. Patriotism, luck, or le bon Dieu may not provide administrators of high quality if pay is inadequate.

Organization may be divided into control and integration. Control is essential in government, industry, or battle. Loss of control is a nightmare of the military commander and all sorts of communication devices are used to provide a mechanical guard against it. Control involves motivation. A General Patton might control where a weaker man might lose control. Control is necessary for a rationing system and for maintaining secrecy in government and the armed forces. Integration means how the parts of an organization mesh together. One aspect is illustrated by the integration of Negro troops into white units in the United States Army. This step multiplied many-fold the power value of the Negro soldiers and removed from them the stigma of "the weakest link." The operations of alliances are generally hampered by imperfect integration. The faulty integration of American railroads early in World War I led to intolerable congestion. The converse of congestion—shortages—may also arise from faulty integration, even when ample materials or goods are available.

The pace of operations is an important aspect of their quality. Equipment of high quality is necessary but not sufficient for fast pace. Whittlesey has pointed out that the time-dimension of human activities has three derivatives, velocity, pace, and timing.[7] A jet airplane may have a velocity near the speed of sound. The pace of air operations depends on many other velocities than those of airplanes. It depends, among other things, on the rate at which intelligence reaches the commander, on the rapidity with which plans are formulated and orders issued, upon the speed of servicing and repair. Pace—"the average tempo of trajections in a specified area"—may thus be more significant than velocity. The sluggishness of bureaucratic pace is notorious. Fortunately, it is also world-wide, though this does not permit us to be complacent about it. One purpose of war games is to step up the pace of operations that may some day be performed in the face of the enemy. Perhaps all branches of administration should hold war games.

Operational quality is roughly synonymous with some meanings of "efficiency"

[7] Derwent Whittlesey, "The Horizon of Geography," *Annals of the Association of American Geographers,* 35 (March, 1945), 23–24.

but not necessarily with that which relates output to input, if we measure output and input in conventional ways. Diplomatic operations of high quality are not necessarily economical of time or money. It is debatable whether the decision of 1953 to concentrate war production in the most efficient factories was wise or unwise as a long-run policy, since dispersal among more plants not only might decrease vulnerability but might permit faster acceleration of production in event of war.

VULNERABILITY AND COST

Vulnerability is a modifier of the power inventory that of course now affects the innermost parts of the home front. The power value of two factories may depend, after war begins, more on their vulnerability than on their efficiency. The vulnerability of Britain to air attack weakened Chamberlain's hand at Munich. Theoretically, the states with atomic weapons have the power virtually to blow each other to bits. Whether they will do so is debatable. Atomic warfare might resemble the strategy of the fleet-in-being, the threat of atomic weapons being used to tie up the resources of the opponent. Vulnerability will nevertheless be a factor, for the side that has attained the best defense against atomic weapons can make the most aggressive threats. Distressingly little attention has been paid to the reduction of vulnerability during the period of rapid construction since World War II. Some records have been stored in underground vaults, but little has been done to safeguard the really essential resources of labor and equipment, without which records have little meaning.

Simplicity is one of the classical principles of war. A major reason is the vulnerability of complicated operations, especially in the face of an active enemy. Simplicity is difficult to attain in industrialized war, in spite of modern methods of communication and control. Simplicity in plan may be obtainable only through complexity of control, as in assembly-line manufacturing. In industry, simplicity is not sought for itself but only if costs can be reduced or sales increased. In fact, the search for cheaper supplies or more extensive markets often results in complicated cross-hauling of materials and goods[8] and in duplication of delivery and marketing systems. Much of this complexity, efficient though it may be in a capitalistic economy in peace, would have to be eliminated in time of war, especially if the home front were heavily bombarded.

Cost as an index of power or a measure of power value has been discussed on an earlier page. In spite of its limitations in these respects, it remains a significant modifier. In part, this is because of the subjective importance given to the cost of national defense by taxpayers and their Congressional representatives. There is a persistent clamor for social security and insurance sells steadily, but that national power is the most basic form of social security and insurance, without which the others are illusory, is commonly forgotten in time of peace. The subjective importance of cost is of course greatest in the democracies where public opinion is most effective in government.

Cost has objective as well as subjective importance. Cost, in relation to national power, implies the question, "How much of our resources are required to increase our supply of a given item, or its readiness for use?" Japan, for example, could build war-

ships with cheaper labor than could the United States, but the cost in terms of available steel was proportionately greater to Japan. Japan could man a warship for a small part of the payroll of its American counterpart, but the oil for fuel came from a much more limited resource. World War II showed that most nations can sacrifice living standards for war to a degree hardly thought possible and that national bankruptcy can be staved off for years. Nevertheless, drain on resources is a reality, if replacement does not keep up with use. The attrition on manpower is perhaps the most obvious form, but drain on equipment, if there is insufficient reinvestment to maintain or replace it, may be serious.

THE STRATEGIC BEAM

The power inventory has now been provided with a set of modifiers—a check-list for a check-list, so to speak. A question may arise: Are the modifiers so numerous and so indeterminate that they reduce the inventory to a pulp? This thought can be dismissed with little comment. So long as there is politics among sovereign states, there will be estimation of power. Even though the best estimates are only rough, they are better than reliance on intuition or emotion. It is true that the modifiers are warning signs rather than guideposts, that they point out traps rather than show where the path lies. Nevertheless, insofar as they conform to realities they should be useful. . . .

If one looks at power along the inventory beam, one is asking, "What have I?" If one looks along the strategic beam, one is asking, "What do I need?" Each question of course connotes the other, but most will agree that, as in personal finances needs run

[8]Edward L. Ullman, "The Railroad Pattern of the United States," *Geographical Review,* 39 (April, 1949), 254-55.

ahead of funds, among nations it is strategic needs rather than love of statistics that sets us counting our power resources. This analogy can easily be strained, however. In the first place, neither the power inventory nor strategic needs can be expressed completely in monetary or even statistical terms. Second, the public purse is much more elastic than the personal one. A nation does not live on a fixed income, and it is production rather than the budget that really counts. Third it is not so much a case of shifting one's line of sight from the inventory to the strategic beam as of looking along both. It takes binocular vision, so to speak, to see national power in full relief. What one can do is influenced by what one has, but what one has is influenced by what one does, in world politics at least. . . .

8　World Power Assessment 1977

Ray S. Cline

The author is director of studies at the Georgetown University Center for Strategic and International Studies.

MEASURING THE POWER OF NATIONS

Obviously a sound U.S. strategy requires an objective calculus of national power and clusters of power in the international arena. This calculus must include an analysis of nuclear weaponry and its potential for the deterrence of war, but other elements of strength constitute crucial factors. Nonnuclear arms and forces, economic capacity, and economic resources materially affect the way national power is perceived and hence its effect. Coherence in formulating concepts of national purpose and the degree of consensus expressed as political will substantially

Reprinted from World Power Assessment 1977: A Calculus of Strategic Drift *(Boulder: Westview Press, 1977.) Excerpts are reprinted by permission.*

alter the way military and economic power can be used.

National power, realistically described, is a mix of strategic, military, economic, and political strengths and weaknesses. It is determined in part by the military forces and the military establishment of a country but even more by the size and location of territory, the nature of frontiers, the populations, the raw-material resources, the economic structure, the technological development, the financial strength, the ethnic mix, the social cohesiveness, the stability of political processes and decision-making, and, finally, the intangible quantity usually described as national spirit.

To ease the task of describing elements of international power in their various combinations, I have evolved a formula relating these factors. It is not a magic measuring rod, for many of the variables are not truly quantifiable. It simply provides a shorthand notation or index system to replace words and judgments once these have been defined.

The formula is as follows:

$$Pp = (C + E + M) \times (S + W)$$

Its terms are defined thus:

Pp = Perceived Power
C = Critical Mass = Population + Territory
E = Economic Capability
M = Military Capability
S = Strategic Purpose
W = Will to Pursue National Strategy

It only takes a careful look at the size and state of the economic development of the nations of the world to realize that the majority of them have relatively little impact on international affairs or even on important developments in their own regions. In a serious strategic assessment, only about 40 to 50 nations determine the pattern of the world balance of power at any one time. The rest either weigh so little in realistic power terms that they can be disregarded, or perhaps viewed as the political equivalent of iron filings, automatically arranging themselves around magnetic fields of force in the geographic zones of alliance systems to which they belong.

This is not to say the people of the less powerful countries are unimportant or that long-range strategic and humanitarian concerns can be ignored, especially since these also motivate citizens and governments. Yet, by any consistent standards of gross measurement, the preponderance of power appears to be in the hands of a relatively few nations.

Actually some very simple quantifications appear to be adequate for the rough approximations of strength in world affairs on which

most broad generalizations about the balance of power rest. We are dealing here in macrometrics, the technique of measuring in a broad context where precise detail is not very significant. The patterns and trends in international relationships are what we want to see, not the details; the forest, not the trees. . . .

STRATEGY AND WILL: FINAL RATINGS

Judgments about this final factor in the formula we have been using are bound to be mainly qualitative, rather than precise and quantitative it would be unproductive to describe and defend in detail the coefficients assigned.

Prudence suggests that no attempt be made to rate most of the less powerful nations of the world for national strategy and national will. A few exceptions, however, are rather compelling. Some smaller powers with strong governments, whether democratic or totalitarian, and clear national goals, must be rated and ranked anew. Some, like Rumania, Cuba, Israel, Singapore, and New Zealand, take on a special significance because of their strategic locations linking them with larger countries. For example, Rumania is on the edge of the Soviet-dominated zone maneuvering for its independence; Cuba is in the U.S. zone of influence but presently committed to the USSR; Israel is virtually a U.S. outpost in a dangerous sea of Mideast states. Singapore is a key commercial entrepot and—with Indonesia—a co-custodian of the Malacca Straits. New Zealand is culturally and strategically tied to Australia and, to some extent, to the United States.

On this basis 56 nations in all are ranked for perceived powers in the following table.

FINAL ASSESSMENT

Zone	Country	Concrete Elements of Perceived Power	National Strategy	Will	Total Coefficient	Total	Perceived Power Weights: Zonal Total
	United States	468	0.4	0.5	0.9	421	
I	Canada	97	0.2	0.4	0.6	58	523
	Mexico	74	0.2	0.4	0.6	44	
	USSR	402	0.8	0.5	1.3	523	
	Poland	48	0.5	0.2	0.7	34	
II	Mongolia	30	0.3	0.1	0.4	12	618
	Rumania	24	0.5	0.5	1.0	24	
	East Germany (GDR)	22	0.8	0.2	1.0	22	
	Cuba	2	0.7	0.6	1.3	3	
	PRC	171	0.5	0.2	0.7	120	
III	Vietnam	48	0.8	0.4	1.2	58	209
	North Korea	22	0.8	0.6	1.4	31	
	West Germany (FRG)	112	0.7	0.8	1.5	168	
	France	112	0.4	0.5	0.9	101	
	United Kingdom	99	0.6	0.4	1.0	99	
IV	Italy	71	0.5	0.3	0.8	57	558
	Spain	59	0.5	0.4	0.9	53	
	Yugoslavia	36	0.5	0.2	0.7	25	
	Sweden	29	0.5	0.7	1.2	35	
	Norway	20	0.5	0.5	1.0	25	
	Iran	80	0.9	0.7	1.6	128	
	Egypt	65	0.5	0.6	1.1	72	
	Turkey	65	0.2	0.4	0.6	39	
	Saudi Arabia	43	0.7	0.7	1.4	60	
V	Algeria	41	0.5	0.5	1.0	41	483
	Sudan	40	0.2	0.3	0.5	20	
	Libya	33	0.5	0.6	1.1	36	
	Morocco	30	0.5	0.5	1.0	30	
	Iraq	25	0.3	0.5	0.8	20	
	Israel	22	0.9	0.8	1.7	37	
	India	97	0.3	0.3	0.6	58	
VI	Pakistan	62	0.5	0.5	1.0	62	164
	Bangladesh	40	0.3	0.2	0.5	20	
	Afghanistan	30	0.5	0.3	0.8	24	
	Indonesia	85	0.5	0.5	1.0	85	
	Singapore	1	0.5	0.5	1.0	1	
VII	Burma	50	0.2	0.1	0.3	15	172
	Thailand	47	0.5	0.3	0.8	38	
	Philippines	41	0.5	0.3	0.8	33	
	Japan	111	0.5	0.8	1.3	144	
VIII	South Korea	38	0.7	0.7	1.4	53	234
	China/Taiwan	23	0.7	0.9	1.6	37	
	Brazil	94	0.5	0.8	1.3	122	
	Argentina	71	0.3	0.2	0.5	36	

Zone	Country	Concrete Elements of Perceived Power	National Strategy	Will	Total Coefficient	Total	Perceived Power Weights: Zonal Total	
IX	Colombia	41	0.5	0.5	1.0	41	282
	Peru	31	0.5	0.5	1.0	31	
	Venezuela	26	0.5	0.5	1.0	26	
	Chile	22	0.5	0.7	1.2	26	
	Nigeria	65	0.4	0.4	0.8	52	
	South Africa	60	0.6	0.4	1.0	60	
X	Zaire	55	0.5	0.5	1.0	55	233
	Ethiopia	45	0.1	0.2	0.3	14	
	Tanzania	30	0.5	0.5	1.0	30	
	Zambia	22	0.5	0.5	1.0	22	
	Australia	60	0.4	0.7	1.1	66	
XI	New Zealand	11	0.5	0.5	1.0	11	77
	TOTAL FOR ALL ZONES (56 nations)						3,553	

The striking fact that emerges from this table and from the entire method of analysis followed in this book is that national purpose and national will make a critical difference in the relative power of nations. A totalitarian system has many shortcomings and its suppression of individual freedom and initiative cripples the development of a high level of achievement within a society. Nevertheless, the fact that the USSR has a coherent strategy and a tightly controlled population multiplies the brute power it projects into the international arena. The rating of 523 derives from the efficiency of Soviet decision-making and the discipline enforced on the Soviet people; it is diminished by the dulled responsivity of a population inured to dictatorship and by the divisive element of tension between Slav and non-Slav peoples.

The Chinese system has some of the same advantages, but it lacks a truly coherent national policy at this juncture, despite its ambition, because Chinese leaders are jockeying for position in the struggle for power after Mao's death. The nation is not yet unified in pursuit of its long-range strategy and hence its coefficient for national will is low.

Clarity of national purpose and coherence of disciplined political will also show up in the ratings of countries like West Germany, Iran, China/Taiwan, and Israel. Most of the coefficients for the nations rated can be derived fairly readily from their current history.

For the United States a below-normal coefficient for strategy and will must be assigned as of mid-1977, but one that is higher than in mid-1975. The political malaise left as a legacy of Watergate, Vietnam, and the illusions of easily attained mutually beneficial detente has yet to be dispelled. The debilitation of the National Security Council decision-making system under Nixon and the breakdown of congressional-presidential cooperation in strategic and international policy formulation leave a legacy of uncertainty and still grave functional handicaps; fortunately, however, President Ford's and President Carter's preferences for more open decision-making and caution, candor, simplicity, and loyalty to alliances have started to move the United States in the right direction.

The best thing that can be said today is that U.S. political moods are volatile and its people are resilient. There is a bubbling up of the American spirit; the pendulum is beginning to swing back from pessimism toward increased confidence. The United States is capable of formulating anew a reasonable strategic policy and building a consensus in support of it. If this occurs, U.S. power will again rise to high levels. National purpose and national will are the most critical factors in determining power. The tremendous power potential of a country like the United States can be fully achieved only when its political leadership is unified and crystal clear in explaining national security strategy and foreign policy. With a new White House team of the same political party as the majority of the Congress, all of this can happen during the course of 1977. In these circumstances, as the highpoints of World War II and the late 1950s-early 1960s show, an open society with the support of the governed becomes virtually invincible in international affairs.

Item	Unit	European OECD	US	Canada	Japan	Australia and New Zealand	Yugoslavia
Population (mid-1976)	Millions	386	215	23	113	17	22
GNP, total[d]	Billion dollars	1,809	1,707	193	554	104	38
Per capita GNP[d]	Dollars	4,691	7,933	8,327	4,912	6,192	1,767
Foreign trade							
Imports (c.i.f.)	Billion dollars	442.2	[e]121.8	[e]38.0	64.8	[e]14.5	7.4
Exports f.o.b.)	Billion dollars	397.9	115.0	38.6	67.2	15.9	4.9
Trade balance	Billion dollars	−44.3	−6.8	+0.6	+2.4	+1.4	−2.5
Exports as percentage of GNP	Percentages	22.0	6.7	20.0	12.1	15.3	12.8
Production							
Coal[f]	Million MT	319	593	22	18	81	18
Crude steel	Million MT	161	116	13	107	8	3
Electric power	Billion KWH	1,505	2,123	293	505	101	44
Crude petroleum	Million MT	42	402	64	1	21	4
Primary aluminum	Thousand MT	3,106	3,856	628	919	344	197
Motor vehicles, total	Thousands	12,338	[g]11,477	1,642	7,584	[h]475	159
Passenger cars	Thousands	10,879	[g]8,498	1,138	5,028	[h]386	139
Commercial vehicles	Thousands	1,459	[g]2,979	504	2,556	[h]89	20

NOTES
1. Data shown are latest available at time of publication but are subject to revisions.
2. Some data represent new estimates and therefore are not comparable with data published in the 1976 edition of the "Indicators."
3. All figures are rounded, but computations per capita data and percentages are based on unrounded data.

FOOTNOTES
a. Includes Albania, Bulgaria, Czechoslovakia, the German Democratic Republic, Hungary, Poland, and Romania.
b. There are no reliable data available for other Asian Communist areas. Their share in the total for Communist countries is insignificant.
c. Data for "Rest of World" are based on Department of State and UN estimates.
d. For the Western countries, data are not adjusted for the purchasing power equivalents of the dollar, which are lower in many countries outside the US; currencies were converted into dollars at average 1976 trade conversion factors, as published by OECD. GNP values for Communist countries are based on Department of State estimates.
e. Imports f.o.b. except for New Zealand and Hungary, which are c.i.f.
f. Hard coal and lignite in terms of hard-coal equivalents.
g. Factory sales.
h. Including assembly.

SOURCE: United States Department of State Publication.

Item	Unit	Total West	USSR	Other Eastern Europe[a]	People's Republic of China	Cuba	Total Communist countries listed[b]	Rest of world[c]
Population (mid-1976)	Millions	776	257	110	951	9.5	1,328	2,040
GNP, total[d]	Billion dollars	4,405	856	318	254	9.3	1,437	1,250
Per capita GNP[d]	Dollars	5,683	3,334	2,906	267	979	1,083	613
Foreign trade								
Imports (c.i.f.)	Billion dollars	688.7	[e]38.1	[e]55.6	6.0	3.5	103.2	228.l
Exports (f.o.b.)	Billion dollars	639.5	37.2	49.3	6.9	2.9	96.3	255.l
Trade balance	Billion dollars	−49.2	−0.9	−6.3	+0,9	−0.6	−6.9	+27.l
Exports as percentage of GNP	Percentages	14.5	4.3	15.5	2.7	31.2	6.7	20.l
Production								
Coal[f]	Million MT	1,051	545	388	444	none	1,377	258
Crude steel	Million MT	408	145	54	23	0.3(1975)	222	45
Electric power	Billion KWH	4,571	1,111	366	130	0.1	1,614	658
Crude petroleum	Million MT	534	520	20	88		628	
Primary aluminum	Thousand MT	9,050	2,500	485	357(1975)	none	3,342	n.a.
Motor vehicles, total	Thousands	33,675	2,025	855	146	none	3,026	n.a.
Passenger cars	Thousands	26,068	1,239	645	none	none	1,884	n.a.
Commercial vehicles	Thousands	7,607	786	210	146	none	1,142	n.a.

NOTES
1. Data shown are latest available at time of publication but are subject to revisions.
2. Some data represent new estimates and therefore are not comparable with data published in the 1976 edition of the "Indicators."
3. All figures are rounded, but computations per capita data and percentages are based on unrounded data.

FOOTNOTES
a. Includes Albania, Bulgaria, Czechoslovakia, the German Democratic Republic, Hungary, Poland, and Romania.
b. There are no reliable data available for other Asian Communist areas. Their share in the total for Communist countries is insignificant.
c. Data for "Rest of World" are based on Department of State and UN estimates.
d. For the Western countries, data are not adjusted for the purchasing power equivalents of the dollar, which are lower in many countries outside the US; currencies were converted into dollars at average 1976 trade conversion factors, as published by OECD. GNP values for Communist countries are based on Department of State estimates.
e. Imports f.o.b. except for New Zealand and Hungar, which are c.i.f.
f. Hard coal and lignite in terms of hard-coal equivalents.
g. Factory sales.
h. Including assembly.

IV

Framing and Implementing
Foreign Policy

One of the most fascinating but difficult problems in the study of international relations is how to explain why nation-states behave as they do. Another aspect of this problem is the determination by decision makers, and the subsequent interpretation by analysts, of the goals and aims which governments endeavor to achieve in their policies toward others.

The term "national interest" has traditionally been used as the key to understanding why governments frame their goals and objectives the way they do. Because most nation-states exist in a relationship of potential insecurity and competition toward each other, it has seemed reasonable to declare that each government acts so as to preserve and enhance its national (or collective) interest vis-à-vis every other state. By the same logic it has been taken for granted by statesmen and theorists alike that each state counted among its vital interests such things as security and survival, independence, economic well-being, power, and prestige (for example, Nixon and Kissinger hesitated to abandon South Vietnam for so long out of fear that its fall would be a blow to American prestige).

The framing of the goals of foreign policy was assumed to follow automatically by deducing what territorial acquisitions, bases, allies, and distribution of power and influence would be most favorable to one's own nation's security, independence, power, and prestige. Unfortunately, as Professor Sondermann observes in his article, the ambiguities associated with the concept of the national interest have prompted many analysts to turn away from the concept altogether, or to try to bring the theory of how governments frame and implement their foreign policy goals into line with a reality that is much more complex than the simple description we have given assumes.

The survival or self-preservation of the nation-state is often cited as the *sine qua non* of its foreign policy. But what is the "self" that is to be preserved, and what do such terms as preservation and survival mean? If fifty million Americans were to die in a nuclear war with Russia, could we say that the nation had been preserved? Another such term used to describe state objectives is independence. Yet no country, not even the most powerful one, is ever fully independent of decisions made in other countries, decisions over which only a very imperfect control can be exercised. Just how "independent" was the U.S. on the day following Pearl Harbor? The decision to declare war on Japan was made by the Congress at the request of the President, but the real choice for war had been made weeks before in Tokyo (which in turn had made its "independent" decision in response to prior moves that had been made elsewhere, including in Washington). Today our economic independence is at the mercy of Arab oil producers.

Another ambiguous expression, "the maintenance of territorial integrity," is often used to define the interest of states; however, it fails to specify precisely which territory is to be defended and against whom. Does the term "territorial integrity" imply that the U.S. would defend only its own territorial boundaries, or does it include the territory of its European allies and the bases established overseas in order to better protect the national realm?

Some students of international politics maintain that all human behavior, including therefore the behavior of actors on the international stage, is characterized by a "power drive." Bertrand Russell, for example, wrote that "of the infinite desires of man, the chief are the desires for power and glory," and he added that some human desires, unlike those of animals, "are essentially boundless and incapable of complete satisfaction." Other competent observers agree, and although some of them might not classify the power drive as either unlimited or omnipresent, they feel that the concept of power provides the best organizing focus for analyzing relations among individuals and groups, including the massive and complex groups whose interaction is the subject matter of the study of international relations.

Before accepting this or any other single-motive explanation of behavior and applying it to the infinite variety of patterns found in international relations, one should recognize (as did Machiavelli, whose *Prince* symbolizes this approach) that there are other values in the minds of statesmen. Considerations of power are hardly a first priority in each and every type of situation. Much will depend upon how power is defined. If it is equated with physical force alone, one finds many contemporary international relationships which simply cannot be explained by sole reference to relative possession of military strength. But if by "power" is implied not only military but also psychological, economic, and even moral influence or control, as Professor Manning's selection in this chapter strongly suggests, then one may wonder whether the concept has not become too broad to be useful for purposes of analysis. On the other hand, it cannot be denied that in today's world, power, however defined, is not only an immediate means, but a long-range foreign-policy objective in itself in many a state's "shopping bag" of things to be acquired.

The difficulty lies in the specific definition of what is in the national interest, how it is to be defined, and what implementing actions must be performed to make the pursuit successful. Thus, after defining the motivations underlying states' behavior in terms of national interest, one is still left with the same problem—defining what constitutes the national interest.

A second complicating factor in attempting to frame and implement goals in light of the concept of the national interest is that it assumes that states or governments are single-purpose organizations, when in fact they are multipurpose organizations pursuing many varied and often competing objectives. It is no longer possible to assume that the definition of national interest includes only those objectives which a group of experts in the State Department or foreign ministry proclaim, because the influence of domestic groups pursuing their own often narrow and selfish objectives has become a more and more prominent feature of foreign-policy decisions. Citizens of democracies, at least, demand that their personal interests and economic well-being be incorporated into the national interest. So greatly do domestic factors impinge on foreign policy that one writer, Bayless Manning, proposes that we no longer speak of international relations but of intermestic relations.[1]

The definition of the national interest, and hence the framing of a nation's objectives, may also be skewed by the personal power drive of the national leadership or by the stake that foreign policy and military bureaucrats have in maintaining the image of another country as an enemy to perpetuate their own power needs. Then, too, powerful economic interests may impose their will upon a government in the name of the national interest when in fact it is really their own profits that they are seeking. If a president or prime minister fails to be responsive to these interests, even though their claims do not represent any interest but their own, he is sure

[1] Bayless Manning, "The Congress the Executive and Intermestic Affairs," *Foreign Affairs* (Jan. 1977), pp. 306–324.

to be punished in the next election. So, in any theory of the national interest (of how foreign policy is made) we have to take into account that states are multipurpose organizations, not simply guardians of abstractions called the national interest, and that any theory of how foreign policy is framed must take into account the influence that domestic or subnational groups exert upon the process—often in ways that may defeat other, more important values and goals of foreign policy.

This brings up another practical matter that qualifies and conditions the determination of a country's goals and of the policies designed to implement those goals. As Bayless Manning observes in his article that follows, "In real life situations, the problems of the policy-maker is usually how to choose between two or more results that are all desirable but conflict with one another; or how to choose between two or more results, all of which are undesirable; or how to move toward a desired result where one has little or no leverage on the situation. . . ." The national and subnational interests of a country are often in conflict with each other, which greatly complicates the practical matter of deciding which value or goal is to be pursued and which one sacrificed.

The choice of goals and policies to be pursued will be conditioned also by what capabilities and leverage a country has at its disposal. This has been covered in the preceding chapter. Clearly, in any situation so complex as international politics no state will be able to achieve all of its interests. Sooner or later it has to make some choices; choices which the concept of the national interest can illuminate, but which it can in no way determine.

In summary, framing and implementing foreign policy involves a problem of means and ends. In addition to knowing how terms are defined, one must also be aware of what priorities are given to various objectives as well as what specific resources and means can and will be devoted to their attainment.

One of the strongest tendencies (or temptations) of the twentieth century has been for states to adopt an ideological, messianic, or moralistic approach to foreign policy. This has the spurious advantage of appearing to give unity and consistency to policy that may only mask a heterogeneity of competing and mutually contradictory interests and motivations in a nation's foreign policy. We are all aware of the claims that Communist governments make, that they have a consistent and unified foreign policy based upon the moral and political truth of Marxism-Leninism and that there can be no permanent peace until history has brought about the overthrow of capitalism. The Soviet and Chinese governments may not frame their goals entirely in terms of that injunction, but to the extent that their convictions and perceptions are shaped by their ideology it is a potent factor in determining their national interest and shaping their foreign policies.

We are perhaps somewhat less aware of the extent to which cultural and ideological messianism has shaped the definition of our own national interest over the last thirty years. The strength and stability, if not the rationality, of United States' policy since World War II has been built upon the moral principles of anti-communism, anti-colonialism, and a messianic determination to shape the world in the image of American society and institutions. Around these principles, successive presidents built a powerful foreign-policy consensus that provided the government with the unity and support necessary to act on a global scale. These principles also served to justify the foreign-policy bureaucracy and the military in world-wide interventions and the economic interests in developing and exploiting overseas markets.

Toward the end of the sixties, if not earlier, these messianic and moral principles had become a touchstone by which our government rationalized an unending war in Vietnam and justified interventions in many parts of the world, interventions that were becoming less and less acceptable to other countries and were in fact weakening U.S. economic power and leadership both at home and abroad—a condition marked by simultaneous disunity at home and decline of the dollar abroad. As Bayless Manning points out in this chapter, the danger in such an ideological and messianic approach is that "we too long retained a consensus as to our perception of reality into a new era in which the reality itself had radically changed (for example China and the Soviet Union no longer formed a monolithic bloc)."[2]

The temptation to reach for a moral issue with which he might once again rally the American people behind foreign policy was illustrated by President Carter's initial emphasis on human rights. By writing a letter to Soviet dissident Andrei Sakharov in support of his call for greater freedom within Russia, Carter immediately encountered the hostility of the Kremlin and endangered detente and the prospects for a new Strategic Arms Limitation agreement. Subsequently, Carter modified his emphasis on human rights in framing and implementing his foreign policy so as not to sacrifice other goals that are also morally and politically valid.

Does this mean that moral ideals cannot find a place in a nation's foreign policy? Not at all. A state may integrate its moral ideals into its foreign policy by consciously weighing the value of its pursuit of stability and security against the aspirations of poorer nations that call for revolution and change, and by weighing the value of an additional military base or increment of economic advantage against the violence we do to our ideals by supporting governments that engage in political repression, torture, and inhuman exploitation. Morality finds its place in the framing of foreign policy,

---

[2]Richard W. Cottam suggests that the fundamental value change in American attitudes toward the Cold War had occurred even prior to 1965; but the Administration—particularly Secretary of State Rusk and Security Adviser Rostow—and the foreign policy bureaucracy still clung to the Cold War view that communist China and Russia were actively promoting aggression in Vietnam, and that aggression there was no different from that of a Hitler or a Stalin. *Foreign Policy Motivation* (Pittsburgh: University of Pittsburgh Press, 1977) p. 19.

not in the pursuit of ethical and moral absolutes, but in the careful determination of what can be done to improve our own performance and to induce other governments to behave reasonably.

One final observation: The policy change that goes by the term detente reflects how markedly a nation's definition of its national interests and objectives can change, reflecting the observation of Frederick Hartmann that

> almost never are all the interests of two states completely opposed or completely common. As time passes the common and opposed interests of each changes, reflecting a reassessment of current conditions . . . and the impact of changing attitudes by third states. The fluidity of this process has limits, but greater changes [in the definition of the national interest] are possible than popular opinion usually assumes."[3]

For these and other reasons we must approach the terms in which a state defines and implements its national goals with great caution. We must be aware that our assumptions about other states' motivations are not always what they claim or appear to be—just as our own are not. As Sondermann concludes, whatever value the concept of the national interest may have, its analysis raises the questions that are crucial to the framing and implementation of foreign policy: Whose interests are being served, how are they being defined, and what implementing actions must be performed to make their pursuit successful?

[3]Frederick H. Hartmann, *The Relations of Nations*, 5th ed. (New York: Macmillan Publishing Co., 1978) pp. 11-12.

10   Goals, Ideology and Foreign Policy

Bayless Manning

The author is President of the Council on Foreign Relations.

A commonly heard comment about American foreign policy these days is that the nation has lost its earlier sense of national goals and ideological objectives and that we should, as a nation, settle upon a new consensus as to our global moral objectives. This is a difficult subject, and, in my view, much of the discussion of it is made up of half-perceptions and half-truths.

In the first place, it is clearly true that there is less consensus today among Americans on foreign policy issues than was the case from about 1940 until about 1965. This is in no way surprising. The goals of World War II were simple and clear: the utter extermination of Hitlerian nazism and its Japanese counterpart. At the end of World War II, the United States developed a grand global vision grounded in traditional American liberal economics, free trade, anti-colonialism and parliamentarianism. That vision inspired American leadership in the construction of the major world institutions that came into being at the end of World War II—the International Monetary Fund,

This article is adapted from one of a series of four lectures delivered at the Claremont Colleges in April of 1975, published by the Claremont Press under the title, The Conduct of Foreign Policy in the Nation's Third Century. *Reprinted by permission from* Foreign Affairs, *January 1976. Copyright 1975 by Council on Foreign Relations, Inc.*

the World Bank, the General Agreement on Tariffs and Trade, and the United Nations.

Very shortly, however, as the outlines of the cold war crystallized, the dominant drive of U.S. foreign policy increasingly became anticommunism and global Soviet containment; a secondary theme was the desire to help develop a united, democratic Europe that would forever preclude another European-centered world war; and a third motif was decolonization and, somewhat less wholeheartedly, assistance in the untried experiment of bringing modern economic development to the unindustrialized world.

The Nazis are now gone. The restoration of Europe and Japan has long since been completed. The colonial empires have been wholly dismantled. The global institutions built at the end of World War II are now demonstrably inadequate to the problems of today. The cold war (at least in its original form) is now history. The comparative moral, political, and economic power of the United States has been measurably reduced. The trauma of Vietnam has intervened, bringing with it for a time a major schism in U.S. public opinion. Basic changes have also taken place in domestic social attitudes. Politically and psychologically, we are in a time of regeneration, in part stunned by the Vietnam debacle and in part fumbling in a dim recognition that world conditions have changed and that old problems have given way to new ones.

On the other hand, despite these developments, the decline of consensus should not be overstated. Public consensus continues to support a number of elements of U.S. foreign policy—and they are the central ones on the basis of which most of our foreign policy rests.

The nation's resolution to defend itself against attack remains unimpaired. Similarly, a direct Soviet military assault on Western Europe, Japan or Canada would be met with American military retaliation. No conceivable U.S. foreign policy would contain as a component the territorial expansion of the United States. The United States will, like all other countries, devote a substantial portion of its international energies to enhance the economic interests of the American people, but the nation will at the same time continue to respond sympathetically to the humanitarian needs of others. The nation's ideological preference remains in favor of parliamentarianism and free market economics. European unity still enlists U.S. support.

Other such continuing components of our international position could be cited. In fact, with the Vietnam issue behind us, the major changes that distinguish U.S. policy today from the continuity of yesterday are seen on reflection to be essentially two: a lowering of the intensity of our cold-war fears and our communist containment policy, and a heightening of our recognition that it will not be feasible to remake the world in our own image.

Indeed, on further reflection, it becomes apparent that our main problem in shaping our foreign policy in the last decade was not that we lost our consensus, but that we too long retained a consensus as to our perception of reality into a new era in which the reality itself had radically changed.

II

It is easy to make up a roster of things it would be nice to have—like peace and health and open opportunity and an end to poverty —and to describe these as the nation's "goals." But they do not provide much headway toward developing public policy or public support for them. In real-life situations, the problem of the policy-maker is usually how to choose between two or more results that are all desirable but conflict with one another; or how to choose between two or more results, all of which are undesirable; or how to move toward the desired result where one has little or no leverage on the situation; or, if something must be traded off, how to see to it that that which is sacrificed is the least valued—that the most favorable mix of costs and benefits is achieved.

A real-world issue of U.S. foreign policy does not give rise to a single question of "policy" but rather provokes a whole series of subdebates, of which the following are only the most obvious:

Facts: What are the facts? What will they be tomorrow?

Stakes: Who has what kind of stake in the outcome, and how much? The United States, generally conceived? Various domestic interest groups in the United States? Who cares about the outcome, why, and with what intensity? What outcome is more compatible with general ideological preferences of the United States? Economic? Strategic? What is the balance between the short-run and the long-run interests of the nation? What are the risks of action? Of inaction?

Management and tactics: To what extent can the United States affect the situation? Assuming some leverage, what is the most effective tactic for using it? Should the United States act in the matter unilaterally, or multilaterally? Who will be in charge of implementing the steps decided upon?

Costs, priorities, and trade-offs: What will it cost to achieve the desired results? As compared with other desired objectives, how important is it that the desired outcome be achieved at this time? Pursuit of any policy line inevitably means that other desired policy lines will have to be given up or postponed: what trade-offs and other costs will be entailed in pursuing the particular objective? And what are the priorities?

Resources to be committed: How much of the nation's limited economic, military and political capital should be committed to the particular objective? With what intensity should the desired outcome be sought?

A list of generalized national foreign policy objectives proves to be of little or no assistance in working through such a typical matrix of questions, disputes and considerations.

Under our form of government, policy decisions on particular matters are hammered out through a pluralistic process that combines elements of official leadership, interest groups, public debate and various forms of power leverage. Every contesting participant in that process is able to invoke in support of his own position—and he invariably does invoke—one or more of the national "goals" that would appear on anybody's abstract list of objectives of the United States. Such "goals" often provide the vocabulary of public policy debate; they usually do little to resolve real problems of policy choice.

III

Despite the example of the Holy Alliance, in the nineteenth century it had not yet become fashionable to consider that every nation's foreign policy should have an ideological component. Although the United States stood far in the vanguard of representative democracy and individual liberty, the nation did not feel obliged to seek to export its governmental forms or ideals. The primary objectives of U.S. policy were to stay out of European politics, to extend U.S. trade, and to keep the seas open for American ships; we carried out those policies very well.

The twentieth century, however, has seen the emergence of titanic international struggles among a variety of competing secular ideologies. "Isms," great and small, fight for control of men's minds and institutions of power. Future historians of foreign affairs will see our era as made up of a mix of two classical elements (balance-of-power struggles and competition for national economic return) and one new element that is remarkably akin to older wars of religion —an ideological struggle over the "right" principles that "ought" to govern patterns of economic distribution among men in society and define the proper relationship between the individual and the collectivity, the state.

The ideological stance of the United States is clear enough. Indeed it is remarkably so, and it has been extraordinarily stable. The nation has a preference for a relatively free-market economy where feasible, and a preference for the individualistic libertarian tenets set out in the Constitution in 1789, as expanded in the years since to bring more domestic groups into full political participation. A major question for debate today is whether and to what extent these ideological preferences should be given weight in determining the nation's posture on foreign policy issues.[1]

Critics who contend for a "higher ideological content" in our foreign policy usually point out, quite correctly, that the nation performs at its best when welded together in a common ideological endeavor. They recall the enthusiasm in World War I for making the world safe for democracy, they point to the public ideological commitment of World War II and the generation following, and they detect a messianic streak in the American people—a latent propensity to go forth to save the world. When that psychological resource is tapped there is almost nothing the United States cannot accomplish; when that resource is not invoked, goes the argument, the American public loses interest in international affairs, tends to withdraw, and U.S. foreign policy wilts. As these analysts see it, therefore, for the United States to have a strong and effective foreign policy over a period of time, our leaders must serve up, and the public must, after debate, accept some large-scale targeted goal, something which the United States is setting out to do. In this view of the matter, the American public should settle upon some long-term ideological objectives: to achieve political or religious

liberty for all; or to put a floor under global poverty and redistribute wealth among all nations and peoples; or to stamp out totalitarianism; or to commit its armed forces to enforce world peace; or to assure free speech and free movement of persons around the world; or to establish a free market economy everywhere; or to eliminate racial prejudice; or something of the sort. Then the U.S. government, supported by such a consensus, should press steadily toward that ultimate goal.

There is something to be said for this perspective. If the American people could be unified by some broad humanitarian theme it would doubtless make the conduct of American foreign policy easier. Depending on the theme chosen, such a course would also have the power to attract some admiration and support in other countries around the world. And there is no doubt that the American people are capable of a kind of exaltation when the right leader sets the right moral target at the right time. But, granting these general points, the argument for a high-intensity ideological foreign policy suffers from a number of defects.

No person can make any decision without some reference to his underlying philosophic preferences and value system. Equally inevitably, foreign policy outcomes perceived by the United States as preferred will in some degree reflect ideological preferences of the public and of government officials. For example, our military alliance commitments to Western Europe, Canada and Japan are in large part based upon a recognition that our own national security and defense posture are inextricably commingled with theirs, but the alliance also obviously expresses our ideological preference for liberal democracy and a free-market economy.

Further, it is evident that tomorrow's international agenda will repeatedly put to us in one form or another at least four basic

---

[1]Whether these traditional national ideological preferences themselves should be abandoned in favor of others is an entirely separate issue—the issue that is pressed by political elements that are for that reason properly denominated "radical," whether of the unreconstructed right or of the un-constructed left. Sometimes persons who argue that our foreign policy has "insufficient ideological content" will be found in reality to be arguing that their own idiosyncratic brand of ideology should be adopted by the nation—quite a different point.

For a recent contribution to aspects of the debate, see William P. Bundy, "Dictatorships and American Foreign Policy," *Foreign Affairs*, October 1975.

questions that contain an unavoidable ethical or ideological component. What will be the American attitude regarding the poor two-thirds of the world? What will be the American attitude regarding persons in other countries whose individual political rights are being suppressed? What will be the American attitude toward such global problems as environmental protection and the use of the world's air space and seabeds? And what will be the American attitude toward the development of new multilateral international institutions that will entail some sacrifice of national freedom or unilateral action? It will require political leadership of the highest order to explain these broad issues to the American public and to work out responsive U.S. foreign policy positions that are compatible with the ethical and ideological predispositions of a majority of the American people.

The question is thus not whether there should be *some* ideological component in foreign policy, but whether that ideological component should be greatly enlarged or made predominant.

IV

In assessing that question, it must first be recognized that even a high degree of ideological content in our foreign policy will not produce consensus, eliminate debate, or provide answers to foreign policy problems. If Nation X decides on ideological grounds to impose economic sanctions against Country Y, that step does not predetermine whether the government of Nation X would also be willing to go to war with Country Y on the same ideological grounds. Regardless of the ideological target, the costs and benefits of each new policy decision must be weighed anew, and the issue decided pragmatically on its own footing as it arises.

The answer arrived at will, of course, vary in accordance as the ideological factor (or any other factor) is differently weighted, but the *process* of decision-making is not altered by changes in the weighting of the factors. Thus, while one may argue that this or that ideological consideration should be given more weight in foreign policy decision-making, one cannot eliminate the necessity for the weighing process itself.

A high ideological content has not historically been an indispensable element in the successful conduct of U.S. foreign policy, as the experience of the nineteenth century showed. Some of the nation's less appealing chapters of history coincided with a high fervor of self-righteousness, notably the Mexican War, the Spanish-American War, and our adventure with old-time imperialism at the turn of the century. Then too, there appear to be hangover costs; when the nation has experienced an ideological "high" in foreign policy, it has tended to be followed by a later "low" and a propensity to withdraw from the world, as the United States did in rejecting the League of Nations, and as many fear the American public may be doing today.

In present-day circumstances it is far from apparent *what* ideological bugle call would arouse a consensus among the U.S. public and spark a moral crusade. The point is not merely that no such consensus of enthusiasm exists at present; it is, rather, that the domestic atmosphere at this time of post-Vietnam and post-U.S. *imperium* is not propitious for a remobilization of the moral energies of the nation for a major overseas initiative. Any effort to embark upon a new ideological push at this time would sharply divide, rather than unify, the American people.

Then there are the special dangers that crusades always bring. Once launched, the *jihad*, the holy war, is the least manageable of all forms of human dispute. For man's greatest suffering at the hands of man we can thank the ideologues and the religious zealots of history—those arrested personalities who cannot live with uncertainty, cannot tolerate difference, are divinely (or atheistically) certain of their own rightness and are ready—eager—to impose their views on others.

The foreign policy history of the twentieth century has been heavily freighted with that sort of thinking, some of it (though by comparison only a small part of it) contributed by the United States. The costs to mankind of this attitude have been unimaginably great. Western Europe, Japan, the Soviet Union, China and the United States all seem to have concluded of late that they have had enough of high ideologies in their foreign policy for a while, and all are moving toward the conference table as a preferred alternative to mutual destruction over ideological issues that are, by definition, irresolvable.

It is the Third World today which has entered upon a period of intense ideological excitation, inspired in part by a new and fevered nationalism in each country and in part by a sense of community directed against the industrialized powers. In these circumstances, even if it were possible to muster a domestic consensus in the United States for some sort of ideological offensive, it is difficult to believe that such an offensive could do other than to isolate the United States further, and further disrupt the fragile international order that now exists.

Finally, it is now commonplace to observe that the agenda of international affairs is today expanding beyond the traditional issues of security and balance of power to include complex issues of economic interdependence, resource management and global preservation. Issues like these by their nature require multilateral negotiatory treatment, and simply cannot be dealt with on an ideological basis.

For these reasons, and others as well, another call to ideological arms does not at this time offer a promising basis upon which to build U.S. foreign policy for the last quarter of this century. The relationship between a foreign policy that contains some component of ideological preference and a foreign policy that is heavily ideologized is the relationship between normal cell activity and cancerous cell activity. For a complex nation in a complex world, single-minded pursuit of some fixed ideological objective will not only deprive that nation of gains that might otherwise have been made in the direction of multiple objectives that are important to it; will not only guarantee a continuously dangerous condition of crisis and confrontation with others; will not only lead to misassessments of objective realities and the nation's capacity to change them; but will also lead to division and self-destructive tendencies within the body politic itself—all as we have recently experienced in our Vietnam involvement.

V

And yet there remains an important moral role for the United States to play in the world.

As the world's preeminent military power, we can expect to produce in others some fear and also some awe. As the world's most efficient producer we can expect to excite criticism and also some admiration. As the world's richest nation we can expect to generate in others some envy and also some esteem. But we cannot expect to achieve the inspiration of others except through spiritual leadership. The United States has in the past provided that inspiration to the world. It is not doing it now. But it can, one day, do it again.

No contemporary American can be un-aware of the deficiencies, shortcomings and blind spots that still mar the social land-scape of the United States today, and the painful slowness with which we have some-times moved to correct these failings. But many Americans, especially younger ones, do need to remind themselves that, for all its blemishes, the United States stands in the forefront of the world in its commit-ment to the proposition that the individual human being should be free—free to think what he wants, write what he wishes, assemble as he will, read as his curiosity leads him, paint as his eye uniquely sees, worship as to him seems right, and espouse whatsoever political position he finds con-genial, so long only as he accords those same privileges to his fellow citizens.

The United States has been imbued with this spirit of individual liberty since its founding, and its institutions are imbued with it today. There is no doubt whatsoever in my mind that this urge for individual self-expression has ever been the ultimate revolutionary aspiration and always will be. In this sense, the United States remains the most progressive revolutionary society in the world.

We are, however, living in a transitory period in which the vocabulary of revolu-tionary aspirations is turned upside-down; today's revolutionary voices have little or no interest in, or are actively opposed to, the ideal of individual expression. The reasons are not hard to find. Over the course of this century, the unindustrialized former colonies of the world, the backward fast-nesses of Russia, and the traditionalist frozen-in-amber static society of China have all grimly determined that they will somehow, at whatever cost, make the twentieth century the era in which they asserted their full nationhood, garnered for themselves the bounty of modern technology, and shattered the atavistic social, political, and wealth structures they had inherited from the past. Future historians will see this century as a period of the most extraordinary achieve-ment for these countries, as they set out to try to bring themselves abreast of the industrialized West and as they are, in vary-ing degrees, making progress in so doing.

The United States has in the main mis-understood the process that is taking place in the unindustrialized countries in this cen-tury. In some degree we have grasped that economic modernization is being pursued and in some degree we have sought to assist in that regard. To a degree we have under-stood that basic human social services are needed in the developing countries and, again, we have done something to try to help with programs for schools, medical care and the like. But we have had little or no understand-ing of the demand for change in the ancient social orders of these countries or the demand for national self-expression. We have, as a result, for the most part comported ourselves toward these countries so as to appear to be (and sometimes clearly have been) opposed to their internal forces of modernization and in league with their domestic forces seeking to maintain the status quo.

In some instances we have been negative toward these new societies because our democratic preferences—especially those of our liberal ideologues—have been repelled by the authoritarian character of their new governments. Sometimes we have been nega-tive toward them because our free market preferences—especially those of our con-servative ideologues—have been repelled by the planned economy preference of some of the new governments. Sometimes we have been negative because some private U.S. economic interest groups stood to suffer immediate losses from a change in the status quo and succeeded in harnessing Washing-ton to their narrow interests. Sometimes the leaders that have arisen in the non-industrialized countries have seemed to us to be demagogues, or worse. Sometimes we have been negative because the economic policies pursued by the new regimes have been not only harmful to U.S. interests, but downright suicidal for themselves. But most often the issues of U.S. attitude toward a newly developing country became wholly confounded with and dominated by the global confrontation of the cold war; we thought it necessary to support the forces of the status quo because the alternative seemed to be an extension of dangerous Russian global influence, "the spread of communism."

In many of the emerging countries there has been some validity in one or a number of these U.S. perspectives. But the ultimate underlying truth was that the time had come for the industrially backward people of the world to move into the twentieth century, and move they have. More often than not, The United States has wound up on the wrong side of the historic evolution. As a result, the United States stands today in deep disfavor among many of the developing countries, and is portrayed as the main external adversary opposing their national development, internal modernization, and economic advancement.[2]

[2]We thus left the door open—we threw the door open—to the Soviet Union to declare itself as friend of the forces of modernization in these countries. As it has turned out, however, the Russians have done little with this opportunity. Despite the openings offered them, they have conducted themselves in such a ham-handed manner that they have been thrown out after having been invited in (as Ghana, Sudan, Egypt, and Indonesia), and have been able to hang on only where their troops are stationed in active occuption or where, as in Cuba, they support a regime by direct subvention. The "spread of communism" has not gone quite as easily in Third World countries as Soviet planners hoped, or American planners feared.

In a similar way, other programs and institutions affiliated with the United States have become suspect or villains in the view of many in the Third World. The CIA is, of course, the most virulently attacked. Ironically, AID—born as a beneficent program for the express purpose of assisting the Third World deveopment process—is calumniated only a little less. And in the eyes of many developing countries, foreign-controlled multinational corporate enterprises—many of which are based in the United States—have come to be identified with the old imperialistic economic order.

As a result, increased taxation, expropriation, and, of late, kidnapping and terrorism have been directed against such companies. Popular attitudes in these countries toward such treatment of multinational companies are evocative of our own dim recollections of Saxon Robin Hood, living dispossessed in his own country and penniless in the woods, and making occasional retributory forays against rich, fat bishops and the symbols of outlander Norman authority—a dangerous legend for the world's richest country to perpetuate. Many (not all) of the charges made in the Third World against the multinational companies are unfair, and the companies have frequently brought employment and other advantages to other countries where they have invested. But though the Normans, too, brought many advanced and elevated benefits to rustic, backward England, it took a very long time for the men in Sherwood Forest to see it that way.

More generally, these attitudes, coupled with precarious economic conditions in much of the Third World, have produced heavy political pressures in the United Nations and other forums for a so-called "new international economic order" and other proposals for major wealth transfers by the industrialized West to the Third World, backed up by efforts to organize raw materials cartels and threats to resort to boycotts and other forms of arm twisting. These efforts at pressure may or may not prove ultimately effective, but they have already introduced new heat, strain and danger into the world's international political relations and will doubtless continue to do so.

It is now obvious to all that our Vietnam policy was a blunder; one cannot help but wonder, too, how different and better a world it would be for the United States today—and for everybody else—if we had worked more actively for the last 30 years to assist the forces for change in the Third World. Given the tensions of the cold war, the U.S, misperception of the Third World's historical situation, and the economic interests of significant elements of the United States, it is probably true that we could not have done significantly better than we did. In any case, we did not do so, and we shall now for a time have to live with the consequences.

And we must look to the future. In part, what happened during the post-World War II era was that the United States completely misunderstood what revolution we were witnessing in the emerging post-colonial countries. Naïvely, though understandably enough, we thought our own history would be relived by these new nations. In keeping with our anti-colonial traditions, our position immediately following World War II was strongly in favor of granting prompt independence to the colonies of England, France, Holland, and Belgium—much to the annoyance of those wartime allies. So far, so good.

But we then expected the newly independent countries to start at once to behave politically like the Commonwealth of Massachusetts in 1776—complete with parliaments, voting, free press, private entrepreneurship, and the like. We based our policy on that premise—and were promptly disappointed, as in almost no case did the emerging countries follow those expectations. Circumstances in the new unindustrialized countries of this century were wholly different from ours in 1776, and it was not yet time for our kind of revolution. It was time instead for the pursuit of three great goals "at whatever cost"—the building of nationhood, economic modernization, and internal social restructuring.

In those three efforts, some (not all) of the new societies have made extraordinary progress. But they have had to pay a large price for that progress. The price has been paid largely in regimentation, submergence of the individual, suppression of dissent, discouragement of inquiry, public misinformation, and imposed conformity. They have become conscript societies. It will be long debated whether up to now it has been necessary to become a conscript society in order to achieve the goals that were set. But now, as collective social progress has been made, the time is coming, so far most noticeably in Eastern Europe and the Soviet Union, when the seeds of individual expression are stirring and seeking an outlet to sprout. The rustlings of personal expression will not be confined there.

It is not a credible proposition, for example, that the magnificently civilized, creative, colorful and sophisticated Chinese people will for long be content to be compelled to look at only the same eight politically authorized operas, and to spend their lives in gray formations doing responsive readings in unison. Throughout the authoritarian world, the stage is slowly being set for the next evolutionary if not revolutionary move forward, the resumption of the ancient craving for individual liberty. No amount of internal secret police work will stop it. And bit by bit, whatever totalitarian communism or totalitarian neo-Peronism may achieve today in the realm of forced-draft social modernization, tomorrow's reformers will see the political structures of these conscript societies for what they are—authoritarian and repressive.

Revolutionary movements of the past century have all begun as movements toward idealized collective economic and social systems. But once installed in power they have become primarily distinguished by, and are likely to be most remembered for, their innovative and unique systems of rigid political control.[3] When eventually the counterpressure to these repressive systems mounts, the thrust will not be toward new social and economic ends, but toward the ancient goals of political freedom and individual self-expression.

Marx, it will be recalled, paid tribute to the rise of the capitalist bourgeoisie as the modernizing agent that swept away the rotting social castle of aristocracy and feudalism in Western Europe and substituted a better, more efficient, more productive and widely sharing society. In the Marxist view, however, the new post-feudal system bore within itself the seeds of its own destruction and will in time be swept into the dustbin of history as it is replaced by the new order of socialism. Socialism will then build upon the social gains that were made during the capitalist era.

This historical prognosis is parallel to the point argued here. In some backward countries during the twentieth century, totalitarian regimes, some of them communist, are acting as the modernizing agent to sweep away the rotting manor house of aristocracy and colonialism and substitute a better, more efficient, more productive and widely sharing society. But these new regimes bear within themselves the seeds of their own destruction, for they can allow no significant room for the expression of the individual human spirit. As the latent drives for personal liberation again become active, the authoritarian regimes of today—musty, ossified, and profoundly reactionary—will be themselves swept into the dustbin of history. The new progressive elements will not then reinstate the earlier pre-industrial order that was but will proceed to build upon the social and economic gains made during the era of conscript modernization.[4]

The time will come—in some countries soon—when the triple tasks of nation-building, modernization, and social restructuring by authoritarian means will be largely completed, or become too costly to be pursued single-mindedly further. When that time comes, if the United States has maintained vital and active the traditions of its own revolution and Constitution, then the banners for the next round of progressive change will be rediscovered safe in Philadelphia.

Whatever policy the United States may follow in economic matters, it is debatable whether the developing nations that have adopted central economic planning systems will ever welcome the return of fully free-market forces to their economies.[5] But if America preserves at home its steadfast stand in favor of the claim of the free individual, and also continues to make progress in dealing with its own internal social inequities, the United States will eventually regain its moral leadership among the nations of the world—not by force of its eco-

[4]Though it is fascinating to note that a reinstatement of the ancient order seems to be what Solzhenitsyn would envision for Russia.

[5]On the other hand, who 300 years ago would have predicted the retreat of centrally planned mercantilism?

[3]Their origins as conspiratorial semi-military undergrounds may account for a part of this.

nomic power and its arms but by virtue of its ideological example as a society of free men.

In the long view, the surest way for the United States to influence for the better the ideological future of mankind everywhere is by being sure that we present an unwavering example of commitment to our principles at home. And that *is* an ideological target that can be—has been—set for all Americans.

In the meantime, in the United Nations and other forums, the United States should do what it can to train the spotlight of international public attention upon the openness of its own society and upon the oppressive closedness of authoritarian regimes, of the right or the left. Such steps

by the United States will not be widely welcomed for some time to come. They will not be welcomed because human liberties are never a favorite topic of restrictive regimes, because most developing countries see the present era as the epoch for industrial and social development and consider the time to be premature for serious concern about the individual, and because the United States is today viewed negatively in many parts of the world. Nevertheless, the United States should continuously speak out internationally to reassert its ideological stance on individual freedom and expression. In time, the audience of the world will once more listen and respond.

11   The Concept of the National Interest

Fred A. Sondermann

The author is Professor of Political Science at Colorado College.

II

. . . . The term "national interest" is of relatively recent vintage. It was and remains an effort to describe the underlying rationale for the behavior of states and statesmen in a threatening international environment. But the idea of preserving and protecting one's values against others, goes back into antiquity. The word "interest" derives from the Latin, meaning "it concerns, it makes a

From "National Interest" by Fred A. Sondermann, Orbis: A Journal of World Affairs, Vol. 21, No. 1. (Spring, 1977). Reprinted by permission. (Most footnotes have been omitted.)

difference to, it is important with reference to some person or thing."

We have the example of the early Israelites' continuing efforts to assert and maintain their characteristics and their values. We know of the Greeks' devotion to their citystates—Pericles' Funeral Oration is a statement to which we still respond. We know of the Romans' pride in their empire and the status of their citizenship within it. These feelings, and the behaviors that followed from them, may have been confined to relatively small groups at the top; the popularization and democratization of foreign policy would come much later. But for those who formulated and executed their tribe's, their city's, their kingdom's, their empire's policy vis-ā-vis the outside world, the idea, if not the term, was always there.

Charles Beard, whose book on national interest was written in the early 1930s, traced the evolution of the concept in the more modern period through several stages. In the first of these the relevant concept was the "dynastic" interest—the desire of each monarch to maintain and, if possible, extend his domain and his control over land and people. As more and more groups within the domain came to attach their specific interests to those of the monarch, the dynastic phase gave way to the concept of *raison d'état*, which became, in turn, intermingled with the idea of national honor. Beard argued that the idea of national honor was weakened as economic issues gained an ever greater share of attention. Honor and profit do not always go hand in hand, it seems. He suggested that "with the emergence of the national state system, the increase in influence of popular political control, and the great expansion of economic relations, the lines of [the] new formula—national interest—were being laid down." Links with the past remained strong, however. The characteristic of unity associated with the dynastic phase remained; so did the element of "compelling absolutism," making national interest "no less sovereign and inexorable than the 'will of the prince' had been."

To understand the impact of the concept of the national interest on a generation of scholars of foreign policy, a brief detour into intellectual history is appropriate. The interwar period was characterized by a high level of academic attention to, reliance upon, and value placed in the processes of international law, international organization and international trade. The hope was that re-

liance on these could reduce the harshness of "realpolitik" which had culminated in a disastrous world war. These hopes were disappointed, and in the post-World War II period a new school of thinkers and writers promoted a "realist" stance on issues of foreign policy and international politics. Charles Beard, having written on national interest in the early 1930s, had in a sense been outside the mainstream of scholarly thought at that time, a situation to which he was accustomed and which he seemed to relish. E.H. Carr weighed in at the end of the decade with his important book *The Twenty Years Crisis, 1919-1939*. By then, World War II was upon us, and it remained for writers like George Kennan, Walter Lippmann, and above all Hans Morgenthau to make the postwar case for the relevance—indeed, the centrality—of the national interest as a focus around which the complex and diverse issues of foreign policy could be organized; as a concept by which the behaviors of states and their governments could be understood.

The crux of the concept, as advanced in the postwar years, was that in a world in which states are "the major units of political life, which command the supreme loyalty and affection of the great mass of individuals," statesmen who are responsible for and to their separate publics, and who operate in an uncertain and threatening milieu, have little choice but to put the interests of their own entity above those of others or those of the international system. National interest, thus, became a synonym for national egoism. One could not rely on others, nor could one rely on international institutions and processes to protect one's key values. These values were thought to be national in scope. Their protection was the concern and responsibility of those who governed each separate entity. Osgood put it as follows: "National interest is understood to mean a state of affairs valued solely for its benefit to the nation. The motive of national egoism, which leads men to seek this end, is marked by the disposition to concern oneself with the welfare of one's own nation; it is self-love transferred to the national group."

It must by now be clear that when we speak of national interest, we speak of values: values held by some, many, perhaps even all of the members of a given society. Whether it be some, many or all is a separate question that will be addressed in the next part of this paper. But the more immediate question is, How can these values be defined? Surely, not everything anyone desires is automatically transformed into an interest, let alone a national one. Hopes, wishes, aspirations and dreams are not the same as practical and concrete interests. They are not always, or even often, reflected in the policies of states and their governments.

The problem of definition, or more accurately of description, has been approached in two ways. Some observers have tried to define the national interest of a given state by looking at the state's actual policy output and, finding repetitive behavior patterns, have deduced from these what the national interest must have been. For instance, John Chase suggested four "aspects of the American national interest which . . . actually guided and motivated the development of our foreign policy": (1) to deprive potential aggressors of bases from which they might launch attacks against the United States; (2) to support self-government and democracy abroad; (3) to protect and advance commerce; and (4) to help establish and maintain a favorable world balance of power. Beard stressed the economic/commercial element in American statecraft throughout the Federalist-Whig-Republican succession. He attached the development

and maintenance of a superior navy to this basic goal, and leaned heavily on the writings of Admiral Mahan, who expanded the reasons for needing a superior navy from mere defense of territory to "defense of our just national interests, whatever they be and wherever they are." Mahan included among those interests the defense of national territory, the extension of maritime commerce, acquisition of territorial positions that would contribute to command of the seas ("when it can be done righteously"), maintenance of the Monroe Doctrine, hegemony in the Caribbean, and active promotion of the China trade. Modern revisionist writers on American foreign policy could hardly express their case more clearly and succinctly.

Other scholars went at the task of defining the national interest in a different manner, basing their analysis on logical reasoning and induction; framing their conclusions in less tangible, more conceptual terms. Thus, Robert Osgood along with many others put national survival or self-preservation at the head of the list, because everything else would clearly depend on the achievement of this goal. He defined survival or self-preservation in terms of territorial integrity, political independence, and maintenance of fundamental governmental institutions.

Osgood proceeded to other categories of national interest: self-sufficiency, prestige, aggrandizement. Beard, on his part, talked about territory and commerce as two of its fundamental aspects. George and Keohane, in a major recent effort to imbue the term with specific meaning, wrote about three "irreducible" national interests: physical survival—by which they meant the survival of people, not necessarily the preservation of territory or sovereignty; liberty—by which they meant the ability of inhabitants of a country to choose their form of government and to exercise a set of individual rights defined by law and protected by the state; and economic subsistence—the maximization of economic welfare.

Finally, since he is clearly the contemporary scholar most closely connected with the concept of national interest, let us consider Hans Morgenthau's work. He defined the "survival of a political unit . . . in its identity" as the irreducible minimum of a state's interest vis-a-vis other units, encompassing in this the integrity of a state's territory, its political institutions, and its culture. He asserted that it had been the perennial national interest of the United States to remain the predominant power in the Western Hemisphere—leading it to support the European balance-of-power system whose breakdown alone could threaten our hegemony in the Americas. With respect to Asia, he stipulated that maintenance of the balance of power there had been the consistent ingredient of American statecraft, hence part of our perennial national interest.

Although there are some variances in all of this, one detects a high degree of convergence of definitions and descriptions. Certain terms and ideas recur frequently. Most of them relate to tangible things—to concrete conditions or advantages, concretely experienced. But a few (culture, liberty, prestige) refer to intangibles—to how a society feels about itself, how it maintains and strengthens its morale, its elan.

III

Yet the picture is clouded. Difficulties and complexities have caused many analysts of the foreign policy process to turn away from the concept altogether, in spite of the fact that the term clearly remains a part of the rhetoric of foreign policy. Its use for analytic purposes has declined from the high point reached in the late 1940s and early 1950s. Some students of the subject suggest that it will not be used much in the future.

One way of explaining this state of affairs is to speculate that in the late 1940s and early 1950s the concept's function differed from the one for which scholars in the field now strive. The idea of the national interest was useful to Morgenthau and others in the then-current debate between "realists" and "idealists." In my judgment, this debate was won by the realists. But the victory was transient. The study of international relations, having conquered that particular piece of intellectual territory, proceeded in directions different from, and in fact somewhat irrelevant to, those staked out by the realists.

Of the many areas of doubt about, and criticisms of, the concept of the national interest, we present five as concisely as the subject matter permits.[1]

The first criticism is, simply, that the concept is too broad, too general, too vague, too all-inclusive to perform useful analytic functions, to serve as guideline for policymakers, as organizing concept for scholars, or as a criterion of judgment and evaluation for the citizen. . . .

Morgenthau, of course, tried to give the concept a specific meaning—namely, that national interest could be ascertained as well as advanced by the possession of power. The difficulty with this formulation is that it merely pushes the analytic task back a

---

[1]One area of criticism omitted is the moral/ethical one—not because it is unimportant, but because the debate is based on assumptions that would require a separate paper to do them full justice. In the final section of this article, we will briefly refer to some considerations pertaining to the moral/ethical dimension of the subject.

step: now one has to determine what "power" means, what it consists of, and how it can be measured. This task, far from becoming easier, has become ever more complex.[2]

But what is true regarding power is also true of other formulations of the content and meaning of the national interest. Such terms as survival, self-preservation, independence, sovereignty—usually said to constitute the rock-bottom purposes of the foreign policies of states—will be found, upon closer inspection, to hide a host of ambiguities.

In short, there is concern that the "great generality" of the phrase "national interest" obscures from the view of policymakers, analysts and the public the fact that foreign policies are designed to achieve specific goals, often short-term in nature; and that the study of these specific goals is likely to provide a better basis for the understanding of a country's political behavior in the external realm than reference to a general, vague, ambiguous term such as the national interest.

A second major problem is that of distinguishing between ends and means in foreign policy. The question the national interest concept is meant to answer relates to the ends, the goals, the purposes of foreign policy. This is an area of inquiry that, in my judgment, has not been satisfactorily addressed in the literature of international relations. It appears that, having tried to

[2]Cf. James Rosenau, "National Interest," *International Encyclopedia of the Social Sciences* (New York: Macmillan, Free Press, 1968), vol. 11, p. 35. See also Vernon Van Dyke, "Values and Interests," *The American Political Science Review*, September 1962, p. 573. Van Dyke quotes Morgenthau as admitting that "the goals that might be pursued by nations in their foreign policy can run the gamut of objectives any nation has ever pursued or might possibly pursue." (*Politics Among Nations*, 3rd ed. [New York: Knopf, 1960], p. 9.) The point may be accurate, but it is not very helpful in limiting and defining the issue.

find the explanation for foreign policies in the external realm—in the behaviors and actions of other states—and having failed at this task, observers have more recently turned inward, and now seek to find that explanation mainly within the motivations and operations of domestic bureaucracies. One may be forgiven for doubting whether this approach, by itself, will provide the desired key to understanding.

In any case, on closer inspection ends tend to become means toward some other ends; and conversely means—because they are desired, because they are thought to be useful—tend to become, at least in the short run, ends. Van Dyke put it this way: "When we use the language of means and ends, we say that means can themselves be ends and that ends can be means." (Unfortunately, however, neither the distinction between, nor the merging of, the concepts is always as clear as it might be.)

This problem was obscured by Morgenthau's formulation that stipulated power as the yardstick by which achievement of the national interest could be measured, thereby making power a goal of foreign policy behavior. But is it? Many would, no doubt, agree with George and Keohane, who suggested that "power is . . . only one subgoal of national interest, and an instrumental goal at that, rather than a fundamental value in and of itself." Furthermore, even if one could use power in the way Morgenthau intended to have it used, the issue would by no means be resolved, because in many ways power is as "elusive and ambiguous" a concept as is national interest itself. How many efforts to specify the components of power, to weigh them accurately, to aggregate them suitably, and to utilize them appropriately have come even close to success? . . .

Thirdly, any student or user of the concept of the national interest must face perplexing questions: Whose interests? How determined? By whom?

One can argue that the national interest is the culmination, the aggregation, of all the specific interests contained in the society. But this is a difficult argument to sustain or to act upon. A modern society, by definition, contains a multitude of interests—personal, ethnic, religious, racial, economic, regional, occupational/professional, ideological, to name some. It is one of the tasks of government to satisfy the largest possible number of these interests, or at least to keep dissatisfaction to a level low enough to avoid instability and upheaval. But it is also in the nature of politics that not every interest can be equally satisfied; some cannot be satisfied at all; and painful choices and tradeoffs are the order of the day. Some interests will gain while others lose—sometimes absolutely, always relatively—from any political act.

This is harsh doctrine, difficult to accept. It has become more difficult as the "revolution of rising expectations" we used to attribute to the developing countries has spread to the developed ones as well and has, in the words of Daniel Bell, led to a "revolution of rising entitlements." Each subgroup in a modern society, including governmental bureaucracy, seems to feel entitled to make claims for the satisfaction of its wants and desires, if need be at the expense of other subgroups.[3] Nor is this new. More than forty years ago, Beard put the case as clearly as anyone could:

> The conception of national interest revealed in the state papers is an aggrega-
tion of particularities assembled like eggs in a basket. Markets for agricultural produce in the national interest; markets for industrial commodities were in the national interest; naval bases, territorial acquisitions for commercial support, an enlarged consular and diplomatic service, an increased navy and merchant marine, and occasional wars were all in the national interest. These contentions were not proved; they were asserted as axioms, apparently regarded as so obvious as to call for no demonstration.

Various subinterests are likely to be at cross-purposes with one another. Given a limited pie to be distributed, the claims of one group are apt to run counter to those of another; the aspirations of the military for additional appropriations, claimed to be in the national interest, run counter to the pleas of cities for additional resources for urban services, equally claimed to be in the national interest. How does one ascertain the truth of the matter? How does one determine priorities? The only possible answer is that it is done through acts of political choice, which are likely to be outside the realm of the national interest concept.

Within any society, including ours, some subinterests are less successfully represented in the policy process than are others. But let us assume, unrealistically, the best of all possible societies; one in which all interests have an equal opportunity to make themselves effectively heard; one in which there is a minimum (there can never be an absence) of conflict among various claims and expectations. We would still have to decide whether these various claims and expectations,

---

[3]The author can testify to the strength of these claims from his experience as a member of a city council. Each group, each section, each neighborhood looked after itself. It was relatively easy to achieve general agreement on such issues as the need for better thoroughfares or for social service agencies, as long as these were located in another part of the community. It was often difficult to perceive what the general interest was, or how many people cared enough about it to be willing to make some sacrifices for it. To serve the general interest, however defined, without injuring some individual or group was impossible.

these values and interests, could be aggregated, and if so, whether the aggregate could be said to represent the national interest. Both parts of this problem are extremely complex. Aggregation is particularly difficult because the depth and intensity of separate goals can never really be known. But the second question—whether such an aggregation, if it could be performed, would constitute something to be known as national interest—is more difficult still.

Is the national interest merely the aggregation of specific interests? Or, assuming that there is such a thing as a national interest, could it be larger than, perhaps even different from, such an aggregation? Is a "general will" à la Rousseau, or a "public philosophy" à la Lippmann something real, reflecting values that transcend the accumulation of specific interests? This is not an easy question to answer with confidence, especially within the framework of a society in which government is said to serve the citizens, rather than the other way around. But however one responds, the question is of surpassing importance.

The third subquestion is, Who specifies what the national interest is? Since that can be debated endlessly, let us be brief. After much agonizing, analyzing and debating; after bravely marching up the sides of hills only to march down the other side, the end result is that most of us, most of the time, accept the definition of the national interest provided by a nation's high officials and policymakers.

There is hardly an alternative to this practice. The term national interest is political in nature. Public disputes arise over its meaning in concrete situations. Policymakers have the penultimate word in such disputes; the ultimate word is spoken by the process by which those policymakers can be replaced if their judgments have been faulty. What

seems less clear is whether those of us who try to understand or predict a nation's policy are entitled to build our structure of understanding and prediction on the words and acts of the policymakers, imbuing these with a sense of purpose and rationality that may not be justified. This brings us to the fourth major area of criticism of the national interest concept.

We all know how self-serving statements of policymakers are apt to be. We know that a given policy may lend itself to quite different interpretations of its basic purposes, and that much of foreign-policymaking is accidental, *ad hoc*, fortuitous. The incremental nature of decision-making is known to us. The input of bureaucracies, both in the early stages of decision-making and in the implementation of decisions made at higher levels, has been the subject of a large recent literature. Thus, while we may have no options but to accept the official definition of the national interest, or to infer interest from behavior, utmost caution is indicated in doing so. The case may well be that by holding on to the only thing we have we may go seriously astray.

For all its shortcomings, the best and perhaps the only available procedure may be to take the official definition and the policy output as the basis for our understanding. If one focuses on such official definitions, on the rhetoric that surrounds the policy output, he must make allowance for the fact that in such rhetoric the term national interest can easily serve to justify actions, hide mistakes, rationalize policies, disarm the opposition. Sometimes one suspects that it may be little more than a debater's point: if your side gets to use the term before the other side comes to it, you win the argument.

Compared to previous eras of statecraft, there is now a much greater need for policymakers to justify their choices to broader publics. In fact, a great deal of discussion in recent years has revolved around the idea of government officials' accountability for their conduct in office. But as everyone knows, public justification is an invitation to the use of the rhetorical arts. And within the rhetorical arsenal, few concepts are more effective than that of the national interest. Some students of foreign policy have suggested that the same ingredients that make the term so difficult to use for analytic purposes make it easy, inviting, tempting to use in political discourse.

Of the concerns surrounding the concept of the national interest, we have spoken thus far of its ambiguity; of the complexity of defining ends and means in foreign policy; of the problem of aggregating special interests into a national interest; of the risk that national interest is retroactively read into public policies in the formulation of which it may have played no, or at best only a marginal, role; and of the problem of attempting to use a phrase so serviceable in public rhetoric as a concept in scholarly inquiry which is supposed to rise above debaters' ploys. There is one other issue.

Professor Rochester framed this final issue as follows: "The two-fold assumption which appears to be embedded in the concept of national interest is that (1) there exists an objectively determinable collective interest which all individual members within a given society share equally; and (2) *this collective interest transcends any interests that a particular subset of those individuals may share with individuals in other societies.*" The traditional critiques of the concept have focused on the first of these assumptions. But what about the second? Rochester argued that it "runs squarely up against what a number of observers believe to be major new forces in world politics."

Much has been written on the old versus the new, the "classical" vs. the "modernist" paradigms of international relations. One has no wish to add to the volume of literature on this subject. Clearly, not everything has changed, not everything is different than it was before. But equally clearly, there have been changes, because there will always be changes in an environment of great variety and complexity. There are new actors, such as multinational corporations, functional organizations, terrorist groups. There are new goals of foreign policy that de-emphasize physical conquest and occupation, and stress instead economic and ideological influence. There are certain disintegrative trends within at least some societies, and some integrative trends within the international system. There are new developments in the means used to affect events in other countries. Power has become more diffused; new interdependencies have arisen, though not evenly across the board. There are new problems, new issue-areas to which some of the devices and categories of traditional statecraft are only marginally relevant: the protection of the environment, the allocation of dwindling resources; problems of food supply and of population increases.

Let us leave the relevance of the concept of national interest to such developments as a question, not presuming to be able to answer it fully. No one would suggest that the classical paradigm of international politics is no longer useful. All that is suggested is that the world is changing; that those of us who find ourselves in the midst of these changes are probably not clearly aware of them and cannot know their eventual outcome; and that in such a situation, a healthy skepticism is most suitable for the policymaker, the observer and the public alike: skepticism about the continuing validity of one's accustomed conceptual and operational equipment. . . .

Whatever our search for a more specific and adequate conceptualization of the national interest may reveal; and wherever that search may take us, it seems appropriate to suggest, in conclusion, that in the long run a system based solely on the self-centered pursuit of goals by its individual members can give no assurance of stability or safety, to say nothing of justice and equity, or of peace.

To make this point clearer, let us counterpose the two great events of the year 1776: the publication in Great Britain of Adam Smith's *Wealth of Nations* and the signing in Philadelphia of the American Declaration of Independence.

Smith held, among many other things not so well remembered, that if each individual were left free to pursue his own self-interests, in the long run—by the operation of an "invisible hand"—he would thereby contribute to the well-being of the entire community. The Declaration also stressed individual rights, including the right to pursue personal happiness. But it clearly sought the ultimate expression of those rights in an act of union, of contract, of "decent respect" for the opinions, judgments and (one can reasonably infer) interests of others.

Both sets of ideas have been influential in the history of the last two hundred years. Both have endured. But the second has worn rather better than the first. Men and women around the globe still believe in the principles of the Declaration, even when they are not being practiced. But how many really still believe in the "invisible hand" that encourages the untrammeled pursuit of self-interest? How many still believe that others, and the community at large, cannot be grievously injured by such pursuit? Some do, no doubt; but most of us feel that there must be limits, there must be restraints on the exercise of the pursuit. Most of us understand that some of us, pursuing purely our own interests, can do great damage to all of us; and that this damage must somehow be restrained and limited.

If this is true within a city, a state, a nation, then it must also be true within an international environment—especially one that has changed and continues to change. The requirements of the situation therefore argue for a possible redefinition of the national interest, one that explicitly takes account of the interests of others. Addressing themselves to the "intensity problem," Kendall and Carey in an important essay some years ago noted that stability is important to an entire community, especially to those of its members who—temporarily or otherwise—are in a majority. They concluded that it was inadvisable to force one's interests on others unless the issue at stake was absolutely vital. What this conclusion amounts to is a counsel to practice restraint, not only out of generosity or other appealing human traits, but as a matter of enduring self-interest, albeit more broadly defined than is usually the case.[4] It seems that a similar case can be made for those who operate within the international system.

Given the international context, given the continuing need to conduct foreign policy, to frame goals and to seek to achieve them, three qualities—modesty, restraint, and openness to change—should be cultivated by decision-makers, observers and citizens alike:

> *modesty* in assuming that one can know what is best for others—indeed, sometimes what is best for oneself;

[4]Willmoore Kendall and George W. Carey, "The 'Intensity' Problem and Democratic Theory," *The American Political Science Review*, March 1968, pp. 5-24.

restraint in the assertion of one's own interests (personal, organizational, group or national) as against those of others. In fact, one might make a conscious effort to frame his interests and goals so as to include those of others as much as possible. Morgenthau, much more sophisticated than some of his followers were or than some of his critics gave him credit for being, said it well: ". . . the national interest of a nation . . . must be defined in terms compatible with [the interests of other nations]." More recently, George and Keohane questioned the tendency to use the concept of national interest in only one context—which they call "self-regarding," excluding "other-regarding" and "collective" interests. They point out that this limited usage may be appropriate in periods of great danger, but that such periods occur only rarely, and that "to argue *a priori* that self-regarding interests must always be given priority over other interests is not morally tenable."

openness can mean two things: (1) a willingness to accept national self-interest as a fact without accepting it as a norm, which was Reinhold Niebuhr's position, and (2) a willingness to entertain alternative forms of the national interest and national policy.

One should try not to close off alternatives, but to leave the future open. Given the world in which we find ourselves—and, let us face it, which we helped make—that may be the best we can do, until such time as others can do better.

Part Three

TOOLS OF STATECRAFT IN INTERNATIONAL RELATIONS

V

The Balance of Power

Balance of power, like national interest, is another concept that has been employed by practitioner and theorist alike, not always with a very clear definition or sense of what it is. As Hedley Bull observes in this chapter, "its vagueness and shifting meaning have cast doubt upon the validity of the balance of power concept." The concept of the balance of power holds that states act so as to balance the threat from one of their members by allying themselves with others who feel similarly threatened. Because a preponderant power may conquer or impose its will upon others, the weaker states may feel they have no choice but to band together to balance off the superior power.

Ambiguity has arisen over the question of whether the balance of power or equilibrium comes into being automatically or whether it is a condition or process that must be consciously pursued by the policymakers if it is to come about.[1]

[1]Frederick Hartmann writes that the term has been employed "to describe one or all of three related but distinct things. It has been used to describe (1) the actions taken in making alliances, (2) the intent or motivation behind such actions, and (3) the result of such action." *Relations of Nations,* 5th ed. (New York: Macmillan, 1977). p. 317.

Traditional views of the balance of power, often inferred from the state of nature or the laws of the universe, held that a balance or equilibrium of power among states was a natural condition toward which the system tended spontaneously or automatically in much the same way as the planets and the sun held each other in equilibrium.

Another version is that the balance of power is maintained by the blind effort of each state to achieve its own security. This is analogous to the theory of the unseen hand which became so popular in the latter part of the eighteenth and early nineteenth centuries. Each individual or participant in striving to serve his own self-interest ends up serving the interests of all by preserving the system in a state of equilibrium and thereby benefitting everyone.

Yet a third view of the balance of power holds that it is consciously brought about by statesmen who feel their nation threatened by a potential aggressor and strive to limit or neutralize the threat by organizing a counter-force. The actual process by which a balance of power comes into being seems to be a combination of (2) and (3). As Frederick Hartmann puts it,

> the balance of power is not a system in the sense that the states involved necessarily have the *common end in mind* of preserving the independence of rival participants, but only in the sense that, as the creation of one power grouping tends to beget another, it is relatively rare to find the one long existing without the other. . . . Further, the balance of power, insofar as a balance is created between the opposing blocs [or powers] is almost entirely an accidental by-product of the existence of two alliance groupings, each formed to counter the power and ambitions of the other.[2]

Neither group is particularly interested in balancing the other as such, but each side is determined to counter the other, and in so doing acts to bring about a balance between the two.

However, this does not mean that such groupings or alliances spring into existence automatically. Statesmen and their countrymen must decide that a threat or potential threat exists, and they are guided in that decision by their understanding and views of the situation and by a variety of interests, many of which are counterbalancing. Hedley Bull argues in this chapter that "States are constantly in the position of having to choose between devoting their resources and energies to maintaining their international power position, or devoting their energies and resources to other ends." As Hartmann too observes, "the balance of power process, and what happens to it, is then not only the product of the power relations involved but also of the concept of interests and the foreign policies consequently followed by the great powers . . . there is no automatic compen-

[2]Ibid. p. 330.

satory gearing in the 'mechanism' of the balance that works apart from conscious policy decisions.''[3]

For example, the British government, weakened by its losses in World War I, confronted by a variety of threats from the dictatorships, and being unable to decide which was the greatest danger until it was too late, found itself unable to form an effective coalition; as a consequence, there was no balance of equilibrium that might have checked Nazi Germany in time. The U.S., ensconced in a policy of isolationism at that time, was even less willing to play a part in organizing a coalition which might have led to a balance of power and kept Germany and Japan in line. So we conclude that the balance of power is the effect rather than the intention.

There are many arguments against balance-of-power diplomacy. First and foremost comes the observation that states and their governments want not equilibrium but superiority (in the sense of having a "balance in the bank"). This, of course, would arouse competition and excesses. The selection from David Hume in this chapter depicts in trenchant words the inevitable temptation of a great power, in this case Great Britain, to go to excess in its pursuit of the balance of power, only to go to the opposite extreme of abandoning all concern for the subject. Hume's analysis has a distinctly modern ring if one considers the excesses to which the balance led the United States in Vietnam—in reaction to which, many observers fear, the pendulum is swinging the other way and Americans are abandoning their global responsibilities. Secondly, it is held that the balance of power generates two rival blocs, which makes war more likely if not inevitable. At a certain point, it is said, the two blocs explode into war, as happened in 1914 and threatened to happen on several occasions in connection with the Cold War (the Berlin crisis of 1961 and the Cuban missile crisis).

Thirdly, the balance of power, it is argued, favors the great powers at the expense of the small, often to the point of partitioning and devouring the lesser states, as occurred to Poland in the eighteenth century and to much of Eastern Europe after World War II when the Soviet Union established a satellite empire as a buffer against Western aggression. Be that as it may, few great powers faced by the existence of a potential rival have felt that they had any other recourse but to act to augment their own power.

One of the most trenchant and compelling statements of the logic of the balance of power, the memorandum Sir Eyre Crowe wrote for the British Foreign Office in 1907, is contained in this chapter. One will find in Sir Eyre Crowe's analysis the basic uncertainty that faced Britain concerning the intentions of imperial Germany, followed by the conclusion that it doesn't matter what Berlin's intentions are; in either case it poses a threat, and Britain must assert itself on the continent and work for the preserva-

[3]Ibid, p. 372.

tion of the balance of power. A similar statement of balance-of-power reasoning is to be found in the excerpts from National Security Council Paper No. 68 (NSC68), which was formulated in 1949–50 when the United States was attempting to lay down its strategy for dealing with Russia.

Defenders of balance-of-power diplomacy, such as Hedley Bull, go so far as to argue that only the existence of a balance of power permits other institutions and methods for maintaining international peace and order to operate—diplomacy, law, crisis management. Only if states feel sufficiently secure in their power position can they agree to subject their conduct to the checks and restraints of international law and diplomacy. Another adherent of this position, former Secretary of State Henry Kissinger, often stated that order, not peace, had to be the goal of foreign policy because peace could only come about as a by-product of order—and the basis of order for Kissinger meant a balance of power with Russia. A succession of American Secretaries of State—Acheson, Dulles, Rusk, Kissinger—would all have agreed with Bull that the preservation of the balance (i.e., the assertion of U.S. defense of its conception of the balance) takes precedence over international law itself: "Wars initiated to restore the balance of power, wars threatened to maintain it, military interventions in the internal affairs of another state . . . bring the imperatives of the balance of power into conflict with the imperatives of international law. The requirements of order are treated as prior to those of law, as they are treated also as prior to the interests of small powers and the keeping of peace."

The processes of international politics have given rise to two forms of the balance in the last thirty years. Immediately after World War II and for the next fifteen years the balance took an essentially bipolar form—Russia versus America. Beginning in the early 1960s, with the defection of China from the Communist bloc, France from the NATO bloc, and with the evident inability of the two superpowers to dictate to their partners on all matters, we have entered what is called, perhaps inaccurately, a multipolar system.

In part, the break up of the bipolar balance of power has occurred because of the emergence of what Bull describes as a special case of the balance of power: mutual nuclear deterrence. In one sense, deterrence is analogous to the balance of power: each side deters the other from risking aggression by conveying a threat to inflict punishment or annihilation so much greater than any possible gain. It is certainly true that mutual nuclear deterrence between the United States and the Soviet Union is only part of the balance-of-power relationship between them.

A mutual nuclear balance of terror does not require complete equality or parity in strength, because so long as either side possesses an invulnerable margin of nuclear weapons sufficient to wreak havoc on the other, equality is not necessary (what is needed, according to the experts, is an invulnerable nuclear retaliatory capability sufficient to survive the enemy's first strike).

To be effective, any balance-of-power strategy must be credible—that is, the other side must be convinced as objectively as possible that a balance exists and will be employed. Mutual nuclear deterrence is essentially a state of belief—the belief on each side that the other has the will as well as the capacity to retaliate to a sufficient level that neither will risk it; if one should actually doubt the other's will and capacity, the consequences would be suicidal—out of all proportion to the value of the gains sought.

Mutual nuclear deterrence has had two profound impacts upon the bipolar balance of power within the last fifteen years following the Cuban missile crisis. First, it has induced the two superpowers to enter into a range of agreements and understandings designed to limit the danger of nuclear war and avoid any confrontation over secondary issues that might escalate into a nuclear war. To this extent it has fulfilled one function of the classic balance of power—that of limiting the possibility of war and thereby making negotiations and rational control of one's actions possible (even necessary).

The second consequence of mutual nuclear deterrence has been to convince other states, including one's allies, that the full utilization of nuclear military power by either is unlikely. The "delicate balance of terror" thus entails also a paralysis of military power, and this paralysis has meant that America's allies no longer feel that they need to purchase U.S. support by acquiescing in its policies or spending too much to provide for their own defense.

For awhile the Nixon administration tried to sustain the idea of a five-power balance: Russia, America, China, Europe, and Japan. To some extent the normalization of American relations with Peking has gained for the United States a margin of diplomatic maneuver, vis-à-vis Russia, characteristic of a three-power balance. By contrast, Europe and Japan have contributed very little to any balance-of-power model. Their power is essentially economic, and they lack the unity and will to act politically or militarily as great powers. If anything, their domestic economic concerns and interests have led them into policies of economic competition with the United States—policies which, together with the 1973 OPEC price increases, greatly complicate Washington's ability to maintain its balance either at home or abroad. As a result, the United States continues to be preoccupied by the threat from the Soviet Union (and vice versa, no doubt) and finds itself obliged to act globally in a world marked by pervasive instability and local power conflicts in which the utility of American military and economic strength is much diminished.

American leadership is concerned that while the Soviets may accept for the time being the existence of a global strategic balance, it is striving to upset local and regional balance, such as in the Middle East, the Horn of Africa, and southern Africa. And, of course, the revolutionary ferment that prevails in most parts of the world today does not lend itself readily to management through the traditional balance-of-power politics, posing yet another problem. The balance of power assumes a stable state system, when what in fact exists is a very unstable and highly volatile system composed of both states and non-state actors. Who, for example, would try to predict the nature, timing, and location of the next terrorist attack? This is why American concern for the nuclear balance and for the global strategic balance continues to exist at a very high level. Increasingly since the end of the Vietnam War, Washington has found itself obliged to rely upon diplomacy and bargaining, and has endeavored to develop the potentiality of regional and local balances to help sustain the global balance.

12   On the Balance of Power

David Hume

The author was a famous British political philosopher in the 18th century.

It is question whether the *idea* of the balance of power be owing entirely to modern policy, or whether the *phrase* only has been invented in these latter ages? It is certain that ZENOPHON, in his Institution of CYRUS, represents the combination of the Asiatic powers to have arisen from a jealousy of the increasing force of the MEDES and PERSIANS; and though that elegant composition should be supposed altogether a romance, this sentiment, ascribed by the author to the eastern princes, is at least a proof of the prevailing notion of ancient times.

In all the politics of GREECE, the anxiety, with regard to the balance of power, is apparent, and is expressly pointed out to us, even by the ancient historians. [Much detail on this follows]. . . .

The reason why it is supposed that the ancients were entirely ignorant of the *balance of power* seems to be drawn from the ROMAN history more than the GRECIAN, and as the transactions of the former are generally more familiar to us, we have thence formed all our conclusions. It must be owned, that the ROMANS never met with any such general combination or con-

David Hume, *Essays, Moral, Political, and Literary,* edited by T. H. Green and T. H. Grose (London: Longmans, Green & Co., 1912), Vol. I, pp. 348-58.

federacy against them, as might naturally have been expected from the rapid conquests and declared ambition; but were allowed peaceably to subdue their neighbors, one after another, till they extended their dominion over the whole known world. . . .

After the fall of the ROMAN empire, the form of government, established by the northern conquerors, incapacitated them, in a great mesure, for farther conquests, and long maintained each state in its proper boundaries. But when vassalage and the feudal militia were abolished, mankind were anew alarmed by the danger of universal monarchy, from the union of so many kingdoms and principalities in the person of the Emperor CHARLES. But the power of the house of AUSTRIA, founded on extensive but divided dominions, and their riches, derived chiefly from mines of gold and silver, were more likely to decay, of themselves, from internal defects than to overthrow all the bulwarks raised against them. In less than a century, the force of that violent and haughty race was shattered, their opulence dissipated, their splendor eclipsed. A new power (France) succeeded, more formidable to the liberties of EUROPE, possessing all the advantages of the former, and labouring under none of its defects; except a share of that spirit of bigotry and persecution, with which the house of AUSTRIA was so long, and still is so much infatuated.

In the general wars, maintained against this ambitious power, GREAT BRITAIN has stood foremost; and she still maintains her station. Beside her advantages of riches and situation, her people are animated with such a national spirit, and are so fully sensible of the blessings of their government, that we may hope their vigour never will languish in so necessary and so just a cause. On the contrary, if we may judge by the past, their passionate ardour seems rather to require some moderation; and they have oftener erred from a laudable excess than from a blameable deficiency.

In the *first* place, we seem to have been more possessed with the ancient GREEK spirit of jealous emulation, than actuated by the prudent views of modern politics. Our wars with FRANCE have been begun with justice, and even, perhaps, from necessity; but have always been too far pushed from obstinacy and passion. . . . Above half of our wars with FRANCE and all our public debts, are owing more to our own imprudent vehemence than to the ambition of our neighbours.

In the *second* place, we are so declared in our opposition to FRENCH power, and so alert in defense of our allies, that they always reckon upon our force as upon their own; and expecting to carry on war at our expense, refuse all reasonable terms of accommodation. . . .

In the *third* place, we are such true combatants, that, when once engaged, we lose all concern for ourselves and our posterity, and consider only how we may best annoy the enemy. To mortgage our revenues at so deep a rate, in wars, where we were only accessories, was surely the most fatal delusion, that a nation, which had any pretension to politics and prudence, has ever yet been guilty of. That remedy of funding, if it be a remedy, and not rather a poison, ought,

in all reason, to be reserved to the last extremity; and no evil, but the greatest and most urgent, should ever induce us to embrace so dangerous an expedient.

These excesses, to which we have been carried, are prejudicial; and may, perhaps, in time, become still more prejudicial another way, by begetting, as is usual, the opposite extreme, and rendering us totally careless and supine with regard to the fate of EUROPE. The ATHENIANS, from the most bustling intriguing, warlike people of GREECE, finding their error in thrusting themselves into every quarrel, abandoned all attention to foreign affairs; and in no contest ever took part on either side, except by their flatteries and complaisance to the victor.

Enormous monarchies are, probably, destructive to human nature; in their progress, in their continuance, and even in their downfall, which never can be very distant from their establishment. The military genius, which aggrandized the monarchy, soon leaves the court, the capital, and the center of such a government; while the wars are carried on at a great distance, and interest so small a part of the state. The ancient nobility, whose affections attach them to their sovereign, live all at court; and never will accept of military employments, which would carry them to remote and barbarous frontiers, where they are distant both from their pleasures and their fortune. The arms of the state must, therefore, be entrusted to mercenary strangers, without zeal, without attachment, without honor; ready on every occasion to turn them against the prince, and join each desperate malcontent, who offers pay and plunder. This is the necessary progress of human affairs: Thus human nature checks itself in its airy elevation: thus ambition blindly labours for the destruction of the conqueror, of his family, and of every thing near and dear to him. The BOUR-BONS, trusting to the support of their brave, faithful, and affectionate nobility, would push their advantage, without reserve or limitation. These, while fired with glory and emulation, can bear the fatigues and dangers of war, but never would submit to languish in the garrisons of HUNGARY or LITHUANIA, forgot at court, and sacrificed to the intrigues of every minion or mistress who approaches the prince. The troops are filled with CRAVATES and TARTARS, HUSSARS and COSSACS: intermingled, perhaps, with a few soldiers of fortune from the better provinces: And the melancholy fate of the ROMAN emperors, from the same cause, it renewed over and over again, till the final dissolution of the monarchy.

13   The Balance of Power and International Order

Hedley Bull

The author occupies the Montagu Burton Professorship of International Politics at Oxford University.

In this chapter I propose to deal with the following questions:

(i)   What is the balance of power?

(ii)   How does the balance of power contribute to international order?

(iii)   What is the relevance of the balance of power to the maintenance of international order at present?

THE BALANCE OF POWER

We mean here by "the balance of power" what Vattel meant: "a state of affairs such that no one power is in a position where it

Reprinted from The Anarchical Society *by Hedley Bull. Copyright © 1977 by Hedley Bull. Reprinted by permission of Columbia University Press. (Footnotes omitted.)*

is preponderant and can lay down the law to others." It is normally military power that we have in mind when we use the term, but it can refer to other kinds of power in world politics as well. The state of affairs of which Vattel speaks can be realised in a number of different ways.

First, we have to distinguish a simple balance of power from a complex one, that is to say a balance made up of two powers from one consisting of three or more. The simple balance of power is exemplified by the clash of France and Habsburg Spain/Austria in the sixteenth and seventeenth centuries, and by the clash of the United States and the Soviet Union in the Cold War. The complex balance of power is illustrated by the situation of Europe in the mid-eighteenth century, when France and Austria, now detached from Spain, were joined as great powers by England, Russia, and Prussia. It is also illustrated by world politics at the present juncture, when the United States and the Soviet Union have been joined by China as a great power, with Japan as a potential fourth great power and a combination of Western European powers as a potential fifth. However, no historical balance of power has ever been perfectly simple or perfectly complex. Situations of a simple balance of power have always been complicated by the existence of some other powers, whose ability to influence the course of events may be slight but is always greater than zero. Situations of a complex balance of power are capable of being simplified by diplomatic combinations, as for example, the six-power balance of the pre-First World War period was resolved into the simple division of the Triple Alliance and the Triple Entente.

Whereas a simple balance of power necessarily requires equality or parity in power, a complex balance of power does not. In a situation of three or more competing powers the development of gross inequalities in power among them does not necessarily put the strongest in a position of preponderance, because the others have the possibility of combining against it.

In a simple balance of power the only means available to the power that is falling behind is to augment its own intrinsic strength (say, in the eighteenth century its territory and population; in the nineteenth century its industry and military organization; in the twentieth century its military technology). Because in a complex balance of power there exists the additional resource of exploiting the existence of other powers, either by absorbing or partitioning them, or by allying with them, it has usually been held that complex balances of power are more stable than simple ones.

Second, we must distinguish the general balance of power, that is the absence of a preponderant power in the international system as a whole, from a local or particular balance of power, in one area or segment of the system. In some areas of the world at present, such as the Middle East or the Indian subcontinent or South-east Asia, there may be said to be a local balance of power; in others, such as Eastern Europe or the Caribbean, there is a local preponderance of power. Both sorts of situation are consistent with the fact that in the international system as a whole there is a general balance of power. . . .

Third, one should distinguish a balance of power which exists subjectively from one that exists objectively. It is one thing to say that it is generally believed that a state of affairs exists in which no one state is preponderant in military strength; it is another to say that no one state is in fact preponderant. It is sometimes generally believed that a rough balance of military strength exists between two parties when this does not reflect the "true" position as revealed by subsequent events; in Europe in the winter of 1939–40, for example, it was widely held that a military balance existed between the Allies and Germany, but a few weeks' fighting in the spring showed that this was not the case. A balance of power in Vattel's sense requires that there should be general belief in it; it is not sufficient for the balance to exist objectively but not subjectively. . . .

But if the subjective element of belief in it is necessary for the existence of a balance of power, it is not sufficient. If a power is in fact in a position to gain an easy victory over its neighbour, even though it is generally thought to be balanced by it, this means that the beliefs on which the balance of power rests can quickly be shown to be false, and a new subjective situation brought about. A balance of power that rests not on the actual will and capacity of one state to withstand the assaults of another, but merely on bluff and appearances, is likely to be fragile and impermanent.

Fourth, we must distinguish between a balance of power which is fortuitous and one which is contrived. A fortuitous balance of power is one that arises without any conscious effort on the part of either of the parties to bring it into being. A contrived balance is one that owes its existence at least partly to the conscious policies of one or both sides. . . .

The most elementary form of contrived balance of power is a two-power balance in which one of the parties pursues a policy of preventing the other from attaining military preponderance. A more advanced form is a three-power balance in which one power seeks to prevent any of the others from attaining preponderance, not merely by augmenting its own military strength, but also by siding with whatever is the weaker of the other two powers: the policy known as "holding the balance." This form of balance-of-power policy was familiar in the ancient world, as David Hume argues, relying mainly on Polybius's celebrated account of the policy of Hiero of Syracuse, who sided with Carthage against Rome.

It is a further step from this to the policy of preserving a balance of power throughout the international system as a whole. This is a policy which presupposes an ability to perceive the plurality of interacting powers as comprising a single system or field of forces. It presupposes also a continuous and universal system of diplomacy, providing the power concerned with intelligence about the moves of all the states in the system, and with means of acting upon them. The policy of preserving a balance throughout the international system as a whole appears to

have originated only in fifteenth-century Italy, and to have developed along with the spread of resident embassies. It became firmly implanted in European thought only in the seventeenth century, along with the notion that European politics formed a single system.

It is a further step again to the conception of the balance of power as a state of affairs brought about not merely by conscious policies of particular states, but as a conscious goal of the system as a whole. Such a conception implies the possibility of collaboration among states in promoting the common objective of preserving the balance, as exemplified by the successive grand alliances of modern times against potentially dominant powers. It implies also that each state should not only act to frustrate the threatened preponderance of others, but should recognize the responsibility not to upset the balance itself: it implies self-restraint as well as the restraint of others. The idea that preservation of the balance of power throughout the international system as a whole should be the common goal of all states in the system was one that emerged in Europe in the seventeenth and early eighteenth centuries, especially as part of the coalitions against Louis XIV, and which came to fruition in the preamble to the Treaty of Utrecht in 1713.

FUNCTIONS OF THE BALANCE OF POWER

Preservation of a balance of power may be said to have fulfilled three historic functions in the modern states system:

(i)   The existence of a general balance of power throughout the international system as a whole has served to prevent the system from being transformed by conquest into a universal empire;

(ii)   The existence of local balances of power has served to protect the independence of states in particular areas from absorption or domination by a locally preponderant power;

(iii)   Both general and local balances of power, where they have existed, have provided the conditions in which other institutions on which international order depends (diplomacy, war, international law, great power management) have been able to operate.

The idea that balances of power have fulfilled positive functions in relation to international order, and hence that contrivance of them is a valuable or legitimate object of statesmanship, has been subject to a great deal of criticism in this century. At the present time criticism focuses upon the alleged obscurity or meaninglessness of the concept, the untested or untestable nature of the historical generalizations upon which it rests, and the reliance of the theory upon the notion that all international behavior consists of the pursuit of power. Earlier in the century, especially during and after the First World War critics of the doctrine of the balance of power asserted not that it was unintelligible or untestable, but that pursuit of the balance of power had effects upon international order which were not positive, but negative. In particular, they asserted that the attempt to preserve a balance of power was a source of war, that it was carried out in the interests of the great powers at the expense of the interests of the small, and that it led to disregard of international law. I shall deal with these latter criticisms first.

Attempts to contrive a balance of power have not always resulted in the preservation of peace. The chief function of the balance of power, however, is not to preserve peace, but to preserve the system of states itself. Preservation of the balance of power requires war, when this is the only means whereby the power of a potentially dominant state can be checked. It can be argued, however, that the preservation of peace is a subordinate objective of the contrivance of balances of power. Balances of power which are stable (that is, which have built-in features making for their persistence) may help remove the motive to resort to preventive war.

The principle of preservation of the balance of power has undoubtedly tended to operate in favor of the great powers and at the expense of the small. Frequently, the balance of power among the great powers has been preserved through partition and absorption of the small: the extraordinary decline in the number of European states between 1648 and 1914 illustrates the attempt of large states to absorb small ones while at the same time following the principle of compensation so as to maintain a balance of power. This has led to frequent denunciation of the principle of the balance of power as nothing more than collective aggrandisement by the great powers, the classic case being the partition of Poland in 1772 by Austria, Russia and Prussia. Those who, like Gentz and Burke, argued that the partition of Poland was an aberration and a departure from the true principles of the balance of power, which enjoined respect for the independence of all states, large and small alike, took as their starting-point an idealised and legalistic conception of the balance-of-power doctrine which misconstrues its essential content. The partition of Poland was not a departure from the principle of balance of power but an application of it. . . .

From the point of view of a weak state sacrificed to it, the balance of power must appear as a brutal principle. But its function in the preservation of international order is not for this reason less central. It is part of the logic of the principle of balance of power that the needs of the dominant balance must take precedence over those of subordinate balances, and that the general balance must be prior in importance to any local or particular balance. If aggrandisement by the strong against the weak must take place, it is better from the standpoint of international order that it should take place without a conflagration among the strong than with one. . . .

It is noticeable that while, at the present time, the term "balance of power" is as widely used as at any time in the past in the everyday discussion of international relations, in scholarly analyses of the subject it has been slipping into the background. This reflects impatience with the vagueness and shifting meaning of what is undoubtedly a current cant word; doubts about the historical generalizations that underlie the proposition that preservation of a balance of power is essential to international order; and doubts about its reliance on the discredited notion that the pursuit of power is the common denominator to which all foreign policy can be reduced.

The term "balance of power" is notorious for the numerous meanings that may be attached to it, the tendency of those who use it to shift from one to another and the uncritical reverence which statements about it are liable to command. It is a mistake, however, to dismiss the notion as a meaningless one, as von Justi did in the eighteenth century and Cobden in the nineteenth, and some political scientists are inclined to do now. The term is not unique in suffering abuses of this kind, and as with such other overworked terms as "democracy," "imperialism" and "peace," its very currency is an indication of the importance of the ideas

it is intended to convey. We cannot do without the term "balance of power" and the need is to define it carefully and use it consistently.

But if we can make clear what we mean by the proposition that preservation of the balance of power functions to preserve international order, is it true? Is it the case that a state which finds itself in a position of preponderant power will always use it to "lay down the law to others"? Will a locally preponderant state always be a menace to the independence of its neighbors, and a generally preponderant state to the survival of the system of states?

The proposition is implicitly denied by the leaders of powerful states, who see sufficient safeguard of the rights of others in their own virtue and good intentions. Franklin Roosevelt saw the safeguard of Latin America's rights in U.S. adherence to the "good-neighbour policy." The United States and the Soviet Union now each recognize a need to limit the power of the other, and assert that this is a need not simply of theirs but of international society at large. But they do not admit the need for any comparable check on their own power. . . .

Criticism of the doctrine that the balance of power functions to maintain international order sometimes derives from the idea that this is part of a theory of "power politics," which presents the pursuit of power as the common and overriding concern of all states in pursuing foreign policy. On this view the doctrine we have been discussing involves the same fallacies as the "power-political" theory of which it is part.

Doctrines which contend that there is, in any international system, an automatic tendency for a balance of power to arise do derive from a "power-political" theory of this kind. The idea that if one state challenges the balance of power, other states are bound to seek to prevent it, assumes that all states seek to maximize their relative power position. This is not the case. States are constantly in the position of having to choose between devoting their resources and energies to maintaining or extending their international power position, and devoting these resources and energies to other ends. The size of defence expenditure, the foreign-aid vote, the diplomatic establishment, whether or not to play a role in particular international issues by taking part in a war, joining an alliance or an international organization, or pronouncing about an international dispute—these are the matters of which the discussion of any country's foreign policy consists, and proposals that have the effect of augmenting the country's power position can be, and frequently are, rejected. Some states which have the potential for playing a major role—one thinks of the United States in the interwar period and Japan since her economic recovery after the Second World War—prefer to play a relatively minor one. But the doctrine I have been expounding does not assert any inevitable tendency for a balance of power to arise in the international system, only a need to maintain one if international order is to be preserved. States may and often do behave in such a way as to disregard the requirements of a balance of power.

THE PRESENT RELEVANCE OF THE BALANCE OF POWER

It is clear that in contemporary international politics there does exist a balance of power which fulfils the same functions in relation to international order which it has performed in other periods. If any important qualification needs to be made to this statement it is that since the late 1950s there has existed

another phenomenon which in some respects is a special case of the balance of power but in other respects is different: mutual nuclear deterrence. In a final section of this chapter I shall consider the meaning of mutual nuclear deterrence and its relation to the balance of power.

There clearly does now exist a general balance of power in the sense that no one state is preponderant in power in the international system as a whole. The chief characteristic of this general balance is that whereas in the 1950s it took the form of a simple balance (though not a perfectly simple one), and in the 1960s was in a state of transition, in the 1970s it takes the form of a complex balance. At least in the Asian and Pacific region China has to be counted as a great power alongside the United States and the Soviet Union; while Japan figures as a potential fourth great power and a united Western Europe may in time become a fifth. However, the statement that there is now a complex or multilateral balance of power has given rise to a number of misunderstandings, and it is necessary to clear these away.

To speak of a complex or multiple balance among these three or four powers is not to imply that they are equal in strength. Whereas in a system dominated by two powers a situation of balance or absence of preponderance can be achieved only if there is some rough parity of strength between the powers concerned, in a system of three or more powers balance can be achieved without a relationship of equality among the powers concerned because of the possibility of combination of the lesser against the greater.

Moreover, to speak of such a complex balance of power is not to imply that all four great states command the same kind of power or influence. Clearly, in international politics moves are made on "many chess-boards." On the chess-board of strategic nuclear deterrence the United States and the Soviet Union are supreme players, China is a novice and Japan does not figure at all. On the chess-board of conventional military strength the United States and the Soviet Union, again, are leading players because of their ability to deploy non-nuclear armed force in many parts of the world, China is a less important player because the armed force it has can be deployed only in its own immediate vicinity, and Japan is only a minor player. On the chess-boards of international monetary affairs and international trade and investments the United States and Japan are leading players, the Soviet Union much less important and China relatively unimportant. On the chess-board of influence derived from ideological appeal it is arguable that China is the pre-eminent player.

However, the play on each of these chess-boards is related to the play on each of the others. An advantageous position in the international politics of trade or investment may be used to procure advantages in the international politics of military security; a weak position on the politics of strategic nuclear deterrence may limit and circumscribe the options available in other fields. It is from this interrelatedness of the various chess-boards that we derive the conception of over-all power and influence in international politics, the common denominator in respect of which we say that there is balance rather than preponderance. Over-all power in this sense cannot be precisely quantified: the relative importance of strategic, economic and politico-psychological ingredients in national power (and of different kinds of each of these) is both uncertain and changing. But the relative position of states in terms of over-all power nevertheless makes itself apparent in bargaining among states, and the conception of over-all power is one we cannot do without.

Furthermore, to speak of the present relations of the great powers as a complex balance is not to imply that they are politically equidistant from one another, or that there is complete diplomatic mobility among them. At the time of writing a *detente* exists between the United States and the Soviet Union, and between the United States and China, but not between the Soviet Union and China. Japan, while it has asserted a measure of independence of the United States and improved its relations with both the Soviet Union and China, is still more closely linked both strategically and economically to the United States than to any of the others. While, therefore, the four major powers have more diplomatic mobility than they had in the period of the simple balance of power, their mobility is still limited, especially by the persistence of tension between the two communist great powers so considerable as to preclude effective collaboration between them.

We have also to note that the complex balance of power that now exists does not rest on any system of general collaboration or concert among the great powers concerned. There is not any general agreement among the United States, the Soviet Union, China, and Japan on the proposition that the maintenance of a general balance of power is a common objective, the proposition proclaimed by the European great powers in the Treaty of Utrecht. Nor is there any general agreement about a system of rules for avoiding or controlling crises, or for limiting wars. . . .

The present balance of power is not wholly fortuitous in the sense defined above, for there is an element of contrivance present in the "rational" pursuit by the United States, the Soviet Union and China of policies aimed at preventing the preponderance of any of the others. It may be argued also that there is a further element of contrivance in the agreement between the

United States and the Soviet Union on the common objective of maintaining a balance between themselves, at least in the limited sphere of strategic nuclear weapons. There is not, however, a contrived balance of power in the sense that all three or four great powers accept it as common objective—indeed, it is only the United States that explicitly avows the balance of power as a goal. Nor is there any evidence that such a balance of power is generally thought to imply self-restraint on the part of the great powers themselves, as distinct from the attempt to restrain or constrain one other.

The United States and the Soviet Union have developed some agreed rules in relation to the avoidance and control of crises and the limitation of war. There is not, however, any general system of rules among the great powers as a whole in these areas. Neither in the field of Sino-Soviet relations nor in that of Sino-American relations does there exist any equivalent of the nascent system of rules evolving between the two global great powers. In the absence of any such general system of rules, we cannot speak of there being, in addition to a balance among the great powers, a concert of great powers concerned with the management of this balance.

Finally, the present complex balance of power does not rest on a common culture shared by the major states participating in it, comparable with that shared by the European great powers that made up the complex balances of the eighteenth and nineteenth centuries. . . . In the European international system of those centuries one factor that facilitated both the maintenance of the balance itself and cooperation among the powers that contributed to it was their sharing of a common culture, both in the sense of a common intellectual tradition and stock of ideas that facilitated communica-

tion, and in the sense of common values, in relation to which conflicts of interest could be moderated. Among the United States, the Soviet Union, China and Japan there does exist, as will be argued later, some common stock of ideas, but there is no equivalent of the bonds of common culture among European powers in earlier centuries. . . .

This presently existing balance of power appears to fulfill the same three functions in relation to international order that it has performed in earlier periods, and that were mentioned in the last section. First, the general balance of power serves to prevent the system of states from being transformed by conquest into a universal empire. While the balance continues to be maintained, no one of the great powers has the option of establishing a world government by force. . . .

Second, local balances of power—where they exist—serve to protect the independence of states in particular areas from absorption or domination by a locally preponderant power. At the present time the independence of states in the Middle East, in the Indian subcontinent, in the Korean peninsula and in South-east Asia is assisted by the existence in these areas of local balances of power. By contrast, in Eastern Europe where there is a Soviet preponderance and in Central America and the Caribbean, where there is a U.S. preponderance, local states cannot be said to be independent in the normal sense. It would be going too far to assert that the existence of a local balance of power is a necessary condition of the independence of states in any area. To assert this would be to ignore the existence of the factor of a sense of political community in the relations between two states, the consequence of which may be that a locally preponderant state is able, up to a point, to respect the independence of a weaker neighbour, as the United States respects the independence of Canada, or Britain respects the independence of Eire. We have also to recognize that the independence of states in a particular area may owe less to the existence or non-existence of a balance among the local powers than to the part played in the local equilibrium by powers external to the region: if a balance exists at present between Israel and her Arab neighbors, for example, this balance owes its existence to the role played in the area by great powers external to it.

Third, both the general balance of power, and such local balances as exist at present, help to provide the conditions in which other institutions on which international order depends are able to operate. International law, the diplomatic system, war and the management of the international system by the great powers assume a situation in which no one power is preponderant in strength. All are institutions which depend heavily on the possibility that if one state violates the rules, others can take reciprocal action. But a state which is in a position of preponderant power, either in the system as a whole or in a particular area, may be in a position to ignore international law, to disregard the rules and procedures of diplomatic intercourse, to deprive its adversaries of the possibility of resort to war in defense of their interests and rights, or to ignore the conventions of the comity of great powers, all with impunity.

MUTUAL NUCLEAR DETERRENCE

Since the 1950s there has existed another institution or quasi-institution which is in some respects a special case of the balance of power and in other respects different: mutual nuclear deterrence. In this final section I shall consider the following:

(i)   What is the balance of terror or relationship of mutual nuclear deterrence?

(ii)   How is mutual nuclear deterrence related to the balance of power?

(iii) How does mutual nuclear deterrence function in relation to international order?

In dealing with the first of these questions we shall begin by considering the meaning of deterrence; then consider the meaning of mutual deterrence; and finally set out what is involved in the special case with which we are concerned, mutual nuclear deterrence.

To say that Country A deters Country B from doing something is to imply the following:

(i) That Country A conveys to Country B a threat to inflict punishment or deprivation of values if it embarks on a certain course of action;

(ii) That Country B might otherwise embark on that course of action;

(iii) That Country B believes that Country A has the capacity and the will to carry out the threat, and decides for this reason that the course of action is not worthwhile.

All three of these conditions have to be fulfilled if we are to speak of deterrence. To take the first, there has to be a threat conveyed by the deterrer to the deterred. If, for example, the Soviet Union desisted from attacking the United States because it believed that the United States would inflict intolerable punishment in retaliation, but the United States had not in fact conveyed any such threat of punishment, we could not say that the United States had deterred a Soviet attack. There has to be the conveying of a threat if the deterrer is to take credit for the result.

To take the second condition, there has to be some possibility that the country that is the object of the threat will undertake the course of action from which the deterrer wishes it to desist. If there is, in fact, no possibility that the Soviet Union will attack the United States in any circumstances, then even though the United States has conveyed threats of punishment and the Soviet Union has desisted from attacking the United States, we cannot say that the Soviet Union has been deterred from doing so. We should note, however, that policies of deterrence may have a rationale independently of whether the country at which they are aimed has a present intention to initiate an attack. It may be argued, for example, that U.S. policies aimed at deterrence of Soviet attack are justified by the objective of creating a feeling of security from attack within the United States, or by the objective of discouraging the emergence within the Soviet Union of an intent to attack, even though there is no evidence of any present intent.

To take the third condition, the country threatened with punishment is not deterred unless it believes that the country making the threat has the capacity and the will to carry it out, and decides for this reason that the course of action it would otherwise follow is not worthwhile. The threat that is conveyed by the deterrer has to be "credible" to the country deterred; and it has to be judged by the latter to render the course of action contemplated unacceptable or not worthwhile. Whether or not the punishment threatened (assessed in terms of the probability of it as well as the extent of it) renders the course of action unacceptable will of course vary with circumstances: what the country (or particular leaders of it) hopes to gain from doing the thing in question or to lose by not doing it, what importance it attaches to the values of which the deterrer threatens to deprive it, and so on. It is for this reason that there is no absolute "level of damage" which is necessary and sufficient to deter a country from doing something.

Deterrence of attacks by other powers has always been one of the objects for which states have sought to use their military forces. What is novel about deterrence in the age of nuclear weapons is that states have been driven to elevate it to the status of a prime object of policy by their reluctance to use nuclear weapons in actual war. The policies or strategies of deterrence that have been evolved vary along three separate dimensions: the range of actions from which it is hoped to deter the adversary; the priority accorded to deterrence in the scheme of policy; and the force threatened to produce deterrence.

Thus in the United States the object of policy has been envisaged as to deter the Soviet Union from a nuclear attack on the United States; from any attack on the United States; from a nuclear attack on the United States or its allies; and from any attack on the United States and its allies. These contrasts have sometimes been referred to in terms of a choice between "finite deterrence" and "extended deterrence."

Deterrence has been envisaged, as in the 1957 U.K. Defence White Paper, as the sole object of policy for nuclear weapons ("deterrence only"), or "deterrence plus defense," or, as in the later years of Robert McNamara's Secretaryship of Defence, in terms of a combination of deterrence and other objectives, such as "damage limitation."

The force required to achieve deterrence has not only been seen in terms of nuclear weapons, but also in terms of a combination of nuclear and conventional weapons: in terms of a single massive threat or a series of graduated threats (Slessor's "the great deterrent" *versus* Buzzard's "graduated deterrents," or Dulles's "massive retaliation" *versus* McNamara's "flexible response").

Mutual deterrence is a state of affairs in which two or more powers deter each other from doing something. In the broadest sense it may be a state of affairs in which the powers deter each other from a wide range of actions by a wide range of kinds of threat. These actions and threats need not be nuclear in nature, nor military at all. Nor need the threat conveyed by the deterrer constitute retaliation in kind; powers may be deterred from a chemical weapons attack by a threat of retaliation with conventional or nuclear weapons, or they may be deterred from military attacks by threats of econmic reprisals. Here, however, I wish to focus upon the special case of mutual nuclear deterrence: a state of affairs in which two or more powers deter one another from deliberate nuclear attack by the threat of nuclear retaliation.

As with the state of affairs we have called a "balance of power," a situation of mutual nuclear deterrence may be realized in a simple, two-power relationship or in a more complex relationship of three or more powers. At the present time there is a relationship of mutual nuclear deterrence between the United States and the Soviet Union, and one growing up also between China and the Soviet Union and between China and the United States. Some would claim that Britain and the Soviet Union and France and the Soviet Union are also in this relationship. A three- (or more) power relationship of mutual nuclear deterrence is the sum of the bilateral relationships involved, not (as inthe case of the balance of power) the product of these relationships involved, not (as in the case of the balance of power, again, mutual nuclear deterrence might in principle be realized either generally or locally. If the spread of nuclear weapons proceeded so far as to enable every state to deter every other state from nuclear attack—or if (to take a more likely hypothesis) all states were consolidated under one or another existing "nuclear umbrella"—there might arise a general situation of mutual nuclear deterrence, the state of affairs which Morton Kaplan calls

a "unit veto system." At present there are only particular or local relationships of mutual nuclear deterrence.

As in the case of the balance of power, again, situations of mutual nuclear deterrence may in principle arise fortuitously or as the result of contrivance. The Soviet-American relationship of mutual nuclear deterrence arose in the late 1950s as the result of efforts on the part of each to deter the other, if not to gain a strategic nuclear ascendancy over the other. A central idea of advocates of arms control has been, that the situation that arose thus fortuitously could be preserved only by conscious, collaborative efforts to bring this about. Left to its own logic or momentum, strategic nuclear competition between the super powers could lead to the undermining of mutual nuclear deterrence, and collaboration in the field of arms control could therefore be directed toward preserving the stability of the relationship of mutual nuclear deterrence.

MUTUAL NUCLEAR DETERRENCE AND THE BALANCE OF POWER

The idea of a contrived relationship of mutual nuclear deterrence is in some respects similar to that of a contrived balance of power, but in other respects different. First, a relationship of mutual nuclear deterrence between two powers is only part of the relationship of balance of power between them, the latter being made up of all the ingredients of national power, of which the exploitation of nuclear force is only one. Where, in a two-power situation, one of the powers has the ability to strike at the other with nuclear weapons, the creation of a relationship of mutual nuclear deterrence is a necessary condition of a balance of power between them. But it is not a sufficient condition. At the present time, as we have noted, there appears to be developing a relationship of mutual nuclear deterrence between the Soviet Union and China and between the United States and China, and some would argue that there is mutual nuclear deterrence between France and the Soviet Union and between Britain and the Soviet Union. But no one would argue that in any of these relationships the two states concerned were equal in power.

Second, whereas in a simple or two-power situation a balance requires equality or parity in military strength, a relationship of mutual deterrence does not; it requires only that each power has sufficient nuclear striking power for the purpose of deterring a nuclear attack. For each power there is a threshold level of damage with which it needs to be able to threaten the other; a degree of nuclear strength that cannot threaten this level of damage will be insufficient for the purpose of deterrence, and a degree of strength that can threaten more than this level will be redundant for this purpose, although it may still be justified by other strategic criteria such as the need to limit damage, to "extend" deterrence so as to cover allies, or to fortify the country's diplomatic position for purposes of crisis bargaining.

The irrelevance of equality or parity to mutual nuclear deterrence in a two-power situation can be seen in the case of the United States and the Soviet Union. From the time when the relationship of mutual nuclear deterrence first arose between the two super powers, at the earliest in the mid-1950s, until the end of the 1960s the United States had a clear superiority over the Soviet Union in all of the relevant indices of strategic nuclear strength: total numbers of strategic nuclear delivery vehicles (ICBMs, SLBMs and long-range bombers), total megatonnage of nuclear stockpiles, and total numbers of deliverable nuclear warheads. By the end of the 1960s the Soviet Union had achieved "parity" in some of these indices. The United States' loss of strategic "superiority," it may be argued, has deprived it of an important diplomatic advantage, and has contributed to a shift in the balance of power away from the United States and towards the Soviet Union. But it has not in itself undermined the relationship of mutual deterrence, which persists independently of fluctuations in the balance of strategic nuclear strength.

In a complex balance of power involving three or more states, as argued above, maintenance of the balance does not require equality or parity because inequalities can be corrected by alliance agreements. In a complex situation of mutual nuclear deterrence such as the three-sided relationship now emerging between the Soviet Union, the United States and China, alliance arrangements or *ad hoc* combinations may also play a role. It is conceivable, for example, that joint Soviet-American threats directed against China could undermine the credibility of Chinese threats of nuclear retaliation in a way that neither the United States nor the Soviet Union could accomplish singly. Similarly, joint American-Chinese threats directed at the Soviet Union might serve to establish China's deterrent *vis-à-vis* the Soviet Union at a time when the ability of China herself to deter Soviet attack was in doubt. A French theorist, André Beaufre at one time argued that the West's ability to deter Soviet attack was strengthened by the fact that there existed three separate centers of nuclear decision in the West— Washington, London, and Paris. But alliance combinations in a many-sided relationship of mutual nuclear deterrence have a different function from those that take place to maintain a complex balance of power: they are still concerned with providing a deterrent that is sufficient for the purpose in hand, rather than with adding the military strength of one country to another in such a way as to ensure that no power is preponderant.

Third, whereas the balance of power is essentially an objective phenomenon, the relationship of mutal deterrence is essentially subjective. The state of affairs we call a "balance of power," it was argued above, is defined by the actual absence of any preponderant power, and not merely by belief that no power is preponderant. Mutual nuclear deterrence, by contrast, is essentially a state of belief: the belief on each side that the other has the will and the capacity to retaliate to a sufficient level. In principle two powers could deter each other from nuclear attack by bluff both as to their will and as to their capacity.

Robert McNamara has argued strongly that the deterrent policy of the United States can be effective only if there is an actual will to carry out threatened nuclear retaliation, together with actual capacity to achieve "assured destruction." It seems likely that this is the actual policy of the United States, and it may well be that any attempt to base nuclear deterrence on bluff as to will or capacity carries great risks that the bluff will be called. Nevertheless, an actual will and capacity to retaliate is not part of the definition of mutual deterrence. McNamara's doctrine on this point, even if it is correct, shows only that the actual will and capacity to retaliate is essential to producing the adversary's belief in it.

Fourth, whereas the balance of power has as its primary functions the preservation of the international system and the independence of states, and has the preservation of peace as only an incidental consequence, the preservation of mutual nuclear deterrence

has (as we shall see) the preservation of nuclear peace as its primary function.

THE FUNCTIONS OF MUTUAL NUCLEAR DETERRENCE

The relationship of mutual nuclear deterrence, which so far exists unambiguously only between the United States and the Soviet Union, may be said to have fulfilled the following functions.

(i) It has helped to preserve the nuclear peace, at least between the United States and the Soviet Union, by rendering deliberate resort to nuclear war be either one of them "irrational" as an instrument of policy.

(ii) It has also served to preserve peace between the two leading nuclear powers, which are reluctant to enter directly into non-nuclear hostilities with one another, for fear of expansion of the conflict; and peace between states that are allies of these two powers, because of the restraint exercised by the latter upon them.

(iii) It has contributed to the maintenance of a general balance of power in the international system by helping to stabilize the dominant balance, that is, the balance between the two global great powers. Thus, indirectly, the relationship of mutual nuclear deterrence has contributed to the functions fulfilled by the general balance of power: maintenance of the system of states, of the independence of states and of the conditions under which other institutions concerned with international order can operate effectively.

It is important to understand the limitations within which the preservation of mutual nuclear deterrence may be said to carry out its major function of contributing to the preservation of the nuclear peace. First, mutual nuclear deterrence can make deliberate resort to nuclear war "irrational" as an instrument of policy only so long as it is stable, that is, it has a built-in tendency to persist. "The balance of terror" is not created by the mere existence of nuclear weapons in the hands of two adversaries, nor does it persist automatically while these weapons continue to be available. In principle a relationship of mutual deterrence may be upset by one or both of two technological developments: the acquisition by one side or both of an effective defense of cities and populations against strategic nuclear attack; or the development by one side or both of an effective means of disarming the other's strategic nuclear retaliatory forces before they are brought into action. It is also vulnerable in principle to change in the political and psychological dimensions of mutual nuclear deterrence: in the will or resolve of the deterrer to carry out his threat, in the ability of the deterrer to cause the deterred to believe that he can and will do so and in the assessment which the deterred makes as to whether or not the risks that the threat will be carried out are worth incurring.

Second, while the relationship of mutual nuclear deterrence persists, and deliberate resort to nuclear war is rendered "irrational," there are still dangers of nuclear war arising by accident or miscalculation, which the relationship of mutual nuclear deterrence by itself does nothing to assuage. It is beyond our present task to consider the steps that have been taken and might be taken to preserve mutual nuclear deterrence. only point here is that the measures which the nuclear powers take, unilaterally or jointly, to reduce the likelihood of war by "accident" or miscalculation, or to control it if it occurs, lie outside the field of actions taken to preserve mutual nuclear deterrence.

Third, mutual nuclear deterrence, while it persists and helps to make nuclear war unlikely in itself, does nothing to solve the problem of limiting or controlling a nuclear war that has broken out. Unilateral strategic policies of "deterrence only" have long been criticised for failing to answer the question: "what if deterrence fails?" Arms-control arrangements founded upon the idea that mutual nuclear deterrence is a self-sufficient goal in the strategic nuclear field are open to the same criticism. "Deterrence only" is an insufficient goal in both strategy and arms control, and proposals drawn up in terms of it may have the effect not merely of failing to insure against the possibility that nuclear war will break out, but of obstructing the business of controlling it if it does.

Fourth, the idea of mutual nuclear deterrence as a source of the nuclear peace places a tremendous burden upon the supposition that men can be expected to act "rationally." When we say that action is rational all we mean is that it is internally consistent and consistent with given goals. There is no such thing as "rational action" in the sense of action dictated by "reason" as against "the passions," a faculty present in all men and enjoining them to act in the same way. When we say that it is "irrational" for a statesman deliberately to choose to bring about the destruction or devastation of his own country, all we mean is that such an action is not consistent with the goals which statesmen are normally expected to pursue. This does not mean that they will not act in this way or have not done so in the past.

Fifth, to say that mutual nuclear deterrence carries out this function in relation to preservation of peace is not to endorse the proposition that international security is enhanced by the presence of nuclear weapons on both sides in international conflicts.

Elsewhere I have argued that if it were possible to return to the world that existed before the development of nuclear technology (which it is not), international security would be enhanced, even if this meant that wars, though less potentially catastrophic, were more likely. I have also argued against the notion that international security is enhanced by the spread of nuclear weapons. But in an international system in which nuclear technology is ineradicably present, and in which possession of nuclear weapons has spread beyond the original custodians of them, one must recognize the positive functions performed by relationships of mutual nuclear deterrence among the nuclear powers.

Sixth, the preservation of mutual nuclear deterrence obstructs the long-term possibility of establishing international order on some more positive basis. The preservation of peace among the major powers by a system in which each threatens to destroy or cripple the civil society of the other, rightly seen as a contemporary form of security through the holding of hostages, reflects the weakness in international society of the sense of common interest. It is for this reason that some theorists of arms control have been drawn to advocate the attempt to base strategic arms policy and strategic arms understandings on defense rather than deterrence, and that the global great powers, even in reaching understandings (like the Moscow Agreements of May 1972) that tend to confirm the relationship of mutual nuclear deterrence, are reluctant to state explicitly that this is the basis of their understanding.

14   British Relations with France and Germany

Sir Eyre Crowe

The author served as one of the leading permanent officials in the British Foreign Office

The general character of England's foreign policy is determined by the immutable conditions of her geographical situation on the ocean flank of Europe, as an island State with vast overseas colonies and dependencies, whose existence and survival as an indepen-

Memorandum by Sir Eyre Crowe on the Present State of British Relations with France and Germany, January 1, 1907, British Documents on the Origins of the War 1898-1914, ed. by G. P. Gooch and H. Temperley (London: His Majesty's Stationery Office, 1928), vol. III, pp. 402-07, 414-20).

dent community are inseparably bound up with the possession of preponderant sea power. . . . Sea power is more potent than land power, because it is as pervading as the element in which it moves and has its being. Its formidable character makes itself felt the more directly that a maritime State is, in the literal sense of the word, the neighbor of every country accessible by sea. It would, therefore, be but natural that the power of a State supreme at sea should inspire universal jealousy and fear, and be ever exposed to the danger of being overthrown by a general combination of the world. Against such a combination no single nation could in the long run stand, least of all a small island kingdom not possessed of the military strength of a people trained to arms, and dependent for its food supply on oversea commerce. The danger can in practice only be averted . . . on condition that the national policy of the insular and naval State is so directed as to harmonize with the general desires and ideals common to all mankind. . . . Now, the first interest of all countries is the preservation of national independence. It follows that England, more than any other non-insular Power, has a direct and positive interest in the maintenance of the independence of nations, and therefore must be the natural enemy of any country threatening the independence of others, and the natural protector of the weaker communities.

Second only to the ideal of independence, nations have always cherished the right to free intercourse and trade in the world's markets. . . .

History shows that the danger threatening the independence of this or that nation has generally arisen, at least in part, out of the momentary predominance of a neighboring State at once militarily powerful, economically efficient, and ambitious to extend its frontiers or spread its influence. . . . The only check on the abuse of political predominance derived from such a position has always consisted in the opposition of an equally formidable rival, or of a combination of several countries forming leagues of defense. The equilibrium established by such a grouping of forces is technically known as the balance of power, and it has become almost an historical truism to identify England's secular policy with the maintenance of this balance by throwing her weight now in this scale and now in that, but ever on the side opposed to the political dictatorship of the strongest single State or group at a given time.

If this view of British policy is correct, the opposition into which England must inevitably be driven to any country aspiring to such a dictatorship assumes almost the form of a law of nature. . . .

For purposes of foreign policy the modern German Empire may be regarded as the heir, or descendant, of Prussia. Of the history of Prussia, perhaps the most remarkable feature . . . is the process by which, on the narrow foundation of the modest Margraviate of Brandenburg, there was erected in the space of a comparatively short period, the solid fabric of a European Great Power. This process was one of systematic territorial aggrandizement achieved mainly at the point of the sword . . . for the avowed object of securing for Prussia the size, the cohesion, the square miles and the population necessary to elevate her to the rank and influence of a first class State.

. . .With the events of 1871 the spirit of Prussia passed into the new Germany. In no other country is there a conviction so deeply rooted in the very body and soul of all classes of the population that the preservation of national rights and the realization of national ideals rest absolutely on the readiness of every citizen in the last resort to stake himself and his State on their assertion and vindication. With "blood and iron" Prussia has forged her position in the councils of the Great Powers of Europe.

In due course . . . the young empire found opened to its energy a whole world outside Europe, of which it had previously hardly had the opportunity to become more than dimly conscious. Sailing across the ocean in German ships, German merchants began for the first time to divine the true position of countries such as England, the United

States, France, and even the Netherlands, whose political influence extends to distant seas and continents. . . . The effect of this discovery upon the German mind was curious and instructive. Here was a vast province of human activity to which the mere title and rank of a European Great Power were not in themselves a sufficient passport. . . . Germany had won her place as one of the leading, if not, in fact, the foremost Power on the European continent. But over and beyond the European Great Powers there seemed to stand the "World Powers." It was at once clear that Germany must become a "World Power." . . . [Many acts and utterances] confirm the impression that Germany distinctly aims at playing on the world's political stage a much larger and much more dominant part than she finds alloted to herself under the present distribution of material power. . . .

It remains to consider whether, and to what extent, the principles so elucidated may be said, on the one hand, to govern actual present policy, and, on the other, to conflict with the vital interests of England. . . .

So long . . . as Germany competes for an intellectual and moral leadership of the world in reliance on her own national advantages and energies, England can but admire, applaud, and join in the race. If, on the other hand, Germany believes that greater relative preponderance of material power, wider extent of territory, inviolable frontiers, and supremacy at sea are the necessary and preliminary possessions without which any aspirations to such leadership must end in failure, then England must expect that Germany will surely seek to diminish the power of any rivals, to enhance her own by extending her dominion, to hinder the cooperation of other States, and ultimately to break up and supplant the British Empire.

Now, it is quite possible that Germany does not, nor ever will, consciously cherish any schemes of so subversive a nature. Her statesmen have openly repudiated them with indignation. Their denial may be perfectly honest, and their indignation justified. If so, they will be most unlikely to come into any kind of armed conflict with England. . . .

But this is not a matter in which England can safely run any risks . . . ambitious designs against one's neighbors are not as a rule openly proclaimed, and . . . therefore the absence of such proclamation, and even the profession of unlimited and universal political benevolence are not in themselves conclusive evidence for or against the existence of unpublished intentions. . . .

[In succeeding paragraphs, Sir Eyre Crowe examines two sets of assumptions about German policy goals: 1) that Germany "is deliberately following a policy which is essentially opposed to vital British interests, and that an armed conflict cannot in the long run be averted except by England either sacrificing those interests . . . or making herself too strong to give Germany the chance of succeeding in a war;" and 2) that "the great German design is in reality no more than the expression of a vague, confused, and unpractical statesmanship, not fully realizing its own drive." He points to the "well-known qualities of mind and temperament distinguishing for good or evil the present Ruler of Germany" who may "be largely responsible for the erratic, domineering, and often frankly aggressive spirit . . . of German public life." He severely chastizes German policy since the fall of Chancellor Bismarck, and concludes as follows]

If it be considered necessary to formulate and accept a theory that will fit all the ascertained facts of German foreign policy, the choice must lie between the two hypotheses here presented: Either Germany is definitely aiming at a general political hegemony and maritime ascendency, threatening the independence of her neighbors and ultimately the existence of England;* or Germany, free from any such clear-cut ambition, and thinking for the present merely of using her legitimate position and influence as one of the leading Powers in the council of nations, is seeking to promote her foreign commerce, spread the benefits of German culture, extend the scope of her national energies, and create fresh German interests all over the world wherever and whenever a peaceful opportunity offers, leaving it to an uncertain future to decide whether the occurrence of great changes in the world may not some day assign to Germany a larger share of direct political action over regions not now a part of her dominion, without that violation of the established rights of other countries which would be involved in any such action under existing political conditions.

In either case Germany would clearly be wise to build as powerful a navy as she can afford.

The above alternatives seem to exhaust the possibilities of explaining the given facts. The choice offered is a narrow one, nor easy to make with any close approach to certainty. It will, however, be seen, on reflection, that there is no actual necessity for a British Government to determine definitely which of the two theories of German policy it will accept. For it is clear that the second scheme

*Editors' Note: A careful reading of these two hypotheses will show how closely they approximate the terms of the debate presently occurring in America over Soviet military intentions.

. . . may at any stage merge into the first, or conscious-design, scheme. . . .

It appears, then, that the element of danger present as a visible factor in one case, also enters, though under some disguise, into the second; and against such danger, whether actual or contingent, the same general line of conduct seems prescribed. . . .

So long as England remains faithful to the general principle of the preservation of the balance of power, her interests would not be served by Germany being reduced to the rank of a weak Power, as this might easily lead to a Franco-Russian predominance equally, if not more, formidable to the British Empire. There are no existing German rights, territorial or other, which this country could wish to see diminished. Therefore, so long as Germany's action does not overstep the line of legitimate protection of existing rights, she can always count upon the sympathy and good-will, and even the moral support, of England. . . .

[But] . . . there is an impression that Germany will think twice before she now gives rise to any fresh disagreement. In this attitude she will be encouraged if she meets on England's part with unvarying courtesy and consideration in all matters of common concern, but also with a prompt and firm refusal to enter into any one-sided bargains or arrangements, and the most unbending determination to uphold British rights and interests in every part of the globe. There will be no surer or quicker way to win the respect of the German Government and of the German nation.

NSC-68. A report to the National Security Council by The Executive Secretary on United States Objectives and Programs for National Security, April, 1950. This report was declassified by Dr. Henry A. Kissinger in February 1975. Following are excerpts from this report, which reflects another approach to the balancing process:

I BACKGROUNDS OF THE PRESENT WORLD CRISIS

Within the past thirty-five years the world has experienced two global wars of tremendous violence. It has witnessed two revolutions—the Russian and the Chinese—of extreme scope and intensity. It has also seen the collapse of five empires—the Ottoman, the Austro-Hungarian, German, Italian, and Japanese—and the drastic decline of two major imperial systems, the British and the French. During the span of one generation, the international distribution of power has been fundamentally altered. For several centuries it had proved impossible for any one nation to gain such preponderant strength that a coalition of other nations could not in time face it with greater strength. The international scene was marked by recurring periods of violence and war, but a system of sovereign and independent states was maintained, over which no state was able to achieve hegemony. . . .

II. FUNDAMENTAL PURPOSE OF THE UNITED STATES

The fundamental purpose of the United States is laid down in the Preamble to the Constitution: ". . . to form a more perfect Union, establish Justice, ensure domestic Tranquility; provide for the common defense, promote the general Welfare, and secure the Blessings of Liberty to ourselves and our Posterity.". . .

Three realities emerge as a consequence of this purpose: Our determination to maintain the essential elements of individual freedom . . .; our determination to create conditions under which our free and democratic system can live and prosper; and our determination to fight if necessary to defend our way of life. . . .

III. FUNDAMENTAL DESIGN OF THE KREMLIN

The fundamental design of those who control the Soviet Union and the international communist movement is to retain and solidify their absolute power, first in the Soviet Union and second in the areas now under their control. In the minds of the Soviet leaders, however, achievement of this design requires the dynamic extension of their authority and the ultimte elimination of any effective opposition to their authority.

The design, therefore, calls for the complete subversion or forcible destruction of the machinery of government and structure of society in the countries of the non-Soviet world and their replacement by an apparatus and structure subservient to and controlled by the Kremlin. To that end Soviet efforts are now directed toward the domination of the Eurasian land mass. The United States, as the principal center of power in the non-Soviet world and the bulwark of opposition to Soviet expansion, is the principal enemy whose integrity and vitality must be subverted or destroyed by one means or another if the Kremlin is to achieve its fundamental design. . . .

IV. THE UNDERLYING CONFLICT IN THE REALM OF IDEAS AND VALUES BETWEEN THE U.S. PURPOSE AND THE KREMLIN DESIGN

A.   Political and Psychological:

Our overall policy at the present time may be described as one designed to foster a world environment in which the American system can survive and flourish. It therefore rejects the concept of isolation and affirms the necessity of our positive participation in the world community.

This broad intention embraces two subsidiary policies. One is a policy which we would probably pursue even if there were no Soviet threat. It is a policy of attempting to develop a healthy international community. The other is the policy of "containing" the Soviet system. These two policies are closely interrelated and interact on one another. Nevertheless, the distinction between them is basically valid and contributes to a clearer understanding of what we are trying to do.

The policy of striving to develop a healthy international community is the long-term constructive effort which we are engaged in. It was this policy which gave rise to our vigorous sponsorship of the United Nations. It is of course the principal reason for our long continuing endeavors to create and now develop the Inter-American system. It, as much as containment, underlays our efforts to rehabilitate Western Europe. Most of our international economic activities can likewise be explained in terms of this policy.

In a world of polarized power, the policies designed to develop a healthy international community are more than ever necessary to our own strength.

As for the policy of "containment," it is one which seeks by all means short of war to (1) block further expansion of Soviet power, (2) expose the falsities of Soviet pretensions, (3) induce a retraction of the Kremlin's control and influence and (4) in general, so foster the seeds of destruction within the Soviet system that the Kremlin is brought at least to the point of modifying its behavior to conform to generally accepted international standards.

It was and continues to be cardinal in this policy that we possess superior overall power in ourselves or in dependable combination with other like-minded nations. One of the most important ingredients of power is military strength. In the concept of "containment," the maintenance of a strong military posture is deemed to be essential for two reasons: (1) as an ultimate guarantee of our national security and (2) as an indispensable backdrop to the conduct of the policy of "containment." Without superior aggregate military strength, in being and readily mobilizable, a policy of "containment"—which is in effect a policy of calculated and gradual coercion—is no more than a policy of bluff.

At the same time, it is essential to the successful conduct of a policy of "containment" that we always leave open the possibility of negotiation with the U.S.S.R. A diplomatic freeze—and we are in one now—tends to defeat the very purposes of "containment" because it raises tensions at the same time that it makes Soviet retractions and adjustments in the direction of moderated behavior more difficult. It also tends to inhibit our initiative and deprives us of opportunities for maintaining a moral ascendency in our struggle with the Soviet system.

In "containment" it is desirable to exert pressure in a fashion which will avoid so far as possible directly challenging Soviet prestige, to keep open the possibility for the U.S.S.R. to retreat before pressure with a minimum loss of face and to secure political advantage from the failure of the Kremlin to yield or take advantage of the openings we leave it.

We have failed to implement adequately these two fundamental aspects of "containment." In the face of obviously mounting Soviet military strength ours has declined relatively. Partly as a by-product of this, but also for other reasons, we now find ourselves at a diplomatic impasse with the Soviet Union, with the Kremlin growing bolder, with both of us holding on grimly to what we have, and with ourselves facing difficult decisions.

In examining our capabilities it is relevant to ask at the outset—capabilities for what? The answer cannot be stated solely in the negative terms of resisting the Kremlin design. It includes also our capabilities to attain the fundamental purpose of the United States, and to foster a world environment in which our free society can survive and flourish. . . .

B. Objectives:

The objectives of a free society are determined by its fundamental values. . . . The Kremlin's challenge to the United States is directed not only to our values but to our physical capacity to protect their environment. . . .

1. Thus we must make ourselves strong (militarily and economically). . . .
2. We must lead in building a successfully functioning political and economic system in the free world. . . .
3. . . .our policy and actions must be such as to foster a fundamental change in the nature of the Soviet system, a change toward which the frustration of the design is the first and perhaps the most important step. . . .

It is only by developing the moral and material strength of the free world that the Soviet regime will become convinced of the falsity of its assumptions and that the preconditions for workable agreements can be created. . . .

C. Means:

The free society is limited in its choice of means to achieve its ends. Compulsion is the negation of freedom except when it is used to enforce the rights common to all. The resort to force, internally or externally, is therefore a last resort for a free society. . . . The resort to force, to compulsion, to the imposition of its will is therefore a difficult and dangerous act for a free society, which is warranted only in the face of even greater dangers. The necessity of the act must be clear and compelling; the act must commend itself to the overwhelming majority as an inescapable exception to the basic idea of freedom; or the regenerative capacity of free men after the act has been performed will be endangered.

The Kremlin is able to select whatever means are expedient in seeking to carry out its fundamental designs. Thus it can make the best of several worlds, conducting the struggle on those levels where it considers it profitable and enjoying the benefits of a pseudo-peace on those levels where it is not ready for a contest. . . .

Practical and ideological considerations therefore both impel us to the conclusion that we have no choice but to demonstrate the superiority of the idea of freedom by its constructive application, and to atempt to change the world situation by means short of war in such a way as to frustrate the Kremlin design and hasten the decay of the Soviet system. . . .

[Section V deals with Soviet intentions and capabilities. It is based, as is the entire paper, on the assumption of an overriding Soviet goal of world domination. It considers political and psychological capabilities, economic capabilities; military capabilities. Section VI then proceeds to a parallel examination of U.S. intentions and capabilities. Since all figures are as of 1950, they are not reproduced here; but the paper does represent an instructive example of capability analysis as practiced at that time—and since.]

[Section VII addresses the subject of "Present Risks." It proceeds on the proposition "that the integrity and vitality of our system is in greater jeopardy than ever before in our history." Section VIII specifically deals with "Atomic Armaments," in which,

as of 1950, the United States had, of course, a clear preponderance; but growing Soviet strength in this field had to be anticipated. Finally, Section IX addresses the subject of "Possible Courses of Action." Below are key quotes from this section.]

Four possible courses of action by the United States in the present situation can be distinguished. They are: Continuation of current policies; Isolation; War; and a more rapid build-up of the political, economic and military strength of the free world than provided for under [a continuation of current policies]. . . .

[The ultimate conclusion of the paper is that no course of action but the fourth one will suffice]:

A more rapid build-up of political, economic, and military strength and thereby confidence in the free world than is now contemplated is the only course which is consistent with progress toward achieving our fundamental purpose. The frustration of the Kremlin design requires the free world to develop a successfully functioning political and economic system and a vigorous political offensive against the Soviet Union. These, in turn, require an adequate military shield under which they can develop. It is necessary to have the military power to deter, if possible, Soviet expansion, and to defeat, if necessary, aggressive Soviet or Soviet-directed actions of a limited or total character. The potential strength of the free world is great; its ability to develop these military capabilities and its will to resist Soviet expansion will be determined by the wisdom and will with which it undertakes to meet its political and economic problems.

VI

Diplomacy

Diplomacy has developed in response to the nature of the state system. Wherever people have existed in separate tribes or nations they have had need of some means of communicating and regulating their relations. In the absence of common councils, the practice developed of establishing permanent missions or embassies at each other's court or capital as a channel of communication and negotiation. Inasmuch as the ambassador was the personal representative of the ruler or monarch, he enjoyed all the privileges and immunities that would be extended to the monarch were he to appear in person. Diplomacy gained its unique status from the special need which the system of sovereign states has for communications and mediation if their relations are not to break down.

Even though the term diplomacy is sometimes used interchangeably with *foreign policy* (e.g., "Israel Diplomacy Seeks Security in Middle East"), the two are not the same. Diplomacy is a *process* and a *method* by which governments pursue foreign policy; it is not the policy itself. It is helpful in clarifying our understanding of how the process works if we draw a distinction between the making of foreign policy and the conduct of diplomacy. Foreign policy is what the President and his advisers decide should be done in order to implement the nation's goals; diplomacy and negotiation are among the methods or techniques whereby the government pursues that policy. Hence diplomacy is not the substance of policy, nor does it constitute the process whereby the government formulates policy, although it may influence that process. The diplomat's primary task is to negotiate with representatives of other countries, to try to arrive at a solution to problems which is acceptable to both sides involved in the negotiating process.

Diplomacy is carried on by governments through the agency of the Foreign Ministry (in the American case, the Department of State). The Foreign Minister or Secretary of State is responsible for the overall co-ordination between the home government and the diplomats serving abroad.

The Department of State is expected to provide the President with the information and advice that he needs in order to make policy. The Department in turn relays these decisions and instructions for their execution to the ambassador serving in the foreign capital, who is expected to take the matter up with the government to which he is accredited. The ambassador is the President's personal representative. Foreign ambassadors back in Washington are performing a similar function for their governments. Ambassadors are expected to carry out the instructions that they have been given and not act upon their own. They may refer questions back to the foreign ministry or make suggestions of their own, but their primary task is to induce the government to which they are accredited to respond favorably to what the home government wants of it. Good ambassadors or diplomats can make personal contributions to understanding by the scrupulousness with which they interpret back to the home capital the point of view of the government to which they are accredited.

Sometimes, of course, diplomacy may take the form of a visit by the President or a Secretary of State to a foreign country to negotiate personally with that country's leadership. On other occasions, diplomats and leaders may involve themselves in complicated negotiations concerning two or more foreign countries, which was what Secretary Kissinger had done and now President Carter and Secretary Vance have been doing in the Middle East. They are usually advised in these matters by a corps of Foreign Service officers and State Department specialists versed in the complicated economic, political, social or religious issues of the area. In these instances, the President or the Secretary of State are themselves acting as diplomats. They must be exceedingly careful when they undertake this role. When a diplomat negotiates he is acting as a professional agent and is professionally versed in the art of negotiation; when a President or any other national leader enters into negotiations, he may be under pressure either to refuse any significant concession so that public opinion will not think that too much is being sacrificed or under pressure to reach agreement for the sake of agreement. As one writer observes, "Negotiation involves a delicate balance between giving what is asked and getting what is wanted. To obtain the desired result, the negotiator must . . . turn everything to account.''[1]

Traditionally, the function of diplomacy has taken its form from the nature of the state system. In the absence of a common forum such as a parliament, states had to regulate their relations indirectly and diplomats were sent abroad to negotiate with other diplomats or directly with foreign sovereigns to accomplish their ends. For hundreds of years foreign policy was seen as the exclusive province of the monarch and his advisers. The preoccupations of traditional diplomacy were war, sovereignty, territory, and the personal ambitions of rulers. Diplomats were sent abroad to win over other monarchs to their master's point of view. Hence a premium was placed upon the arts of charm, guile, flattery, threat, and persuasion. As relations became more complex, diplomats had to be knowledgeable about the state to which they were sent, skilled in representing their country's interests to a foreign government (and vice versa), and adept at bargaining. Kenneth Thompson describes the background to nineteenth-century European diplomacy as follows:

> In theory at least, it sought to mitigate and reduce conflicts by means of persuasion, compromise, and adjustment. It was a diplomacy rooted in the community of interests of a small group of leaders who spoke the same language, catered as often to one another as their own people, and played to one another's strengths and weaknesses. When warfare broke out, they drew a ring around the combatants and sought to localize and neutralize the struggle. The old diplomacy . . . carried on its tasks in a world made up of states that were small, separated, limited in power, and blessed, ironically enough, by half-hearted political loyalties. Patience was a watchword; negotiations and talks would be initiated, broken off, resumed, discontinued temporarily, and reopened again by professionals in whose lexicon there was no substitute for "diplomacy."[2]

A good deal of modern diplomacy still involves secrecy and bargaining over conflicts of interest. The United States and the Soviet Union could only reach agreement on strategic arms control after extensive secret bargaining. In fact, two bargaining processes went on simultaneously, both secret. In Vienna the Soviet and American delegations engaged in the formal negotiations. But behind the scenes in Washington, and unbeknownst to the American negotiators in Vienna, National Security Advisor Kissinger and Soviet Ambassador Anatoly Dobrynin were secretly negotiating to remove the roadblocks encountered in the deliberations going on in Vienna. The formal negotiating positions on the Soviet and American sides were severely circumscribed by the interests of the military in maximizing their weapons advantages; Nixon's overwhelming desire to reach an agree-

---

[1]Frederick H. Hartmann, *The Relations of Nations*, 5th ed. (New York: Macmillan Publishing Co., 1978) p. 102.

[2]Kenneth Thompson, *Christian Ethics and the Dilemmas of Foreign Policy*, (Durham, N.C.: Duke University Press, 1959) pp. 81-82.

ment prompted him to bypass these limitations in having Kissinger explore other alternatives directly with Brezhnev in the Kremlin. Had they not been able to bargain in secret, they would have been under such pressures from opponents of the treaty that neither could have made the necessary concessions to the other's point of view. The same was true of the negotiations to end the war in Vietnam, to settle the Arab-Israeli conflict, and to establish terms for ending U.S. control of the Panama Canal. It is in the nature of many issues that only after the bargaining has been consummated and the terms of an agreement reached can results be revealed to the public. It is then to be hoped that, with the knowledge of the whole package including what each side has conceded, the public can be persuaded to accept the agreement.

Nevertheless, diplomacy has changed a great deal in the twentieth century and especially in the last thirty years. As Gilbert Winham points out in the next selection, diplomacy today is less an art than a management process. This is because states and societies are more interdependent and the issues are increasingly complex. In the old days, the outcome of negotiations was likely to have little effect upon the people at home unless it led to war. But today there are endless problems that can only be solved in conjunction with other nations, and they are not problems that can be neglected or easily postponed. Nuclear arms control, tariff and monetary matters, agreements to regulate air travel and communications, the avoidance of danger from pollution or terrorism or economic collapse, all are less a matter of conflict over issues than a matter of finding solutions to common problems. The difficulty encountered in obtaining landing rights for the Concorde at New York's Kennedy Airport is a perfect example of the way in which technology has created problems at the domestic level, the solution to which must be found at the international level if conflict is to be avoided.

Internal pressures have also affected the negotiation process. Many more private as well as public interests in each country must be taken into account. The complexity of the issues frequently requires large teams of experts on both sides. In effect, many problems we face can no longer be solved exclusively at the national level or left to the uninhibited play of national self-interest. As Winham observes in the selection that follows,

> Modern international negotiation represents a meshing of great systems. It is commonplace today to observe that the world is becoming more interdependent. . . . Today, negotiators function as an extension of national policymaking processes rather than as a formal diplomatic representation between two sovereigns. . . . It is now more akin to the art of management as practiced in large bureaucracies than to the art of guile and concealment as practiced by Cardinal Mazarin.

Governments need more control over forces in the international system than they can achieve independently. In the absence of the policy debate and consensus that occurs at the national level, they must have resort to diplomacy and negotiations. Much of modern diplomacy requires quite a different psychology and perspective from that of the past. Negotiators must approach their task with a problem-solving orientation rather than with a view to winning points at the expense of someone else, although the latter may still be an element in the bargaining process. They must also be able to bring about change in their own government's negotiating position. One diplomat remarked to Winham that as much as ninety percent of his delegation's time was spent in securing modifications of position from the government back home. In this sense, much of modern negotiation is indeed the extension of the national bureaucratic bargaining and policy process to the level of the international system.

Nevertheless, nations often come to the negotiating process with important differences of style and motive. The most persistent questions about style and motive have been raised concerning Soviet diplomacy. The Bolshevik government came to power in 1917 foresworn to the overthrow of the capitalist system. Lenin made no secret of his belief that all relations with capitalist countries were to be conducted on the presumption that friendly or even normal relations were not possible between two ideological systems, one of which was historically destined to triumph over the other. According to the Marxist-Leninist interpretation of history, capitalism is an outmoded system against which socialism must carry on a life-and-death struggle. That does not mean that capitalism will not fight back. Under the socially determined laws of history, peaceful or harmonious relations between socialist and capitalist states are not possible; the only relevant question is "who will kill whom?" The Soviet view that it is incumbent upon a good Bolshevik to advance the victory of Communism wherever possible, and to be ever on guard against the efforts of the capitalists to reverse the gains of socialism, does not make the task of diplomacy an easy one. Short of war, diplomacy presupposes some degree of mutual interest and trust in the relations between states; but given the Marxist-Leninist view that relations between capitalist states and Communist states must be governed by historically determined laws of conflict, it is not possible for Soviet diplomacy to possess that degree of common interest and trust that usually has marked diplomatic relations between states not on the verge of war.

This outlook has led the eminent diplomatic historian Gordon Craig to write,

> Despite the excellence of their training in the external forms of diplomacy, and their skill in using it, Soviet negotiators have always had a fundamentally different approach toward diplomacy from that of their western colleagues. To them, diplomacy is more than an instrument for protecting and advancing national interest; it is a weapon in the unremitting war against capitalist society.

Diplomatic negotiations, therefore, cannot aim at real understanding and agreement; and this has profound effects upon their nature and techniques.[3]

It should be noted that a considerable evolution has occurred in the Soviet approach to diplomacy. In the first stages of the Communist rule there was a tendency to regard diplomacy as an outworn bourgeois institution. There is still a dual commitment by the Soviet government to pursue a two-track course in its relations with other states—one track being that of conventional diplomacy and government-to-government relations; the other being that of support for revolutionary movements aimed at the overthrow of established governments. Still, the trend of Soviet diplomacy has been in the direction of exploiting the possibilities of diplomacy as much as possible to achieve the objectives of the Soviet state—objectives which are less and less those of world revolution and more and more those characteristic of every great power with global pretensions. Still, there is the strong suspicion that the Kremlin views negotiations less as a means of achieving a mutual accommodation of national interests than as another terrain on which the struggle to defeat capitalism must be carried on at all times. Hence Gordon Craig notes that not all negotiations entered into by the Soviet government are intended to eventuate in settlements, but rather serve as a means of testing the tenacity of the parties on the other side or for purely propaganda purposes designed to win the sympathy of potential recruits to the Soviet side against the West. Once entered into, the Soviets may not intend to make any concessions of their own so much as to gain concessions from the other side. "Soviet inflexibility is generally combined with the skillful use of tactics designed to wear out the patience or weaken the judgment of their adversaries."[4] By contrast, western governments are often under public pressure for quick results and are therefore prone to accept illusory concessions or dangerous agreements in principle. Soviet negotiators are free to proceed with infinite patience knowing that they may be in a position sooner or later to exploit the Western need for agreement. This does not necessarily mean that the Soviets are duplicitous, but rather that their operational principles and conditions give them negotiating advantages that are denied to western diplomats. On the other hand, it is often argued that the rigidity and secrecy with which the Kremlin surrounds its diplomacy limits its negotiators from securing terms that would be more in the Soviet interest to secure than would prolonging negotiations and worsening relations. This was probably more true in Stalin's day than it is today.

The greatest criticism advanced by those who fear that the United States is giving away too much in the Strategic Arms Limitation Talks is that

---

[3]"Totalitarian Approaches to Diplomatic Negotiations," in A. O. Sarkissian, ed., *Studies in Diplomatic History and Historiography* (London: Longmans, Green & Co., 1961), p. 120.

[4]Ibid, p. 122.

the United States does not approach the talks as a bargaining process or a competitive one, but as a cooperative process, whereas the Soviets have regarded SALT as another competitive endeavor designed to catch up or get ahead of the U.S. and to make gains in other political areas. "Arms control has, after all, become a normative term in the United States. Viewed as inherently good, arms control is difficult [for Americans] to see in terms of political competition or struggle for advantage."[5] It is alleged by critics of SALT and of detente that the United States negotiators enter the negotiations "with an excessive preoccupation with technical details and specifics at the expense of a thorough consideration of the basic [political and strategic] questions involved"[6]—namely, how is the outcome likely to affect America's overall political and strategic position in the world? By contrast, it is argued by critics of SALT I and detente that the Soviets approach these negotiations with a comprehensive strategico-political view as to what kind of agreement will most enhance Soviet strategic and political superiority. "Arms negotiation, like diplomacy and politics, is to the Soviets a means to maximize political or strategic advantage and gain *when possible at the expense of the other side.*"[7]

No doubt the American national psychology tends to put an emphasis upon the technical aspects of a problem and to assume that both sides to a negotiation view it as a bargaining process and not that one side might be coming at it as part of a larger political strategy designed to make gains at the expense of the other. Nevertheless, as is made clear by the interview with Marshall Shulman, special assistant to Secretary of State Vance for Soviet affairs, American negotiators are highly aware of the pitfalls of negotiating with the Russians. The interview in this chapter with Ambassador Shulman provides several interesting examples of the indirect negotiating technique. Shulman has taken advantage of the interview on the eve of Vance's departure for Moscow to signal the Kremlin that unless productive results are forthcoming the ability of President Carter to deal with domestic critics of arms control will be much more difficult. He has also taken the occasion to remind Soviet leaders that they signed a solemn agreement in June, 1972 to behave with a great deal more restraint in local conflict situations than they were then showing in Africa. The entire interview presents a fascinating exercise in tacit diplomacy. The tenacity which marked the U.S. approach to the SALT I negotiations, and the intense concern of President Carter and his strategic arms advisers to come up with a SALT II agreement that can withstand the assault of even its most dedicated critics, suggests that whatever diplomatic advantages the Soviet approach may have given them in the past has been offset by American experiences with Communist diplomatic style and motives.

⁵Testimony by William R. Van Cleave. *International Negotiation.* Hearings before the Subcommittee on National Security of the Senate Committee on Government Operations. Part 7. July 25, 1972. p. 200.

⁶Ibid, p. 201

⁷Ibid, p. 201

16   Negotiation As A Management Process

Gilbert R. Winham

The author is Associate Professor of Political Science and Director of the Centre for Foreign Policy Studies, Dalhousie University, Canada.

I. INTRODUCTION

Negotiation is an enduring art form. Its essence is artifice, the creation of expedients through the application of human ingenuity. The synonyms of the word "art" are qualities we have long since come to admire in the ablest of negotiators: skill, cunning, and craft. We expect negotiators to be accomplished manipulators of other people, and we applaud this aspect of their art when we observe it in uncommon degree. Negotiation is considered to be the management of people through guile, and we recognize guile as the trademark of the profession. . . .

In contemporary times we continue to acknowledge cunning. In a recent article on the Vietnam cease-fire agreement, Tad Szulc recorded with obvious enthusiasm the performance of Henry Kissinger in achieving a negotiated settlement to the war. As Szulc's account makes clear, Kissinger certainly demonstrated on this occasion that the hoary tactics of manipulation and concealment were important tools in the contemporary management of international relations. However, lest we overstress the

Reprinted from World Politics, *30, No. 1 (October 1977). Copyright © 1977 by Princeton University Press. Most footnotes have been omitted. Reprinted by permission of Princeton University Press.*

importance of these tools, it is well to ask ourselves why brilliant performances in diplomacy seem so few and far between, and why there are apparently so few diplomats today who enjoy the equivalent of Kissinger's reputation. Perhaps it is because negotiation, like leadership, is a skill applied in a situation, and there are relatively few situations in international relations today that call forth the skills Kissinger so ably demonstrated. Times are changing, and the world is a less suitable stage for the diplomat's machinations in the 1970's than it was in the time of Monsieur de Callieres.

The typical negotiation situation today bears little resemblance to those that obtained in the service of Louis XIV. Most diplomacy is conducted less discreetly and more under the surveillance of domestic interests than was the case previously. Negotiations are often more multilateral than bilateral; even when relationships are pursued on a bilateral basis, "reality is not bilateral," as Neustadt has observed. Both the operations of domestic groups and the incidence of multilateral negotiation enormously complicate the task of the diplomat. But more complicating yet are the changes in the subject matter of contemporary negotiations. The preoccupations of traditional diplomacy were war, sovereignty, territory, and the personal ambitions of rulers; although these could be painful subjects, they at least were comprehensible through the application of political acumen and common sense. Negotiators today spend more time discussing technology than did their predecessors, because technology—whether it takes the form of information systems, industrial processes, or nuclear weapons—has a proportionately greater impact on human existence now than it did in the past. And technology is in a state of rapid change, often at an exponential rate; it creates an enormous problem of comprehension and adaption for contemporary society.

Unquestionably, modern negotiation continues to be a contest of will and wit, but the emphasis has shifted. The principal problem for most contemporary negotiators is not to outwit their adversaries, but rather to create a structure out of a large mass of information wherein it is possible to apply human wit. The classical diplomat's technique of the management of people through guile has given way to the management of people through the creation of system and structure. The process is not as glamorous and individualized, but it requires no less the application of human intelligence than did the trickery of the classical diplomat.

Modern international negotiation represents a meshing of great systems. It is commonplace today to observe that the world is becoming more interdependent—and one symptom of this interdependence is the fact that complex political and economic problems are increasingly handled at the level of international negotiation rather than exclusively at the domestic level. Today, negotiators function as an extension of national policy-making processes rather than as a formal diplomatic representation between two sovereigns. The number of people involved in international negotiation has increased sharply, with consequent depersonalization of the process. It is unlikely that the "true feelings" of leaders or diplomats are as important as they once were, but it is erroneous to assume that personalities are irrelevant—particularly as they combine in various decision-making settings. In past eras it was fashionable to describe negotiation as art, and art it continues to be, but it is now more akin to the art of management as practiced in large bureaucracies than to the art of guile and concealment as practiced by Cardinal Mazarin.

Rapid changes have been occurring in the negotiation process, and these changes should be reflected more than they now are in our thinking about international relations. . . . The changes affect the nature of negotiation, and . . . an understanding of this fact is important in evaluating the usefulness of conducting negotiations. The changes also affect certain theories about the practice of negotiation, and they affect especially the importance of concessions and convergence in the negotiation process. Most important, the changes reflect different tactics which are employed by negotiators and which should be understood in order to propose improvements in the process.

II. POLITICIZATION

Since 1945, international negotiation has been under pressure from two sides. External pressure has occurred from significant changes in the international system—principally from the increased number of nation-states and the consequent trend toward multilateral diplomacy in the United Nations system. Internal pressure has occurred from the increasing impact of citizen input and bureaucratic politicking on the negotiating process. International negotiation is a more politicized affair than previously, and as a consequence the distinctions between foreign affairs and domestic affairs are blurring.

Some aspects of the external pressure on negotiations are well known. Some time ago, Sir Harold Nicolson called attention to the increasing trend toward conducting negotiation by public conference, and observed that the process violated the rule that sound negotiations must be confidential and continuous. More recently, certain developments have occurred that Nicolson did not foresee. The increased number of nation-states since 1945 has ensured that national positions are more varied and more difficult to reconcile than ever before. New states tend to raise issues that more established ones consider as settled; as a consequence the negotiation process can rely less on precedent to create a common referent for bargaining. This problem was illuminated in a study of the Law of the Sea negotiation in 1958, where some of the newer states objected to the concepts of international law and the administrative-legalistic style of negotiation with which Western countries had long been familiar. A similar example occurred at the U.N. Environmental Conference in Stockholm, where less developed countries were successful in forcing the issues of human poverty and under development into the definition of environment, and hence onto the agenda of the conference.

Internal pressures have also affected the negotiation process. In de Callières's day, the process of representing a sovereign abroad was simpler than it is now. Monsieur de Callières viewed negotiation neither as troubled by bureaucratic constraints nor as a bureaucratic process in itself. The contrast between this image and that of modern negotiation could not be more striking. Most modern negotiations are carried on between teams that represent bureaucracies, and in large negotiations the teams themselves approach the status of small bureaucracies. That this system would increase the scope of bureaucratic politics in negotiation is self-evident, and there are many examples. John Newhouse, writing on the Strategic Arms Limitation Talks, observed that the U.S. SALT delegation replicated the SALT bureaucracy in Washington, and that "most importantly, SALT [was] an internal negotiation." A similar sentiment was expressed by an experienced U.S. negotiator: "I would say about nine-tenths of my time of negotiation was done with my own side.". . .

The bureaucratic dissensus that negotiators must contend with is often a reflection of the demands of pressure groups at home. In any major negotiation the interests of large groups must be accounted for, and this creates a problem of organization, distillation, and representation for the negotiating team. The problem was accurately, if perhaps unjoyously, portrayed by a U.S. official in connection with the American position at the current trade negotiations in Geneva: "The U.S. negotiating team is particularly restrained by having to respond to 45 private-sector committees composed of 900 knowledgeable people who are well aware of their own interests. . . . The E.C. confronts the same problem." Nor is this problem appreciably lessened in a smaller system. In connection with the same trade negotiation, the Canadian Government received a request from the Province of Manitoba to include representatives from the Province during the final stages of the negotiation. Since the positions of the Federal and Provincial Governments on trade and tariff matters are not congruent, the outcome of Manitoba's request will probably complicate the work of the Canadian delegation no matter how the issue is resolved.

TECHNOLOGICAL CHANGE

The increased complexity in negotiation due to human factors is matched by an equivalent impact from non-human factors. Technological change is occurring in all countries, and with increasing intensity. The rate of change poses two principal problems that frequently create difficulties at the negotiating table. One is the scale, or variety, of relationships. International relationships today encompass an enormous variety of interaction which gives rise to an equivalent variety of items in the negotiation process. Consider one example. In the Kennedy Round, the negotiators dealt with levels of protection on tens of thousands of products traded by 82 states, and in addition considered questions such as problems of dumping and assistance to less developed countries. Most states were therefore burdened by a portfolio of staggering complexity, which would be unknowable in any sense in which we might apply the term. Nor was this problem a special product of economic relations, trade negotiations, or the Kennedy Round in particular. A similar situation obtained in the SALT talks and in the current Law of the Sea negotiation. Indeed, it seems that when one looks at the areas where major negotiations have been held, the complexity of the sort described in the Kennedy Round is the rule rather than the exception.

A further problem is uncertainty. If technological progress creates variety, it also creates uncertainty, for in many areas we are simply unaware of the implications of modern technology on human life. Moreover, we are uncertain about the means for managing such technologies. These observations apply to defense, to off-shore mineral exploitation, and to food distribution (all areas in which there have been international negotiations), but they pertain especially to problems of the international economy. Economists are simply uncertain about some of the most important questions regarding the international economy, and this uncertainty is reflect at the bargaining table when governments negotiate on various problems. In trade negotiations, for example, there are no satisfactory ways to measure the effect of tariff reductions on trade, and hence this creates the difficulty of not having any ultimate guidelines by which to evaluate the results of the negotiation. The same is true of weapons negotiations, where there are no clear and unambiguous ways to assess the relation between numbers of nuclear weapons and the national security. The conclusion, then, is that the environment within which states must conduct their relationships is becoming increasingly complex, both because of the operation of technological progress and because of certain changes that have occurred in the structure of domestic and international politics. . . .

The main thesis of this paper is that much international negotiation, especially multilateral negotiation, occurs as an attempt by the parties to manage some aspect of their environment. Negotiations often do not occur simply to resolve specific points of dispute between the parties, although disputes are certain to be embedded in the fabric of any negotiation. An important purpose of negotiation is to reduce complexity; the technique is to achieve, through negotiated agreement, a structure that will limit the free play of certain variables in the future.[1]

[1] Clearly there are many negotiations in which control of complexity is a lesser problem, such as disputes over fishing quotas or beef imports. However, negotiations on specific issues (for instance, Canadian-

...The SALT negotiation affords an excellent example. The impetus behind SALT, as Newhouse's excellent analysis has made clear, was not a desire to reduce arms, but rather a need to stabilize defense relations between the United States and the Soviet Union. The main threats to stability were a competitive arms race, uncertainty about future force levels, and the consequent need to assume the worst in projecting defense needs in the future. SALT did not reduce arms appreciably, but it did permit Soviet and American planners to exercise greater control over the environment in which they project defense needs. As in the case of the Kennedy Round, an underlying purpose of SALT was control of uncertainty, as was made clear by the U.S. chief delegate to SALT, Gerard C. Smith:

> A major driving force behind the strategic arms competition—at least from the American standpoint—has been uncertainty as to what future Soviet force levels would be. If the Vladivostok accords evolve into a formal limitation agreement, the U.S. will be assured of the maximum number of Soviet launchers during the next decade. Even though the number is high, it will be known. . . . Assurance about the future maximum size of the forces . . . should encourage stability in the American-Soviet strategic relationship.

The attempt to reduce variety and uncertainty through negotiation, and consequently to increase international stability, is not a new feature of international diplomacy. Indeed, as Nicolson has noted, the chief aim of diplomacy is international stability, and governments have long tried to reduce their uncertainty about the intentions or capabilities of their adversaries through negotiated agreements. What is different is that the complexities of the present age are greater, due largely to technical change, and as a result environmental control is a more urgent task than before. National leaders are uncertain about the future, and, as Newhouse reminds us "it is the unknown, not the known, that fosters instability." Many statesmen today feel under pressure to create values or structures in international politics that will replace the uncertainties of unilateral action with the certainty of negotiated agreements. Secretary of State Henry Kissinger expressed such a sentiment when he said of the U.N. Conference on the Law of the Sea (L.O.S.): "Unilateral legislation would be a last resort. . . . It [the Conference] must succeed. The United States is resolved to help conclude the Conference in 1976—before the pressure of events and contentions places international consensus irretrievably beyond our grasp. . . ."[2]

IMPLICATIONS

To view international negotiations as a process for reducing uncertainty involves important implications for our understanding of the negotiation process. One implication is that negotiation is no longer viewed principally as a dispute-settlement or distributive procedure. This distinction was apparently appreciated by Dr. Kissinger when he

---

Egyptian negotiations on cotton textile imports) often occur within the context of a more general negotiated framework. Thus, the Cotton Textile Agreement of 1964, established to regulate international textile trade, sought the purpose of reducing uncertainty as outlined here.

[2] ADDRESS BY SECRETARY OF STATE KISSINGER, "INTERNATIONAL LAW, WORLD ORDER, AND HUMAN PROGRESS," delivered before the American Bar Association at Montreal, Canada, on August 11, 1975. *Department of State Bulletin*, Vol. 73, September 8, 1975, 335–62; quote from p. 359.

described the L.O.S. negotiation in the following terms: "We are at one of those rare moments when mankind has come together to devise means of preventing future conflict and shaping its destiny, rather than to resolve a crisis that has occurred or to deal with the aftermath of a war." Dispute settlement, or crisis resolution, is the common model we usually adopt for understanding most international negotiation. This model usually entails the tabling of an opening position, and the movement (or convergence) toward a compromise position through step-by-step concessions. The burden on the negotiator is to maintain as much of his position as possible while moving toward an outcome that will be mutually acceptable. This process emphasizes concealment, competitive strategies, and the ability to persuade.

The model of dispute settlement continues to be appropriate in international politics, and certain elements of it can operate in negotiations where dispute settlement is not the main purpose of the negotiation. At the Kennedy Round negotiators certainly engaged in haggling and compromise; they exchanged concessions; and they vigorously tried to persuade other parties of the justice and merit of the positions they had staked out. However, the basic structure of the negotiation, viewed in its entirety, was quite different. A more appropriate model for negotiation in a complex situation is one that replaces strategy with search for information, and is concerned with process as opposed to outcome. Negotiators tend not to estimate acceptable outcomes, because outcomes are distant and unknowable. They focus instead on the process of negotiation and what they want the process to achieve, such as exchange of information about both parties' principal concerns, decision-making procedures, or the like. The process of nego-

tiation involves a search for acceptable solutions, where strategy is more a matter of forestalling the consideration of certain unattractive solutions than a matter of extracting a change of position from an adversary. This process is akin to the tactics of integrative bargaining as described by Walton and McKersie, or the procedures of "debate" as described by Rapoport.[3]

The second implication of viewing negotiation as a process for reducing uncertainty is that the development of common perceptions becomes more important to the negotiating process than the exchange of concessions. In complex situations, negotiators tend to negotiate over the "definition of the situation," and theories of how people develop common perceptions of complex information are more likely to be useful than theories of how people outwit others in bargaining contests. When negotiators deal with each other over complex subjects, they often represent societies that have evolved entirely different methods of accomplishing certain social tasks, and as a result the first problem is to establish a definitional basis from which to proceed. Newhouse has appreciated this aspect about the SALT negotiations; he concludes a description of the first negotiating session with the state-

---

[3]Richard E. Walton and Robert B. McKersie, *A Behavioral Theory of Labor Negotiations* (New York: McGraw-Hill 1965); Anatol Rapoport, *Fights, Games and Debates* (Ann Arbor: University of Michigan Press 1960). See also Sawyer and Guetzkow: "The process of devising more favorable alternatives and outcomes may be characterized as one of 'creative problem-solving' since it involves innovation rather than mere selection among given possibilities. As with creative processes more generally, however, relatively little is understood of its operation." Jack Sawyer and Harold Guetzkow, "Bargaining and Negotiation in International Relations," in Herbert C. Kelman, *International Behavior* (New York: Holt, Rinehart & Winston 1966), 466–520; quote from p. 485.

ment: "The two sides parted as they met, still speaking a different strategic vocabulary." He further quotes an interviewee: "We were so absorbed in our own definitional problems we made no serious effort to anticipate theirs." In Zartman's words: "The whole process of the Strategic Arms Limitation negotiation is a search for referent principles and then for the implementing details."

The process described above normally requires some agreement on the negotiating rules, or some similar formula for standardizing the approach of different parties. In the Kennedy Round, the problem of negotiating rules was dealt with explicitly, but it may be more common for negotiators to establish referents or formulas implicitly as part of the discussion of a problem. Also, establishing such formulas can be an ongoing procedure during a negotiation, and will be part of the process that occurs naturally when parties take up new issues. An analogous procedure to the use of negotiation formulas is the creation of a bargaining language to assist negotiators to exchange proposals. A bargaining language essentially consists of cognitive structures that facilitate communication between negotiators. These structures can be very general, such as the notions of "parity" in weapons negotiations, or "reciprocity" in trade negotiation, or they can be common definitions or evaluation procedures that enable negotiators to evaluate their progress in the negotiation. In complex negotiations, a bargaining language can serve as a mechanism for simplifying the information that negotiators must handle in the course of moving toward an agreement. It is a means of developing common perceptions about the bargaining environment, and its use in itself constitutes some measure of agreement between the parties. . . .

PROGRAMMED OPERATIONS

The reality of negotiation is not a rapid exchange of creative ideas, even though creative ideas are part of the process. The reality of negotiation is tedium. There are good reasons why this is so. First, the barriers to agreement are political, not intellectual, and it takes time and patience for governments to persuade themselves to accept change.[4] Second, the search for agreement is a combination of trial and error plus insight, and it takes time for the process to be played through. Negotiations reflect the cutting edge of change in the international system, and the process of accepting change is a discontinuous and drawn-out affair.

Most actual negotiation is a form of programmed operations that follows from general principles established by the parties. As one Kennedy Round interviewee put it, "The orchestration of negotiation is almost mechanical." Problem areas are broken down into their constituent parts, and are taken up by small working groups of negotiators. Working groups have agendas, and these agendas call for a sequential treatment of the topics scheduled for discussion. Topics are usually discussed rather than haggled over (admittedly, this is a fine distinction), particularly through the early and middle stages of the negotiation. Bargaining is exploratory and communication is relatively free.

There are several principles that govern the programmed operations in a large negotiation. One is the quasi-resolution of con-

[4]This observation was made by Robert W. Barnett in the course of explaining the function of trivia in negotiations. Newhouse has made an analogous point ("tedium has its place in the negotiating process") in the course of criticizing the fast-paced strategy of the U.S. SALT delegation.

flict. Issues are brought up sequentially and the positions of the parties are explored. Where disagreement exists, various suggestions are pursued to resolve the disagreement. Trade-offs are discussed, and alternative compromises are attempted. In some cases, the conflict will be resolved through concession, compromise, and convergence. Where conflict is resolved, the issue is put aside and is usually not raised again. As the area of agreement widens, the parties develop a greater stake in the negotiation, and this creates a positive momentum toward a final, overall agreement. If in this process parties are unable to agree, they will drop the issue and hence postpone the conflict. The issue in question will be moved up for consideration at a higher level in the negotiating bureaucracy. The same procedure will be used; hence, the most difficult and conflictual issues will be put off until the end of the negotiation.

A second principle is that negotiators do not try to deal with all the material that comes under their cognizance in a complex negotiation. They solve the problem of too much variety in the situation by ignoring much of that variety, concentrating instead on simple operational feedback variables. These variables tend to be internal, relating to the organizational work of the negotiating team or relations with the home government, rather than external. The reason is that negotiators are more concerned with presenting their own position than with relating to their adversary. That point has been made in both classical and modern literature, and has also been observed in the runs of the trade negotiation simulation.[5]

There are several feedback variables that negotiators focus on especially in complex negotiations. One is their organization and control over their own negotiating position. Problems of control over the negotiating position stem from bureaucratic politics on the negotiating team, from the constant need to obtain new information to defend the position and its changes, and from the inherent difficulties of maintaining consistency when a large body of data is in constant change. It is especially important that negotiators be able to project an image of being in control of their portfolio; failure to do this provides ammunition for whatever opposition may exist at home. Another key feedback variable is the extent to which negotiators can maintain domestic consensus for the negotiation. Objectively this variable is always important, but it has a profound subjective impact on negotiators because of the difficulty of communicating structural problems to the adversary. In the Kennedy Round, American negotiators worried about Congress, and their anxiety was increased by E.E.C. negotiators who apparently did not appreciate the need to maintain support for the negotiation in Congress. Conversely, E.E.C. negotiators worried about the uncertainties of decision making in the E.E.C. and the fragility of support for the Kennedy Round, and *their* anxiety was increased by apparent American insensitivity to Brussels.[6]

---

[5] "Most men handling public affairs pay more attention to what they themselves say than to what is said to them," De Callières. "And yet, we found

in our experiments that our subjects were overwhelmingly 'introverted,' that their demands were primarily determined by their own past demands, and that they paid little attention to one another's offers." Otomar J. Bartos, "Concession-Making in Experimental Negotiations," in Joseph Berger, Morris Zelditch, Jr., and Bo Anderson, *Sociological Theories in Progress* (Boston: Houghton Mifflin 1966) 3–28; quote from p. 21.

[6] These anxieties often are expressed as principles. For example, one E.E.C. negotiator stated: "It was difficult for our partners to understand our decision-making process . . . we faced a *simultaneous* negotiation . . . it was part of the *democratic* process."

Another feedback variable that is monitored, and one that relates primarily to the adversary, is the "will to negotiate." Governments enter a negotiation to achieve certain principles, and they monitor the behavior of their adversaries to ensure that it does not represent a pulling back from the principles of the negotiation. Individual concessions are not a major concern—they are a fairly structured and hence unimportant phenomenon—but the failure to resolve certain problems, or the failure to "move in a certain direction" can become a major stumbling block in the negotiation. In such cases, disputes crop up, often on fairly trivial matters. A case in point was the bitter dispute in the Kennedy Round between the Common Market and the United States over the matter of the American Selling Price (A.S.P.) in chemicals. This issue, as the American negotiators correctly pointed out, was of little direct consequence to trade, but the form of the restriction gave the American Government the unilateral right to decide the issue, either in applying the restriction or in dropping it (which required congressional confirmation). The Common Market found the A.S.P. repugnant because, maintaining a unilateral freedom of movement for the Americans, it created uncertainties for the Common Market countries and hence was contrary to one of the fundamental purposes of the Kennedy Round negotiation. From the perspective of the E.E.C., the A.S.P. was a matter of principle bcause it raised the question of the United States' "will to negotiate" reductions in trade restrictions.

A third principle inherent in the programmed operations of negotiation is organizational learning, a concept which has been analyzed in the literature of organization theory. Negotiating teams are usually assembled from governmental bureaucracies on an *ad hoc* basis, and are disassembled at the conclusion of their task. These teams confront problems that are often novel in substance, and are certainly novel in terms of procedures and personalities. In the succession of encounters that constitute day-to-day negotiation, the teams achieve various kinds of organizational learning: they gather and store information, they develop procedures for communication, and they adapt organizational goals to fit the possibilities in the situation. Above all, negotiating teams learn how other countries perceive the problems that are up for negotiation, and what priorities these countries place on different issues.

Over time, negotiating teams learn to develop concepts, or to create relationships in the bargaining situation that are not obvious to internal decision makers, but that may be necessary to facilitate bargained exchanges between states. Negotiators accomplish this partly through the creation of a bargaining language, which, like other bureaucratic languages, is a collection of task-oriented symbols or concepts that facilitate the work of the organization. There were several examples of bargaining language in the Kennedy Round; the concept of "reciprocity" has aleady been mentioned in this context. The notion of reciprocity was itself refined into more specific concepts, such as measures (e.g., weighted average reductions) for making quantitative assessments of reciprocity. By common agreement, such measures were not accurate in an economic sense, but they did give negotiators a language for communicating and for exchanging tariff reductions.[7] These measures allowed negotiators to build an agreement, but they had inherent limitations

[7] One highly placed interviewee commented: "The advantage of tariff negotiations is that you can put phony numbers on things."

from the standpoint of reaching a final settlement. In order to reach a final settlement, negotiators had to develop the flexibility to move beyond the structures and the bargaining language that had been successful throughout most of the negotiation.

FINAL AGREEMENT

Most negotiations have a deadline for the completion of the work. Occasionally such deadlines are beyond the immediate influence of negotiators. However, even when deadlines can be manipulated, they create a pressure to conclude the negotiation, since senior members of governments cannot be detained indefinitely in an exercise that appears to be going nowhere. The expectation that negotiation must soon be concluded not only increases the tempo of the exercise, it also changes the nature of the task. Concluding a negotiation puts more emphasis on decision making than occurs in the early phases, and proportionately less emphasis on bargaining and communication.

The situation, as complex negotiations like the Kennedy Round or SALT negotiations conclude, is that many outstanding issues must be woven together into a package deal. In different areas of the negotiation, issues which have proven troublesome have been postponed. Conflicts have only been partially resolved. The negotiators must bring the unresolved problems together in the concluding period of the negotiation in a way that the various governments can accept. Usually, difficult issues cannot be resolved by dropping them: they have become interlocked in a complex negotiation, and to drop any major issue late in the game leads to an unravelling of other agreements that are contingent on its solution. Negotiators are thus put in a position where they must find a formula to resolve the principal issues or

acknowledge that the negotiation has failed to produce the agreements that had been envisioned.

The elements in the conclusion of a negotiation inescapably increase the pressure on the negotiators. There will usually be considerable political momentum behind a negotiation, especially where the negotiation is publicized, visible to internal politics, and where it is obvious that much effort has been put in. The negotiation normally will represent a considerable sunk cost in terms of government decision-making time, and there will be a major personal and professional investment for the negotiators concerned. Furthermore, there will be an increasing awareness of the political values that will be lost if the negotiation fails, especially the value of extending greater control over the international environment through international agreement. All these factors will militate toward compromise and settlement of the outstanding issues. On the other hand, as the conclusion nears, negotiators will be under increasing pressure not to give way on issues of concern to home governments and domestic interests. Those issues are outstanding precisely because they are areas where change is least easily accepted. The conclusion of a negotiation tends to expose these areas, and the government and domestic interests involved counter by bringing pressure not to reach settlement in the negotiation. One Kennedy Round negotiator summed it up simply: "The pressure comes from everywhere."

The conclusion of a negotiation increases the complexity and uncertainty that have faced the negotiators throughout the exercise. The sequential handling of issues gives way to a situation that demands that many issues be handled at once. Negotiators find it more difficult to resolve problems within established categories (e.g., the category of industrial products in trade negotiations);

they are required instead to seek relationships between dissimilar categories (e.g., agricultural versus industrial sectors). This means that the programmed operations that have evolved for achieving balances thus far in the negotiation are less helpful as a guide to negotiators in the last stages of the negotiation. Striking a final overall balance is less a bargaining process with the other side than a political process of convincing capitals to accept what negotiators are prepared to deliver. New methods must be evolved to deal with what have become old problems in the negotiation.

The task of concluding a negotiation necessarily falls to senior negotiators, and Kennedy Round inverviewees agree that it is more political than administrative in nature. The bureaucratized procedures, programmed operations, and technical notions of balance that delegations may have relied on previously have become less relevant. There is a need for negotiating teams to change "set"; that is, to shift from procedures that facilitate interdelegation bargaining (e.g., procedures for calculating reciprocity in trade negotiations) to procedures that permit general overarching restatements of the problem. A clear example of this need was observed in the trade negotiation simulations. As in the real negotiation, simulation subjects used various quantitative measures to calculate reciprocity. However, subjects were unable to use these methods profitably at the end of the negotiation because there was insufficient time to make the needed calculations and because the methods produced results that were too precise for the needs of the moment. In fact, subjects who persisted in such calculations lost their grip on the overall developments in the negotiation, usually to their own disadvantage. The simulations support the contention that the conclusion of a negotiation requires the same

kind of general, formula-oriented solution as does the start of a negotiation. It is primarily an exercise in creative problem solving, where educated political guesswork is more important than shrewd calculation of advantages.[8]

There is ample evidence that the last-minute decisions in a large-scale negotiation are taken amid great confusion. Interviewees from the Kennedy Round admitted as much, and in an interesting way. Senior political members of negotiating teams asserted that much of the competence to understand the accords rested with the technical people, while the technical people maintained that much of the Kennedy Round was "political" and hence outside the scope of their competence. In short, each group professed a lack of competence to understand the overall process, albeit for different reasons. Others as well have remarked on the confusion and uncertainty that obtains at the conclusion of a large negotiation. One of the most perceptive journalists covering the Kennedy Round started his story about the completion of the negotiation with the following paragraphs:

> Deep and very widely shared satisfaction over settling the major Kennedy Round controversies is alternating here with genuine ignorance as to what the settlements may mean in detail. At this stage even senior officials in the various delegations have not yet broached the task of analyzing the precise contents of the agreements reached.
>
> It is not just a matter of detailed information remaining unpublished until the accord has been formally signed a few weeks hence. The hasty deals reached by top negotiators in the frantic final hours often have not yet been translated into actual texts, nor

[8]An interviewee summed it up in the following terms: "Negotiation is a subjective affair: At the end you just take the best guess."

sometimes even communicated to those on the next steps of the hierarchy.[9]

Lest this observation be thought confined to trade negotiations, one can cite a similar observation by Newhouse about the conclusion of the SALT negotiation in Vladivostok: "As confusing as all this may seem, it was only slightly less so to the experts themselves. After the White House party returned to Washington, several meetings of the verification panel were spent largely in trying to establish exactly what had been agreed to on SBLM's and what precisely it all meant."

The fact that the negotiation becomes increasingly difficult to comprehend does not mean that negotiators are incapacitated by complexity, or without a strategy for concluding the process. For one thing, negotiators tend to focus on aspects that are relatively certain, such as the positions that governments take on the issues, and pay less attention to those that are less understandable, such as the significance or value of those positions. Thus, the conflict that is inherent in any negotiation helps to clarify and structure that situation, and it is taken advantage of by negotiators. Second, negotiators try to structure the way they handle conflict. For example, a Kennedy Round interviewee indicated that on conflictual issues, negotiators at different levels tended to argue their position "to a point of incompetence," after which (as we have seen) the issue would be taken up in the next higher level in the negotiating bureaucracy. This procedure brings new faces and new ideas to difficult problems. Also implied in this procedure is a stratagem that was followed by

some delegations in the Kennedy Round, namely that of keeping senior people at home and away from the negotiation until late in the game. This stratagem helps to avoid delegations from becoming psychologically committed to single interpretations of difficult problems, and it creates the flexibility and freedom to make decisions on the solution of issues. . . .

Today what has changed most about international diplomacy is (1) the need to manage information, and (2) the fact that important societal decision making occurs at the level of international negotiation, at the expense of the processes of national government. For the first, the skills needed are those of a systems analyst, which fortunately are not wholly native, but can be imparted through training. Computer programing might well be a valuable ability, not because computers are necessarily useful in international negotiation (for instance, they were not useful in the Kennedy Round), but because the process of thought that is involved in computer programming is one that leads to the handling of information in a systematic fashion, and to the development of a hierarchical, recursive style of search and decision making.

For the second change in diplomacy, the quality needed is political courage. This did not occur to Monsieur de Callières because in his day diplomats represented sovereigns; the actions of these diplomats were not visible to many, and consequently the pressures on them were less burdensome. Today the situation is different. Modern international negotiation is more like representng a labor union than a king, and union negotiators confront problems dealing with their constituents that classical diplomats never had to face. Moreover, negotiation today generates new issues and new problems that negotiators

[9]H. Peter Dreyer, "Tariff Talks Package Gets Mixed Reaction," *New York Journal of Commerce* (May 1967), 1.

themselves are better aware of than anyone else. Negotiators have to take final responsibility for making some decisions (or at least for making recommendations that effectively become decisions) because no one else is in a position to do the job better. This fact itself raises questions about the public accountability of the negotiation process, and it is an issue that will increasingly confront democratic societies in the future. From the negotiator's standpoint, however, it cannot be gainsaid that the job has become more difficult. Negotiators must often make decisions in highly uncertain yet bureaucratically visible situations, with the full knowledge that they may be seriously criticized at home for whatever they do. They need to have political courage to do their job properly.

17   How Shulman Views Soviet Motives and Strategies: An Interview

Marshall D. Shulman

The author is the former head of Columbia University's Russian Institute. He is now the special adviser to Secretary of State Cyrus R. Vance on Soviet affairs and holds the title of Ambassador.

Question. General Secretary [Leonid I.] Brezhnev gave what appeared to be a fairly tough speech the other day suggesting that the Carter Administration was vacillating in its SALT policy. Was this supposed to set a cool tone for Secretary Vance's meetings in Moscow?

Answer. I read the speech as doing several things. It was a very sober assessment of the importance of the SALT negotiations as the most urgent item on the Soviet-American agenda. Secondly, it was clear that Brezhnev was making an effort to rebut the criticisms of Soviet positions that that been coming from the United States. Thirdly, it seemed to me that there were

Reprinted by permission of the New York Times *from the News of the Week in Review, April 16, 1978.*

elements in the speech that were addressed to the domestic Soviet audience defending his policy of seeking agreements with the United States.

Q. Is it your impression then that the Soviets intend to make this a productive meeting with Vance, more productive at least than last March when the talks ended in sharp disagreement?

A. Yes. I think the indications of the Soviet attitude that we've received are that they do want the negotiations to succeed. The issues are very complicated and even with the best will on both sides they would be difficult. But I do have hopes that the negotiations will be much more productive than they were last March.

Q. Given the massive propaganda campaign from Moscow, will the neutron bomb

be discussed, and particularly the President's decision to link future production to Soviet actions?

A. The President's decision in deferring the present production and deployment of the neutron weapon should not be regarded as an act of weakness. It was a sober decision and it took great courage on President Carter's part to take full responsibility for it without allowing himself to be swayed by the pressures of the moment from any quarter, including the Soviets.

Soviet public pressures on the issue made the decision more difficult for the President. His decision to postpone the deployment of the neutron weapons was made not because of the Soviet pressure but in spite of them.

Sometimes the Soviet Union seems not to perceive the differences between serious substantive proposals on arms control matters and propagandistic approaches. And in this case, the Soviet propaganda campaign if anything tended to increase the pressure for moving ahead with the present deployment of the neutron weapons.

I just want to add that the President has said that the reason why the neutron weapon has been considered and is being considered is as a response to the very large Soviet deployment of forces in the European theater. And if the Soviet Union wishes to do something constructive to reduce the necessity of looking to weapons like this, they could reduce their tank forces and personnel and other weapons that bear on the European theatre.

Q. Aside from these specifics how would you describe the overall relations?

A. On the surface right now, the tone is somewhat sharper than it has been in the past—we have been through such periods before. But there are two new factors: One is that the two societies are really involved

with each other to a much greater degree than they were a decade ago. The other is that the most fundamental aspect of the relationship is reflected in the SALT negotiations.

If we are successful in negotiating a good SALT treaty, it will provide a floor under the relationship and will give a measure of stabilization to the other aspects so that the fluctuations that occur—and they inevitably will because of Soviet-American political competition in various parts of the world—will be minimized.

And then this raises the more general point, that in thinking about United States-Soviet relations, we tend in this country to think of there being only two attitudes, hard and soft. What is desirable is to develop an understanding that there needs to be a policy which is neither hard nor soft, that is based on a realistic understanding of the nature of the Soviet system and the problems presented by Soviet policies, but at the same time has a clear view of what our own self-interest requires. That means, in the first instance, the stabilization of the military competition, and over the longer run an effort to enlarge the cooperative rather than the competitive side of relations.

Q. You've been a student of Soviet affairs for a long time. Are there any historical parallels with the present?

A. The one lesson from our past experience is that we oughtn't to be surprised by ups and downs in the relationship, that we ought to expect that the process of moving out of the long years of intense hostility is bound to, first of all, take a long time and, secondly, to move unevenly. Each movement toward easing tensions generates its own backlash effect.

For example, if you get a reduction of tension in relations, this creates problems for the whole [Soviet] security apparatus.

They tend to tighten up. You have vigilance campaigns, you have crackdowns, you have narrower margins within which people can write or discuss things, and then you get prominent cases that emerge from it, people who are the victims of this action, which in turn generates reactions abroad and that sets in motion a cycle.

Q. But before you entered the Administration, you wrote that if there is a general relaxation of international tensions, this improves the domestic climate inside the Soviet Union?

A. Over the long run, yes. But the short-run effect of periods of reduced tension is to produce a tightening, almost a convulsive tightening of the control mechanisms. Since you raised parallels before, the 1930's was the period of the great purges but also the period of the united fronts abroad.

Q. Referring to this Administration, why have relations seemed so bad with Moscow?

A. It hasn't been altogether that way. But your general impression I think reflects the fact that when the new Administration came in, the Soviets obviously had hoped that they would be able to pick up where they left off with the previous Administration. It came as a surprise to them and a disappointment that there was a somewhat new situation that developed and that the halcyon days of 1972 were never going to be recaptured. Probably the reason why it could not be recaptured is that the hopes and expectations about what detente meant were pretty unrealistic in 1972. To some extent we had a backlash of our own here against those too high expectations. The absence of restraint in local competitive situations came as a shock to people who thought that detente meant that there would be surcease of competition.

Q. Talking about lack of restraint, the Administration in the last six months has been very upset by the Soviet actions in the Horn of Africa. How do you explain Soviet motivations there?

A. Well, first of all, it shouldn't come as a surprise to anyone that the Soviets have moved into an area where they felt they had an opportunity to expand their influence. This has been characteristic of Soviet behavior. The Soviets were able to be on the side of legitimacy of the issue, in defense of territorial integrity, which is the side on which most of the African states were.

Now, the problem from our point of view arose from the fact that they did so with obvious lack of restraint. The scale of the weapons they put into the area and the large number of Cuban soldiers they transported there exceeded any reasonable definition of restraint.

In 1972, the United States and the Soviet Union signed a statement of basic principles of coexistence in which there was a commitment to behave with restraint in local conflict situations. It seemed to us that in this case the Soviets went beyond any reasonable definition of restraint.

Now, it appeared to them, I think, that because they were on the side of legitimacy of the issue, and because the number of Soviet personnel involved was on the order of a thousand, that they couldn't be held culpable for what they were doing. They were inclined not to appreciate what impact their actions would have, both regarding the number of weapons they sent and also the number of Cuban troops they transported. I think one reason why they did this is that, as in the case of Angola, they seriously miscalculated what the American reaction would be.

Q. The United States has, of course, spoken out strongly on this, but is there

anything that can be done or should be done?

A. Yes. The most important thing that we have been doing and are able to do is in the diplomatic field. We have made an effort to work with the leading African states and the Organization of African Unity to support them in what measures they are able to take in order, in the first instance, to mediate, bring about a cease-fire, and then to deal with the larger problems of Africa and to deal with them without the intervention of outside troops. And that effort to bring about a diplomatic solution is the long-term strategy for our relations with Africa. It also applies to the efforts to moderate the conflict around Rhodesia which may be a larger scale problem.

Q. **How wise would it be for the United States to link Soviet behavior in the Horn with bilateral relations with the United States, to hold it hostage in some fashion to economic relations or even the SALT negotiations?**

A. Well, it is a question of what we have to work with. Economic relations are not a feasible instrument because we don't have the trade agreement in force and we aren't able to put, say, limits on credits because these simply aren't being granted.

There may be some other actions we can take, but SALT is not a desirable instrument to use because the SALT agreement, if and when we get one, would be in our own security interest. It would not be done as a favor to the Russians. It would not be of more advantage to them than to us, so it doesn't offer very good leverage.

What the Administration has been saying to the Russians is that lack of restraint in Africa would affect the general climate in this country and that may have its effect in many ways.

Q. **Can we just talk a minute about SALT? Would you say this is a crucial period in negotiations;**

A. Well, we are at an important stage. Both countries have expressed a desire to break through the remaining unresolved issues and it is clear that a determined effort is required. What gives the matter its urgency is that if there is not a SALT agreement in the reasonably near future, it is likely that both countries will proceed to develop and deploy additional systems which they would not do under the limitations of a treaty. This will produce several effects.

One is that it will create new problems in any future effort to stabilize the strategic balance. That is, the new systems that come into play will be more difficult to verify and less stable and there will be many more weapons systems spread around. It will make the job of trying to negotiate a treaty a lot more difficult.

And the second effect is that the climate in which both countries are developing and procuring and deploying new systems is one that tends to generate its own mobilization of determination and militance. All problems are likely to be more difficult in that kind of a situation.

Q. **Do You think the Soviet leadership really wants an agreement?**

A. Yes, I do. In general the Soviets give the impression that they have looked very seriously at what the consequences would be in the absence of an agreement. And although they would, I have no doubt, be willing to keep pace with us in the higher level of military competition, I think that would be an inversion of priorities for them.

This leadership in the Soviet Union now has committed itself ever since the middle sixties to the proposition that the most urgent requirement for future Soviet power is the repair of its economic problems, to overcome the problems of productivity and lag in advanced technology. And if they were obliged now to divert still more resources than they are now doing into the military sector instead of into industrial technology, it would have the effect of slowing down still more their rate of growth in the industrial sector.

Q. Yet many experts seem to feel that the Russians are going all out for military growth and want to surpass the United States militarily. What do you think?

A. The Soviet Union is still striving in our judgment to try to overcome the position of inferiority in which it has perceived itself to be. Now, although they have clearly surpassed us in some attributes of the central strategic capabilities, they are inclined, as military men quite naturally tend to do, to be most concerned about those attributes in which we have the lead, and among those the most important from their point of view is the advantage we have in a superior technological base which provides the possibility of military innovation. And they have sought to offset this advantage by doing more of the kinds of things they can do most easily such as more missiles, heavy missiles. As they haven't been able to miniaturize the electronics, they have tended historically to go the route of heavy missiles.

Now, we don't know what they will do if ever they reach a situation which you can clearly and unequivocally say was beyond parity, whether they would keep going. I would assume it would depend upon how they assessed the risks and the costs of doing so. If they did see benefits, I don't believe that they would abstain just out of benevolence of spirit. But this is what the SALT negotiations are about. It is an effort to limit not only the numbers involved but also to limit the qualitative changes. If we are successful in not only this round of SALT but in setting in motion the next round, this will take a deeper bite at the problem and perhaps we can avoid a situation in which the Soviets can exceed parity.

Q. Speaking about the Soviet leadership, is Mr. Brezhnev so ill that he no longer is in charge?

A. His health has seemed to fluctuate and perhaps the reports about his health fluctuate even more. But according to all appearances, although he experiences the disabilities of a man his age, he does appear to be functioning effectively and very much in charge.

Q. Who are the leaders who will replace Mr Brezhnev, and what are they like?

A. We don't really know enough to make any solid predictions either about who are likely to be the next leaders or even what the next generation will be like when it takes over the leadership power.

It is clear that the people who are now [in their] forties to early fifties in the ascendance of Soviet leadership are not a homogeneous group. And it would be a mistake I think to be beguiled by our hopes and think that, because people are younger than they are necessarily more flexible. They might be, but there are also some among them who are really quite nationalistic, some among them who may be quite as rigid and inflexible as their elders.

Q. Let me ask you about the problem of how the United States speaks on Soviet policy. There seem to be different views voiced and even the President seems to speak with different voices. Do you find it unsettling?

A. It is clear that there are multiple aspects of the relations and that at times the President addresses one aspect and at times another. Now he made it clear, for example, in his Charleston [S.C.] speech that his objective was to try to move toward a moderation of relations. But at other times it becomes necessary to make it clear that the moderation of relations depends upon a military equilibrium and therefore he turns to that aspect in another speech.

Q. You and Dr. [Zbigniew] Brzezinski, the President's national security adviser, are old friends from Columbia and you have had different approaches going back to then. [Mr. Brzezinski has been publicly more skeptical of Soviet intentions and more inclined to warn about the possible linkage of SALT and other issues than Mr Shulman] How would you describe your working relationship now?

A. Our working relationship is very good. As you say, we have known each other for a long time, and we have had stimulating exchanges through the years, and I have never found him doctrinaire or inflexible in his thinking. And while we sometimes do have differences of emphasis between us, it has always been possible to discuss and to develop our thinking, and it seems to me that is a very useful thing to have in the Administration.

Q. We haven't talked about the human rights problem in the Soviet Union. How repressive is it now in historical terms?

A. Well, if you compare the situation now with what it was under Stalin, there is no doubt that there has been some easement of the repressive aspects, but it has had its ups and downs. If you compare it now with what it was in '56, it is less good than it was then. That was a time of hope, of the so-called thaw, and many of those hopes have not been borne out. There has been quite a fluctuation.

At the moment, for reasons which we discussed earlier, this is a fairly restrictive time. The Soviet security people have been anxious to limit the effects of the Helsinki agreement. They have tried to contain, to isolate, to reduce the dissidents, and as a

consequence this is not a period of great liberalization in Soviet intellectual and artistic life.

Q. How should the United States react to these rather distasteful developments in the Soviet Union?

A. Well, what we are learning is how to use our influence so that it is effective. What does effective mean? It means that in the cases that come to our attention that we hope that the spotlight of world attention can give some measure of protection to individuals involved. And effective also means that we encourage long-term trends in the Soviet Union toward a moderation of some of the restrictive practices of the Soviet security apparatus. But it is clear that frontal pressure directed against the system, demanding of it steps that go beyond any reasonable scale of feasibility in the near future, can and does have counterproductive effects.

Q. If Anatoly Shcharansky [an imprisoned Jewish dissident] is put on trial and convicted, should the United States respond in some drastic way, such as suspending SALT talks?

A. Well, as much as is politically feasible, I think we should keep in mind that our objective interest is in trying to improve our security by a good SALT treaty, no matter what kind of a regime is in power in the Soviet Union. SALT isn't a favor. It isn't a way of rewarding. It doesn't depend upon the Soviet Union being a democratic society. Our interest in SALT is because the two countries are engaged in a military competition with each other and that means that we can't put it off until some millenial future when the Soviet Union may have become more democratic.

Q. I have always been struck by a paradox in relations. The first time I visited the Soviet Union was as an exchange student

in the summer of '59 when Soviet internal policy was no more liberal, probably less so than it is today. Yet there was a great hope and expectation in the West that somehow these kinds of contacts would over a period of time liberalize Soviet society. The public perception is now much more negative toward the Soviet Union than it was in '59. Do you have any thoughts on that?

A. It is a familiar experience in history that the most dangerous period is when hopes are aroused and are not fulfilled as quickly as expectations lead one to hope for. That is the period when you tend to get the reaction against earlier hopes. Now, if you compare the situation now with 1959, in many ways there have been steps forward.

In 1959 Khrushchev was making his trip to this country and was then expecting President Eisenhower to make his return trip to the Soviet Union, and unfortunately there intervened the episode of the U-2 which led the Soviets to call off the summit and led to the cancellation of the Eisenhower trip. I think that was a very serious mistake on the part of the Soviets and the whole course of our relations might have been quite different if it had been possible to go foward with the Eisenhower trip as planned.

Many of the initiatives that Khrushchev was groping for in his own way have been carried forward somewhat more systematically or in more a regularized way by the Brezhnev leadership. But this is a historical process and it takes many years.

You refer to the effect of exchanges. I have no doubt that the widening of the knowledge of each other's country is useful although not in any immediate dramatic way. Just the fact that there are now thousands of people in the Soviet Union, many of them in positions of responsibility, who know the outside world better, are less provincial, makes the regime less likely to make reckless mistakes than it would do if it were still operating with the kind of parochialism that characterized the Stalin period.

VII

Economic Processes

One of the fundamental dilemmas of the sovereign-state system has been the fact that states divide people into self-enclosed political entities whereas economic life prospers from the greatest possible exchange of goods and investments among people. During much of the nineteenth century under the influence of British laissez-faire and free-trade principles it appeared that the two realms—the political realm of the state and the world realm of economic capitalism—might be made to coexist successfully. Few of the advanced capitalist states adhered completely to free trade, however. Like the U.S., France, and even Germany, many pursued protectionist policies such as high tariffs and subsidies for agriculture and industry in order to develop their domestic economies before venturing to compete with England.

Lenin and other neo-Marxists developed their theories of war and imperialism upon the adduced contradictions between the explosive needs of the capitalist economy and the limitations imposed upon it by the artificial compartmentalization of the world into political entities called states.

The capitalist owners of the means of production, unable to squeeze profits out of domestic production, were theoretically driven to expand overseas into Latin America, Africa, and Asia. In order to do this they had to use the apparatus of the state to conquer and govern colonies. But sooner or later, it was argued, even these outlets would prove insufficient and the great European powers would be driven into wars against each other for control of the globe. It was against this background of global imperialism that World War I occurred, giving apparent support to Leninist and other neo-Marxist theories. The facts are, however, that the war began in the Balkans over the assassination of an Austrian archduke, that it was prompted by the fear on the part of the Austrian government and, more indirectly, by the German government's fear that if it did not help to crush the Serbian challenge, the Austro-Hungarian empire would crumble and Germany would be at the mercy of its Russian and French enemies; capitalist and colonial rivalries were not the precipitating cause of World War I.

The theory that capitalist competition causes imperialism and war has also been challenged by findings on the part of historians that frequently it is governments in the pursuit of political and strategic advantages that support financial interests in their penetration of other countries and areas so that the governments would then have a pretext for becoming politically involved. Inasmuch as states employ economic policies in various ways and for various purposes, a distinction needs to be made between policies pursued for essentially economic ends and policies pursued primarily for political or strategic ends—a point we will return to a little later.

What is clear is that after World War I the capitalist world economy had become increasingly interdependent, and a breakdown anywhere would produce convulsive results throughout the system. Unfortunately, the inability of governments to appreciate this new condition during the interwar period led to a series of economic catastrophes—the German inflation of the early twenties, the uncontrolled banking and stock market speculation of the twenties, the 'Great Depression,' and mass unemployment—all of which contributed to the victory of Nazism in Germany and of militarism in Japan. By adopting protectionism and cutthroat competition to protect its own economy, the modern states destroyed the basis for peaceful management of the global economy, thereby helping to bring on World War II.

As a result of this interwar folly, and out of an emplicit belief that American capitalism could only flourish in a stable and well-regulated world economy, the United States government took the initiative after World War II to establish a set of institutions and policies designed to avoid a repetition of these events. Because the two most important institutions of this American design—the International Monetary Fund and the World Bank—were brought into existence at a meeting of the allied nations at Bretton Woods, New Hampshire in 1944, the system is sometimes called the Bretton Woods system.[1] Whatever we call it, this sytem consisted of a set of arrangements designed to cushion shocks to the international economy and to avoid the need for states to resort to cutthroat economic practices to protect their citizens against unemployment. The Monetary Fund provided for a pool or reserve of funds available to help any country going through a period of economic dislocation to surmount the crisis without devaluation of its currency. The World Bank was designed to facilitate loans by the industrially advanced countries to the underdeveloped Third World countries. There were also agreements among the advanced countries to reduce tariffs and increase trade between them. Above all, the United States provided an economic shot in the arm to the international economy by granting Europe $18 billion in Marshall Plan assistance after 1947 and in providing upwards of $100 billion in economic grants and aid to other countries (principally in the Third World) between 1950 and 1970.

The result of these measures was an era of unprecedented economic growth and prosperity for the advanced capitalist world and for some fortunate parts of the Third World.[2]

The table labeled "Indicators of Comparative East-West Economic Strength, 1976" shown in Chapter Three will give some idea of the magnitude of the economic benefits that have accrued to the developed capitalist world. Real income increased by four and five times between 1945 and 1965, especially that of the Europeans and Japanese; trade quadrupled and then quadrupled again; the European Common Market came into existence; and multinationals led by the Americans undertook overseas operations that sought out profitable new investment and production. There has never been an era in world history in which the material wealth of so many people increased so markedly and so rapidly.[3]

Unfortuntely, this boom was marked by unhealthy traits and developments that have once again put the stability of the international economy in doubt and given rise to national rivalries and cutthroat competition. First and foremost, the U.S. government tried for too long to use the strength of the dollar to sustain a global strategy of containment of communism and of nation-building. On the one hand, it incurred an annual military expenditure of $75 billion, climaxed by the Vietnam War in which labor and resources were consumed in an unproductive and non-income-earning activity. Secondly, other billions were expended each year in economic and military aid programs to a dozen or so selected countries—principally to

[1]The Soviet Union attended these wartime conferences but chose not to join, and set about creating its own economic system linking Russia and the communist states of Eastern Europe.

[2]The economic plight of the Third World will be treated in later chapters.

[3]For a time the nationalist rivalries of the non-communist countries appeared to recede before the benefits of a world-wide economic boom.

America's anti-communist allies like South Korea and Taiwan. Other billions were transferred overseas by American multinationals to purchase or establish businesses abroad. Meanwhile, Europe and Japan, having concentrated on modernizing their economies, were increasingly America's competitors as well as partners. As a result, more dollars went out than came in, and the dollar became overvalued in relation to the German, Swiss, and Japanese currencies.

The weakness of the American economy and of the dollar were covered from 1968 until 1971 by the willingness of other governments to hold onto their surplus U.S. dollars, but this entailed increasing nationalist resentment of America's privileged position. Moreover, the deficit in the American balance of payments and the adverse effect of an overvalued dollar on the American economy could not be postponed indefinitely. Finally, in August 1971, Nixon abandoned the American attempt to sustain and exploit the overvalued dollar by devaluing it cumulatively by almost 30 percent, by ending the right of countries to exchange their surplus dollars for U.S. gold, and by putting a 10 percent surtax on all U.S. imports. In effect, the Nixon economic shock of the summer of 1971 brought an end to the Bretton Woods system. In the absence of American leadership and of the unique economic conditions that made American leadership possible, the international economy must now depend upon collective agreement of all the leading economies, in the absence of which there is a tendency to resort to nationalistic protectionism.

Devaluation was followed two years later by a fourfold increase in the price of oil. Cheap oil had fueled the world economic miracle of 1950–1973. The additional $100 billion in annual oil charges meant that that much less would be available for investment and profits to western capitalist economies and would place an almost unmanageable burden on Third World economies. The oil-price increase was followed almost immediately by the recession of 1974–1975, from which the world has still not recovered. After a century of cheap resources, the capitalist economies are having to face up to the fact that the world is going to have to pay more and more for increasingly scarce minerals.

The cumulative impact of these changes has had a drastic effect upon the economic context of world politics:

(1) The world economy, increasingly fragmented, is in serious trouble;

(2) The U.S. economy is slowing down—the dollar has reached an all time low in value;

(3) World trade is slowing down from 11.5 percent growth in 1976 to 6 percent in 1977, and only 5 percent is projected for 1978;

(4) The world economy of floating exchange rates has not proven as satisfactory in a recession-threatened world as was hoped: and finally,

(5) The debt burden of the poor nations has become so great that interest and debt repayment consumes 20 percent to 40 percent of their export earnings.

As a consequence of these conditions, there has been a marked upsurge inprotectionism, and the advanced capitalist states no longer find it as easy to manage the world economy as they did a decade ago. This is the context in which this chapter's selection by Richard N. Cooper, Under Secretary of State for Economic Affairs, must be read. Despite Cooper's hopefulness, it must be recognized that the adjustments and sacrifices that are bound to be imposed upon people who have either grown accustomed to affluence or are still very poor is likely to have a destabilizing political effect both domestically and internationally. Unless more profound solutions can be found to inflation and unemployment at home and to poverty in the Third World, the capitalist world is in danger of reverting to the destructive economic nationalism that marked the 1930s. Already the movement toward European economic integration has come to a halt and America and its allies are increasingly at odds over economic matters. Should the international order that fosters trade, investment, and access to vital materials break down, we would once again face a situation in which resort to war becomes acceptable. The warning by Secretary of State Kissinger that the United States might have to resort to force should another OPEC oil embargo or price hike threaten the economic life of the advanced industrial countries may have been a bluff, but it was also an intimation of what might really occur.

International economics is not only a process; it is also a form of political power. Economically advanced nations have always exploited their economic power to gain advantages at the expense of weaker societies. This sometimes takes the form of outright imperialism, but it also takes more indirect forms such as in setting terms for the right of access to investment capital, terms that are more advantageous to the lender than to the borrower. Of the many types of economic pressures which an advanced state may employ, the following are among those most often used:

1. financial manipulations to diminish the value of an opponent's currency and enhance that of one's own country;
2. economic penetration of weaker countries, with the eventual objective of exerting pressure on the government of the penetrated society;
3. exploitation of a strategic economic position through such policies as price fixing, dumping, the imposition of quotas, exchange controls, and so forth;
4. boycotting or a refusal to buy from another country;
5. the use of economic subsidies;
6. preemptive buying of goods produced in other countries in order to withhold them from other purchasers; and
7. the stockpiling of important goods.[4]

[4]Charles C. Abbott, "Economic Penetration and Power Politics," *Harvard Business Review*, 26 (1948), 410–24.

Another form of economic power is that of economic bribes and military subventions, by which a more powerful state ties lesser states to it in a form of dependence. For decades, Great Britain subventioned Prussia and other allies on the continent as a means of keeping them actively opposed to the hegemonial ambitions of the Hapsburg and Napoleonic empires.

As the Cold War developed and the United States found itself engaged in a struggle with the Soviet Union for influence in the Third World, a far more elaborate use of economic assistance as a weapon of foreign policy began to be deployed. On the premise that unless the newly emergent nations were helped to develop they would either fall into anarchy or go Communist, or both, the United States began a massive program of economic and military aid to the Third World. An elaborate ideology dubbed "nation-building" was concocted to justify to the American people the transfer of billions in foreign aid. It probably is wrong to say that the ideology was "concocted," because the American leadership and the American people were equally convinced that the U.S. had a duty and a self-interest in tiding the newly emergent countries over their period of economic growth until they were sufficiently developed to take their place as democratic, independent, and, naturally, anti-communist societies. The plausibility of the United States being able to guide and subsidize the transformation and development of societies as culturally diverse and impoverished as India, Indonesia, Ethiopia and Peru was never really questioned by the idealists and ideologues of foreign aid. Perhaps, as Morgenthau suggests in this chapter, the American government found it convenient to maintain the assumption that economic development could actually be promoted through such transfers of money, investment, and services because it helped to sweeten the real purposes of such aid programs—which were to bribe governments to align themselves with the U.S. in the cold war and, more concretely, to provide the U.S. military with bases and U.S. business and banks with investment opportunities.

Much economic aid, of course, has taken a multilateral form. That is to say, the U.S. and other countries have made annual contributions to international organizations such as the World Bank and the United Nations to finance humanitarian and development purposes. But the fact that America's contribution was sufficiently large gave it a veto power over grants or loans to countries whose regimes were offensive to the U.S.— such as Allende's Chile—thereby enabling it to punish and weaken them.

In effect, the foreign aid and military programs, like U.S. policy generally (as those of our European allies), were increasingly directed toward maintaining the status quo; while a similar Communist economic and military aid program was aimed at supporting countries opposed to the United States.[5] As a result, economic and military aid (and sales) has

[5]Charles Reynolds, *Theory and Explanation in International Politics* (London: Martin Robertson, 1973) pp. 231–233. C. R. Hensman, *Rich Against Poor: The Reality of Aid*

become one of the most significant of methods used in contemporary world politics. However, as the U.S. has experienced deception with the results of foreign aid and economic stringency in its own position, economic aid has formed a smaller and smaller percentage of America's gross national product, and aid has either been increasingly tied to narrowly American interests or it has taken the form of loans and investments by private banks and multinationals. There has also been a rising nationalist resistance on the part of Third World countries against subordinating their foreign policies to any form of foreign aid control and toward demanding aid as an obligation that the rich countries owe to the poor. The plight of the Third World, and these efforts to exploit an ideology that the rich are obligated to assist the poor nations, will be analyzed at greater length in a later chapter. Because people are so dependent on the modern state for their economic well-being, and because the economies of states are so intertwined and interdependent that they cannot achieve self-sufficient economic existence, the potential for catastrophic breakdown in the present situation is enormous.

(Baltimore: Penguin, 1971). R. D. McKinlay and R. Little report that "our findings indicate that power and security concerns [not economic] are the central interests supported by and controlled through the U.S. aid program." This does not mean that there is no relationship of dependency. Quite the contrary. "The foreign policy model that provides the most satisfactory explanation of the U.S. aid program conforms to a general view of international relations characterized by the political interpretation of imperialism." "A Foreign Policy Model of U.S. Bilateral Aid Allocations," *World Politics*, Vol. XXX, No. 1 (October 1977), p. 80.

18   The International Economic Situation

Richard N. Cooper

The author is Under Secretary for Economic Affairs in the U.S. Department of State.

I would like to cover several areas—events leading up to our present situation, the current state of the international economy, foreign policy considerations, and our overall foreign economic strategy.

THE RECENT PAST

A quick review of the recent past is helpful in understanding the current environment. Two developments are of particular significance.

In the early 1970's the Western industrial economies began to experience a relatively synchronized economic expansion, the culmination of exceptionally rapid world growth during the previous decade. In 1972-73 the growth rate of the OECD [Organization for Economic Cooperation and Development] area* exceeded 6 percent, approaching the

*OECD members are Australia, Austria, Belgium, Canada, Denmark, Finland, France, Federal Republic of Germany, Greece, Iceland, Ireland, Italy, Japan, Luxembourg, Netherlands, New Zealand, Norway, Portugal, Spain, Sweden, Switzerland, Turkey, the United Kingdom, and the United States.

The following statement was made before the Subcommittee on Foreign Economic Policy of the Senate Foreign Relations Committee during his confirmation hearings, March 18, 1977. Reproduced from "The Department of State, Bureau of Public Affairs.

limits of productive capacity in that area and outstripping the ability of many producers to expand supplies. By 1973, in reaction to rising inflation, several countries were already pursuing contractionary policies to cool their overheated economies, accepting the prospect of a slowdown in growth.

Then came the oil embargo and quadrupling of the price of oil in the winter of 1973-74. This was the largest single global economic shock in modern history. Because of the suddenness and magnitude of the impact, the increased price for oil acted as a major drain on purchasing power in the oil-consuming world. Coming on top of the mild slowdown already in progress, the oil price rise plunged the industrial economies into full recession.

Individual countries reacted differently. The United States, Germany, and Japan accepted the recession and permitted aggregate demand to contract. Others—particularly the weaker European economies and several semi-industrialized developing nations—delayed domestic adjustment. They financed their balance-of-payments deficits with borrowings, gambling that the recession would be short and that resumed economic growth would enable them to bring payments back into balance. The bet was understandable, even rational, but it turned out to be wrong: The recession was longer and deeper than originally expected, large oil deficits added to the problem, and those attempting to ride it out by financing these deficits saw their indebtedness continue to mount.

THE CURRENT SITUATION

Today the world is slowly emerging from the worst recession of the last 40 years. Recovery, which had begun in the latter half of 1975, picked up steam in the first half of last year but then began to slow in many countries. This pause, combined with pressures in foreign exchange markets associated with external payments strains in a number of countries, created renewed uncertainty. The fear that simultaneous recovery in the OECD countries would overheat the world economy was replaced in the second half of the year with the concern that a flattening of the recovery might lead to insufficient growth.

As 1977 began, however, the outlook appeared more positive. The recovery began to pick up in many of the OECD countries. However, because of the different underlying conditions in various countries before the recession and the different ways they reacted to the recession, individual countries are now emerging in widely different positions of strength. Several factors characterize the present state of recovery.

First, We Can Expect Moderate but Sustained Growth Throughout the Rest of this Year.

Real growth rates in the industrial countries are projected to average about 4 percent in 1977, somewhat lower than the 5 percent attained in 1976. The stronger economies—the United States, Germany, and Japan—are well into the cyclical upswing. This year we may see a growth rate somewhat below last year's average for the group, which was above 6 percent. In several other major economies—such as the United Kingdom, France, and Italy—stabilization measures will lead to slower growth than the 1976 average growth rate of about 4 percent.

Real growth in the oil-importing developing countries is likely to be somewhat below the estimated 5.4 percent of 1976. Brazil, India, and Korea were among the major countries helping to pull the LDC [less-developed country] average up in 1976. This year adjustment and slower growth in several larger countries will slightly reduce the overall average.

Aggregate inflation rates in the OECD area will remain disturbingly high, although less than the 8 percent rate of 1976. At the upper end of the OECD spectrum, consumer prices are likely to rise about 20 percent this year in some countries. At the opposite extreme, price increases in the order of 2-4 percent might be expected.

Unemployment will remain a major problem as approximately 15 million men and women are out of work in the OECD area, half in the United States.

Second, There are Areas of the Recovery That Need to be Strengthened.

Sluggish investment in the OECD area is perhaps the most important weakness in the recovery. The severity of the recession led to reduced real investment and a consequent lower growth in productive capacity. New capacity requirements in several key industries, the need to replace a portion of existing capital stock made obsolete by high-cost energy, and special future requirements in energy and pollution control facilities require substantial new investment.

Additional oil price increases, coming on

top of the already high price levels, could also upset the current growth pattern. U.S Government analysis, in advance of the last OPEC [Organization of Petroleum Exporting Countries] price decision in December, indicated that each 5 percent increase in the cost of crude oil would cost oil-consuming countries approximately $6 billion in higher oil import bills, with the United States paying about $1.7 billion of that total. Absent compensating domestic policy actions, each 5 percent increase costs the seven largest industrial countries an average of 0.3 percent of GNP growth and adds roughly 0.3 percent to consumer prices.

Third, OPEC [Organization of Petroleum Exporting Countries] Members* Can be Expected to Amass Annual Current Account Surpluses in Excess of $30 Billion for at Least the Next Few Years, and the Accumulation of Financial Assets by Several Arab Oil Exporters Together Could Easily Surpass $300 Billion by the End of 1980.

The total oil import bill, which was $35 billion in 1973, will be on the order of $140 billion in 1977. The large chronic OPEC surplus is matched by aggregate deficits in both developed and developing oil-importing countries, which can be reduced but not eliminated in the medium term. Only the distribution of the deficit among importers can change.

Borrowings to finance balance-of-payments deficits each year have meant *an increase in the external indebtedness of many nations in the OECD, the developing world,* and *the East European nonmarket countries.*

The debt issue is complex. As an illustra-

*OPEC members are Abu Dhabi, Algeria, Ecuador, Gabon, Indonesia, Iran, Iraq, Kuwait, Libya, Nigeria, Qatar, Saudi Arabia, and Venezuela.

tion of the situation, we can look at the developing countries. Those with access to private capital markets borrowed heavily to finance deficits, in preference to making difficult domestic adjustments, which, if undertaken, would have aggravated the world recession. While in many cases the rate of inflation has reduced the burden of past debts, debt-service payments of the non-oil producing LDCs are now in excess of $21 billion in 1976, or an increase of about 75 percent over the 1973 level. Over 80 percent relates to payments on private and official commercial debt. In 1976 these payments consumed about 20 percent of their income from merchandise exports as compared to 17 percent in 1973. These large debt-service payments will cause several countries to continue the search for new financing at the same time that they make necessary internal adjustments. Collectively, debts must be accumulated beyond present levels because of the OPEC surpluses. Absent sufficient financing, several countries would be forced to take the 1974-75 recession in 1977 and 1978. This could threaten the process of recovery itself, particularly in Europe where dependence on external markets is considerably larger than is that of the United States. But the American economy would also be affected adversely by a major slump in export markets, brought about by deflation and import restrictions.

Fourth, the Danger of Protectionism is Growing and Remains a Constant Threat to the Recovery.

The OPEC surpluses will lead to unaccustomed deficits. At the same time unemployment will exert pressure for expansion which, unless coordinated, will worsen deficits. Import restrictions would seem to be the way out, especially since imports are a natural scapegoat for what is basically deficient total demand. Import restrictions, however, will never work collectively—unemployment will only be exported. Thus far governments have generally followed prudent trade policies, but the possibility of protectionism is real. Trade restrictions would spread in the current environment, and it could easily take another decade to get back to where we are today.

Fifth, Recession and Weak Export Markets, Inflation and Higher Cost Imports, and High Energy Prices Have Adversely Affected Many LDCs.

Our own economic welfare is increasingly intertwined with trade and with investment in the developing world. Many of these critical issues are under discussion in the "North-South" dialogue where a failure to maintain a constructive atmosphere could undermine global economic cooperation.

This then is where we are in the recovery—modest growth ahead which must be reinforced by reduced inflation, increased employment, expanded investment, strengthened energy policies, adequate financing for payments imbalances and adjustment, turning back protectionism, and the improvement of global economic cooperation among all countries.

FOREIGN POLICY CONSIDERATIONS

The current economic situation has major foreign policy implications. Two general considerations are paramount.

The growing interaction of national economies means that problems in some countries can easily become contagious and that they can be effectively addressed only by nations working closely together. Among the market economies the United States is relatively less dependent on the world economy, but our

economic welfare and security cannot be divorced from the economic health of other nations and are becoming increasingly intertwined with it.

Economic concerns preoccupy governments everywhere. They require economic stability and progress to maintain the confidence of their electorates. Economic problems can generate political and social instability and undermine the network of international cooperative arrangements which have been painstakingly erected in the last 30 years.

In the last few years the fabric of international cooperation has held together extraordinarily well despite severe economic strains. Indeed, we have made some major advances, including the first comprehensive reform of the international monetary system since Bretton Woods, an agreement by the industrial democracies to avoid unilateral trade restrictions despite the pressures of the recession, the conclusion of the OECD investment declaration strengthening the framework for private investment among the Western democracies, and the provision of additional sources of finance to developing countries from the IMF Trust Fund and a greatly expanded IMF Compensatory Financing Facility.

The general foreign policy challenge before us is not only to preserve this cooperative framework but to strengthen and extend it to insure global economic growth. I turn now to the specific issues we face and our strategy for dealing with them.

FOREIGN ECONOMIC STRATEGY

Let me discuss our overall strategy in the context of our broad macroeconomic objective—a strong recovery characterized by steady, sustained, noninflationary growth and expanding job opportunities in the OECD area and the developing world. The key elements of our approach are the coordinated stimulation of the stronger economies, adequate international financing conditioned on timely adjustment, reduced dependence on foreign energy sources, continued trade liberalization, and progress in the North-South dialogue.

Coordinated Stimulation

We should look first at President Carter's recovery program, which is designed to strengthen the domestic economic performance and create jobs without triggering inflation. The program should not be seen only in domestic terms but as part of an overall plan in which those countries in a strong financial position expand as rapidly as they can consistent with sustained growth and the control of inflation, thereby absorbing a greater portion of the aggregate deficit of the oil-importing countries and stimulating growth in the weaker economies.

The Administration has formulated its program with both domestic and international considerations in mind. It contains tax features to provide quick injections of purchasing power into the economy as well as encouragement for increased private investment, and it includes programs to increase employment directly. The program will extend over two years and is adjustable as conditions warrant.

We have been encouraging other strong economies to follow our lead in stimulating their economies. Thus far the degree of stimulation varies widely among these countries, and we will be paying close attention to the evolution of their policies.

Financing and Adjustment

In some individual cases countries which chose to rely heavily on external finance to cover their deficits over the past few years must take domestic adjustment measures to strengthen their payments position and avoid the risk of impairing their credit-worthiness. As noted before, however, we must accept the need to sustain considerable increases in aggregate debt for the near future. Individual requirements vary considerably, but for many countries the economic adjustment process will take years and require difficult economic decisions. For some, there is an immediate requirement to channel new funds away from financing consumption to expenditures which increase future production through investment. Over the last few years, ad hoc responses to the major international shocks resulted in large amounts of private borrowing being used to finance imports for consumption without adequate sums being directed to increase productive capacity. In addition, in some countries budget deficits must be severely reduced as government expenditures have exploded without comparable tax collections.

Unless there is international growth, countries cannot make necessary adjustments without painful and severe dislocations. Adjustment and recovery thus go hand-in-hand. It is also imperative that those initiating adjustments are able to find external financial support for responsible stabilization programs. The necessary financing will have to be rechanneled one way or another from OPEC countries in surplus. In the past private commercial institutions have been the principal mechanism for this intermediation. We will continue to rely primarily on the private sector to perform this function. But we are also examining new ways to insure adequate amounts of financing from international institutions and the proper mix of official and private financing in individual cases. The IMF in particular is skilled at facilitating necessary domestic stabilization as a condition for financial support, which is the type of lending that will be most appropriate for many countries.

Energy

The events of the past four years have clearly demonstrated the vulnerability of the United States and its major allies to OPEC decisions to raise prices and to the threatened or actual use of an oil embargo by some oil-exporting countries as an instrument of national policy. As already noted, uncertainty over the course of future OPEC price policy hangs over the recovery and prospects for global economic growth and stability. And for the longer term there is more to the energy question than OPEC's actions. A profound shift in global supply and demand patterns has taken place. Oil is a depletable asset. We must not only reduce our short-term vulnerability but we must begin preparing for the post-oil age.

The key element of U.S. energy strategy is the development of a comprehensive domestic energy policy. The full plan is evolving in close cooperation with Congress and our partners in the International Energy Agency [IEA]* and will be detailed by April 20. Clearly one major thrust will be to reduce dependence on imported oil.

Internationally, we will be supporting several important efforts. The United States has made the International Energy Agency the principal vehicle for energy cooperation with the other industrialized countries, and we will continue our policies there to develop

---

*IEA members are Austria, Belgium, Canada, Denmark, Federal Republic of Germany, Greece, Ireland, Italy, Japan, Luxembourg, Netherlands, New Zealand, Norway (associate member), Spain, Sweden, Switzerland, Turkey, United Kingdom, and the United States.

coordinated national programs for conservation, development, and reduced dependence. We shall continue our efforts to integrate key OPEC countries into the world economic structure so that decisions affecting international economic welfare and stability can be made cooperatively. And we shall focus attention and resources on assisting the non-oil LDCs to improve their energy positions.

Trade Policy

I have already described the impact that renewed protectionism would have on the recovery. In addition, we would undoubtedly pay the price of any resurgence of protectionism in other areas of international cooperation.

In the next several weeks the Administration will face difficult decisions concerning trade policy toward such sensitive imports as shoes and color TV sets. Our own actions will have a major influence on the trade policy of other countries. We are also examining our trade strategy in the Multilateral Trade Negotiations in Geneva, where we expect to make significant progress before the authority of the Trade Act of 1974 expires.

North-South Dialogue

We plan to redouble our efforts in the North-South dialogue in order to strengthen global cooperation generally.

Economic developments of the past four years have caused the developing nations to accelerate their search for international policies which increase resource transfers to them and enhance their role in international decision-making. They have called for increased levels of foreign assistance, permanent trade preferences, technology transfer on more favorable terms, commodity price stabilization, and debt forgiveness.

The Carter Administration is still reviewing its overall North-South policies, but several elements of our general approach are already clear.

> The interests of all countries are best served in an open and buoyant world economy.
> We have many mutual interests with the developing world and will emphasize those issues where all countries can derive benefit, as opposed to those where some countries' gain is others' loss.
> The dialogue must be a two-way street. All countries must accept obligations to the world system. We shall approach problems of the developing world with a desire to assist in any reasonable way possible. But we shall also expect that within their capabilities they maximize their own resources for development, adhere to standards of basic human rights, and respect our interests.

This coming year commodities and official debt will be particularly important to the overall discussions.

Over the next several months we will be engaged in a series of meetings on ways to strengthen individual commodity markets and on the possibility of common funding for individual commodity stockpiles.

A number of serious problems in the commodities area must be addressed cooperatively by producers and consumers. For a large number of developing countries, earnings from commodities are critical to economic development. At the same time, all countries have a major interest in assuring that our goal of a stable, expanding world economy is not threatened either by excessive fluctuations of commodity prices and export earnings or by an inadequacy of resources.

Within this framework of mutual interest we are prepared to act on commodities issues. The problems faced in the commodities area

require an integrated approach addressing price stabilization, trade, the improvement of market structures, the stabilization of export earnings, resource development, and investment. The new Administration is currently formulating policies toward all these issues. We are prepared to deal with them constructively in the coming months in a number of meetings, including the work now underway in UNCTAD [UN Conference on Trade and Development] and elsewhere on a number of individual commodities.

We believe the existing international institutions can play a very helpful role here. The IMF Compensatory Financing Facility, which lends for shortfalls in LDC export proceeds, has been a particularly key element, and we will be open to possible future improvements. In addition, the World Bank might usefully facilitate resource development.

A second major issue will be the demands for general debt relief for official debt of the low income countries. The issue should not be confused with the indebtedness issue discussed before, which involves mainly commercial borrowings of the higher income LDCs, none of which have advocated any type of general debt relief. The developing countries have made forgiveness of official debt a principal demand in the Conference on International Economic Cooperation [CIEC] in Paris, which is due to wind up late this spring. The United States and other industrialized democracies have remained firm that this would be a mistaken policy.

In general official debt burdens can be serviced and are not major impediments to development. In addition generalized debt relief would provide indiscriminate benefits to those countries which had not pursued effective domestic policies and would be unrelated to currently appropriate burdensharing among the aid-giving countries. Finally, since individual country situations differ so widely, debt relief can be meaningfully considered only on a case-by-case basis.

As one examines demands for debt relief, however, it is clear that the developing countries' objective is to increase resource transfers. Looked at this way, the United States, in conjunction with other donor countries, can make a major contribution to development via higher levels of foreign assistance—both multilateral and bilateral. The Administration is convinced that larger resource transfers to the Third World are required in order to meet legitimate development requirements. Furthermore we believe that foreign assistance is the most direct and effective way to do this and that an improved economic assistance performance by the United States not only advances global economic development but is a sensible alternative to LDC proposals for general debt relief, as well as other resource transfer schemes which we believe to be poorly conceived. However, we will want to insure that our foreign assistance resource transfers are efficiently used and actually reach the people who need them.

In recent weeks Secretary Vance and other Administration officials have testified in support of a larger bilateral U.S. foreign assistance program and prompt U.S. participation in the capital replenishment of international development banks, particularly the International Development Association [IDA]— the soft loan window of the World Bank. The 1978 budget calls for budget authority of $1.35 billion for bilateral development assistance, $2.6 billion for the World Bank

group (of which $1 billion is callable capital), $130 million for the UN Development Program [UNDP], and $1.9 billion for security supporting assistance. The support of this subcommittee and your colleagues in Congress will be essential to fulfillment of the President's objective in this area.

CONCLUSION

The economic situation will present a major challenge to our foreign economic policy in the coming years. We will have to deal with the complex interrelationship among the pace of economic expansion, the distribution of large trade deficits, the system of international financing, energy policy, the degree of protectionism, and the strengthening of cooperative relationships among all countries. If the deep strains in the international economy force each country to go its own way, everyone will be the loser.

To date the structure of international cooperation has worked well, thus justifying the continuing effort we and other countries have devoted to building it over the last quarter century. In the face of difficulty we must now preserve and reinforce this structure. This will require the willingness of the United States and others to adapt to new circumstances. As in the past others will be looking to us to lead the way in fashioning effective policies. The Administration looks forward to working closely with the Congress in meeting this challenge.

19 A Political Theory of Foreign Aid

Hans Morgenthau

The author served for many years at the University of Chicago, after which he became Leonard Dawes Distinguished Professor at the City College, City University of New York.

Of the seeming and real innovations which the modern age has introduced into the practice of foreign policy, none has proven more baffling to both understanding and action than foreign aid. The very assumption that foreign aid is an instrument of foreign policy is a subject of controversy. For, on the one hand, the opinion is widely held that foreign aid is an end in itself, carrying its own justification, both transcending, and independent of, foreign policy. In this view, foreign aid is the fulfillment of an obligation of the few rich nations toward the many poor ones. On the other hand, many see no justification for a policy of foreign aid at all. They look at it as a gigantic boon-doggle, a wasteful and indispensable operation which serves neither the interests of the United States nor those of the recipient nations.

The public debate on foreign aid has contributed little to understanding. . . . Only when glaring abuses and inefficiencies are uncovered . . . is the question of the substance of our foreign aid policy raised in public, and even then it is put in the negative terms of remedying the abuses and inefficien-

American Political Science Review, *56 (June 1962),* pp. *301–9. Reprinted by permission of the American Political Science Association and Professor Morgenthau. The paper was originally prepared for the Public Affairs Conference Center, University of Chicago.*

cies rather than in the positive terms of the purposes our foreign aid policy may be supposed to advance and the kinds of measures best calculated to serve these aims.

It is in fact pointless even to raise the question whether the United States ought to have a policy of foreign aid—as much so as to ask whether the United States ought to have a foreign political or military policy. For the United States has interests abroad which cannot be secured by military means and for the support of which the traditional methods of diplomacy are only in part appropriate. If foreign aid is not available they will not be supported at all.

The question, what kind of policy of foreign aid we ought to have, can then not be evaded. As it has developed in recent years, the kind we have is fundamentally weak. It has been conceived as a self-sufficient technical enterprise, covering a multitude of disparate objectives and activities, responding haphazardly to all sorts of demands, sound and unsound, unrelated or only by accident related to the political purposes of our foreign policy. The United States, in short, has been in the business of foreign aid for more than two decades, but it has yet to develop an intelligible theory of foreign aid that could provide standards of judgment for both the supporters and opponents of a particular measure.

I. SIX TYPES OF FOREIGN AID

The first prerequisite for the development of a viable foreign aid policy is the recognition of the diversity of policies that go by that name. Six such can be distinguished which have only one thing in common: the transfer of money, goods and services from one nation to another. They are humanitarian foreign aid, subsistence foreign aid, military foreign aid, bribery, prestige foreign aid, and foreign aid for economic development.

Of these distinct types, only humanitarian foreign aid is *per se* nonpolitical. The aid which governments have traditionally extended to nations which are victims of natural disasters, such as floods, famines and epidemics falls in that category. So do the services, especially in the fields of medicine and agriculture, which private organizations, such as churches and foundations, have traditionally provided in Asia, Africa, and Latin America. . . .

Subsistence foreign aid is extended to governments, such as those of Jordan and Niger, which do not command the resources to maintain minimal public services. The giving nation makes up the deficit in the budget of the recipient nation. Subsistence foreign aid is akin to the humanitarian type in that it seeks to prevent the breakdown of order and the disintegration of organized society. But it also performs the political function of maintaining the *status quo,* without, however, as a rule, increasing its viability. Where a political alternative to a nonviable regime may exist, subsistence foreign aid diminishes the chances of its materializing.

Bribes proffered by one government to another for political advantage were until the beginning of the nineteenth century an integral part of the armory of diplomacy. No statesman hesitated to acknowledge the general practice of giving and accepting bribes, however anxious he might be to hide a particular transaction. Thus it was proper and common for a government to pay the foreign minister or ambassador of another country a pension, that is, a bribe. . . .

Much of what goes by the name of foreign aid today is in the nature of bribes. The transfer of money and services from one government to another performs here the function of a price paid for political services rendered or to be rendered. These bribes differ from the traditional ones exemplified above in two respects: they are justified primarily in terms of foreign aid for economic development, and money and services are transferred through elaborate machinery fashioned for genuine economic aid. In consequence, these bribes are a less effective means for the purpose of purchasing political favors than were the traditional ones.

The compulsion of substituting for the traditional businesslike transmission of bribes the pretense and elaborate machinery of foreign aid for economic development results from a climate of opinion which accepts as universally valid the proposition that the highly developed industrial nations have an obligation to transfer money and services to underdeveloped nations for the purpose of economic development. Thus, aside from humanitarian and military foreign aid, the only kind of transfer of money and services which seems to be legitimate is one ostensibly made for the purpose of economic development. Economic development has become an ideology by which the transfer of money and services from one government to another in peace time is rationalized and justified.

The present climate of opinion embraces another assumption as universally valid: that economic development can actually be promoted through such transfers of money and services. Thus economic development as an ideology requires machinery that makes plausible the postulated efficacy of the transfer for the stated purpose of economic development. In contrast to most political ideologies, which operate only on the verbal level and whose effects remain within the realm of ideas, this political ideology, in order to be plausible, requires an elaborate administrative apparatus serving as an instrument for a policy of make-believe. The government of nation A, trying to buy political advantage from the government of nation B for, say, the price of 20 million dollars, must not only pretend, but also act out in elaborate fashion the pretense, that what it is actually doing is giving aid for economic development to the government of nation B.

This practice of giving bribes as though they were contributions to economic development inevitably creates, in the giver and the recipient, expectations which are bound to be disappointed. Old-fashioned bribery was a relatively straightforward transaction; services were to be rendered at a price, and both sides knew what to expect. Bribery disguised as foreign aid for economic development makes of giver and recipient actors in a play which in the end they may no longer be able to distinguish from reality. In consequence, both may come to expect results in terms of economic development which in the nature of things may not be forthcoming. Thus both are likely to be disappointed, the giver blaming the recipient for his inefficiency and the recipient accusing the giver of stinginess and asking for more. The ideology, if taken for reality, gets in the way of the original purpose of the transaction, and neither side believes that it has received what it is entitled to. . . .

Foreign aid for military purposes is a traditional way by which nations buttress their alliances. Rome used to receive tribute from its allies for the military protections it provided. The seventeenth and eighteenth centuries are the classic period of military subsidies, by which nations, and especially Great Britain, endeavored to increase the military strength of their allies. Glancing through the treaties of alliance of that period, one is struck by the meticulous precision with which obligations to furnish troops, equipment, logistic support, food, money, and the like were defined. . . .

In contrast to traditional practice, military aid today is extended not only to allies but also to certain uncommitted nations. The military aid the United States has been giving to Yugoslavia is a case in point. The purpose is here not so much military as political. It seeks political advantage in exchange for military aid. It obligates by implication, the recipient toward the giver. The latter expects the former to abstain from a political course which might put in jeopardy the continuation of military aid. Military aid is here really in the nature of a bribe.

What appears as military aid may also be actually in the nature of prestige aid, to be discussed below. The provision of jet fighters and other modern weapons for certain underdeveloped nations can obviously perform no genuine military function. It increases the prestige of the recipient nation both at home and abroad. Being in the possession of some of the more spectacular instruments of modern warfare, a nation can at least enjoy the illusion of having become a modern military power.

As bribery appears today in the guise of aid for economic development, so does aid for economic development appear in the guise of military assistance. In the session of 1961, for instance, Congress appropriated 425 million dollars for economic aid to strategic areas, and it is likely that in the total appropriations of over 2 billion dollars for military aid other items of economic aid are hidden. This mode of operation results from the reluctance of Congress to vote large amounts for economic aid in contrast to its readiness to vote virtually any amount requested for military purposes. Yet the purposes of aid for economic development are likely to suffer when they are disguised as military assistance, as we saw the purposes of bribery suffer when disguised as aid for economic development. The military context within which such aid is bound to operate, even though its direct administration be in the hands of the civilian authorities, is likely to deflect such aid from its genuine purposes. More particularly, it strengthens the ever-present tendency to subordinate the requirement of aid for economic development to military considerations.

Prestige aid has in common with modern bribes the fact that its true purpose, too, is concealed by the ostensible purpose of economic development or military aid. The unprofitable or idle steel mill, the highway without traffic and leading nowhere, the airline operating with foreign personnel and at a loss but under the flag of the recipient country—all ostensibly serve the purposes of economic development and under different circumstances might do so. Actually, however, they perform no positive economic function. They owe their existence to the penchant, prevalent in many underdeveloped nations, for what might be called "conspicuous industrialization," spectacular symbols of, and monuments to, industrial advancement rather than investments satisfying any objective economic needs of the country.

This tendency sheds an illuminating light upon the nature of what is generally referred to as the "revolution of rising expectations."

We are inclined to assume that the urgent desire to improve one's lot by means of modern technology and industry is a well-nigh universal trend in Asia, Africa, and Latin America. Actually, however, this trend is universal only in the sense that virtually all underdeveloped nations want to appear as having achieved industrialization, while only a fraction of the population, and frequently only small elite groups within it, seek the social and economic benefits of industrialization and are willing to take the measures necessary to achieve them. For many of the underdeveloped nations the steel mill, the highway, the airline, the modern weapons, perform a function that is not primarily economic or military, but psychological and political. They are sought as the outward show of modernity and power. They perform a function similar to that which the cathedral performed for the medieval city and the feudal castle or the monarch's palace for the absolute state. Nehru is reported to have said, when he showed Chou-En-Lai a new dam: "It is in these temples that I worship." And the more underdeveloped and less viable a nation is, the greater is likely to be its urge to prove to itself and to the world through the results of prestige aid that it too, has arrived in the mid-twentieth century.

The advantage for the giver of prestige aid is threefold. He may receive a specific political advantage in return for the aid, very much like the advantage received for a bribe. Also, the spectacular character of prestige aid establishes a patent relationship between the generosity of the giver and the increased prestige of the recipient. The giver's prestige is enhanced, as it were, by the increase of the recipient's prestige. Finally, prestige aid comes relatively cheap. A limited commitment of resources in the form of a spectacular but economically useless symbol of modernity may bring disproportionate political dividends.

The giver of foreign aid is therefore well advised to distinguish between prestige aid and aid for economic development, though both are justified by the prospective recipient in terms of genuine economic development. The prospective giver, if unaware of the distinction, is likely to fall into one of two errors. By mistaking prestige aid for aid for economic development, he may waste human and material resources in support of the latter when the purpose of prestige aid could have been achieved much more simply and cheaply. Or else he may reject out of hand a request for prestige aid because he cannot justify it in terms of economic development, and may thereby forego available political advantages. The classic example of this error is the American rejection of the Afghan request for the saving of the streets of Kabul as economically unsound. The Soviet Union, pursuing a politically oriented policy of foreign aid, did save the streets of Kabul. . . .

[Editors' note: in the succeeding portion of this article, dealing with foreign aid or economic development, the author makes the following major points: that this hope of foreign aid has been primarily the object for economic rather than political analysis; that the popular version of foreign aid for economic development has proceeded from a series of uncertain assumptions. These assumptions involve correlations between the giving of foreign aid and the economic development of the recipient society; between economic development and social stability; between social stability and the emergence and strengthening of democratic institutions; and between the existence of these institutions and a peaceful foreign policy. He concludes that "however attractive and reassuring these correlations may sound to American ears, they are borne out neither by the experiences we have had with our policies of foreign aid nor by general historic experience."]

II. CONCLUSIONS FOR POLICY

The major conclusions for policy to be drawn from this analysis are three: the requirement of identifying each concrete situation in the light of the six different types of foreign aid and of choosing the quantity and quality of foreign aid appropriate to the situation; the requirement of attuning, within the same concrete situation, different types of foreign aid to each other in view of the over-all goals of foreign policy; and the requirement of dealing with foreign aid as an integral part of political policy.

The task of identifying concrete situations with the type of foreign aid appropriate to them is a task for country and area experts to perform. Can country A not survive without foreign aid? Is its government likely to exchange political advantages for economic favors? Would our military interest be served by the strengthening of this nation's military forces? Does this country provide the non-economic preconditions for economic development to be supported by foreign aid? Are our political interests likely to be served by giving this nation foreign aid for purposes of prestige? Can a case be made for foreign aid in order to alleviate human suffering? What kind and quantity of foreign aid is necessary and sufficient to achieve the desired result?

To answer these questions correctly demands first of all a thorough and intimate knowledge and understanding of the total situation in a particular country. But it also requires political and economic judgment of a very high order, applied to two distinct issues. It is necessary to anticipate the receptivity of the country to different kinds of foreign aid and their effects upon it. When this analysis has been made, it is then necessary to select from a great number of possible measures of foreign aid those which are most appropriate to the situation and hence most likely to succeed.

In most cases, however, the task is not that simple. Typically, an underdeveloped country will present a number of situations indicating the need for different types of foreign aid simultaneously. One type given without regard for its potential effects upon another type risks getting in the way of the latter. One of the most conspicuous weaknesses of our past foreign aid policies has been the disregard of the effect different types of foreign aid have upon each other. Bribes given to the ruling group, for instance, are bound to strengthen the political and economic *status quo*. Military aid is bound to have an impact upon the distribution of political power within the receiving country; it can also have a deleterious effect upon the economic system, for instance, by increasing inflationary pressures. Similarly, the effect of subsistence foreign aid is bound to be the support of the *status quo* in all its aspects. Insofar as the giving nation desires these effects or can afford to be indifferent to them they obviously do not matter in terms of its over-all objectives. But insofar as the giving nation has embarked upon a policy of foreign aid for economic development which requires changes in the political and economic *status quo*, the other types of foreign aid policies are counterproductive in terms of economic development; for they strengthen the very factors which stand in its way.

This problem is particularly acute in the relations between prestige aid and aid for economic development. The giving nation may seek quick political results and use prestige aid for that purpose; yet it may also have an interest in the economic development of the recipient country, the benefits of which are likely to appear only in the more distant future. Prestige aid is at best only by accident favorable to economic development; it may be irrelevant to it, or may actually impede it. What kind of foreign aid is the giving country to choose? If it chooses a combination of both it should take care to choose an innocuous kind of prestige aid and to promote economic development the benefits of which are not too long in coming. Afghanistan is the classic example of this dilemma. The Soviet Union, by paving the streets of Kabul, chose a kind of prestige aid that is irrelevant to economic development. The United States, by building a hydroelectric dam in a remote part of the country, chose economic development the very existence of which is unknown to most Afghans and the benefits of which will not appear for years to come.

It follows, then, from the very political orientation of foreign aid that its effect upon the prestige of the giving nation must always be in the minds of the formulators and executors of foreign aid policies. Foreign aid for economic development, in particular, which benefits the recipient country immediately and patently is a more potent political weapon than aid promising benefits that are obscure and lie far in the future. Furthermore, the political effects of foreign aid are lost if its foreign source is not obvious to the recipients. For it is not aid as such or its beneficial results that creates political loyalties on the part of the recipient, but the positive relationship that the mind of the recipient establishes between the aid and its beneficial results, on the one hand, and the political philosophy, the political system, and the political objectives of the giver, on the other. That is to say, if the recipient continues to disapprove of the political philosophy, system, and objectives of the giver, despite the aid he has received, the political effects of the aid are lost. The same is true if he remains unconvinced that the aid received is but a natural, if not inevitable, manifestation of the political philosophy, system, and objectives of the giver. Foreign aid remains politically ineffectual—at least for the short term—as long as the recipient says either: "Aid is good, but the politics of the giver are bad"; or "Aid is good, but the politics of the giver—good, bad, or indifferent—have nothing to do with it." In order to be able to establish a psychological relationship between giver and recipient, the procedures through which aid is given, and the subject matter to which it is applied, must lend themselves to the creation of a connection between the aid and the politics of the giver which reflects credit upon the latter.

The problem of foreign aid is insoluble if it is considered as a self-sufficient technical enterprise of a primarily economic nature. It is soluble only if it is considered an integral part of the political policies of the giving country—which must be devised in view of the political conditions, and for its effects upon the political situation, in the receiving country. In this respect, a policy of foreign aid is no different from diplomatic or military policy or propaganda. They are all weapons in the political armory of the nation.

As military policy is too important a matter to be left ultimately to the generals, so is foreign aid too important a matter to be left in the end to the economists. The expertise of the economist must analyze certain facts, devise certain means, and perform certain functions of manipulation for foreign aid. Yet the formulation and over-all execution of foreign aid policy is a political function. It is the province of the political expert.

It follows from the political nature of foreign aid that it is not a science but an art. That art requires by way of mental predisposition a political sensitivity to the interrelationship among the facts, present and future, and ends and means. The requirements by way of mental activity are two-fold. The first is a discriminating judgment of facts, ends and means and their effects upon each other. However, an analysis of the situation in the recipient country and, more particularly, its projection into the future and the conclusions from the analysis in terms of policy can only in part be arrived at through rational deduction from ascertainable facts. When all the available facts have been ascertained, duly analyzed, and conclusions drawn from them, the final judgments and decisions can be derived only from subtle and sophisticated hunches. The best the formulator and executor of a policy of foreign aid can do is to maximize the chances that his hunches turn out to be right. Here as elsewhere in the formulation and conduct of foreign policy, the intuition of the statesman, more than the knowledge of the expert, will carry the day.

COMPARATIVE AID PERFORMANCE

Official Development Assistance as Percent of GNP—1975

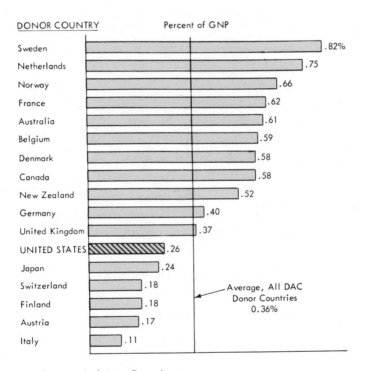

Development Assistance Committee

The United States ranks 12th among the non-communist developed countries providing aid.

From AID Publication, January 1977

175

INTERDEPENDENCE FOR U.S. INDUSTRY

Imports from Developing Countries as % of Consumption

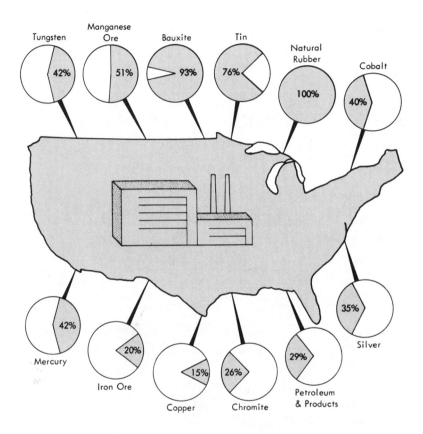

Based on 1974 data from the U.S. Bureau of Mines.

From AID Publication, Jan. 1977

VIII

The Threat and Use of Force

So long as war and the danger of war lurk in the background of international politics, there is no question of whether or not states require coercive power. They do. What is at issue is the determination of what kinds of military power are most appropriate for achieving a given state's goals, and especially how much power is required to enable that state to threaten its use, even though the state may not actually have to (or wish to) use it. To be effective, threats must be credible. Otherwise, if a bluff is called, the state's position will be weakened.

The answers to these questions involve more than calculations of relative technological or productive capacity. The psychological climate engendered may profoundly affect the entire international climate; an arms race, like war itself, seems to possess its own inner dynamic. Military capabilities seem to transform themselves from means to ends. While diplomats prefer to negotiate from what Secretary of State Acheson like to call "positions of strength," policies of building positions of strength are often pursued with such energy and dedication that the ultimate purpose—negotiation and settlement—tends to be overlooked. As one leading analyst of power politics has put it, "The most serious wars are fought in order to make one's own country militarily stronger, or more often, to prevent another country from becoming militarily stronger, so that there is much justification for the epigram that 'the principal cause of war is war itself.' "[1]

Nations resort to war for reasons other than defense. A state that is dissatisfied with its economic and territorial status may resort to war in the hope of achieving a more favorable situation. Sometimes states are dominated by elites or ruled by leaders for whom war has a positive value in and of itself. The Prussian officer class or the Samurai warrior caste in Japan are examples of elites for whom war was an honorable and attractive undertaking. Similarly, war was justified for a Hitler or a Mussolini because they believed in the virtue of war and expansion as evidence of a nation's vitality. There is also a theory that a state facing domestic divisions may seek to unify the country through a war waged against a foreign power.

Military power is also an element of any great power's bargaining strength. Even if the leadership does not desire to change the status quo, it may have to count upon the credibility or the utilization of its military might to maintain the balance of power against a potential threat. The presence of American forces in Europe is almost certainly indispensable to the security and stability of our allies, and hence to the balance of power. Finally, there are the wars fought to avenge an insult or to redeem national honor. The Arab vendetta against Israel is in major part a desire to vindicate Arab honor that has been violated by the creation of Israel.

The association of war with the state system is no accident. As Nieburg points out in this chapter, all social life is marked by tension and conflict among groups competing to assert their will and interests. Following the thinking of Lewis Coser, Nieburg argues that conflict serves a functional purpose: "Conflict, in functional terms is the means of discovering consensus, of creating agreed terms of collaboration." More important, conflict within a society is a means of challenging the status quo and opening the way for long overdue changes in response to new social demands.

In the international system, there is no supranational authority with a monopoly of violence to preserve order among states. Instead, states look to war and the threat of war to assert their self-interest and to defend against their extinction. War in the modern state system may be considered from three perspectives. From the perspective of each state, war appears as an instrument of national policy, "as a means by which the state's objectives may be attained."[2] From the perspective of the international system—that is, from the perspective of the relations that exist among its

---

[1]Edward Hallett Carr, *The Twenty-Years' Crisis, 1919–1939* (London: MacMillan and Co., Ltd., 1951), p. 111.

[2]Hedley Bull, *The Anarchical Society* (New York: Columbia University Press, 1977) p. 186.

members, "war appears as a basic determinant of the shape the system assumes at any one time."[3] For example, one might consider the transformation that had occurred in the world at the end of World War II: Germany, Italy, and Japan were defeated, and the U.S. and the Soviet Union emerged as the dominant powers.

From the perspective of those who believe in an international society which has common values, rulers, and institutions, war is both "a manifestation of disorder in international society, bringing with it the threat of breakdown of international society itself into a state of pure enmity, or war of all against all."[4] But it is also a means by which society carries out changes in relationships and yet still attempts to keep disorder and insecurity within limits. For example, many wars have been caused in the twentieth century by the efforts of subjugated nations and colonies to achieve independence; there was simply no alternative but war. Under the nation-state system there is no supranational authority with a monopoly of force which could impose these changes and preserve security and order the way a domestic society does. It is the paradox of war that its threat and even its outbreak may be the only means of preserving a stable order, provided the war does not get out of control. States are deterred from aggression and war by the knowledge that other states won't let them get away with it. The more appropriate the state's preparation for violence, the less likely it will have to use it. And it is certainly true that more states are at peace than at war most of the time.

There are as many causes of war as there are types of social and political dissatisfaction and disorder. One study, by Stephen Rosen and Walter Jones, lists twelve proximate causes of war:

1. Power asymmetry—an unfavorable tilt in the distribution of power;
2. Nationalism, separatism, and irredentism—the desire of a people to throw off foreign rule or to annex nationals living under foreign rule;
3. Social Darwinism—the belief that societies, like biological species, evolve and advance through competition resulting in survival of the fittest;
4. Communications failure—misunderstanding and hostility due to stereotypical images and mutual misperception of intentions;
5. Arms races;
6. The exploitation of a foreign war to achieve unity at home;
7. Instinctual aggression—the psychological predisposition of people toward aggression;
8. Economic and scientific stimulation—new economic and scientific innovations stimulate expansionist tendencies;
9. Military-Industrial complexes—groups within a society, principally the

---

[3]*Ibid.*, p. 187.

[4]*Ibid.*

military, the defense industry, and their political allies, acquire a vested interest in maintaining a state of conflict;

10. Relative deprivation—to achieve greater benefits or to relieve the frustration of denial, groups may turn to aggression and political violence;
11. Overpopulation;
12. Conflict-Resolution—war as a device for challenging and changing unacceptable or incompatible conditions between two or more states.[5]

Unfortunately, if war is an unavoidable condition of the nation-state system, one must recognize that is has been getting increasingly murderous and destructive. Ever since the twentieth century began, technology has been working a revolution in the relationship of war to foreign policy and human values. First it was the machine gun and the submarine that produced the horrible war of attrition on the Western Front in 1914 and at sea throughout the war; then airpower and tank warfare destroyed much of Europe, Russia, and Japan in World War II. Today, nuclear weapons and missiles have undercut the traditional relationship of war to foreign policy and human values. Traditionally, a nation expected to use its full military might in a war. Today, the suicidal consequences of a resort to nuclear war by either side has raised the question of whether war between nuclear powers is any longer thinkable. As Klaus Knorr observes in the selection that follows, "the nuclear balance of terror, which is assumed to be safely stable, has inhibited any large-scale use of force between powerful states, whose leaders, as rational actors, are completely self-deterred." Nevertheless, while nuclear weapons may make resort to war unthinkable except as an act of complete national desperation, their deterrent function prompts each side to maintain an enormous arsenal of such weapons, and so long as such arsenals exist their use cannot be ruled out. In fact, military authorities in both the Soviet Union and the United States have stated quite clearly that under certain circumstances of crisis or war a resort to nuclear weapons *cannot* be ruled out. Still, it does seem to be the case that fear of a nuclear holocaust has acted as a restraint upon the two superpowers.

Nevertheless, the nuclear deadlock only seems to have displaced each side's preoccupation with security and with the utility of war and the threat of war away from the nuclear terrain to attention to the possibilities of subnuclear war. The limited use of force has been frequently resorted to by both superpowers in the postwar era: by the United States in Korea and Vietnam and by the Soviet Union in Hungary, Czechoslovakia, and Ethiopia. Secondly, neither side has renounced the exploitation of the threat of force for political ends.

While each of the contestants may possess force sufficient to produce damage the other would regard as unacceptable, they may be unequal in demon-

---

[5]Steven J. Rosen & Walter S. Jones. *The Logic of International Relations* (Cambridge, Mass.: Winthrop Publishers, 1977), pp. 283–312.

strating resolve to use the force at their disposal. Superior technique in "brinksmanship" or "crisis management" may establish the greater willingness of one side to go to war rather than back down, and so bring a diplomatic victory in its train, as was demonstrated by the United States in the Cuban missile crisis of 1962.[6]

Hence, enormous wealth is still expended by both sides, but particularly by the Russians, on building up all their military forces to higher levels.

While the balance of terror seems to have reduced the incidence of war among the advanced industrial states (Communist and Western), there has been a great upsurge in the numbers and types of war being fought in Africa, Asia, and the Middle East. Klaus Knorr observes in this chapter that "military conflicts have occurred mostly in the Third World, mainly between Third World countries, and this shift is paralleled by the fact that the proportion of world military spending, manpower, and weapons imports outside the capitalist states has sharply increased." The increased frequency of war in the Third World is in part due to: the absence of consensus among many of the new states as to where their borders really are; the unresolved presence of white regimes in southern Africa; national xenophobia; and the eagerness with which the Western powers and Soviet Union alike have been willing to supply them with arms and even help them fight these wars. Here again, there is always a danger that one or both superpowers will become bogged down in a war such as the U.S. did in Vietnam, or come into direct conflict as they almost have on occasion in the Middle East.

As yet, no one has been able to devise a formula which would enable the powers to dispense with such weapons. While they seem to be essential both as deterrents and as symbols, it is not clear what, if any, positive or affirmative functions are served by having such weapons in one's arsenal. How can their possession be translated into concrete political advantage when their threat value is very limited? Weapons of such massive destructive capacity carry with them the greatest inhibitions to their employment. The argument that the threat of force is no longer the most effective way of exercising power because it may call forth violent resistance is particularly appropriate today.

In order to reduce the danger of nuclear war, each side has adopted what is called a "second-strike" strategy. The second-strike strategy was enunciated in 1962 by Secretary of Defense Robert McNamara. By installing U.S. missiles in underground silos where they could not be destroyed, Washington was in a position to inform the Kremiin that it renounced any resort to a preemptive, or first-strike, attack on Russia. Instead, it would henceforth rely upon the threat from America's invulnerable nuclear retaliatory force to deter the Soviet Union from a resort to war. It was hoped that the Kremlin, knowing that the U.S. would not attack first, would

[6]Bull, *op. cit.*, 194.

be persuaded to adopt a similar strategy and thereby minimize the uncertainty and instability that characterized a situation in which each felt it had to get in the first blow if it were to have any hope of surviving.

In the ensuing years, both superpowers have tacitly or actively shaped their deterrence strategy around the concept of the second-strike. Each has hardened its missile sites to render them less vulnerable, and among the Strategic Arms Limitation agreements reached at Moscow in June 1972 was an agreement to abandon the construction of anti-ballistic-missile (ABM) defenses on the principle that any attempt to reduce one's vulnerability to the opponents second-strike would weaken the stability of deterrence. Until the last few years each side's missiles were generally targeted on population centers (called a countervalue strategy), rather than on each other's rockets (called a counterforce strategy). In effect, each held the other side's population hostage against a surprise attack. This has been the paradox of nuclear deterrence: security and stability have rested upon each side knowing that the other could not 'knock out' its retaliatory capability in the form of land based ICBMs, bombers, and, more potently, in the form of missiles fired from submarines 200 to 2000 miles off each other's coast. In the last several years, however, uncertainties have arisen due to technological advances in the throw weight, megatonnage and accuracy of Soviet rockets, the accuracy and warhead numbers of American missiles, and a shift on both sides toward targeting on each other's missiles (counterforce). As Hedley Bull observes, "mutual deterrence can make deliberate resort to nuclear war 'irrational' as an instrument of policy only so long as it is stable."[7] Moreover, the move on both sides to build mobile missiles that cannot be located by surveillance satellites threatens to recreate the environment of fear and instability based upon uncertainty about the other's capability (and hence intentions) that marked the fifties and early sixties.

There are, therefore, a number of reasons why war, including major wars fought with nuclear weapons, may still be possible. One side or the other may miscalculate the effects of an aggressive action, convincing itself that it can get away with achieving its goals through the threat of force. Or one side may believe that the other side is about to launch a military action and that it must strike first; this is the strategy of preemption, and it was effectively applied against three Arab states by Israel in 1967. In addition, wars may break out, not because of miscalculation arrived at by deliberation (however faulty), but simply by accident, unlikely as this may seem. Or one side or the other may achieve a genuine technological breakthrough in weapons, delivery systems, or defense capabilities, which might drastically shift the existing balance and make war once again appear to be a rational policy choice. Just as America's monopoly on nuclear weapons gave way to duopoly, and just as America and Russia have since been joined by Great Britain, France, and China as nuclear powers, so other states may well be

---

[7]H. Bull, *op. cit.*, p. 124.

on the threshold of joining the nuclear club, despite the efforts of statesmen to prevent it. Local, limited conflicts may grow in area and scope (such as in the Middle East) until they embrace powers with nuclear capabilities. One can easily imagine that nuclear weapons may not be used at the outset of a war; but it stretches the imagination to assume that a country would prefer losing a war or its very existence to using its full arsenal.

One of the mockeries of the modern age is that peace itself seems to rest upon the mutual fear inspired by the magnitude of nuclear destructiveness. The nature of the entire concept of threat takes on new meaning. States have arrived at such a deadlock in their search for security that peace seems to depend upon the degree to which the superpowers can maintain the so-called balance of terror. On the other hand, the possibility that massive destructive weapons may soon be in the hands of many can only add to the insecurity and instability of the entire international system. The threat now lies in the system itself rather than in the actions of a state's immediate neighbors, as before. Although, in a sense, apprehension of what others can do has always been a basis for restraint in international behavior, this is a dubious foundation upon which to rest hopes for continued peace and stability. The system is highly volatile; there are no guarantees against the kinds of miscalcultions, destructive impulses, or even accidents which could lead to an explosion. The task of leadership is, in the words of McGeorge Bundy, President Kennedy's chief adviser on national security policy, "to cap the volcano."

As the magnitude of the security problem grows and the military claims upon the lives, resources, and direction of society continues to mount, there is the latent danger of the transformation of the nation in the direction of a garrison state. There is an even more subtle aspect to the problem, and that is the risk that military considerations will take precedence over political considerations in the conduct of foreign policy itself.

When relations with the Soviet Union during the 1950s and early 1960s were virtually tantamount to a state of war, and when American foreign policy was defined so completely in terms of national security, it was almost inevitable that the military would exert a major influence on policy.[8]

Even more in doubt in recent decades has been Clausewitz's famous aphorism that "war is nothing but the continuation of political relations by other means." One may wonder if this maxim of cautionary wisdom

[8]Richard K. Betts, *Soldiers, Statesmen, and Cold War Crises* (Cambridge: Harvard University Press, 1977). Betts argues, with examples, that America's military advisers were no more hawkish (or dovish) on balance than the civilian leaders.

This is a case that can be argued on both sides. The Pentagon is not just another bureaucracy, but a rather unique institution. Civilians were conditioned by the Cold War to think in perspectives often attributed only to military men. For additional and alternative formulations of this issue, see F. C. Ikle, *Every War Must End* (New York: Columbia University Press, 1971); Bernard Brodie, *Politics and War* (New York: MacMillan, 1973); Robert Gallucci, *Neither Peace nor Honor* (Baltimore: Johns Hopkins University Press, 1975).

retains the meaning it had when the concept of limited war was rooted in the temper and technology of a simpler age. In the memory of living men, the political restraints on victor and vanquished alike have twice been swept away by the passion of total war, and even so-called limited wars such as Vietnam have been fought with the objective of victory heavily in mind. There now exists abundant evidence that wars are often embarked upon by civilian and military alike without adequate knowledge or with a serious underestimation of the enemy, and without any clear idea of what political end might realistically be expected to be gained from the war. Once engaged, the war is conducted on the basis of faulty strategy and tactics, exaggerated hopes, inadequate and doctored intelligence, and misrepresentation of the truth by the leadership. It is conducted on the part of the military on the basis of counterproductive and often tremendously wasteful and destructive strategy and tactics. It is invariably marked by an attitude on the part of the military that once war has been entered upon, only the military should any longer have a say as to its conduct. (It is true that President Johnson set limits upon the all-out use of military power against North Vietnam, but it is far from clear that had such limitations not been in effect North Vietnam could have been defeated, as the military claim.) Defeats are denied, painted as victories, or attributed to the treasonous influence of appeasement at home. People and leaders alike become locked into a face-saving effort to deny reality and therefore reject the political terms for ending the war until it is too late. So we see that although war may be an unavoidable concomitant of the nation-state system, even limited wars are often entered into and carried on in ways that have no reasonable relationship to the national interest or to the maintenance of a stable world order.

21   Uses of Violence

Harold L. Nieburg

Harold L. Nieburg teaches in the Political Science Department at SUNY Binghamton.

. . . The argument of this essay is that the risk of violence is necessary and useful in preserving national societies. This specifically includes sporadic, uncontrolled, "irrational" violence in all of its forms. It is true that domestic violence, no less than international violence, may become a self-generating vortex which destroys all values, inducing anarchy and chaos. However, efforts to prevent this by extreme measures only succeed in making totalitarian societies more liable to such collapses. Democracies assume the risk of such catastrophes, thereby making them less likely.

Violence has two inextricable aspects: its actual use (political demonstrations, self-immolation, suicide, crimes of passion, property, politics, etc.), or its potential use. The actual demonstration of violence must occur from time to time in order to give credibility to its threatened outbreak, thereby gaining efficacy for the threat as an instrument of social and political change. The two aspects, demonstration and threat, cannot be separated. The two merge imperceptibly into each other. If the capability of actual demonstration is not present, the threat will have little effect in inducing a willingness to bargain politically. In fact, such a threat may provoke "preemptive" counter-violence.

The "rational" goal of the threat of violence is an accommodation of interests, not the provocation of actual violence. Similarly, the "rational" goal of actual violence is demonstration of the will and capability of action, establishing a measure of the credibility of future threats, not the exhaustion of that capability in unlimited conflict.*

. . . Within each system there are conflicting values among members which are constantly adjusted as roles change, maintaining a state of tension. Political systems have an objective, dynamic interrelationship, structured into the hierarchy of macrosystems. Within the latter, each subsystem has a role much like that of the individual in smaller constellations. Each subsystem may be part of several macrosystems, imposing conflicting demands upon it. Consequently, within macrosystems there is maintained a state of constant tension between subsystems. This objective tension, existing on all levels, is seen subjectively in terms both of competition and consensus, depending on the comparative degrees of collaboration

These excerpts from "Uses of Violence" by H. L. Nieburg are reprinted from Journal of Conflict Resolution Vol. 7, No. 1 *(March 1963) pp. 43–54 by permission of the Publisher, Sage Publications, Inc. Some footnotes omitted.*

*By "rational" here is meant: having a conceptual link to a given end, a logical or symbolic means-ends relationship which can be demonstrated to others or, if not demonstrable, is accepted by others (but not necessarily all) as proven.

and conflict which exist in the situation at any given moment.

Any two or more systems may appear as hostile at any given time. From the viewpoint of the participants, the conceptual framework of competition overrides underlying consensus. Decisions and policies of the rival elites are rationalized in terms of hostility to the values and leaders of the other system. However, if events conspire to place a higher value on a hostile tactical situation involving the macrosystem of which both smaller systems are a part, their relationship will be transformed quickly to a conceptual framework of consensus which will override and mute the unresolved competitive elements. Such an event may also bring about internal leadership changes in both subsystems, if the elites were too firmly wedded to the requirements of the now-irrelevant competitive situation.

Objectively, tension is always present among all roles and systems; that is, there are always present both elements of competition and consensus. The subjective emphasis which each pole of the continuum receives depends on the value which the tactical situation places on acts and attitudes of hostility or collaboration among the various systems at various times. Degrees of hostility and collaboration are structured by a hierarchy of values within and among all roles and systems all the time. All are involved in a dynamic process.

Conflict, in functional terms, is the means of discovering consensus, of creating agreed terms of collaboration. Because of the individual's personal role in the macrosystem of nation-states, he tends to view the Cold War in terms of competition. Similarly, because of his role in the subsystem of the family, he tends to view family problems in terms of consensus (until the system breaks down completely). . . .

The commitment required by a credible threat of violence, able to induce peaceable accommodation, is one of a very high order. Not all individuals nor all political systems are capable of credibly using the threat of violence in order to induce greater deference by others to their values. There is general recognition by all of the kinds of values which can and cannot elicit the high degree of commitment required to make the threat credible.

By and large, all violence has a rational aspect for somebody, if not for the perpetrator. All acts of violence can be put to rational use, whether they are directed against others or against oneself. This is true because those who wish to apply the threat of violence in order to achieve a social or political bargaining posture are reluctant to pay the costs or take the uncertain risks of an actual demonstration of that threat. Many incoherent acts of violence are exploited by insurgent elites as a means of improving their roles or imposing a larger part of their values upon a greater political system. The greater the logical connection between the act and the ends sought, the easier it is to assimilate the act and claim it as a demonstration of the threat available to the insurgents if their demands are ignored. The rapidity with which insurgent movements create martyrs, often from the demise of hapless bystanders, and the reluctance of governments to give martyrs to the opposition, are evidence of this. . . .

THE INTERNATIONAL PROCESS

Many people blithely argue for law as a substitute for violence, as though there were a choice between the two. They call for international law and world government to eliminate war. This point of view reveals a blissful ignorance of the functions of violence in domestic legal systems. A viable system based on law protects the conditions of group action. Law always rests on violence. The threat of violence and the fear of the breakdown of law and order act to moderate demands and positions, thereby setting into peaceful motion the informal political processes of negotiation, concession, compromise, and agreement. Although there is no centralized police power in the international forum, the processes of mediation and negotiation operate in much the same way. The credible threat of violence in the hands of the nations has a similarly stabilizing effect, provided statesmen are attentive to maintaining their national capability for demonstrating violence, and provided their ambitions are commensurate to the bargaining position which their armaments achieve. More comprehensive legal codes and a world government may not improve the stability of the world community in any case, since the possibility of civil conflict exists in all political systems. Civil wars are frequently bloodier and more unforgiving than wars between sovereign nations.

In international politics, the threat of violence tends to create stability and maintain peace. Here the threat is more directly responsive to policy controls. The nation-state has greater continuity than the informal political systems that coalesce and dissolve in the course of domestic social change. The threat of violence can be asserted much more deliberately and can be demonstrated under full control, as in "good will" navy visits, army maneuvers near a sensitive border, partial mobilization, etc. Because of the greater continuity of these macrosystems, the national leaders must strive to maintain the prestige of a nation's might and will. If the reputation of a nation's military power is allowed to tarnish, future bargaining power will be weakened. It may be forced to reestablish that prestige by invoking a test of arms, as a means of inducing greater respect for its position from other nations. All strong nations are anxious to demonstrate their military power peaceably in order that their prestige will afford them the bargaining power they deserve without a test of arms.

Because the threat of violence is a conscious instrument of national policy, it generally lacks the random character which violence has domestically. This means that if the armaments of nations fall out of balance, if the prestige of nations is no longer commensurate with their ambitions, if the will to take the risks of limited military conflicts is lacking, if domestic political considerations distort the national response to external threat, then the time becomes ripe for the outbreak of violence, escalating out of control.

In general, the dangers of escalating international conflict induce greater, not lesser, restraint on the part of national leaders in their relations with each other. Attempts to achieve infinite security for the nation are as self-defeating as such attempts are for domestic regimes.

The functioning of consensus and competition between nations is not fundamentally different from that of domestic politics. The most striking difference is that in domestic politics the level of centralized violence available to the state creates a high threshold of stability against the threats brought to bear within the system by private groups. In the international forum, the closest approximation to such a threshold is the decentralized forces available to the Great Powers. A power interested in modifying the status quo must raise the level of its threat of violence, in order to induce other powers to choose between concessions to its demands or the costs and risks of an arms race. To the extent that the status quo powers are capable and willing to pay the costs and take the risks, their own levels can be raised, depriving the challenger of any political advantages from his investment. When all of the great powers are attentive to the equations of potential violence, no nation can hope to gain conclusive political advantages from an arms race. This situation makes possible international agreements for stabilizing arms and bringing about political settlements.

Diplomatic ceremonials, like the ceremonials of personal relations which we call "manners," serve to minimize the dangers of provocation and threat in the day-to-day relations between nations. Conversely, manners tend to minimize the dangers of provocation and threat in relations between people. . . .

22   On the International Uses of Military Force in the Contemporary World

Klaus Knorr

The author is Professor of Public and International Affairs at the Woodrow Wilson School, Princeton University.

In 1965, this author wrote a book (published by Princeton University Press in 1966) —*On the Uses of Military Power in the Nuclear Age*—in which he was one of the first to advance the thesis that the usability and usefulness of military force in interstate relations, compared with previous historical periods, had been diminished by several changes in underlying conditions. Twelve years later, it seems interesting to review this proposition in the light of subsequent writings that greatly amplified it, on the one

Excerpted from "On the International Uses of Military Force in the Contemporary World" by Klaus Knorr. Orbis: A Journal of World Affairs, Vol. 21, No. 1. Reprinted by permission. (Some footnotes have been omitted.)

hand, and in consideration of the actual uses of military power and the preparations for its use that have occurred since, on the other. Do the relevant events of the past decade or so, and what they foreshadow, confirm or disconfirm the thesis and the amplifications it has received? . . .

In *On the Uses of Military Power in the Nuclear Age*, I argued that some traditionally important goals for going to war had lost appeal, that the anticipated costs of doing so had markedly risen, and that the expected utility of using military forces internationally had therefore probably declined, in the sense that governments and elites found their useful employment more restricted than was previously the case.

The following were the principal points.

The desire for territorial conquest has been the most powerful motive for using force throughout recorded history. Economic and security considerations are among the major concerns that have propelled governments to conquer or defend territory. Prior to the Industrial Revolution, an expansion of territorial possessions meant more control over manpower and resources, sources of supply, markets and outlets for investment. In recent decades, elites have gradually learned, in large part as a result of modern economics and education, that the prime sources of national wealth are ultimately domestic (i.e., savings and investments, technological progress and the upgrading of human resources). They also came to believe that international trade and investment do not require territorial control so long as there is an international economic order that fosters such intercourse. Historical experience has confirmed these expectations. Several countries became highly developed and wealthy while remaining strictly confined to a small home base (e.g., Switzerland and Sweden), and West Germany and Japan became rich after they lost territories in World War II.

Until not long ago, expansion of territory and territorial control also appealed on grounds of security. Territorial expansion meant more population, more assured access to raw materials and food, which could not be cut off in times of war, and more space than an enemy had to cross in order to reach the local centers of power. These strategic values have also tended to diminish. Manpower is a military asset only to the extent that it is loyal and skillful, and sophisticated technological capacity has become a base of military strength more important than sheer numbers of people. Dependence on foreign supplies that can be cut off in wartime is a serious vulnerability only if war is protracted. The expectation of prolonged warfare, how-ever, has decreased in recent decades because the most powerful modern technology has lent to offensive weapons a vast superiority over defensive arms. Moreover, the development of nuclear missiles has greatly lowered the protective value of territory and distance from prospective enemies.

Four factors have been operating on the cost side. First, memories of the stupendous destructiveness of World Wars I and II, the watching of recent televised conflicts (e.g., Vietnam and Lebanon), and profound anxieties about a possible nuclear holocaust have sensitized an increasing number of people to the costliness of war, and this sensitivity has become particularly important in societies that are no longer governed by traditional warlike elites. Second, nuclear weapons technology has rendered the most destructive arms useless for anything but deterrence between states encapsuled in a balance of terror. In fact, the fear that lesser conflicts between them might escalate to the level of strategic nuclear exchanges gives nuclear powers a strong incentive to refrain from employing conventional forces against one another. Third, the global spread of nationalism, and of the capacity for political and military mobilization, and the export of modern arms to the less-developed parts of the world have made these unattractive targets for intervention or conquest by great powers. The opportunity for cheap colonial aggrandizement and overseas military intervention that the great powers enjoyed from the fifteenth century to the beginning of the twentieth has disappeared. Fourth, while roughly until the end of the nineteenth century aggressive war was generally regarded as natural, legitimate and inevitable, recent decades have witnessed a growing normative revolution; as a result, at least the aggressive use of military force is increasingly held to be illegitimate—a rule imbedded in the charter of the United

Nations. The normative costs of resorting to military aggression have thus risen palpably.

Although these developments seemed to this author (in 1965) to point at least tentatively to a diminishing utility of the international use of armed force, he noted (though in retrospect not emphatically enough) two significant qualifications. For one, even if the appeal to use force in behalf of certain economic and security objectives has become deflated, this does not, of course, exhaust the reasons for which governments may resort to arms. Ideological goals, especially, ethnic unification (or liberation) and world order objectives may suggest worthwhile gains. Changes on the cost side appeared to be more conclusive. Even here, however, it was doubtful that military force for purposes of deterrence and defense had lost utility. The ability to threaten nuclear reprisal was felt to be highly useful as an instrument of deterrence. The enhanced capacity of less-developed countries to resist military attack by great powers had high utility to the former. In addition, normative changes had engendered no normative costs in regard to defense against aggression. The other qualification—about which more will be said below—noted that the various changes in expected utility were not evenly distributed over the world. They had much more of a hold in some societies, especially the capitalist-democratic countries, than in others.

This theme of the declining value of military forces has been pushed a great deal further in more recent writings. For the sake of economy, I will briefly sum up these opinions and propositions without attributing them to individual authors.[1]

This new school of thought asserts that

[1] Stanley Hoffmann has written an excellent analysis of this school of thought, which he calls the "modernist" school. "Choices," *Foreign Policy*, Fall 1973, pp. 3–42.

international relationships have recently been experiencing, and are still undergoing, a revolutionary transformation in the following terms. First, the nuclear balance of terror, which is assumed to be safely stable, has inhibited any large-scale use of force between powerful states, whose leaders, as rational actors, are completely self-deterred. Second, societies everywhere are now preoccupied with the solution of economic and social problems on which national welfare depends. The fading of serious questions of military security has facilitated this emphasis on domestic priorities over the previous stress on defense budgets and military service. Third, rapidly growing international interdependence, particularly economic, has been accompanied by the vigorous growth of transnational forces and organizations, including multinational business corporations, which in turn have undermined the primacy of governmental interstate behavior in favor of that of private actors and have greatly reduced the significance of state boundaries. Indeed, as many see it, the classic nation-state, in which military sovereignty reposed, is being increasingly hemmed in and dominated by these forces and is probably on the way out. Fourth, contemporary international affairs are more and more devoted to problems—economic, environmental and normative—that generate negotiations in which military power is irrelevant, which are more subject to international economic power, and which in any case increasingly require management by authorities and institutions that transcend national boundaries.

The world, according to this concept, is being shaped by forces and visions that are creating new forms of "international life," in relation to which the realities and teachings of the past are largely, if not wholly, irrelevant. The extent to which the members of this new school assert the presence of novel realities or express a vision of the future is often unclear. They apparently believe they are addressing themselves to an international reality that is in the process of swift and irresistible change and that is evidently escaping from the grim shackles of the premodern world.

If these are the arguments alleging that the utility of force is declining, what do we find if we turn to the actual behavior of governments in military matters? Taking the period from 1964 to 1975,[2] and excluding civil wars in which no country intervened directly with troops, we find the following major armed conflicts erupting: (1) the war in Indochina (already under way since 1962); (2) the Six-Day War between Israel and Arab states (June 1967); (3) the invasion of Czechoslovakia by troops from the Soviet Union, Poland, Hungary, Bulgaria and East Germany (1968); (4) repeated armed clashes between Soviet and Chinese troops (1969); (5) the war between India and Pakistan after Indian forces intervened in the civil war in East Pakistan (1971); (6) the Yom Kippur War between Israel and Arab countries (1973); (7) the landing of Turkish troops on Cyprus to intervene in a local civil war (1974); and (8) Soviet-Cuban and South African interventions in Angola's civil war (1975).

In addition, the period witnessed numerous local clashes between Israeli and Arab forces as well as Israeli raids on Arab targets. There were also many minor military violations of the truce between North and South Korea; for example, in January 1968, North Korean commandos raided Seoul, and in January 1974, North Korean gunboats sank a South Korean patrol boat in waters south of the boundary.

[2]The following account is based on David Wood, *Conflict in the Twentieth Century* (London: International Institute for Strategic Studies, Adelphi Paper no. 48, 1968), for the period from 1964 to 1966, and on the IISS's annual *Strategic Survey* for the subsequent years.

The list of border clashes and small-scale fighting over disputed territorial claims is lengthy: the low-level Indonesian-Malaysian conflict (1963-1966); Kenya versus the Somali Republic (1963-1967); the Rann of Cutch incident between India and Pakistan (1967); the so-called Soccer War between El Salvador and Honduras (1969); Guyana and Surinam (1969); El Salvador and Honduras (1970); the Soviet Union and China (1972); India and Pakistan over Kashmir (1972); the second phase of the Cod War between Iceland and Britain (1972-1973); South Vietnam and China over the Paracel Islands (1974); Iran and Iraq (1974); the third phase of the Cod War (1975); Thailand and Cambodia (1975); Morocco and Algeria over former Spanish Sahara (1975); and India and Pakistan over Kashmir (1975).

Other direct interventions in civil wars occurred: Egypt and Saudi Arabia in Yemen (beginning in 1962); Syria in Jordan, when the Jordanian government fought to subdue the local Palestinian guerrillas (1970); intervention by South Yemen, on the one hand, and Iran and Jordan, on the other, in the Shofar rebellion in Oman; and the seizure of ex-Portuguese Timor by Indonesian forces (1975).

The United States was involved in the following minor incidents: the North Korean capture of the U.S. intelligence ship *Pueblo* (1968); North Korea's shooting down of a U.S. reconnaissance aircraft over the Sea of Japan (1969); and the recapture by American forces of the *Mayaguez* and its crew, which had been seized by Cambodia (1975). Military forces are, of course, also used to threaten other countries. The period from 1964 to 1975 was studded with military threats. Some were dramatic, such as the military alert on which American forces were placed during the Yom Kippur War in order to deter the Soviet Union from intervening militarily. Many were minor, such as when Spain, in February 1975, dispatched gunboats to its North African enclaves of Ceuta and Melilla in response to the assertion of territorial claims by Morocco.

Another body of evidence worth examining is the range of defense efforts maintained by states during the priod. While domestic concerns may be an important—and in some instances the dominant—factor in determining the scale of these costly efforts, few will dispute that their chief purpose was to provide for international deterrence and defense, if not aggressive action.

Expressed in constant dollars (current 1973 prices in the United States)[3] world military expenditures rose from $222 billion to $286 billion, or about 28 percent, from 1965 to 1974. Total outlays of the NATO countries, the Warsaw Pact countries and the less-developed countries (LDCs) increased by 23 percent, 29 percent and 100 percent, respectively. Of course, these aggregate data conceal large individual differences between states, but it is precisely the group data that interest us here. When military expenditures are expressed as a proportion of GNP, total world outlays decreased from 6.7 percent to 5.7 percent; that is, by around 15 percent over the period. Expenditures by the European NATO countries fell by more than 18 percent in these terms, and those by the United States and Canada decreased by 20 percent while those of the LDCs as a group mounted by 22 percent. (Owing to statistical difficulties, no comparable figures were computed for the

[3]The data that follow were taken from U.S. Arms Control and Disarmament Agency, *World Military Expenditures and Arms Transfers 1969–1974* (Washington: GPO, 1975). The reader should be warned that, because of various conceptual and statistical problems, these comparative data do not represent a precise picture of reality, but they probably do reflect gross changes in the real world. (The difficulties are detailed in *World Military Expenditures. . .*, pp. 6–11.)

states of the Warsaw Pact, but the figures do suggest that the world decline in percentages of GNP devoted to defense is accounted for by the reduced expenditures of the NATO nations.

We are now ready to assess, to the extent that it can be done, recent scholarly theses on the contemporary utility of force in the light of actual state behavior. . . .

VI

The frequency of armed conflict in recent years, the rise in global military expenditures and manpower, and the expansion of the international trade in arms does not appear prima facie to support any thesis asserting a secular diminution in the use of force or in the expected utility of military capabilities. If there is a pronounced trend, it expresses a remarkable international shift. Military conflicts have occurred mostly in the Third World, mainly between Third World countries, and this shift is paralleled by the fact that the proportion of world military spending, manpower and weapons imports outside the developed capitalist states has sharply increased.

All this is incontrovertible. Nevertheless, it is arguable that most government behavior in these respects is lagging behind changes in underlying realities. Whether it is or is not we cannot know. But we can subject to critical analysis the components of the theses asserting a decline in the utility of force. To what extent is it true or plausible that the costs of employing force have been rising relative to the gains that may be expected from its use?

The evidence concerning the range and imputed value of expected gains is naturally very poor because motivations are involved. It does seem, though, that the notion of economic gain as a justification for the aggressive use of force is far less in evidence, at least superficially, than it was for millennia prior to World War II. . .

It would nevertheless be imprudent to disregard or unduly belittle economic motives that might fuel military conflict in the future. Severe shortages of food and raw materials, combined with the attempt of states controlling scarce supplies to exploit such control for economic and political purposes, may well serve to preserve some potential—even if a lesser one relative to other issues—for dangerous conflict. Current moves to extend territorial control over the sea are indicative of this prospect.

The use of force to seize or control territory for reasons of military security, also a traditionally important motive, likewise seems to have lost attraction. Yet is has not disappeared altogether. The 1968 Israeli conquest (or at any rate, retention) of the Sinai as a glacis vis-à-vis Egypt and (in 1973) of the Golan Heights, vis-à-vis Syria, come to mind. Since it is doubtful that the Soviet divisions now stationed in Czechoslovakia are required to assure Soviet domination over that country, it is conceivable that their deployment on the Czech-German boundary was an objective of the Soviet invasion from the beginning. But perhaps it was a mere afterthought. Finally, while the United States and the Soviet Union, rivals in the exercise of worldwide naval power, secure overseas bases and support facilities by diplomacy and contract, or by the invitation or consent of allies, it is possible that their activities to support friendly countries and to help overthrow hostile regimes, at times by direct intervention, has had the retention of such facilities, or their denial to the rival power, as a significant objective.

However, the fading importance of some objectives does not mean that there are not other goals that may justify the use of military force. Several other traditional objectives of this kind have lost little, if any, of their urgency or legitimacy, either internationally or domestically. Deterrence of, and defense against, attacks on political or territorial integrity as well as the rescue of citizens facing organized violence abroad fall into this category. Nor is there any lack of grounds on which to justify force for the purpose of revising the status quo. Aside from the Arab-Israeli conflict, which is in some ways unique, the recent military conflicts listed above suggest the contempoary importance of three major issues capable of generating the decision to go to war. One involves disputes over established boundaries that are regarded unjust by one side or the other. A second, sometimes overlapping with the first, is the protection or liberation of ethnically related peoples; that is, ethnic unification or national reunification. The third issue, apparently the one most productive of international conflict in the world today, is intervention in civil strife, either to support or help combat incumbent regimes. The precise objective or combination of objectives no doubt varies from case to case, but ideological commitments and the desire to maintain or extend spheres of influence, or reduce the interest of a rival power, evidently play an important part. Anyhow, contemporary governments do not seem to lack incentives to consider force or to be militarily prepared for executing that option.

Turning to the cost side, the deterrent effect of the nuclear balance of terror has figured as a major reason for speculations about the declining utility of military force. The risk of a nuclear war that would destroy both sides, it is argued, keeps each side from using lesser military force against the other. So long as this balance of terror prevails, the aggressive use of military force is undoubtedly curbed. But if deterrent power is needed for this purpose, that power has extremely high utility as an insurance of self-protection. Moreover, because strategic nuclear reprisal against lesser military attacks, including attacks against allies, is suicidal under these conditions, and because its threat therefore has low credibility, the maintenance of adequate conventional forces for defense also has a great deal of utility. The effective balance of both types of forces accounts for the military stability in Europe in recent decades—provided, of course, that deterrence was needed to stifle the emergence of aggressive designs. The claim that nuclear technology has engendered a decline in the utility of military force can only refer to one thing: namely, fear that a serious conflict might increase the risk of escalation to the strategic nuclear level has restrained adventurism. This consequence, however, will endure only so long as the nuclear balance of terror and that of associated defense capabilities remain solid. The future is by no means certain in this regard. New technological choices or an unreciprocated decay of the will to retaliate or to provide sufficient capabilities for deterrence and defense could upset this balance.

States without nuclear weapons are apparently little, if at all, restrained in their behavior toward states possessing nuclear arms. (The behavior of North Vietnam and North Korea toward the United States is illustrative.) This is so because a powerful moral stigma has become attached to the use of nuclear weapons, especially against a non-nuclear opponent. The magnitude of the expected moral and political costs constrains their use and reduces their utility in these relationships. The fact that states possessing nuclear weapons are thus inhibited from bringing their most effective military technology into play against the vast majority of countries is greatly to the advantage of the latter. It tends to increase the utility of *their* military forces against the nuclear superpowers, thereby making the distribution of military deterrence and defensive power less unequal than it would otherwise be. . .

Heightened awareness of war's destructiveness, claimed to have greatly increased in recent decades, should lead to greater reluctance to use military power. Indeed, numerous surveys in highly developed countries provide evidence that confirms this awareness of the costs of using military force. The historical experience of World Wars I and II has apparently lost little impact in Europe and Japan. Such sensitivity is also a function of the development of higher education and communications systems in these societies. Sophisticated news media, in particular television, have reinforced this awareness by the rich display of violence and destruction in more recent conflicts (e.g., Vietnam), and more widespread education has enabled more and more people to appreciate the effects of nuclear war. Freedom of speech and press in these democratic countries facilitates the diffusion of this sensitivity to the physical and psychic costs of warfare, and democratic constitutions permit the awareness to become politically influential.

However, there is far less evidence that this sensitivity is equally developed in other parts of the world, specifically in the communist societies and the LDCs. Of course, restricted access to opinions and attitudes in these countries obstructs the assembly of relevant evidence one way or the other. Such evidence is sparse. But it would not be surprising if this awareness were more thinly spread in those societies where some of the conditions that seem to account for its development in the capitalist-democratic nations are absent or nearly so: namely, a strong sensitivity to the destructiveness of war, broad-based higher education, a huge volume of news production and dissemination under conditions of freedom of speech and press, and lively media competition. . . .

The frequency of recent armed conflict in the Third World does not encourage the view that the new norm has attracted more than a shallow adherence. This is not surprising. After all, the prohibition of aggressive warfare in the UN Charter was a Western, particularly an American, idea, and it was lodged in the charter at a time when relatively few Third World states were present—at a time when decolonization had only begun. Given their historical experience, countries in the Third World are primarily anxious about aggression by great powers.

Thus, it is not difficult to be skeptical about the profound systemic transformations that, as a number of writers have proposed, governments will increasingly be compelled to adapt to, and that tend to make war less feasible and relevant. We have already dealt with the consequences believed (with inadequate justification) to stem from the evolution of nuclear arms. The thesis that contemporary societies are primarily preoccupied with solving domestic political, economic and social problems seems to be true by and large. How much of a systemic change this sense of priorities represents is problematic. Moreover, the thesis often associated with this finding—that the forementioned preoccupation has generally caused societies to turn "inward"—is implausible. The economies of the highly developed capitalist countries are far too dependent on one another to encourage this sort of isolationism, and the vast majority of the LDCs seek the solution of their economic problems predominantly through the establishment of a new world economic order. While these are not problems that commend the use of military force as a solution, the historical record does not suggest that other pressing issues cannot come to dominate the agenda and the international behavior of states. In the past, certainly, societies have not rarely been content to devote themselves for considerable periods of time primarily to domestic problems, only to be seized by, or have foreced on them, international issues that claimed priority. There are a number of countries whose struc-

ture of priorities is largely shaped by international considerations that do not rule out the use of force. . . .

One can only conclude, unhappily and disappointingly, that the global picture is far from clear so far as the utility of military force is concerned. The components of this picture do not encourage the prediction that the use and usefulness of military force are definitely on the decline. What look like considerable changes in parameters are too ambiguous and have been with us for too short a time to permit confident answers to the questions we have raised. The changes on the cost side (actual, probable, possible?) certainly do not establish the disutility of force, and they could not do so even if we accepted the changes as substantial and if their impact were uniform throughout the world. Rational actors, to be sure, will not resort to force unless they expect gains to exceed costs. But aside from the circumstance that deviations from rationality are not unknown among political leaders, there is a powerful subjective element and a great deal of unavoidable guesswork in estimates of costs and gains. All we can argue is this: if cost-increasing factors persist and become less unevenly distributed, then war will become a less likely choice of action statistically speaking. This would be an important change, but such a downgrading effect would be acting only marginally on a historically high level of readiness to consider military options when vital, or seemingly vital, values are at stake. Even if the costs of using force rose substantially, rational actors would be willing to meet them when expected gains have exceeding appeal. The recent behavior of governments in regard to military conflict, both engaging in it and preparing for it, is in line with this judgment.

The conclusion I arrived at more than ten years ago did maintain that the utility of military power was on the decline, but several qualifications were attached. Among them, I noted the uneven global distribution of the relevant changes in parameters. Yet I did not then perceive their importance nearly so much as I do at this time, and I regard my overall assessment now to justify less optimism than I expressed then. The world would seem to contain plenty of state actors for whom the avoidance of violence, including international violence, is not the supreme good; and, as if in recognition of this fact, there are even more actors who still find the aura of military power attractive, if only for reasons of security. I now expect international military conflict and direct foreign intervention in civil wars to continue at a high level, and I expect, too, that the superpowers will have diminishing military influence in the Third World. Whether or not the military relationship between the Soviet Union and the United States, both on the strategic level and in Europe, will stay calm and stable depends on the ability of each to maintain solid deterrence. Conflicts in the Third World are likely to remain localized so long as this condition obtains.

It seems to me also interesting that the appreciably more optimistic analyses and predictions that have been offered in more recent years are virtually all the product of scholarship in those societies wherein the new distaste for the use of force is most highly developed. This suggests the possibility that these comforting interpretations suffer from being a bit culture-bound, unless one takes the patronizing view—which seems to be congenial in the West—that revolutionary, systemic transformations have been first generated in the West, that the rest of the world is only lagging behind, and that it is therefore only a matter of time before it catches up.

IX

Crisis and Crisis Management

One of the most dangerous moments in international relations is the point at which mutually exclusive aims develop between two or more states. There has been no crisis for Americans in recent years comparable to the Cuban Missile crisis of 1962 although the Arab-Israeli War of 1973 threatened for a time to involve the United States and the Soviet Union in a showdown. Consequently, most of us have no recent personal experience with the dreadful and obsessive atmosphere in which such crises unfold. Nevertheless, the world has experienced so many wars and crises in the twentieth century that the subject deserves serious study.

While the onset of an international crisis or threat of war usually occurs in a context of long-standing rivalry and hostility between two states, it nevertheless acquires a life of its own in which leaders appear chained to the great wheel of events, seemingly helpless to arrest the fatal movement toward disaster. Man is never more at the mercy of his emotions and of the remorseless logic of the nation-state system than at the moment when his government has determined that there is no alternative but war or the threat of war as a means of securing a particular end. Once the threat of war is involved the potential exists for the situation to escape from the control of statesmen who are then swept into a war which they either did not want or hoped the enemy would find some way to avoid. While war should, in the classic phrase of von Clauswitz, represent the continuation of politics by other means, it all too often represents the abandonment of politics as a process of rational calculation in favor of an emotional release from the strain and tension of the situation.

Because of the price that man has paid for the folly of war, a great deal of scholarly attention has been focused on the dynamics of an international crisis. While certain leaders and nations have determined upon war as the only means of attaining their ends, there is a great deal of evidence that crises take on a life of their own and that, in the process, governments are heavily influenced by non-rational factors. To begin with, crises are often the outcome of a stimulus-response pattern in which the words and actions of one side are perceived and interpreted as hostile and threatening by the other. This, in turn, stimulates counter-expressions of hostility, touching off a vicious cycle of constantly escalating actions and emotions. A constant, unrelenting crisis situation such as that which characterizes the Arab-Israeli conflict fosters attitudes of fear and hostility that are almost impossible to overcome. Egyptian President Sadat's November visit to Jerusalem was a major effort to cut through the accumulated hostilities of more than thirty years.

Secondly, as stress increases in a crisis situation, the decision maker's perceptions of the factors that are involved change also. In his study of the coming of World War I, Holsti observes that "In a crisis situation, decision-makers will tend to perceive their own range of alternatives [and that of their allies] to be more restricted than those of their adversaries; that is, they will perceive their own decision making to be characterized by necessity and closed options, whereas those of the adversary are characterized by open choices."[1]

As the crisis mounts there seems less and less time available to examine options and arrest the race to war. As a result, decision makers limit the range of information available to them and foreclose alternatives more quickly than necessary. In desperation, they may also overlook or downgrade questions of relative capabilities of their own countries vis-à-vis others with whom there is conflict. Members of the decision-making groups tend to abandon their individual judgments and to coalesce around the group judgment. Hostility and threat are perceived to be greater than they really are. The sense of "injury" done to one by the adversary grows apace, as does the degree to which one feels one's honor and prestige to be at stake. "Finally,

Ole R. Holsti "Perceptions of time, perceptions of alternatives, and patterns of communications as factors in crisis decision-making." PEACE RESEARCH SOCIETY PAPERS (3) pp. 79–120.

stress may cause an actor to misperceive the actions of another, thus giving him an inaccurate definition of the situation."[2] Thus even when the adversary endeavors to make reassuring signals, they are perceived as threats or dissimulation.

There is also the evidence that a group such as the nation may, through its leaders, be willing to take greater risks than would be true of individuals. A collectivity cannot calculate the consequences of its action in quite the same direct and personal way that we, as individuals, calculate the likely consequences of our actions. Amidst all this, the decision maker may feel himself under pressure from the public and press, or from his rivals for power. As a result, we can see that there is really no limit to the failure or breakdown that is capable of afflicting the processes of rationality in a crisis situation.

Because of their suicidal potential, nuclear weapons seem to have fostered a greater concern to avoid war in the thinking and policy decisions of Soviet and American statesmen. This is really what is meant by the term "crisis management." Beginning with the Korean War (1950-1953), both the American side and the Chinese side acted in ways designed to limit the war to the Korean peninsula. Subsequently, both the Soviet and the American sides have sought to exploit the coercive possibilities of their position while consciously avoiding actions which might escalate into a nuclear war.

The differential consequences that would ensue from a nuclear war as opposed to a conventional war have served as a "fire break," prompting both superpowers from reaching the point in a crisis at which one or the other might feel compelled to resort to nuclear weapons. Under conditions of crisis, the most powerful signal that one superpower can send to the other is the warning that a resort to nuclear weapons is being contemplated. The holocaust that would ensue upon any use of nuclear weapons constitutes a threshold in the calculations of the two superpowers between a crisis outcome that would be tolerable and one that would be intolerable.

There are, as Professor Amos Perlmutter points out in the selection in this chapter, two different types of crisis management situations:

(1) an adversary type of crisis management such as comes into play when the United States confronts the Soviet Union or, as was the case in the 1950s and 1960s, the People's Republic of China; and

(2) a crisis-management situation such as confronts the United States in the Middle East where it has endeavoured to manage and mediate the Arab-Israeli conflicts.

As Perlmutter observes, the practice of crisis management developed principally in crises affecting the power relationship in the central nuclear

[2]McGown, Patrick J. and Howard B. Shapiro. THE COMPARATIVE STUDY OF FOREIGN POLICY: A SURVEY OF SCIENTIFIC FINDINGS. Vol. 4 (Beverly Hills: Sage Publications, 1973) p. 59.

balance; that is, between the United States and the Soviet Union. Crisis management and the avoidance of war have been possible because both sides share a single overwhelming preoccupation—to avoid nuclear war and to control the chances of a confrontation that might escalate into nuclear war. Crisis management between the U.S. and the communist side is characterized by the sending of signals and the application of a range of coercive measures of a military, political, and psychological nature designed to induce the other side to yield or abandon some position (e.g., Berlin). Such a crisis is not simulated; it is quite real. But it is undertaken with a conscious intent to control its implementation so as to escape the fatal consequences to which showdowns in the past have all too often led. Without abandoning the attempt to employ coercive tactics in the pursuit of their objectives and to take advantage of the adversary's weak points, the two superpowers have sought to do so while consciously intending to avoid a war. This is a dangerous game, aptly entitled "brinksmanship" by John Foster Dulles, the American Secretary of State who seemed to view it as his personal contribution to the art of statecraft—going to the brink of war without actually falling into the chasm.

In the wake of their experience in the 1961 Berlin Crisis and the 1962 Cuban Missile Crisis, both superpowers have gone a step further and signed an agreement by which each solemnly promises to refrain from any action that might result in a confrontation involving the danger of war. Still, in the October 1973 Middle East war, in Angola, and in the Horn of Africa the exigencies of their power rivalry have exerted a fatal attraction, especially upon the Soviet Union, to score points at the other's expense, even at the risk of some degree of confrontation.

It cannot be assumed that, in order to behave rationally in crisis situations, each side will recognize limits to the gains that are to be made, or that each side acts in awareness of the values and rules on which rationality is based. There is nothing that compels or guarantees governments to adhere to rational behavior in a crisis involving the nuclear powers. For example, the point is made that tacit negotiations are possible between opponents in the sense that both sides recognize specific limits and constraints upon their conduct. But there is no way that these limitations are known until one or the other side chooses to make them known by refraining from certain actions. Such restraint may have to do with considerations outside the actual theater of conflict—such as global political considerations—but these considerations may just as easily compel a state to reject the logic of a local setback and escalate the crisis into an all-out confrontation.

The other form of crisis management, that which Amos Perlmutter's article treats, involves the attempt by a third party—in this case, Henry Kissinger—to manage, control, end, and mediate a conflict between two other parties. There have always been mediators—third parties who try to bridge the gap between two parties to a conflict. But crisis management goes well beyond mediation to include the employment of threats and coercion, conditioning of the disputants to respond to one's perception of a satisfactory solution to the conflict, and by stretching the adversaries to the limit so that they are willing to accept his views of what each side can and should surrender. Crisis management of this type may involve the tacit or active participation of other parties.

23   Instruments and Techniques of Crisis Management

Coral Bell

The author is Professor of International Relations at the University of Sussex.

Every crisis is an exceedingly complex set of interactions, a confluence of decisions some of whose sources are very difficult to trace. Each of the historical episodes which I intend to dispose of in a paragraph or two . . . would warrant examination at book-length, and some of them, for instance Cuba '62 and Suez '56, have already been the subject of several such studies. Here I shall be looking at them in shorthand outlines, so to speak, simply as illustrations of particular modes of handling crises which seem to me to have grown up in the postwar period. There are considerable similarities . . . between the contemporary conventions and those of earlier periods of crisis management, but these similarities have not often been recognized by the decision-makers or even the academic analysts of the process. Perhaps every generation feels obliged to re-invent its world, and to assume that its conventions are new.

The distinction between instruments on the one hand and techniques on the other in crisis management is not altogether easy to sustain, but I shall take the former word to indicate *what* is used, and the second *how* it is used. On this distinction, the basic instru-

ment of crisis management is what I shall call the signal, and the techniques are mostly ways of using signals. By signal I mean a threat or offer communicated to the other party or parties to the crisis.

Such signals are not necessarily verbal messages. Some of the sharpest and most effective of them are movements of military resources of various sorts. For instance, when the Russians appointed the second-in-command to their most noted rocket expert as Commander-in-Chief of their Far Eastern military district at a time of sharp border clashes between themselves and China, the appointment was a more brusque signal about the possible nature of future hostilities there than words would have been.[1] Similarly, the Russian sending of Victor Louis, a "journalist" who does ill-defined diplomatic odd jobs for the Russian government, to Taiwan at a time when the Chinese were hinting at the possibility of a settlement with America, was probably a signal that the island might have another protector than the Seventh Fleet. This obviously is the sort of thing that it would be politically difficult to say in words, until the hinted shift of a relationship was an accomplished fact. The hint may prevent the actuality being necessary. Border hostilities themselves are a kind of signal: it is hard to make sense of Russian incursions over the Sinkiang border save as a

From The Conventions of Crisis *by Coral Bell, published by Oxford University Press under the auspices of the Royal Institute of International Affairs,@RUA 1971. Reprinted by permission of the publisher. [Some footnotes have been omitted.]*

[1]General Tobulko, appointed in July 1969.

signal to the Chinese of the vulnerability of their nuclear installations there. In fact, in the obscure border crises of March—October 1969 between China and Russia, one might interpret the whole of Russian policy as an exercise in crisis management by signal, i.e. by communicated threat. The means of communication were most elaborate and varied, including a Russian letter to Communist parties outside the Communist world, apparently constructed to be interpreted as a bid for support in the case of a Russian strike at China.

Signalling is as essential to crisis management as to a busy airport. But there is a good deal more scope for ambiguity in signalling in the diplomatic field than in that of transport. An ambiguous signal when driving may be a prelude to disaster, but in diplomacy ambiguity in signalling may be creative.

A good instance of this is what came to be known as the "Trollope ploy" in the Cuban missile crisis. The "Trollope ploy" has been defined as "the acceptance of an offer that has not been made, in order to induce the adversary to accept the acceptance." The name (apparently conferred by Robert Kennedy) derives from those many Victorian heroines in the novels of Anthony Trollope who interpret a squeeze of the hand on the hero's part as a proposal of marriage, and who are successful in making this interpretation stick. In the Cuban case the ambiguity of communication was Mr. Khrushchev's: he sent two letters, one inplying a hard line about the American blockade, the other a mild and even yielding one. To deepen the confusion, it was not clear whether the "hawklike" letter (which was received second) had been written before or after the "dovelike" one. The American policy decision (the Trollope ploy) was to treat the "dovelike" letter as the true communication, more or less ignoring the

other (though it was received second, was probably written second, and might normally have been interpreted as the Russians, final position). It was this creative use of ambiguity which enabled the settlement to be reached.[2]

It may be objected that this was an exceptional case, and that ambiguity is more usually a dangerous and potentially disastrous element in crisis signalling. Many eminent practitioners in the field have implied as much. Mr. Dulles, for instance, maintained and perhaps believed that the Korean war had been precipitated by a misleading or ambiguous signal by Dean Acheson when he was Secretary of State: Acheson's definition of the US defense perimeter in Asia as running down the island chain from Japan through Okinawa to the Philippines. This, according to the Republican interpretation, was assumed in Moscow to mean that South Korea would not be defended by US troops, and so led to the Russian miscalculation of allowing the North Koreans to initiate their take-over bid for South Korea. It was, of course, a very partisan version of the events which produced the Korean War, but short of the production of the North Korean equivalent of Cabinet minutes for the period concerned, there is no way of actually disproving it. Mr. Dulles, however, was himself uncommonly proud of a diplomatic success which must be held to have been gained largely by a conscious or unconscious use of ambiguity in diplomatic signalling. This was during the Quemoy-Matsu crisis of 1958, the management of which he sometimes described as his finest achievement. The ambiguity resided in the difference between the line apparently signalled by President Eisenhower's speeches during this crisis (mild, conciliatory, and seemingly ready to aban-

[2]See Robert Kennedy, *Thirteen Days* (New York: W. W. Norton & Co., Inc., 1969).

don the islands to the Chinese Communists) and the line signalled by Mr. Dulles during the same period (tough, intransigent, and ready to back the Chinese Nationalists' determination to retain the islands by all means including atomic weapons). These conflicting signals were differentially received by the adversary alliance, China and the Soviet Union, which still at this time functioned as such, even though the Lebanon-Jordan crisis a few weeks earlier had made a large crack in it. The Russians "selected" the tougher American signals, as transmitted by Mr. Dulles as the true definition of the American posture. The Chinese "selected" the milder line, as transmitted by the President, since it was more compatible with their overall view of the balance of forces in the world, and the Maoist propositions that the "East Wind was prevailing over the West Wind" and that "all imperialists are paper tigers." Since it was the Russians who actually controlled the weaponry, their view of the situation prevailed, and the Chinese had to retreat to the ritualized expression of the conflict by shelling Quemoy and Matsu on alternate days. The Americans not only obtained their optimum objectives in the crisis area (retaining the islands without having to fight for them) but a very large bonus indeed in the fact that the Sino-Soviet alliance never recovered from this difference of interpretation. Within a year the partners had gone their separate ways: Mr. Khrushchev symbolically on his journey to meet Eisenhower at Camp David, and the Chinese along the road to independent nuclear status. So Mr. Dulles had some reason to count this among his prime successes, though I do not know that he ever conceded that ambiguity was among his techniques. . . .

There are, however, more straightforward instruments that must seem entitled to claim a role in crisis management: law,

economic pressures, intermediaries, arbitration and conciliation procedures, international institutions. One would not deny that all these are potentially useful, yet examining the crises of the postwar period one would not say that they have been very conspicuously used and successful. Concepts of what is internationally legal no doubt influence the choices made by decision-makers in crisis situations, but on the evidence the influences have been rather marginal. Economic pressures have been used: for instance, the threat of oil sanctions in the Suez crisis was part of the combination of factors which modified British policy. But when used alone, as in the Rhodesia case, they do not seem decisive. Intermediaries of various sorts have had their successes (and rather more often their failures). The ability of the UN to provide inspection teams, peace-keeping forces, truce commissions, and the like has been an essential element in the success of what may be called the "tidying-up" phase of many a crisis. Yet when the UN role is examined more closely in particular crisis situations, it will be seen very often to consist of conferring legitimacy on crisis management by the great powers, and the same is true of the roles of other organizations such as NATO, or the OAS.

Most importantly, we must look at the question of the choice of particular kinds of weapons systems, and military structures, as an influence on crisis management. This is a very large subject, and full of uncertainties. Theoretically, the choice of weapons systems ought to be one of the most useful modes of controlling crises, but the "lead time" for modern weapons systems is five to ten years, or even longer in some categories, and predicting what the crises of ten years hence are going to look like, and what forces-in-being will be most useful for reducing their dangers is thus a somewhat difficult project.

One can of course point to the obvious desirability of built-in devices against the unauthorized or accidental tripping of retaliation systems in times of crisis, such as the "permissive action" link, the "fail-safe" system, and various "two keys" sets of arrangements. Luckily this is a field in which the interests of the two dominant powers are so nearly identical that a surprising amount of information has been deliberately passed. President Kennedy was the decision-maker on this. Just after his inauguration there was a near-disaster of a nuclear kind, when a bomber on a training flight with two 24—megaton bombs crashed in North Carolina. The bombs had six interlocking safety devices, but on one of them five of these devices had been triggered by the crash, so that only one switch prevented a detonation. This incident, and the information that there had been about sixty near-accidents since the end of the Second World War, including the launching of two actual missiles with nuclear warheads, alarmed Kennedy into the consciousness that it was desirable not only that the US should improve its accident-proofing, but that the Russians should have equally good techniques in this field, and should know what the American systems were. He therefore authorized a Pentagon man, John McNaughton, to provide a good deal of information on these devices at an Arms Control symposium in December 1962, and via US scientists to Russian scientists at a Pugwash conference.[3] The Russians are now known to have developed similar accident-proofing devices. One hopes that in due course information of these techniques also reached the Chinese, and has been used.

Even this kind of precaution is not without its ambivalences. Better accident-proofing means that missiles are more readily put on "full alert" and this has some uncertain side effects on crisis decision making. . . .

Having said so much about these instruments and techniques, we have now to look a little at how they have worked out in some of the crises of the postwar period, both adversary and intramural. . . .

Let us start by considering the Suez crisis, because it lay more or less on the border between the two categories, adversary and intramural, and to my mind shows that the management of a crisis may determine its very nature.[4] Oddly enough, the outcome in this case seems to have depended partly on the insistence of some members of the State Department on playing up, in fact exaggerating, its alleged dangers as a potential adversary crisis. Robert Murphy, who was by no means sympathetic to this point of view, quotes some of his colleagues as wailing that they might be "burned to a crisp,"[5] meaning presumably that they took seriously the heavy Soviet hints of military action (rockets) on behalf of the Egyptians. The Foreign Office entirely discounted this threat, and was, I think, right to do so. What we know of the weakness of Soviet missile forces even six years later, in 1962, plus the caution with which the Soviet Union has always avoided any military involvement with the Arabs in their encounters with Israel (other of course than the supply of arms and instructors) inclines one to feel even more convinced now than at the

---

[4]Rather on the analogy of the infant bee, which, if fed on royal jelly, will become a queen bee, but if sustained on more prosaic stuff will become a worker.

[5]*Diplomat among Warriors* (Garden City, N.Y.: Doubleday & Co., Inc., 1964), p. 476.

---

[3]This incident has not, as far as I know, been officially acknowledged but there was some leakage to the press about it, see *Newsweek*, 5 May 1969.

time that there was never any real possibility of a military initiative by Russia in reaction to the British and French collusion with Israel. Nevertheless the Russian threat, empty though it was, provided a considerable part of the rationale for the arm-twisting American technique of managing this episode as an intramural crisis of the Anglo-American alliance. (The French simply acquiesced, somewhat resentfully, in the British decisions. It was also, of course, an intramural crisis of the American-Israeli tacit alliance, managed by similar methods though separate measures.) In the British case, the effective arm-twisting was undoubtedly economic: the threat of oil sanctions and the necessity of stopping the run on the pound.[6] Britain is peculiarly vulnerable to this kind of technique, and so in a slightly different way is Israel. But the number of other countries of which this is true is surprisingly small, and on the whole economic sanctions have shown themselves relatively ineffective as a mode of management of either adversary or intramural crisis, a point which later became painfully obvious to British policy-makers in connection with Rhodesia.

I said that this was successfully managed as an intramural crisis of the Anglo-American alliance, and I think in terms of my three criteria for success this was fairly clearly the case, as far as Britain was concerned, though one might put up the contrary argument as far as the Franco-American alliance was concerned. At least in the British case, the alliance was no less effective from 1957 than before it: in many ways closer than ever, in fact, on matters

such as nuclear weapons.[7] The British were not permanently shaken in their attachment to the alliance: the credibility or credit of the US as an ally was not diminished. But one might, as I said, give different answers on all these criteria with regard to France, and I think one must concede that the Anglo-American situation is rather exceptional among alliances in that the sense of an overriding common interest is or has been so strong as to sustain, without undue fraying, some exceedingly sharp clashes of specific interests in particular areas. One cannot generalize from this particular alliance-relationship to others: the French attitude is nearer the norm. . . .

Every crisis raises the question of whether there is any function for an intermediary, and who will be the one most likely to be useful. And in every case many voices will suggest that it should be the UN, probably the Secretary-General. This is, so to speak, a convenient shelf onto which any awkward diplomatic package tends to be shoved. But it is by no means true that every crisis benefits by the services of an intermediary, or that the Secretary-General or any other official of the UN is necessarily the right intermediary if one is required. And it is furthermore always necessary to offset the real costs to the intermediary institution (in terms of its later usefulness) against the advantages of its use in the particular crisis concerned. Counting up all the costs to the UN of its intermediary role in [the Congo] case (including Hammarskjold's death, and all that stemmed from it), I am not entirely sure that the sum comes out positive.

There is one mode of adversary crisis which offers no scope for being turned into

[6]For an examination specifically of the Anglo-American relationship in the Suez crisis see Richard E. Neustadt, *Alliance Politics* (New York: Columbia University Press, 1970).

[7]This question is treated in more detail in the author's *The Debatable Alliance* (London: Oxford University Press, 1964).

an intramural crisis (though it may have intramural repercussions on either or both sides) and that is the direct head-on collision of interests between two dominant powers: America and Russia, America and China, China and Russia. I shall take the Cuban '62 crisis as the model for the first of these. There is indeed a prevalent tendency to take it as a model for all crises, largely I think because it had such an attractive cast of characters. But this tendency should be resisted, because Cuba as a model for crises generally is misleading in the same way as a child's model of a farm is misleading for farms generally: it is neater, brighter, more *determinate* than life. Most crises tend to have a more sprawling, formless, unsatisfactory, repetitive shape.

However, if the crisis itself is not a universally applicable model, the behavior of the chief decision-maker and his advisers on the Western side still seems to me to be so, informed by great moral and intellectual sensitivity, perception, imagination, and courage. The mode of resolution of the adversary crisis is so well known that there seems no need for further analysis. The factors in the American success were, first, local superiority in conventional forces (in this case, naval) which meant that the adversary decision-maker, if he wanted to raise his stakes, had to raise them to the level of nuclear encounter; secondly, the overall strategic superiority, which in fact inhibited him from doing that; and third, the skill and judgment with which the President and his advisers built bridges behind the adversary to facilitate his retreat.

There are some aspects of the crisis which are less well understood, and may therefore warrant more examination. It was, one might say, the first crisis of the age of surveillance. That is to say, the form that the

crisis took, and the moment of its precipitation, were determined by intelligence gathering in the modern manner, i.e. the discovery of the missile sites by U-2 overflights. The instrument of surveillance has since become the satellite-mounted television camera rather than the U-2, and this is a more extreme form of a growing class distinction between America and Russia on the one hand, and their respective allies on the other. The US, and the USSR, with a vastly greater knowledge of the technology in this field (one of the fringe benefits from the space race), must increasingly be confronted by the problem of how much of the information so gathered to communicate to allies, and at what stage, and how to convince them that the information is reliable, means what it is taken to mean, and warrants the action proposed. In such episodes there must be tension between on the one hand the desire to have military plans completed before disclosure, even to allied decision-makers under pledges of secrecy, and on the other hand the necessity of carrying those allies and public opinion with the chief decision-maker. . . . Clearly President Kennedy took great trouble in this instance, by the dispatch of Dean Acheson and others to Europe, to ensure that the information turned up by the CIA carried suitable diplomatic weight. But it can hardly be said that he consulted his NATO allies in the crisis management (though one could regard the informal role of the British Ambassador in the policy-making process as akin to such consultation with Britain, the Ambassador acting as a proxy for the Prime Minister, if not the government, by a process of telephone communication). One can argue that a greater appearance of consultation would have prevented such intramural repercussions from the crisis as did develop within

NATO. But I would be inclined to make the contrary argument. When a crisis blows up so fast, the other members of the alliance are somewhat in the situation of passengers in a car going into a skid: it is not necessarily advantageous for them to have time to develop lines of advice to the chief decision-maker. Nor is it true that a known or assumed process of crisis decision-sharing on an allied basis would necessarily conduce to the safer management of crises. The crucial element is the expectations of the adversary decision-makers, and their ability to predict reactions correctly. Anything which complicates this calculation for them (such as having to allow for the influence of allies) probably increases the risk of error, and thus the chance of disaster. In the Cuban case this risk was largely removed by the known existence of an arbitrary time limit for decision, imposed by the length of time known to be necessary for the completion of the missile installations. Since the time span was very short, the prospect of real consultation, and real allied influence on the Washington decision-making, was ruled out *and was known to the Russians to be ruled out*. So their calculations had to encompass only American attitudes and, luckily, they got the answer right.

Nothing fails like failure, as the saying goes, and so the intramural (and perhaps domestic) repercussions of the Cuban crisis were much greater on the Soviet side of the balance than on the American side. The most important of these repercussions were with China rather than Cuba—Dr. Castro was indignant enough, but was mollified by lavish financial aid. For China, however, Mr. Khrushchev's management of the crisis provided reasonably substantial grounds for Chinese accusations of both "adventurism" (for putting the missiles in) and "capitulationism" (for taking them out). All in all, it was certainly the largest and most effective item in the Chinese case against general Russian strategy in the long-drawn-out struggle of "peaceful coexistence" with the capitalist world.

The recurrent Berlin crises offer a clear contrast to Cuba in respect of the possibilities of consultation, and the development of some kind of allied crisis management, even though with an overriding vote for the United States. The primary reason for this distinction is the difference in military responsibilities and potentialities in the two areas. In the Caribbean the United States neither wants nor expects military help from its European allies, and the whole tenor of American foreign policy tradition since the Monroe Doctrine has been to look with suspicion and resentment on any European claim for a voice or influence in the Latin American area. Of all the areas of potential crisis, it is perhaps the one in which allied management or serious consultation with the Europeans is least likely. Would it be too harsh to say that consultation with Latin American states is also rather a formality? It is somewhat difficult to believe that American policy on Cuba or the Dominican Republic or Guatemala would have been changed if the government of Argentina or Brazil or Mexico had raised an objection to the proposed action. The diplomatic support of Latin American countries is useful to the United States, but their military cooperation is not necessary, and in moments of crisis, distant prospects of diplomatic resentment are not likely to be a major preoccupation.

The Berlin situation illustrates the opposite case: the military co-operation as well as the diplomatic support of America's major NATO allies is necessary if reaction to any kind of challenge is to look credible. Therefore it is a quite exceptional candidate for allied crisis management. Possibly the history of the city also helps in this respect. There is a general recognition that Berlin has been an area of latent crisis over the whole period since 1948, or even 1945, and thus by the time of the most recent dangerous-looking rise in tension, that of 1958--61, joint contingency planning was a long-standing routine. This was not necessarily an unmixed blessing: familiarity with a problem seems sometimes to result in the overlooking of some of the options available to the adversary. That the Russians might build a wall actually across the city was not one of the contingencies for which plans were prepared (though walls elsewhere had been thought of) and so Western policy was in fact rather hesitant in the first week or so of the Russian operation.

However, one can see the building of the wall as part of the resolution phase of the Berlin crisis, rather than its development phase. In fact, there is a certain hopefulness in the history of Berlin as a *locale* for crisis since 1948. If it illustrates the reality of the conflict between the Western powers and the Soviet Union, it also illustrates the resourcefulness both sides have devoted to preventing this conflict from flaring into actual hostilities over a period of more than twenty years. And in that span of time, one might argue, Berlin has been turned from a true *source* of crisis, to a *symbol* of crisis, where tension is consciously turned on and off as a gesture or a signal. . . .

24   Crisis Management: Kissinger's Middle East Negotiations (October 1973-June 1974)

Amos Perlmutter

College of Public Affairs American University

With the advent of nuclear weapons and competition among the great powers, both

AUTHOR'S NOTE: I am grateful to Professor Thomas Schelling of Harvard University for a concise definition of crisis management and for recommending that I examine the approprite literature. I am also grateful to Robert Jervis of UCLA and Murray Feld of Harvard for their help.

This excerpt from "Crisis Management: Kissinger's Middle East Negotiations (October 1973-June 1974)" by Amos Perlmutter is reprinted from International Studies Quarterly, Vol. 19, No. 3 (September 1975) by permission of the Publisher, Sage Publications, Inc. [Footnotes omitted.]

the nature and structure of the international crisis have been revolutionized. In the three decades since 1945, no major war among the great powers has erupted. As Bell has written, the postwar period may be characterized as "a period of limited and peripheral wars."

The new nature of the nuclear international system demands a new method for resolving international conflicts. This new structure is called "crisis management," and is an innovation of nuclear diplomacy. Buchan sees two different types of crisis management structures: "an allied system of crisis management and a bilateral system

(U.S.-U.S.S.R.)." Bell identifies two major types of crisis management on two different levels: adversary crisis, which is conducted on the central level, and intramural crisis, conducted on the local level (Kashmir, the 1967 war, and the Arab-Israeli conflict).

The structure of crisis management has mainly developed in crises affecting the power in the central nuclear balance. Crisis management between the nuclear powers is not a cordial type of exercise; it is "a consciousness between the dominant powers, that they have solid common interests as well as sharp conflicting interests."

The main purpose of forming structures for crisis management is to develop rational procedures to meet unexpected contingencies and to search for options which minimize the adversary's threats and maximize one's own self-interests, without turning to war. In the United States a major structural reform took place during the Kennedy and Johnson administrations when the National Security Council (NSC) was reestablished (it was first formed in 1947) to research, consult, plan, and take appropriate action to meet the adversary's challenge. The function of the NSC became one of crisis management. . . .

When Henry Kissinger took over NSC he substituted personal diplomatic management for institutionalized crisis management, which he saw as being needlessly encumbered by its bureaucratic structure. Although the term crisis management is still used academically to refer to an institutionalized system of decision-making for contingency planning, the practices have changed the structure and, therefore, the purpose of the post-1962 crisis management thinking and procedures. The term has come to mean solely the personalization of international diplomacy, the technique developed by Kissinger.

THE CRISIS MANAGER

Crisis management calls for "crisis manager" types. According to Bell such a person must: (1) possess "information about the other side's military capabilities and disposition"; (2) exploit surveillance; and (3) the relations between antagonists based on "adverse partnership"; (4) have access to intelligence information. Crisis managers must share a common strategic ideology "built around the military means of the nuclear age." Above all, a crisis can be managed only when there is a "preponderance of power on the side of the status quo coalition, formal or informal."

The chief and most brilliant practitioner of Western contemporary crisis management is, in fact, Kissinger. He must be endowed, says Bell, with "great moral and intellectual sensitivity, perception, imagination and courage." Whether Kissinger is endowed with all these qualities will be subject to continued historical and political controversy. But whatever his own particular successes and failures, there can be no doubt that he has set the standards for the art of crisis management.

By these standards, the crisis manager, if he is to succeed, must be a super diplomat. His method is to set himself above the battle, to affect a style of innocence. The super diplomat must appear to stand to gain nothing from the negotiations; he must only see to it that the adversaries do. A super diplomat is not necessarily a statesman. The two types have converged in only a few exceptional individuals, such as Masaryk, Bismarck, and Chaim Weizmann. The super diplomat is a highly skilled technician; he is not necessarily endowed with the statesman's vision.

The post of super diplomat has not been institutionalized and probably never will be. Nevertheless, men have taken the role on themselves throughout history, and all with different styles. The purpose of this analysis is to examine how Kissinger has adapted the super diplomat role to suit his background and personality. To this end we shall look at the first phase of negotiations in the Middle East (October 1973-June 1974) and examine the workings of Kissinger's technique, that of crisis management.

THE KISSINGER MODUS OPERANDI

Two types of behavior are evident in this super diplomat: first, the understanding empathizer; and second, the mean man, the master of "coercive diplomacy."

The Diplomat As Empathizer

The technique is one of intimacy and empathy with adversaries and negotiations.

Networks

When he was a professor at Harvard, Kissinger established a strategy-defense seminar which was designed to attract promising international politicians. In a little over a decade, Kissinger made close contacts with men who by the late 1960s and early 1970s would become key political leaders in the Western world. In his seminar he taught such men from the Middle East as Allon, several key advisers of Sadat and Faisal, and a few key senior Syrian civil servants.

Several senior members of national and international media also "served their time" in Kissinger's summer seminars and in the one-year Fellow appointments at Harvard's Center for International Affairs. Kissinger is intimate on a first-name basis with his former students and has increased his entourage considerably since 1968, especially with the addition of Dayan and Rabin.

Understanding

The Kissinger diplomat must convince the adversary or adversaries that he "understands" their aspirations, goals, and fears and is willing to modify his own goals as a result of this understanding.

Advocacy

The super diplomat must convince the adversary that he knows all about the latter's apprehensions concerning security interests. He even relates to the adversary his "understanding" of the latter's maximum and minimum national security aspirations.

Surrogate-Arbitrator

In negotiations Kissinger's ideal type of diplomat acts as a surrogate for everybody's national interests, supposedly at the exclusion of his own interests. The super diplomat is above the battle, the arbitrator of everybody's fears, the universal man who understands and sympathizes with all causes. This attitude he relates to each actor only in private. He never gathers all adversaries in one room or conference. He disdains international collective propaganda and ceremonial conferences. The approach is tete-à-tete, secretive, confidential, and most intimate, in contrast to the conference approach of traditional diplomacy.

Insulator

The super diplomat acts as an insulator in negotiations. He "loves" both Chinese and Russians, Egyptians and Israelis, South and North Vietnamese. Since "unfortunately" all of these nations are in conflict with one another, he finds himself as the only person who can act as go-between. It is essential that he give the impression of gaining nothing for himself. All he gains must seem to be dedicated to the adversaries.

Confidant

Throughout negotiations the super diplomat must take the role of being the only person whom all belligerents and adversaries can trust. Since he thus seems to be their trust personified, he is in a position to demand that adversaries reward him with further confidence.

KISSINGER AS THE MASTER OF COERCIVE DIPLOMACY

The diplomat who practices the Kissinger technique learns to turn the failure of negotiations onto the shoulder of the adversary, leaving the latter to think he is helpless once the mediator threatens to end his services on the adversary's behalf.

Threat

An example of Kissinger's use of this technique himself can be seen in his warning to Dayan in which he said, in effect, "If you do not trust me, General Dayan, I do not know whether the U.S. will once again airlift supplies and weapons to Israel as it did in October, 1973." Or in his advice to Sadat, "If you do not trust me, President Sadat, how can I prevent the Israelis from resorting to a war of preemption?" Similarly, to Asad he might have said, "If you do not trust me, President Asad, how can I guarantee return of the Golan Territory now occupied by Israel? How can I restore the rights of Palestinians?"

Having made the threat, the super diplomat's next step is to bring forth his own solution. In Kissinger's case, such a plan was usually known as an "American initiative" or "American proposal." After the adversaries have confided in him, after he knows their weak points as well as those on which they will be least persistent, he "sums up" the belligerents' demands and makes known what was really a preconceived American plan. In effect he pulls out of the hat the rabbit that has been there since he left Washington, acting as if it were only one hour old. By threatening the worst possible, he has "convinced" the adversaries that what they have as a result of his efforts is the best solution they could ever have achieved.

Responsibility

It is important for the diplomat to make it appear that should the negotiations collapse, it is the fault of the adversary. He must convince them that if only they could have seen the situation as he did, then the outcome of the negotiations would have been positive.

Using this line of reasoning, Kissinger might have said to adversaries in the Middle East, "You people in Israel and in the Arab world must plan your own future. The best I can do is to help you bring your ideas together so that no one's aspirations are realized at another's expense. But if you do not want to see things as they are [the American initiative], then do not come to me, Israelis, and ask for more weapons; and, Egyptians, do not ask me to pressure Israel to withdraw from occupied territories. If you do not accept the American initiative, you are on your own and at the mercy of conflicting self-interests. Do not come to me in a crunch if you fail to accept my reasonable proposal for negotiations."

If negotition fails, the adversary is to blame, not the insulator. The adversary is responsible for his own faith. He is a political criminal if he does not heed the "noninterested" righteous advice of the arbitrator. The super diplomat maintains his posture of having given all that could humanly and morally be expected.

The Unthinkable

Examination of the diplomat's threats to the adversaries shows that they are rarely carried out. Nevertheless, most of the time the harness of coercive diplomacy binds each adversary and makes him believe the worst possible. The function of speed—the force of shuttle diplomacy—is designed to baffle the adversaries into believing that if the diplomat's mission fails, the unthinkable may occur. Such a blitz is the super diplomat's most effective weapon.

Tranquilizers

Another popular super diplomat maneuver could be called use of the "pill," in this case, pain-killing pills administered to belligerents wounded during the process of securing their agreement to the diplomat's blitz proposal. The tranquilizing process is one of reinforcement and of lowering the aspirations of the adversaries. It is furthered by a tacit message to each adversary that this may be his last operation.

Administering the anti-depressant, Kissinger said in effect, "Now that you Israelis have withdrawn from the Kuneitra and some kilometers on the Golan Heights, you are in a more secure position. The Syrians will no longer shoot." Giving the Syrians their medication he might have said, "Now that Israel has withdrawn from some of your territories, this is the beginning of a new life for Syria." And to the Egyptians, he would have said, "Now that Israel has withdrawn from the Suez Canal, you can concentrate on rebuilding the canal and rehabilitating its cities."

Thus Israel was promised some tranquility, as were Egypt and Syria. All three were exhausted by the shuttle blitz, confused by the promises, and given the hope that their national aspirations had not been compromised. But tranquilizers are not a cure in themselves, and whether the operation was successful can only be seen when the medication wears off. Thus, while the patients are being lulled into thinking that the worst is over, the super diplomat may be busy contemplating further surgery. Conversely, the diplomat may mistake the calm of the adversaries for lasting satisfaction only to find their disagreements and discontent as strong as ever, once his painkillers wear off.

213

Satellites

. . . In order to rationalize the system of crisis management, the super diplomat has encouraged and, indeed, "created" crisis managers in the Middle East—notably, Sadat, Dayan, Allon, Rabin, Eban, and Fahmy. These Middle Eastern leaders have adapted the new style of diplomacy, presumably to further their own national goals. That Kissinger approves of this turn of events is seen in his praise of his "student" crisis managers. He has remarked, for example, that "Dayan is a man with original ideas"; "Asad, although tough, is a tenacious man"; "Rabin is a brilliant analyst"; "Fahmy is a forward looking and pragmatic negotiator."

The creation of satellite crisis managers lubricates diplomatic procedures and makes all the participants feel that they are partners in a common pursuit, carefully guided by their mentor.

THE DYNAMICS AND PROCESSES OF CRISIS MANAGEMENT

The aftermath of the 1973 war in the Middle East offers a clear illustration of the dynamics of super diplomacy as refined by Kissinger. . . .

The 1973 war certainly called for crisis management. Kissinger harnessed himself to crisis management on the day of attack, October 6, 1973, and that process, which began with the negotiation over the Suez and the Golan Heights for the disengagement of Egyptian, Syrian, and Israeli forces, was still going on a year later. By October 1974, it had resulted in the total withdrawal of Israel from territories occupied in 1973 and in a partial withdrawal from territories occupied in 1967. . . .

The newly institutionalized super diplomacy can be divided into the following processes, which embody the variables of the Kissinger style: (1) the conditioning of the belligerents for negotitions; (2) the promotion of their hopes; (3) the system of threat-making; and (4) the breakthrough.

The Conditioning of the Belligerents

To persuade the belligerents, the super diplomat must first act as the sympathizer and convince them that he understands them. . . .

Once the empathy/sympathy phase of the diplomatic maneuvering is completed, the next step is to exploit the belligerents' trust and channel it into mutual self-serving praises between the crisis manager and satellites.

Abba Eban had this to say on March 16, 1974: "Mr. Kissinger's personal role refutes the view that history is the product of impersonal forces and objective conditions in which the personal human factor doesn't matter. I believe that the association of American prestige with Secretary Kissinger's skills has been crucial in creating a new climate."

When President Anwar el-Sadat was asked, "To what extent do you think that your personal rapport with Secretary Kissinger has been a factor in the change between the U.S. and Egypt?" he replied, "I always believe in personal contacts, and when you find a secretary of state who knows the full details about the problem, *who is a man of trust and a man of vision*, our friendship and relations survive. I was accused by my Arab colleagues of betrayal (that is, of establishing cordial relations with the U.S.), but it has been proved that with imagination, effort, and trust, we have reached the best conclusions (mutually). We (Kissinger and I) talk lots—lots. He is a man of strategy; myself, I am a man of strategy also; so when we sit together one cannot imagine what we discuss (that is, we discuss the range of strategic questions)—not only the area here, the Middle East, but all over the world. Dr. Kissinger and I are friends. We discuss everything that friends discuss: business . . . exchange jokes, everything.''. . .

The Promotion of Hopes

Acting as a surrogate, above-the-battle arbitrator, and not taking sides, Kissinger has managed to lift the level of adversaries' hopes.

The technique is rather simple. First, the crisis manager claims little or nothing for his own personal or national interests. . . . He tries to create hopes (ones which supposedly have not existed before) that the adversaries' aspirations can be fulfilled and their fears alleviated. . . .

Aware of Israel's fears, its mistrust of Syria, and its sense of hopelessness concerning the Syrian attitude toward conflict resolution, Kissinger made this statement on his arrival in Jerusalem on May 2, 1974, ''I come not to discuss concessions but to discuss security. The issue is not pressure, but a lasting peace.'' In this way, Kissinger raised Israeli hopes by substituting Israel's most cherished symbols, ''security'' and ''lasting peace,'' for the two symbols of fear, ''concessions'' and ''pressure.'' He was also protecting Dayan, who in Washington on March 30 had conceded more than the Israeli cabinet had formally authorized. Finally, by using the language of the adversary's aspirations, Kissinger offered Israeli decision

makers and his students of crisis management a demonstration of using language to put forth a more favorable image of an unhappy situation.

Using the adversary's own words, phrases which symbolize his fears and hopes, has been proved an effective psychological technique in diplomatic management. For instance, in mid-May 1974, Kissinger told journalists accompanying him that ''Asad has gone a long way toward drumming up domestic support for a settlement and it could be too late for him to turn back.'' Thus by raising the hopes of adversaries, he hoped to reduce their resistance and to make his own demands (in form of a ''solution'') seem suddenly reasonable.

Kissinger's next step is to portray the hope he has promoted as being *new conditions* that could not have been realized previously. Thus, in negotiating troop disengagement, he has promised Israel secure borders and the Arabs that the pre-October 6, 1973 conditions will be tolerable and the process of Israeli withdrawal will begin. He avoids defining the secure or final borders for Israel (perhaps even to himself), nor has he told the Arabs how much territory lost in 1967 will be returned. These conditions have been left to the imagination, craftiness, and persistence of the belligerents. The secure Israeli border and the final Israeli withdrawal are not the American concern.

Incrementalist crisis management demands a minimum from the belligerents and inspires them with hope. To alleviate their frustration at not realizing their hopes—which is often the outcome—Kissinger supplies them with a version of what transpired during negotiations which is more positive. For instance, he tells the adversaries that they will *lose* still more if they refuse to negotiate or compromise. Then what they might have lost by failing to negotiate, he tells them they have gained. In effect, the adversaries are thus persuaded that each of their losses can become a gain.

On October 12, 1974, Kissinger reiterated this statement made in the midst of the October war: "Stalemate is the most propitious condition for a settlement." He had worked hard to achieve that type of stalemate by October 22, 1973. The strategy was to create "gains" out of domestic frustrations in Israel and to minimize Arab "losses" by gaining for the Arabs all the territories in 1973 and some of those lost in 1967.

The System of Threat Promotion

After establishing confidence, creating conditions of credibility, and securing maximal information on the adversaries' apprehensions and fears, Kissinger will often then use another technique, that of making a double-edged threat. On one side it appears as another element of understanding. Such a statement as "Since I know your apprehensions, let me see what I can do for you" is presented not as a threat, but as friendly advice. But the other edge is a direct threat to withdrawing support, after which the adversary is made to believe he will collapse. The threat, then, combines misinformation and friendly advice with an actual statement (or sometimes an allusion) concerning the withdrawal of support. Its purpose is to lead the adversary to think that the only possible situation is to accept the American proposal. Finally, Kissinger uses a third type of threat, this one better known as deterrence.

A classic example of a threat which incorporated all three elements of ambiguity, withdrawal of support, and deterrence, was the U.S. alert of October 25, 1973. According to one of Washington's national security specialists, the alert was conceived after the Soviet Union boasted that it has "mobilized seven Russian divisions to fight for Egypt." Whether this information was correct, whether it was part of a diplomatic maneuver by Sadat, demonstrating his fidelity to the Arabs, the fact remains that the week of October 26, 1973 was climactic in the American-Soviet struggle. After the alert Brezhnev faced a real dilemma: was the United States withdrawing from detente, or was crisis management being stretched to the limit?

The fear of a Russian withdrawal from detente must have played a key role in the American alert, which, according to the New York *Times,* was managed by Kissinger and Secretary Schlesinger alone. "It is now certain," wrote David Binder of the *Times* in November, "that both the timing and exact nature of the alert were acted upon without the President's specific prior approval." Binder described all the elements of the alert, which were faithful to the style of crisis management. The actors were Kissinger, Schlesinger, Brezhnev, Gromyko, and Dobrynin (one of Kissinger's chief partners in the system of super diplomacy). "From all this," wrote Binder, "it seems clear there was no *actual* crisis, but a *potential* crisis. That is why the President stayed upstairs and that is why the hot line was not used. Only after the news of the alert was broadcast, did Mr. Nixon decide to *dramatize* it as a crucial, personal face-off against the Russians."

The other side of the threat, the technique of appearing extremely understanding and sympathetic to adversaries' positions, was demonstrated when Kissinger imposed a cease-fire on the Israeli army advancing into the Western Territory of Egypt. Kissinger arrived in Tel-Aviv from Moscow on October 22 with a fait accompli—an American-Soviet agreement on a new Middle Eastern cease-fire, which was adopted by the U.N. Security

Council as Resolution 333. Kissinger had advocated a ceasefire as early as October 6, 1973, but as this idea was not accepted by Egypt and Syria or by the USSR, he waited to see what the Arabs could and would do. According to Leslie Gelb of the New York *Times,* "Informed American officials [in the White House and Pentagon] related that Mr. Kissinger moved as soon as Moscow was prepared to support the ceasefire. These officials said he [Kissinger] was arguing that a total *Israeli victory over Egyptian* forces would make negotiations impossible." Kissinger himself claimed that he had "requested Israel to accept the ceasefire in view of the Soviet military threat to the advancing Israeli armies." Thus, Kissinger approached Israel in the spirit of "understanding," warning the Israelis of the supposed Soviet threat.

Kissinger used the same technique to persuade Israel to help him in negotiating a Syrian-Israeli troop disengagement. Arriving on May 9, 1974, he persuaded the Israelis of his interest in their security and lasting peace. While the Israeli cabinet was discussing the Syrian proposals submitted by Kissinger, he recruited Nixon to send no less than three cables, "asking Mrs. Meir to support Dr. Kissinger in his efforts, while emphasizing that, he, Nixon, was monitoring his secretary's trip with great *personal* interest."

Then Kissinger moved to threaten the Israelis. He must have said something like this, "If war breaks out again, many people may blame Israel for it. I doubt if it will be possible to airlift supplies to Israel as the United States did after the tenth of October. U.S. public opinion will not understand Iraeli stubbornness [its unwillingness to compromise on the Golan negotiations], and I doubt if another alert such as the one issued on October 25 could be taken under the circumstances, even if the Soviets should threaten direct intervention." Support withdrawal,

Kissinger's last resort, is his most effective way of reducing the adversary's highest hope and aspirations to the super diplomat's own level. Once this has been achieved, negotiations verge on the step known as "breakthrough."

The Breakthrough

When the process of diplomatic attrition reaches a point at which the secretary believes that: (1) by threatening the adversaries' most cherished national interests, he has persuaded them of the "advantages" of compromise; (2) they are now convinced that their interests converge with those of the super diplomat's; and (3) he has stretched the adversaries' nerves to the limit, he pulls out a plan which embodies *his* views of what the adversaries can and should surrender. The plan—variously labeled the breakthrough, the American initiative, or the American proposal—defines the nature and structure of the compromise. The decision about the time for the breakthrough is crucial. The adversaries are not permitted to decide on their own time and place, for the breakthrough is the super diplomat's most guarded domain. Even his closest advisers are not aware when he will declare that the impasse has been broken.

The possible parameters for the breakthrough are conceived in advance, based on various proposals secured from the adversaries even before the secretary leaves Washington. Since the breakthrough consists of the secretary's own ideas for compromise, what takes place during the early and middle phases of negotiations can only be termed attrition diplomacy.

Marilyn Berger of the *Washington Post* described the breakthrough phase in negotiations between Israel and Syria as follows:

"Kissinger's negotiating style is to wait until the last moment, so that *any American proposal* does not become a subject for negotiations." Or, as Joseph Kraft puts in, "In sum, the Secretary's essential method is to leash the dogs of war which he himself has previously unleashed. It is not nice, but it works what looks like wonders."

Past successful American proposals have been accompanied by a frantic blitz of diplomatic activity. The major ingredient is surprise. "Diplomatic momentum produces success, success feeds success, and leads to strengthening one's position at home. Each negotiation partner is to be given the impression that everyone else is about to compromise and agree . . . the technique is to seek whatever agreement is possible." And should the technique appear to be failing, Kissinger may suddenly announce that he is desperately needed in Washington. He may thus further press the adversaries by saying that if they do not hurry up, they may find him on the way to Washington in the next hour. . . .

The process of Israeli attrition had begun even before the secretary left for his first shuttle diplomacy. In December 1973, he invited a group of leading Jewish intellectuals, Harvard Zionists, and pro-Israeli professors to Washington and lectured them on the "plight" of Israel. He told them that Israel had lost the war, that if it had not been for him there would have been no airlift, and that Israel was politically isolated

and mortally wounded. He said that its political leadership lacked vision, its strategists lacked ideas, the malaise in the country was serious, and the Israeli government could not carry the burden of negotiations. This method of diplomatic attrition had three purposes: (1) to convey to the Israeli leadership the need to withdraw from territories, thus "softening" the Israeli opposition; (2) to protect Kissinger's flank from a Jewish and intellectual-liberal backlash; (3) to signal to Israel that he could be rude and ruthless. Similar ideas were related to the Executive Council of NATO late in March 1974. . . .

In the words of a key Egyptian official in Cairo on January 18, 1974, "Kissinger produced a proposal and we accepted." What looks like an agreed compromise can be described, with a knowledge of the workings of crisis management, as a solution *imposed* on the adversaries. In the long run this type of diplomacy may prove to be little more than a whirlwind. Tactics of switching from ruthlessness to understanding, from empathy to meanness, and from love to hate make an impact, to be sure. Such emotional manipulations have produced two troop separations. But will they produce a lasting peace? . . .

Clearly, Kissinger's super diplomacy in the Middle East has made a considerable contribution to crisis management. But despite his brilliance, imagination, energy, and persuasiveness, the Middle East still faces the threat of war.

X

International Organization

Given the fact that international law does not appear noticeably to restrain or affect states in the actual pursuit of their "vital national interests," which are often narrowly self-seeking, doubts have often been expressed that international law is really law at all. But this is not the point. In the absence of a value consensus and a common power base for the entire world, international law is qualitatively different from domestic law, and in many ways is hardly comparable to it. What is important for the student to understand at the outset, however, is that legal processes *are* at work in the international system and have been for three centuries or more. They operate more for the convenience of states than to control their behavior. Once there is sufficient consensus of value, enforceable law on that foundation will follow—but not before then.

Prevailing assumptions about the relevance, efficacy, or potential utility of world law tend to vary with the degree of stability in the interstate system at any given time. Before the turn of the century there was more stress upon the universal applicability of international law than there is today. On the other hand, there is more urgency expressed today about the *need* for a world rule. of law. The reason is clear: before World War I, the "civilized states" shattered the illusion, it was widely believed that there existed among the leadership of these Great Powers a consensus of values which was sufficiently general to support and sustain the development of a rule of law throughout the world. This turned out not to be the case even then, and with the Bolshevik revolution in Russia, and later the emergence of the Fascist powers which were determined to overturn the existing system, there was not even an illusion of value consensus between the wars.

During that period, those who believed that there were at least the beginnings of a world community tended to concentrate their attention and hopes upon the League of Nations, at least until that body proved incapable, less than twenty years after its inception, of meeting the challenge of totalitarianism.

To speak of a world rule of law assumes that among the many countries of the world there exists a sufficiently high degree of consensus that a universal legal system can be created. Obviously such a degree of consensus does not exist, because neither the communist states nor Third or Fourth World states can agree with the advanced capitalist states upon what values such a legal system would be founded. But, to repeat, this is not to say that extensive legal processes are not constantly at work in the adjustment of differences and in the daily conduct of affairs among states which could never accept each others' basic values and legal norms. Diplomats are exchanged and granted diplomatic immunity; transportation and communications are regulated by universally accepted legal rules; and detailed agreements with the virtual force of law have been reached on everything from monetary policy to non-proliferation of nuclear weapons. Nevertheless, it is difficult to contest the view expressed by Hans Morgenthau that merely to recognize that international law exists is not tantamount to saying that, as a legal system, it is as effective as the legal system that operates within each state. Nor does it follow that it is "effective in regulating and restraining the struggle for power on the international scene." By way of summary, let us refer to the useful delineation made by the late Wolfgang Friedman, in which he sets forth the following basic principles of international law;

1. International law is based upon a society of sovereign states, regardless of structure and ideology.
2. Any attempt by a foreign power to interfere with internal change by assisting either rebels or the government is probably contrary to international law.
3. It is within the right of any sovereign state to surrender its national sovereignty, by federation or amalgamation with another state (or states).
4. Any state is, under international law, at liberty to tolerate or suppress a

subversive political movement by whatever means it chooses, except insofar as its action threatens the security of a third state by demonstrable preparations for aggressive action.
5. The evolution of lesser and indirect forms of aggression, falling short of armed attack, justifies countermeasures that are intermediate between peace and war. . . .[1]

In an effort to make international law more effective, states have resorted to the creation of international organizations. Prior to World War I, a number of international organizations and commissions had been established to manage specific areas of international relations—the Universal Postal Union, international fisheries commissions, and the like. But the first international organization with a political mandate was the League of Nations. The League was intended to provide an institution through which states acting collectively might identify threats to the peace and take measures such as sanctions and even military action to stop an aggressor. Unfortunately, the strength of the League was sapped from the beginning by the failure of the United States and Russia to join, and by the difficulty of the remaining great powers in deciding to act when first one (Japan) and then another (Italy) and another (Nazi Germany) country committed aggression.

During World War II the American government determined to take the lead in creating the United Nations Organization. The keystone of the United Nations was to be the Security Council, on which were permanently represented the five great powers—the United States, the Soviet Union, Britain, France, and China (now represented by the Peoples' Republic of China)—plus seven (now nine) other states periodically elected by the General Assembly. Recognizing that it would be impossible for the United Nations to act against one of the great powers if it was unwilling to be restrained, the U.N. Charter provided each permanent member of the Security Council with the power to 'veto' any resolution with which it did not concur. Almost immediately after the cessation of hostilities, the Cold War erupted between the Soviet Union and the West, and the actions of the Security Council were largely stymied by the Soviet veto. It was only by chance that the Soviet Union was boycotting the United Nations for failing to admit the government of mainland China, when the Korean War broke out (June 25, 1950), thereby permitting the U.S. to secure the endorsement of the Security Council for the United Nations armies to intervene.

When the UN was founded in 1945 it had fifty-one members each of which was represented in the General Assembly. By October 1977 the number had grown to 147. So long as the UN remained small the United States enjoyed an automatic majority among the membership (principally

[1]Wolfgang Friedman, *The Changing Structure of International Law* (New York: Columbia University Press, 1964) p. 378.

the Latin American states and NATO allies), and the UN consistently endorsed or legitimized American foreign policy.

After 1956 the majority of the new members were either opposed to Western capitalism or determined not to become involved in the Cold War struggle. For years a majority of the Assembly, invariably assisted by the communist bloc, concentrated on pushing for the independence of the remaining colonial possessions. They refused to view the Soviet suppression of Hungarian freedom as being of the same illegality as the Franco-British attack upon Egypt in 1956. In fact the majority refused to support the Western position on Berlin in 1961 and was even less willing to give its sanction to the U.S. operations in Vietnam.

In the course of the past decade the Third World voting majority has concentrated upon pushing for the advancement of economic development as the UN's first concern. As the selection in this chapter by Richard Bissell illustrates, almost the entire thrust of the underdeveloped two-thirds of the world is upon the need for more investment funds and a more equitable redistribution of wealth. On a whole succession of issues in the recent past, the West, and the United States in particular, has found itself isolated, such as on the Middle East, on condemnation of PLO terrorism, and on the financing of economic development. On all these issues the U.S. has found itself at loggerheads with a UN majority comprised of Third (or Fourth) World and communist states. The terms may require some amplification. The "first world" consists of the highly developed capitalist/democratic countries; the "second world" consists of highly developed communist states. The rest of the world used to be lumped together as "Third World," but more recently it has become apparent that there are large distinctions among these countries. Now "third world" is defined as those societies, still underdeveloped, who have the capacity to develop and modernize rapidly (Iran, and other members of the Organization of Oil producing states (OPEC) clearly fall into this category). But in addition, there are countries so poor that it remains doubtful whether they can develop without massive foreign assistance. These states are now referred to as the states of the "fourth world."

As a result of these changes Americans have felt disillusioned and frustrated with the United Nations. Having invested too much ideological faith in the UN as a panacea and then finding it to be at the mercy of hostile majorities, many Americans have called for us to withdraw. In his selection in this chapter, Inis Claude suggests that Americans would do better to view the United Nations as "a symbol of the inhibitions that their country should respect, of the limitations that it should observe in the conduct of foreign policy." We should see the United Nations as a forum in which the collective destiny of states must be worked out in place of unilateral U.S. efforts to remake the world. The UN cannot act in the absence of the United States, and we should continue to belong.

It is Claude's contention that the value of the United Nations role should not be overlooked. At a time when there are many tendencies toward chaos and anarchy in the international system, the UN and its associated organs provide a medium through which the most desperate and extreme demands of the Third World may be heard and attended to. "The United Nations is an effective agency of international communication, socialization, and integration. Despite its shortcomings in the area of conflict resolution, it remains an effective arm of international law in the realization of these tasks."[2] By belonging to and participating in the one organization that most fully exemplifies the principles and norms of law and justice in the international system, members are conditioned to act in conformity with those principles and norms.

As the preceding chapters have tried to make clear, states and their governments remain the most important actors on the international scene, but they have more recently been joined by other, non-state actors as well. International organizations have attempted, with varying degrees of success, to link states and governments in networks of contact and communication; and also to draw into that network the non-state actors in international relations—multinationals, ethnic groups, and the like. Usually this has taken the form of placing the non-state actors in a consultative capacity to the organs of international organizations, with primary emphasis on the work of the Economic and Social Council and various specialized agencies. International organizations thus play an important integrative role. While it is easy to overstate their effectiveness, one must also avoid under-estimating the role that they play.

Secondly, the United Nations has managed to perform a crucial peace-keeping function in such places as the Congo, the Middle East, and Cyprus. Despite the furious indignation of the conservative press in the United States and Europe and of the Soviet government over these peace-keeping operations in the Congo, on a number of occasions the capacity of the United Nations to dispatch a military force drawn from the armies of its members to enforce cease fires and truces, and even to establish internal order, has not only provided the *only* basis for establishing peace between the parties (Arabs and Israeli), but has kept the Soviet Union and the United States from becoming embroiled. In line with our discussion of the balance of power in a previous chapter, Inis Claude has defined the peace-keeping function of the United Nations, not as a device for defying aggression and certainly not for coercing great powers, but as a means of helping them to contain their conflicts.

> The greatest political contribution of the United Nations in our time to the management of international power relationships lies not in implementing collective security or instituting world government, but in helping to improve

[2]A. Sheikh. *International Law and National Behavior* (New York: John Wiley and Sons, 1974) p. 126.

and stabilize the workings of the balance-of-power system, which is, for better or worse, the operative mechanism of contemporary international politics.[3]

The United Nations Organization is only the most important of a vast array of international organizations. Some, such as the Food and Agricultural Organization, the World Health Organization and UNESCO (UN Educational, Scientific, and Cultural Organization) are affiliated with the UN. Others, such as the International Monetary Fund, the World Bank for Reconstruction and Development, and the Universal Postal Union, operate independently of the UN. Then, of course, there is a vast array or organizations to which only a limited number of states belong, but which are international in their character and impact. Usually they exist to provide their members with security, economic benefits, or greater political influence in world politics. Some notable examples are the European Economic Community, the North Atlantic Treaty Organization, the Organization of African Unity, and OPEC.

[3]Inis Claude, *Power and International Relations* (New York: Random House, 1964) p. 285.

25 The Symbolic Significance of The United Nations

Inis L. Claude Jr.

The author is Professor of Government and Foreign Affairs at the University of Virginia.

For twenty-five years, the United Nations has been a part of the American scene. The impetus for its creation came largely from the United States. . . .

As the host country and the most prominent and powerful member, the United States has displayed an unusual degree of interest in and concern about the world organization. While such sentiments as pride of authorship and presumption of ownership may have entered into the American attitude toward the United Nations, the dominant factor making for strong interest and active concern has probably been the novelty of the engagement of the United States in a massive effort to organize the operation of the international system. . . .

The attitudes and expectations directed toward the world organization by interested Americans have, naturally enough, been mixed and variable. Considerable currency has been gained by the notion that the United Nations was oversold to the American people in the beginning, and that the subsequent decline in popular enthusiasm is a reaction to disappointment of unrealistic hopes. This strikes me as something of a myth, for the evidence of which I am aware fails to lend substantial support to the proposition that there was either marked overselling or marked overbuying of the fledg-

From the Virginia Quarterly Review, *Vol. 47 (Autumn 1971), pp. 481–504. Reprinted by permission.*

ling organization. As I read the record, the potentialities of the United Nations were described by most officials and commentators with restrained optimism and were regarded by most Americans with moderate pessimism. The United Nations appears to have been presented and accepted as an experiment worth trying, not as a panacea worthy of uncritical confidence. The mood of 1945 was one of resolution to make a determined effort to save the world from chaos, not one of naive conviction that an easy and infallible method had been found. Nevertheless, it is true that many Americans, both in official positions and in private life, initially approached the United Nations in a spirit of idealism, giving at least lip service to the notion that it provided man's best hope for a just and lasting peace and sometimes acting on the premise that the highest duty of the United States was to support its development as an effective institution.

From the inception of the United Nations, Americans have been strongly inclined to treat the question of the attitude one should adopt toward the organization as an ideological matter, an issue of political faith and morals. This suggests that the appropriate imagery of the United Nations is that of a church rather than a political institution. The organization has its creed of orthodoxy, its conventional liturgy, its component of hypocrisy, and its gap between the performance willed by the spirit and that dictated by the weakness of the flesh. The question of conviction about the United Nations has frequently been put in terms of believing *in* rather than believing *that*, thus indicating that the issue is thought to fall within the realm of political theology. . . .

Negative attitudes toward the United Nations within the United States have been no less ideological in character. If the United Nations is a church, it is for some Americans the wrong church, leading its adherents to whore after false gods and to abandon the true faith. Friends of the organization approve it as a symbol of the destruction of National Sovereignty, or the insidious advance of International Communism, or the undermining of European Civilization. The view of the United Nations as the embodiment of lofty idealism is countered if not matched in American public opinion by the conception of it as a manifestation of nefarious conspiracy or utopian foolishness. Against the vision of the organization as the hope of mankind is set the notion that it is a snare, a delusion, and a confounded nuisance.

If enthusiastic dedication to the United Nations has declined in the United States, as I think it has, the trend has run not toward militant ideological opposition but toward the dominance of indifference; the organization has tended to be neglected, not rejected. Ideological passions regarding the United Nations have cooled, not so much because agreement has been reached as to the values that the organization should or does epitomize as because it has come to be considered less relevant to the important issues of world affairs. The United Nations has been relegated to a less prominent place on the agenda of public interest and concern.

Is this an unfortunate development? It is if it reflects an actual decline in the usefulness and usability of the United Nations for worthwhile international purposes. To some degree, this is the case; some of the loss of popular interest in the United Nations, favorable and unfavorable, must be considered symptomatic of the diminishing effectiveness of the organization in producing results that excite either strong approval or strong disapproval. On the other hand, this development may tell us more about the ideologically-based attitudes of friends and enemies of the United Nations than about the evolution of the organization itself. . . .

On the whole, I am inclined to regard public indifference to the United Nations, involving the diminution of both dedicated support and passionate distrust, as a healthy development. This judgment is based on the premise that the world organization is inappropriately cast as an object of ideological fervor. I have long contended that the United Nations has too many supporters and opponents, and too few students. I have reacted with discomfort to the question of whether I am "for" or "against" the United Nations; to ask the question seems to me to betray an immature attitude toward international organization.

Nobody asks whether I am "for" or "against" Congress, or the state board of education, or the local fire department. I am presumed, correctly, to take the view that such agencies as these are parts of the necessary mechanism for carrying on the public business, to regard it as normal that their policies and acts should sometimes win my approval and sometimes arouse my wrath, and to consider that it is more sensible for me to ponder the question of how I can influence their performance than to raise the question of whether they should continue to exist. We take such agencies of domestic government for granted. We have no illusions that they will achieve the definitive solution of the problems with which they deal, and we are frequently dissatisfied with their efforts, but few of us are tempted to imagine that a complex society could dispense with the imperfect apparatus that they constitute.

[The United Nations] will have achieved a firm footing when it has come to be taken for granted, when it is routinely regarded as a part of the apparatus for the conduct of international relations, when nobody feels compelled to consider or announce whether he is "for" or "against" it—when, in short, it comes to be treated and evaluated as a political institution, in pragmatic terms, rather than as a Cause, in ideological terms. This is the proposition that underlies my belief that popular indifference toward the United Nations is essentially a good thing. In so far as it can be interpreted as casual acceptance of the view that institutionalized arrangements and procedures are as indispensable to the running of the international system as to the operation of the domestic system, in so far as it indicates a disposition to judge the United Nations according to how it is used, by whom, and for what, that indifference seems to me to represent a salutary change in attitude.

To a considerable degree, the recent decline of popular interest in the United Nations does, I think, represent the development of a more matter-of-fact attitude toward the organization. At the very least, it tends to free responsible American public officials to treat the United Nations less as the symbol of an ideological crusade and more as an instrument to be appraised according to estimates of its utility. The shift is a partial one; from the beginning, American popular opinion and public policy have been influenced in some measure by calculations of the practical merits of the United Nations. Despite verbal emphasis

upon what the organization has been thought to stand for, the actual behavior of the United States in and toward the United Nations has never been altogether divorced from consideration of what practical objectives can and cannot be achieved within the network of facilities that it provides for the managers of international affairs. The weakening of pressures against the dominance of such an instrumentalist view is, from my standpoint, to be welcomed.

Nevertheless, it would be unrealistic to deny that the United Nations has had, still has, and will continue to have symbolic significance that is only imperfectly related to the shifting boundaries of its potentialities and accomplishments as a working institution. What it is believed, or hoped, or feared that the organization symbolizes is no less important an object of study than its operating experience. The symbolic meaning attributed to the United Nations by Americans has some impact upon the character of American participation in the processes and programs of the organization. More than this, it provides a valuable clue to American perceptions of the nature of the international system and of the necessary and proper role of the United States in that system. Recognizing the persistence of the ideological, as distinguished from the pragmatic, approach to the United Nations, I propose to exploit its analytical value. This requires brushing aside such questions as what the United Nations is, what it does, and how it can be used, in favor of questions pertaining to its symbolic significance. What is it taken to *mean?* What image of the world does it convey? What changes in the world does it stand for? What place in the world and what kind of performance in the world can be envisaged for the United States as derivatives of its acceptance of the Charter and its occupancy of a seat in the United Nations? The task is to examine the symbolic meanings attached to the United Nations by Americans—the hopes and fears, promises and expectations, commitments and inhibitions that have been tied to the idea of the United Nations rather than derived from its record of operation.

During the period of the designing, building, and launching of the United Nations, the organization symbolized above all the commitment of the United States to permanent involvement and reliably continuous and vigorous leadership in global affairs. In sponsoring its creation, in joining it, and in accepting the role of host state, Americans were deliberately affirming such an intention; they regarded the United Nations as a vehicle for the solemnization and the institutionalization of the resolve that the United States should henceforth play a major role in international relations.

The self-consciousness of this symbolic act can be understood only in the light of American history and of the reaction of Americans to the results of their twentieth-century performance in world affairs. The United States had a tradition of isolationism, dating back to its origin as an independent state, that argued against any avoidable involvement in the central arena of international politics. It had undertaken, in the early twentieth century, to play an auxiliary role in that arena exercising the discretion to intervene on an emergency basis, but without the expectation of sustained involvement. Although President Wilson had led the United States into World War I on that basis, he had changed his mind before the fighting was finished; pondering the future requirements of world order, he had concluded that the avoidance of major war would depend heavily upon the willingness of the United States to serve continuously as a leading member of an organized community of states, conspicuously dedicated to upholding world order against all who might attempt to disrupt it. This was, in my view, the central meaning of Wilson's scheme for the League of Nations. For him, the League was to be a symbol of the transformation of American foreign policy, of America's adoption of the position and role that he had come to consider requisite for the maintenance of global peace and order. Wilson's campaign for American adhesion to the League conveyed this message; he warned that the investment of blood and treasure in World War I would prove to have been wasted, that the horrors of major war would recur, if the United States did not, by joining the League, commit itself to the policy that he advocated. . . .

Wilson's campaign . . . failed; the United States had rejected the lesson that he had learned, the challenge that he had presented, and the responsibility that he had urged the nation to assume. America had resumed its auxiliary role, and had then in fact reverted to a more extreme version of isolationism than the founding fathers had championed. World War II had begun, and the United States had been drawn inexorably into the struggle, which entailed costs for the world and for America far in excess of those exacted by the earlier conflict.

What was to be learned from all of this? What conclusions did Americans draw from it? Isolationism was discredited. It had neither prevented wars nor prevented American involvement in those wars. The isolation of the United States from the disasters of international politics no longer appeared feasible. The auxiliary role seemed hardly more attractive. The United States had eventually intervened in both global conflicts, but it had risked doing so too late to save the situation, and the uncertainty as to whether it would intervene at all or in time to be effective had encouraged aggressors to drive ahead. The United States had helped to cause these terrible wars by not helping to prevent them; if it had not tempted potential disrupters of the peace to disregard the weight of American opposition, the United States might well have forestalled the execution of their plans. By its refusal to commit itself to join in action against aggression, the United States had not avoided the necessity. A contrary policy of promising and threatening to fight in resistance to aggression, to do what in fact it ultimately did, might well have averted the occasions for fighting. In the acid of this logic, the virtues of the auxiliary role were converted to vices. The retention of national freedom of action took on the appearance of international irresponsibility; desirable flexibility of policy came to appear as disastrous indecisiveness; commendable maneuvering to avoid being drawn into other peoples' wars was translated as giving the green light to those ambitious for global conquest. The United States should deter aggressors, not defeat them by belated and unpredictable entry into the ranks of their opponents. Through all of this ran the confident assumption that American power was formidable enough to make the decisive difference; in two World Wars, the military strength of the United States had turned the tide. The tragedy lay in the fact that this power had been used only to affect the ending of the struggles, not to inhibit their beginning.

This analysis boiled down to the conclusion that Wilson had been right as to what the United States could and should do in the world. He had urged the country to symbolize its adoption of a new role of leadership in keeping the world at peace by joining the League of Nations; the League now became the symbol of the folly and irresponsibility of the United States, of America's relinquishment of the task that only it could have performed. Small wonder then that the United Nations became the symbol of America's repentance, its enlightenment as to what was required for maintaining world order, and its determination to undertake the responsibility that it had previously spurned!. . .

The twin themes of the San Francisco Conference in 1945 [at which the UN Charter was adopted] were that the defection of the United States had doomed the League to failure and that only the loyal adherence of the United States to the new organizational plan could give the world a chance to achieve peace and order under the United Nations. Getting the United States firmly and irrevocably committed to playing an active role in world politics was generally regarded as the central task of that conference. If ever an international leader was "elected," it was the United States at San Francisco. Fears directed toward the United States related to what it might refrain from doing; hopes directed toward it related to what it might be prepared to do. The symbolic act of joining the United Nations represented not an assertion but an acceptance by the United States of a central position in world affairs. Statesmen at large had urged and hoped, and Americans had now agreed and resolved, that the Wilsonian transformation of American foreign policy would take place. . . .

A second—and, as I shall argue, secondary—element in the early symbolism of the United Nations was the view that the new organization stood for, and promised, a new and better kind of international system. The United Nations was identified with One World. Some men thought in terms of structure and process; World Federation was on the way, a universal Rule of Law was in prospect, or a system of institutionalized

International Co-operation was being established. Others concentrated more on policy and program; aggression was to be frustrated, national self-determination was to be promoted, human rights were to be safeguarded, and economic and social welfare was to be fostered. The Charter was widely regarded as a definitive affirmation of the ideals of a nascent international community. One could retain his doubts and fears, even his sophisticated awareness of complexities and difficulties, and yet treat the United Nations as a powerful symbol of human hopes and aspirations for peace, justice, and welfare. The organization was envisioned as an augury of change for the better in the quality of state behavior and in the manner of operation of the multistate system.

For many human beings, the United Nations undoubtedly stood primarily for the transformation of the international system into a more orderly, rationally managed, humanely oriented, democratically run system, in which it might be hoped and expected that the United States, along with all or most other states, would be included. The focus of this point of view was on the global system, not on the American component of that system. Among statesmen concerned with the strategy of advance toward international order, however, a more acute sense of the linkage between the transformation of American foreign policy and the transformation of the international system prevailed. . . .

This background provided the basis for the strategy of peace-building that was adopted during and after World War II. The objective remained that of securing the commitment of the United States to active international leadership. The method employed was to assure the United States that its leadership was sought not in the bad old system but in a bright new system. In short,

Wilson's prescription was again applied—and this time it worked. The United Nations symbolized the purification of international relations, the creation of a global system fit for American participation and worthy of American dedication. The United States responded, as Wilson had vainly hoped that it would do a generation earlier, by taking the position that membership involved not the abandonment but the fulfillment of its principles, that the engagement represented not the world's dragging the United States down to the level of old-style power politics but America's lifting the world up to the level of co-operative endeavor to achieve justice and peace. The two transformations, of American foreign policy and of the international system, were envisaged as having been successfully linked in this second attempt. The United Nations was the symbol of this dual success.

In this original conception of the symbolic significance of the United Nations, the emphasis lay upon the positive, constructive tasks that were to be performed in order to promote the realization of a just and stable world order. One thought in terms of building a peaceful world. States were to join as partners, with the United States taking the leading role, in assuming the responsibilities and carrying the burdens entailed by this ambitious project. The evils of international relations—anarchy, oligarchy, and widespread misery—were to be reduced by a vigorous and concerted multilateral effort. The anarchic element, war, was to be tackled directly by the mobilization of persuasion, pressure, and—where required—coercion, an enterprise in which the power of the United States ranked as a critical resource. International oligarchy, identified as colonialism and other forms of imperialism, was to be ameliorated by programs looking toward the preparation of suppressed and underprivileged peoples for the exercise of national self-determination. The inadequacies of the resources and capabilities of these and other peoples for liberating themselves from the bonds of poverty and associated ills were to be remedied by cooperative assistance, in which the contribution of the United States would be a vital element. In all of these undertakings, heavy reliance would have to be placed upon the power, the wealth, the political initiative, and the political support of the United States. . . .

III

This version of the meaning to be attached to the United Nations and to American membership in that organization has not been abandoned, but it has lost its standing as the unquestionably orthodox view. The chief contender for predominance is one that has a distinctly negative flavor, as contrasted with the positive emphasis of the originally dominant viewpoint. Positive and negative elements have always been, and continue to be, mixed in the symbolism of the United Nations. The point I wish to make is that the former have tended to become less, and the latter to become more, prominent.

The negative syndrome may be analyzed, first, with reference to its implications concerning the position and policy of the United States, both in the United Nations and in the world at large. American membership in the organization is interpreted less as a proclamation of commitment to act than as a registration of restraint. What the United States is willing to refrain from doing replaces what it is prepared to do as the key question. The United Nations Charter is conceived mainly as a list of restrictions laid upon states, and the contribution of the United States to the success of the organization is measured by its acceptance of limitations and prohibitions stated in the Charter or in the resolutions adopted by organs of the United Nations. The ultimate responsibility of the United States is to refrain from intervening, particularly with military force, in external situations unless such intervention is authorized or demanded by the United Nations. The proper role of the United States in the world organization is no longer conceived as that of doing what no other state can do, but, in this version, as that of refraining from doing what every other state should also refrain from doing. What is wanted from the United States is not dynamic leadership but faithful followership.

It is hardly surprising that this shift of emphasis concerning the symbolic significance of American membership in the United Nations should have occurred among leaders of other states. International political memories are notoriously short, and a quarter of a century has gone by since the world was preoccupied with the urgent importance of securing a guarantee that the United States would assume primary responsibility for action to maintain world order. For most states, the world has come to seem more settled and the need for a vigilant and powerful protector of the global system less pressing; the possibility of worrying about irresponsible American action instead of irresponsible American inaction is a luxury of this situation. . . .

America's performance of the role [of guarantor of the international order] that it was elected to play at the end of World War II has not been flawless. All along, nervousness as to how well the United States would play the role has competed with nervousness as to whether it would stick with the role. The demand that the United States be active in the effort to maintain international stability is not a demand that it be gratuitously, or stupidly, or recklessly active, and it is altogether possible that some of the activity undertaken by the United States may have been, or may have seemed to some honest and reasonable men, misguided in one or more of those senses. The urgent request for leadership cannot be expected to carry with it a guarantee of automatic and unquestioning approval for all that the leader does. As the international political situation has evolved, the danger has increased that American activism may in some cases be counter-productive, in that it may be more likely to rock than to discourage the rocking of the international boat.

On balance, however, the record of the United States as the leader of postwar efforts to achieve a modicum of international order has been, in my view, a creditable one. The fact that this leadership was essential is now obscured by the fact that it has been successful. Widespread doubts that it is now being exercised wisely, whether justified or not, are permitted by the fact that it has been exercised faithfully. . . . For the present, however, the international emphasis lies upon the dangers posed by American activity on the global stage, and the United Nations is widely conceived as the symbol of the multilateral constraint that ought to be brought to bear upon, and accepted by, the United States.

The shift to negative symbolism has been quite as pronounced among Americans as among foreigners, and its importance is probably greater on the domestic than on the foreign scene. For a variety of reasons, the general American disposition to engage in strenuous international activity has diminished. The fear that the United States might fail to do what it should do has largely given way to the conviction that it has been doing what it should have abstained from doing. Preventing unwise or improper American action looms as more important than facilitating necessary and proper action.

The reasons for this alteration of attitude are numerous and complex, and only a sketchy analysis will be offered here. One generation of Americans is tired and discouraged—weary of the carrying of burdens and the running of risks, nostalgic for the blissful days of freedom from responsibility for the state of the world, wistful for a "normalcy" that shows no signs of arriving, apprehensive about the domestic costs of continuing the effort to hold the world together, and resentful of America's being too little assisted, too little understood and appreciated, and too much suspected and condemned. Here we encounter the self-image of the overworked, underpaid, and much-maligned policeman. Another generation has never known an America that threatened world peace by weakness, neglect, and indifference, and it tends to interpret postwar American policy as that of a bumptious imperialist, ambitious to dominate and enamored of military action. From this perspective, the American image is that of the overweening tyrant, not the overburdened policeman. . . . Contradictory as they are, [these two views] point in the same direction: whether impelled by weariness in well doing or by a sense of guilt for wrong doing, whether it be undertaken as a prudent reduction of obligations or as a penitent renunciation of pretensions, the United States should restrict its engagement in international affairs.

This conclusion, however reached, finds expression in a drastically revised version of the meaning that should be attached to American membership in the United Nations. The world organization becomes, for Americans, a symbol of the inhibitions that their country should respect, of the limitations that it should observe, in the conduct of foreign policy. Membership should be taken to imply America's surrender of the right of unilateral intervention in situations external to itself, and acknowledgment of multilateral authority to restrict and regulate American activism.

It is not clear whether the United States should do what the United Nations authorizes or orders it to do—would the approval or sponsorship of the organization have been recognized as having purified and justified the American entanglement in Vietnam, or would it have been cited as evidence that the United States had corrupted the United Nations? It is certain, however, that, according to this view, the United States should not intrude into external situations without the blessing of the organization. The United Nations is the symbol of what the United States must not do.

It is also, for those of this persuasion, a symbol of what the United States *need* not do. Advocates of American retrenchment, thinking more wishfully than realistically, have displayed an inclination to regard the United Nations as a substitute for the United States, eligible to take up the burdens that this country might cast off. "Let the United Nations do it" is a slogan of those who are more weary of bearing responsibility than concerned about the responsibility's being successfully borne, whose eagerness for abdication surpasses their interest in the problem of succession. There is a certain irony in the fact that the United Nations, originally conceived as a device for insuring steadfast American involvement in world affairs, is now increasingly regarded by Americans as a means for encouraging and facilitating their retreat from such involvement.

More broadly, this newly prominent syndrome represents a shift toward an essentially negative conception of the task of achieving international peace. It substitutes pacifism for peace-building. The American contribution to peace is put in terms of withdrawing from foreign entanglements, minimizing internatioal commitments, minding one's own national business, reducing military expenditures, and limiting executive authority to respond to international exigencies. Peace is seen as a function of what states are incapacitated for doing and resolved not to do. The United Nations is conceived no longer as a state-building, state-activating, state-mobilizing enterprise, but as an agency for restraining, limiting, and—in some vague sense—replacing states. The state is regarded as an evil to be suppressed and supplanted. A sort of zero-sum game is thought to be in progress between the United Nations and its member states, a game in which a gain in the strength and effectiveness of one side involves a corresponding loss on the other side; the attainment of world peace is considered dependent upon the flourishing of the United Nations—which means the withering away of the state. In these terms, the United Nations is the symbol of a movement to achieve peace and order by controlling and subordinating states, and ultimately by putting them out of business. In such a scheme, submissiveness is the criterion of the loyalty of the performance of any state, including the United States.

IV

In my judgment, the first of the two versions of the symbolic significance of the United Nations that I have discussed is both more realistic as a description of the enterprise is which the world is engaged and more convincing as an approach to peace. The United Nations is in fact not a competitor of states but a stimulator of states; its business is not to put them out of business, but to help them to help themselves and each other to develop their capacities for handling their business. The antithesis between positive and negative approaches to peace is ultimately false, since they are related as the two sides of a coin, but placing emphasis upon the responsibilities that states should assume, rather than upon the restraints that they should accept, seems to me a sound approach to the ordering of international relations. World peace is not so much a status quo to be protected by the dictates of a multilateral nay-sayer as a situation to be promoted by the action of states cognizant of their stake in the state of the world. Such success as the United Nations may have in the building of a peaceful world will depend upon its ability to inspire the positive action of states.

In particular, the success of the United Nations will be determined by what the United States is able and willing to do. American restraint is obviously essential; both in the national interest and in the interest of world peace, it is important that the United States refrain from acting foolishly or wickedly. To say that not just any American action will conduce to international order is not to say, however, that the prime requirement for peace is to establish safeguards, domestic and international, against improper or imprudent action by the United States. An America preoccupied with the problem of avoiding mistakes and abuses will not break the peace, but is very likely to permit it to be broken. American innocence is not enough; American responsibility is the critical ingredient in any workable formula for world peace in our time. The world is more likely to survive unwise American activity than unwise American passivity.

No formula is available for the easy and certain calculation of what the United States should and should not do to enhance the prospects for a stable international order. . . . [The] contribution that falls peculiarly within the province of a major power such as the United States [is] to work at establishing and maintaining the kind of world situation that permits the United Nations to survive and to have the chance to accomplish something. Performance of this task may not be consistently compatible with observance of the rules of "good citizenship" described above. It may sometimes require taking actions that are unpopular among members of the United Nations and that constitute bypassing rather than utilization of the organization. The truest form of great-power support for the United Nations may involve not heeding its resolutions or funding its programs but providing a favorable international context for its operation.

This is clearly not a task for the United States alone, but for all major powers, including particularly the Soviet Union. Despite all the global troubles that can be attributed to antagonism between the United States and the Soviet Union, it must be said that these two superpowers have performed the task rather well, in rivalry more than in partnership. In pursuing the arms race, for instance, they have ignored or violated many resolutions of the General Assembly, but they have stabilized the international situation to the degree necessary for the survival and development of the United Nations. Rivalry between the giants, originally dreaded as the nemesis of the world organization, has in fact proved to be its principal dynamic force. Thus far, the survival of the United Nations has depended far more upon the kind of world we have than the survival of the latter has depended upon the United Nations. The maintenance of the kind of world in which it has been possible for the United Nations to take root has been, under all the circumstances, a remarkable achievement—which should be credited primarily to the United States and the Soviet Union.

To divide this credit between the superpowers is not to insist or to concede that it should be distributed equally. Both have contributed something, positively and negatively, but the record seems to me to confirm the general international judgment expressed at the end of both World Wars: the conviction that the basic requirement for global order is the firm and resolute commitment of the United States to active leadership in world affairs. . . .

Americans today are tired, disillusioned, confused, and divided. They are a captive audience for a "peace movement" that conceives peace in narrow and negative terms, that interprets peace as the immediate or nearly immediate cessation of fighting by one of the two sides involved in the Indochinese struggle,* that concentrates on peace *now* and peace *there,* and that defines the essential American contribution to peace in terms of what the United States should stop doing, refrain from undertaking again, and diminish its capability for attempting in the future. They are confronted with a "peace movement" that seeks to intimidate those whom it may not be able to persuade, that asks while arrogantly refusing to take "No" for an answer, that proclaims the right of dissent while rejecting the possibility that decent and responsible men might dissent from its dissent, and that threatens to destroy the capacity of the United States to follow any approach to peace other than its own. Understandably, Americans are tempted to adopt a short-range and narrow view of peace, and one that requires only that the United States exhibit a virtuous passivity.

Peace, however, is too important a matter to be left to those who think that they are pacifists. It is not a "whether" issue but a "how" problem. It is not a matter of local ceasefire but of global stability. It is not an immediate withdrawal but a long-term building project. Nobody knows with certainty how to achieve world peace; there is no necessary correlation between passionate commitment to the idea of peace and intelligent understanding of the problem of peace. . . . Only one thing seems to me reasonably certain: the future peace of the world depends more heavily upon the vigilance, far-sightedness, wisdom, courage, persistence, and power of the United States than upon any other factor. The founders of the League of Nations and the United Nations were on the right track, I think, when they undertook to make those organizations serve as symbols of an American commitment to active leadership in the quest for a just and lasting peace.

---

*[This article was published in 1971 at the height of the anti-war movement.]

26   The 'Fourth World' at the United Nations

Richard E. Bissell

Dr. Bissell is Visiting Research Fellow at the Center of International Studies, Princeton University.

. . . As the Afro-Asian and Latin American group of independent countries, commonly called the Third World, expanded in the 1960s and early 1970s, a new type of state appeared on the international scene: countries with all the trappings of formal independence that existed only by virtue of the movement of decolonization to its illogical conclusion. The initial, sound, rationale for the freeing of colonies was that certain societies were ready to adapt to independence in a world of sovereign states, and could maintain themselves politically, socially, and economically. Just as the UN Charter, in relation to the admission of new members, speaks of states as 'able and willing' to abide by the Charter, so it was assumed for some time that a country would achieve independence when it *wanted* it and was *able to keep it*. When translated into policy, however, these fine principles were lost as the process of decolonization became far more important than the underlying logic. Many of the new states could not support themselves economically, and had such fragile political structures that the domestic political process became something akin to the children's game "king of the castle"; moreover, they capriciously decided on random occasions to ignore the traditional

From The World Today, *March 1977, monthly journal of the Royal Institute of International Affairs, London, pp. 81-89. Reprinted with permission.*

rules of the diplomatic game. Although such a description may not apply across the board to the Fourth World, any one of its members will consistently fit at least one of those qualifications, and thereby assume a certain role in the international system.

Needless to say, no formal organization yet exists for the Fourth World, for the widespread umbrella of LDC groupings, such as the 'Group of 77' in UNCTAD, took in these new proto-states, gave them ideological shelter, and has recently found itself controlled by their concerns as well as their whims. Various observers have attempted to define criteria for identifying the Fourth World: economists suggest that any state whose citizens earn less than $100 per year is in that category; political scientists point to the lack of evidence of orderly transitions of power; and sociologists measure the missing cohesion in the society. Those less concerned with theoretical frameworks simply call members of the Fourth World the 'have-nots', though no list is definitive.

THE UN MAJORITY COALITION

What is important about the Fourth World in connexion with the UN is its role in what the then US Ambassador, John Scali, called the "mathematical majorities" of the General

Assembly: he was referring to coalitions mustered to oppose the United States and Western Europe on many issues at the 29th General Assembly, including the Third World "haves," the Fourth World "have-nots", and the Communist states. Even allowing for a few defections from Latin America or Asia, that type of coalition guaranteed a majority view of at least 100 states on most issues. How this grouping came into being, however, is not explained by any single factor.

Its ideological bonds are clearly most important for the Communist states, and help to explain the bitterness of the contest between China and the USSR in their efforts to prove their alignment with the Third and Fourth Worlds. The anti-imperialist and anti-capitalist bias of their ideology is negative in orientation; what positive ideology the groups have in common is more difficult to ascertain.

In terms of economic allegiance, the coalition maintains its revisionist unity fairly well. On occasional issues, the Communists may find it costly to follow their LDC allies, but most concessions to anti-capitalist unity mean little in operational terms. At the 1968 UNCTAD, for instance, the USSR magnanimously eliminated all tariffs on products from the LDCs. What was not stated, however, was that the effect of tariffs on the price mechanism in the USSR is nil, and that they therefore fail to determine the level of Soviet external purchases.

It is in the realm of issue alliances that the three groups mass their 100-plus majorities most effectively. On a whole succession of issues, the West has found itself isolated: the Middle East, terrorism, South Africa, decolonization, the structure of economic development, etc. Thus the United States and Britain, in particular, have been forced into postures of intransigent opposition to resolutions that are proposed at each General Assembly, passed, and ignored by those developed states controlling effective application. As the British Ambassador, Ivor Richard, stressed during the General Assembly debates in December 1974:

> To create a new international economic order is to create a new set of international economic relationships based on firmness and equity between the developing and the developed world. We cannot create it solely by debates on a series of resolutions which ignore the major differences which still exist, or which brush aside interests of those developed countries whose co-operation is necessary for their implementation.

Similar comments have been heard in various forms from Western delegates in increasing volume during the past decade.

THE 29TH GENERAL ASSEMBLY SESSION

The Fourth World manages at each session of the General Assembly to swing this large coalition of states in the direction of radical change. During the 29th session, their attention was focused particularly on three areas: Israel, South Africa, and the economic disasters of the poorest nations.[1]

The South African question was a dramatic example of how the Fourth World polarizes the world organization. Not content with the exclusion of South Africa from nearly all the specialized UN agencies, the antiapartheid radicals launched an initiative to throw her out of the United Nations as well. Their efforts inevitably failed in the Security Council with the triple veto of the United States, Britain, and France. In the General Assembly, however, the President, Algeria's Foreign

[1]See Sydney D. Bailey, "Some procedural problems in the UN General Assembly", *The World Today,* January 1975.

Minister, Mr. Bouteflika, was pressured into making an unprecedented (and unconstitutional in the view of many legal observers) ruling that suspended South Africa from the 29th session. There has been much tolerance of diplomatic irregularities at the UN, but it is questionable that the West will continue to put up with perceived illegalities.

The moves against Israel were closely tied to the South African issue, since the Arabs and Africans had agreed to trade votes on their respective causes. The result was the royal reception accorded to the leader of the Palestine Liberation Organization (PLO) by the Assembly. The radical tactics used against South Africa during the last three decades are now being applied to Israel, causing the confrontation between the support actors on each side: the United States (as the principal ally of Israel) and the Fourth World and the Communist states (as the backers of the Arabs and Palestinians). A curious aspect of this formation is that there is at present a natural "have-not" affinity between the Palestinians and the Fourth World, so that the Arabs welcome the support of the latter. Yet the granting of statehood to the Palestinians on the West Bank would hardly eliminate the poverty of the Palestinian people that is an embarrassment to the oil-rich Arabs. Indeed, a radical Palestinian state with sovereign rights may be more trouble to Arab allies in the Third World than the present role of Yasser Arafat's legions. Such underlying tensions and conflicting interests make policy-making among the anti-Israeli forces at the UN rather tortuous and occasionally impossible.

The last issue that preoccupied the Fourth World at the UN was the spreading spectre of starvation and regressing per capita incomes in their own states. Here the Fourth World could only play on the consciences of allies and enemies alike, as its economic condition had greatly deteriorated during 1974 through climbing costs of food and energy. Though there was little overt censure of the Third World states with a growing oil income, the complaints of Fourth World diplomats were clearly audible in the corridors of the UN. The strident speeches were reserved for the industrialized and food-rich nations of the West, but the implications were there for the new rich of the Middle East as well. In the closing sessions of the General Assembly, the Fourth World managed to lead a successful movement for a special emergency fund aimed at raising billions of dollars to help the thirty-two most needy states, but the votes of the "mathematical majority" could not be translated into reality. The Arabs ignored the fund in most instances, and the US said that she would continue relief aid on a bilateral basis. Thus the manipulation of the majority by the Fourth World clearly was reflected more in words than in actions.

The efforts of the Fourth World extended beyond UN Headquarters to the specialized agencies and conferences. At the Unesco General Conference, an attack was mounted on Israel over an issue where she was clearly vulnerable: alteration of the cultural environment of Jerusalem. The move was politically inspired, given the amount of cultural desecration that goes on in other parts of the world and remains uncensored, but it was remarkable that a relatively trivial issue could be used to punish Israel with a loss of cultural aid ($12,000 annually) and termination of membership in Unesco regional meetings, thus effectively expelling her from this organization. The Fourth World deliberately missed two points at Unesco: it chose to condemn Israel, rather than negotiate for the preservation of Muslim monuments in Jerusalem (which might imply recognition of Israel's right to exist as a state), and it repeated the tactics of ostracism that had manifestly failed against South Africa. If the goal is really to preserve the ancient assets of Jerusalem, the Fourth World would hardly achieve it by banning Israel from the only agency that might have some influence in this respect. This was yet another example of the "victories" of the Fourth World, which are symbolic rather than material.

The diplomacy displayed at the World Food Conference in November, 1974 also followed a predictable pattern. The tensions between those interested in long-range planning (stable food stocks and population control) and those concerned only with their immediate difficulties decimated the ranks of the optimists. Where the West failed, and particularly the US erred, was in not giving the Fourth World the symbolic handout—an implicit assurance that there would be no widespread starvation; then the Conference might have arrived at a conclusion more amenable to long-term planning. But the atmosphere of confrontation was too strong, and the new American President felt obliged to prove that he was in charge. The price of prestige politics was a tragic delay in meaningful food planning for several years.

It seems increasingly clear, however, that the alliance of forces at the UN between the Communist states, the Third, and the Fourth worlds will not be strained by confrontation with adversaries. Indeed, intransigence by the West may give them an incentive to preserve their cohesion, though growing internal divisions over several major issues are causing large fissures in their majority.

BREAKDOWN OVER COMMODITIES

The very cause of the Fourth World's coming into existence is creating increasing bitterness between it and the Third World. Their interests are not in tandem any longer, and it is rapidly becoming a question of "haves" versus "have-nots".

Competition among the LDCs has never been absent. The conflicts between coffee-exporting states, for instance, hampered their ability to obtain an operational international coffee agreement for decades. Willingness to stab one another in the back and inadequate diplomacy caused the competitors also within other commodities to fight bitterly: this was the case with substitutable commodities, such as coffee versus tea producers. On the other hand, what was so remarkable about the OPEC cartel was the demonstration that the producers within one commodity had the political will to co-operate, to maintain prices, and to show that such efforts could be applied to other commodities as well. One can readily understand the mushrooming of commodity conferences, on bauxite, copper, coffee, and so forth.

Old-fashioned commodity conflicts, however, were mild compared to the treacherous effects of increased energy prices on the Fourth World. The balance-of-payments situation for countries such as Tanzania, Senegal, Congo, Sri Lanka, and many others deteriorated so rapidly as a result of higher energy costs that their economic plans were thrown into ruin. The afflicted Fourth World asked the oil producers for aid, or at least concessionary prices on oil, but little was forthcoming (although that may be changed with the present oversupply of petroleum products). The oil producers insisted that the misfortunes of the Fourth World were the responsibility of the rich developed West, causing particularly bitter resentment amongst the Africans whose ancient feelings of enmity against the Arabs are easily revived. For most of the less-developed world, such commodity disputes balance out in that most states have at least one important commodity that gives them a stake in the rapidly rising price structure. Zambia, for instance, may not have oil, but if she can keep copper prices up the oil can be paid for. The Fourth World is distinct in that it is composed of states without such a card to play. Thus the hard core of thirty to thirty-five states, mostly African, have been willing to channel their radical inclinations towards political demands in recent international gatherings, including the 29th General Assembly. Economic questions, which are the root of their troubles, have been the object of several resolutions, none of which the Fourth World can realistically expect to see implemented by the states with the resources to do so.

TEMPORARY ALLIANCE WITH THE COMMUNISTS

There exist long-standing logical differences in the interests of the Communist states and the Fourth World: developed versus less developed, resource-endowed versus poverty-stricken, and orthodox versus radicals. Such potential conflict has meant little in the face of the overwhelming Communist desire to demonstrate ideological solidarity with the underdogs.

The 29th session of the General Assembly, however, revealed a serious split that is likely to be exacerbated, not healed, in the future. It is in the area of basic political power that the Soviet Union finds herself unable to compromise. In the General Assembly, this meant that the unplanned debate on the role of the United Nations in early December threw the Soviet Union off-balance. The polarized positions of the Fourth World and the group led by the United States left little room for compromise for the Russians. At first, the USSR refused to participate in the debate and later she voted against the resolution calling for the re-examination of UN structures for peaceful change. According to the Soviet representative, Mr. Malik, such a step might weaken the Security Council; what he had in mind was clearly the power of veto of the USSR, which would be undermined if powers were transferred from the Security Council to the General Assembly. The issue of political power remains crucial and, with the impending review of the UN Charter, is more alive in 1975 than in any previous year since 1945. It is likely that the meeting which will re-examine the Charter will reveal the limited nature of the coalition between the Fourth World and the Communist states. Not a genuine alliance, this coalition can be valid for certain times on certain issues, but not when it strikes at important Soviet interests.

THE FUTURE

A look at the group of countries defined by the UN as most needy, and comprising the core of the Fourth World,[2] prompts the question of where salvation lies for these underprivileged states. The solution will obviously vary from country to country. Not all of them can hope for an oil discovery. Some may alter their economic conditions through population control or simple industrial growth. Certainly India's basic problem is economic and not political. Others may look to substantial outside aid; after all, it would take a small diversion of oil royalty revenue for the two Yemens to make substantial progress. But it may be that the Fourth World will always exist, unless its members

[2]Bangladesh, Central African Republic, Chad, Dahomey, Democratic Yemen, El Salvador, Ghana, Guinea, Guyana, Haiti, Honduras, India, Ivory Coast, Kenya, Lesotho, Madagascar, Mali, Mauritania, Niger, Pakistan, Senegal, Sierra Leone, Somalia, Sri Lanka, Sudan, Cameroun, Tanzania, Upper Volta, and Yemen.

choose to merge with wealthier neighbours. Prosperity and power are relative concepts, and a group of states is bound to be worse off than the rest of the world for the foreseeable future.

What can be said with some certainty is that their role in the international system, and particularly in the United Nations, will never again be as strong. Part of the Charter review by the General Assembly Special Committee, due to meet in Peru in August, will include discussions of "associate membership" for those entities which are not "able" to carry out the obligations of UN membership, and which deserve aid to become viable. Such a concept of trusteeship for the UN is being given increasing consideration.

Even if such a scheme were not launched, the Fourth World will no longer be able to afford to spend scarce political capital on issues such as Israel or South Africa; all available energy will have to be applied to the pressing economic problems of starvation, the cost of energy, and at least minimal efforts at development—all available through bilateral ties. Whatever the results, the perspective on this era, and the role of the Fourth World at the UN, will be that these states have made their point. They were in desperate straits, and had to disrupt a reasonably orderly process in order to get attention. And one hopes that it will be possible to look back and say that their problems were met.

PART FOUR

ISSUES IN CONTEMPORARY INTERNATIONAL RELATIONS

XI

Population and Food Supplies

Why a chapter on population and food supplies in a text on international relations? The answer is reasonably simple. There are now four billion people living on the planet earth and two-thirds or more are living under conditions of extreme poverty. The total number is likely to increase to six billion by the end of the century (see Fig. 11-1). It is not a matter of feeling guilty or idealistic to be concerned about this problem. Overpopulation is a source of extreme pressure on many Third World societies, producing domestic unrest and repression; to some extent, poverty and the upheaval connected with overpopulation are causing not only the violation of human rights but the breakdown of society itself. Ted Robert Gurr, James Davies, Eric Wolf, and a host of other students of violence in Third World countries have noted that peasant fatalism and the sheer time and effort required to stay alive are the only things keeping poverty from taking an explosive form. But how long will this continue while the population piles up in the great shanty towns around the principal cities?

World society cannot be insulated against the consequences of over-

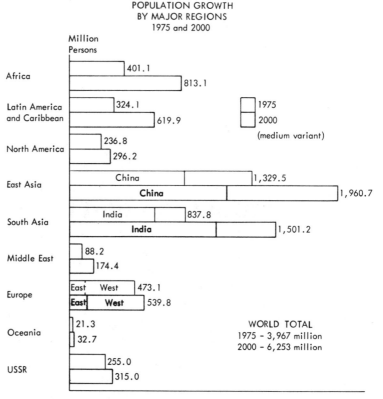

FIGURE 11-1 From The Department of State Bulletin Reprint, 11/3/1977.
SOURCE: U.N. Population Division

population and hunger. Most Third World countries presently exist under conditions of extreme instability or some form of dictatorship. They are increasingly manifesting their dissatisfaction with the present distribution of the world's wealth through anti-Western criticism in the United Nations. More fundamentally, it is difficult to maintain normal economic and political relations with states which are under such intense pressure. Secondly, the effects of overpopulation are being felt directly. Millions of Mexicans and Caribbean people enter the United States and England legally or illegally each year in an effort to escape their fate. The sending back of upwards of a million Italian laborers who had been working in Switzerland, France, and Germany accounts for some of the extreme unrest Italy has been experiencing. The magnitude of the population increases in a number of countries such as Brazil, Mexico, Egypt, India, Indonesia, and the Philippines is likely to reach a critical mass that may have explosive military or political consequences. At the same time, rulers in underdeveloped countries may note the fact that in the Indian elections which displaced Indira Gandhi from power, enforced population control was one of the issues.

Population and food problems present themselves in another form for Americans. What course of action are we to take? The economist P. T. Bauer takes the view that population growth reflects a fall in mortality and therefore an improvement in the position of Third World people.

> Acceleration of growth of population in underdeveloped countries does not by itself provide a valid argument for aid. It is debatable to what extent people would reduce the number of their children if they had access to more sophisticated methods of preventing conception. But even now there is no reason why they cannot reduce the number of children they have, and they will certainly do so if they value higher living standards for themselves and their children.[1]

Bauer believes that all the babies born to Third World mothers are really wanted; that the mother and father sit down and weigh the satisfaction of seeing another child at the mother's breast against the economic and nutritional consequences for themselves and the child. On the basis of this and other arguments, economists like Bauer dismiss the population problem as not being our responsibility.

Another point of view is that the imbalance between overpopulation and the potential for economic growth is so great in some countries that they are beyond helping. This is the argument of the "triage," or "lifeboat," school, which argues that since there is not sufficient room in the lifeboat for everyone, the hopelessly impoverished third of the world will just have to be written off.

Another alternative, advanced in the selection that follows by Robert McNamara, President of the World Bank, is for the developed world to face up to the fact that it has not done all that could have been done had we really devoted the necessary resources of education, money, and effort to the task. Even allowing for the obstacles which cultural patterns, poverty, and attitudes put in the way of birth control and economic achievement, more can be done. Up until now western governments have made assistance available for their own political and economic motives. As a result, recipient governments have felt free to use the aid, not necessarily with regard for the impoverished masses or with an eye to fundamental, long-term solutions to such things as overpopulation. Countries like Communist China and Brazil have actually encouraged rapid population growth in order to hasten their nation's arrival at great-power status. "Brazil, which counted 50 million inhabitants in 1949, reached 100 million in 1972, giving its population a doubling time of 23 years."[2]

American aid has been used to finance the existing elites and to preserve the status quo. This has permitted Third World elites to avoid coming to grips with the problems of agriculture and overpopulation. What is needed,

[1]P. T. Bauer, *Dissent on Development* (Cambridge: Harvard University Press, 1976), p. 123.

[2]K. P. Erickson. *The Brazilian Corporative State and Working-Class Politics.* (Berkeley: University of California Press, 1977), p. 191.

according to such distinguished and hard-headed economists as Gunnar Myrdal and Jagdish Bhagwati, is an approach that involves a very broad agreement on objectives and moral values among the donor and recipient nations to assure that assistance programs will really deal with the needs of people, including the need for birth-control techniques.

Of course, such an approach would require the governments and political elites in both the donor and recipient countries to put the solution of these problems ahead of their immediate self-interest.

"Governments have considerable capacity," writes McNamara, "to help create a generalized atmosphere of social consensus in an antinatalist direction. Allocations of [foreign aid] and central government funds for community improvements . . . can be conditioned on evidence of [reform] and new-style family norms." One can be permitted to wonder: if the same zeal, effort, and money that is spent on armaments or putting men on the moon had been devoted to population control, would the problem still be as acute as it is?

27   Population and International Security

Robert S. McNamara

A former U.S. Secretary of Defense, Mr. McNamara is President of the World Bank.

THE POPULATION BACKGROUND

Last year [1976] the world's total population passed the four billion mark. On the face of it, the event was not very dramatic. It marked, of course, the largest number of human beings ever to have been alive simultaneously on the planet—and thus was a record of sorts. But that particular record is broken every year. And will continue to be broken every year long beyond the lifespan of anyone alive today.

Barring a holocaust brought on by man or nature, the world's population today is the smallest it will ever be again. How did it reach a population of four billion? For the first 99 percent of man's existence, surprisingly slowly. For the last 1 percent of his history, in a great rush.

Man has been on earth for a million years or more. . . . Until the dawn of agriculture around 8000 B.C., the population, after ten thousand centuries, had reached only an estimated eight million. During this immense interval, the average annual rate of increase was only about one additional individual for every 150,000 persons.

With the advent of agriculture and the

From INTERNATIONAL SECURITY (Fall, 1977). Copyright 1977 by the President and Fellows of Harvard College, all rights reserved. Reprinted by permission. (Some footnotes have been omitted)

domestication of animals, the food supply became more dependable, and the eight million population of 8000 B.C. rose to about 300 million by the beginning of the Christian era. This means an average annual rate of increase of 65 persons for every 150,000—or as demographers would express it today, a growth rate of .046 percent.

From A.D. 1 to the middle of the eighteenth century, the population ebbed and flowed, gaining in prosperous periods, and falling back sharply in times of trouble. . . By 1750, the total had reached only about 800 million. Then, as the industrial revolution gathered momentum, population growth began rapidly to accelerate. By 1900 it had doubled to 1.6 billion; by 1964 it had doubled again to 3.2 billion; and by the end of the century it is projected to double again to about 6.3 billion.

Now these numbers—as abstract as they may seem—illustrate an important point about population dynamics. The doubling time is extremely sensitive to very minor increments in the average annual growth rate. It took mankind more than a million years to reach a population of one billion. But the second billion required only 120 years; the third billion 32 years; and the fourth billion 15 years. If one postulates that the human race began with a single pair of parents, the population has had to double only 31 times to reach its present huge total.

At the current global growth rate of about 2 percent, the world's population will add a

TABLE 1
The Rate of Growth of the World's Population

Year	Total Population	Rate of Growth Per Year Since Previous Date	Doubling Time
1,000,000 B.C.	A few thousand	—	—
8,000 B.C.	8 million	.0007%	100,000 years
1 A.D.	300 million	.046	1,500
1750	800 million	.06	1,200
1900	1,650 million	.48	150
1970	3,600 million	1.0	70
2000	6,300 million	2.0	35

fifth billion in about 11 years. But these global totals, of course, obscure wide demographic differences between the developed and developing countries. During the period from 1750 to 1850, the two groups of countries grew at similar average annual rates: .6 percent for the developed, .4 percent for the developing. From 1850 to 1950, the rates were .9 percent and .6 percent. From 1950 to 1975 the rates changed dramatically and became, respectively, 1.1 percent and 2.2 percent. The recent growth rates in the developing countries are not only twice as great as those in the developed countries today, but exceed by an equally large margin the most rapid growth ever experienced by the developed countries.

Translating these growth trends, and relative population sizes, into absolute numbers of people demonstrates the historical pattern even more graphically. From 1750 to 1850 the developed countries grew annually by 1.5 million people and the developing countries by 3 million; from 1850 to 1950, by 5 million and 7 million respectively; and from 1950 to 1975, by 11 million, and 48 million.

Demographic Dynamics

To grasp fully what is happening here it is helpful to recall the fundamental dynamics of population increase. On the surface they seem simple enough: population growth for any given society is the excess of births over deaths, as modified by migration. If we disregard, for the moment, the influence of migration, it is apparent that so-called stationary, or steady-state, populations are those in which births and deaths are in balance. For thousands of centuries the world had something very close to just that.

To achieve a steady-state population there must be a stable age structure and replacement-level fertility: a child must be born to replace each person in the parent generation. That seems obvious enough, but since some females die before or during childbearing age, the average number of children that parents in a given society must have to keep the population stationary is a function of the mortality conditions in the society.

In the Ivory Coast, for example, the death rates in the late 1960s of potential childbearing women were such that 3.5 births per woman would have been required to replace the parent generation; whereas in the United States, where death rates were much lower, only 2.1 births per woman were needed. In actuality, of course, fertility in the Ivory Coast, as in almost all of Africa, is much higher than that; and fertility in the United States has, since 1972, been below the replacement level. . . .

We know, too, what are the outer limits

of the various female mortality-fertility combinations that can produce a stationary population. Today in the developed countries over 95 percent of women survive through childbearing years. Under such conditions, a total fertility rate of only 2.1 children per woman suffices for replacement.

On the other hand, average female life expectancy of 15 is the highest feasible mortality rate any large population could sustain, since in such a case only about 25 percent of women live to have children, and they would have to have an average of almost 9 children apiece to keep the population from declining. While it is, of course, physiologically possible for individual women to give birth to more than that number, no large grouping has ever been observed with a total fertility rate much higher than 8 to 9 births per woman.

This explains how near zero growth prevailed in the world's population for thousands of centuries. Life expectancy at birth was very low, probably about 20 years. This meant that only about a third of the females born survived to the mean age of childbearing, and that those who lived to the age of menopause had an average of about 6.5 children: a birth rate of 50 to 55 per 1,000. . . . .

Developing countries today typically have a female life expectancy at birth of about 55; total fertility rates averaging about 5.3 children per woman; and crude birth rates of about 37 per 1,000.[1] This, combination results in a growth rate of approximately 2.3 percent, doubling the population every 30 years. To reach replacement level fertility,

[1]There is, of course, a great range of differences between developing countries. Some have average life expectancies as low as 38; crude birth rates as high as 50 per 1,000; and annual growth rates as much as 3.5 percent, which double the population every 20 years. Women throughout these countries have an average number of children ranging between four and eight.

at current mortality rates, would require a reduction in the total fertility rate to 2.6, and the crude birth rate to about 20 per 1,000.

But when a net reproduction rate of 1.0—replacement-level fertility—is reached in a society, it does not mean that the population immediately ceases to grow. It will continue increasing for decades. That is a function of the society's age structure.

The population will continue to grow because the higher birth rates of the past have produced an age distribution with a relatively high proportion of persons currently in, or still to enter, the reproductive ages. This in turn will result in more births than deaths until the population changes to the older age distribution intrinsic in the low birth rate. Thus, even at replacement-level fertility, the population does not become stationary until the age structure stabilizes, which takes 60 to 70 years. . . .

And here we come to a point of immense importance—one that is not well understood, and one that I want strongly to emphasize: the speed at which fertility in the world declines to the replacement level will have a very significant effect on the ultimate size of the stationary population.

For every decade of delay in achieving a net reproduction rate of 1.0—replacement level—the world's ultimate steady-state population will be about 15 percent greater. The significance of this statement can be understood by applying it to the present outlook. If current trends in fertility rates continue, i.e., if crude birth rates in developing countries decline by approximately 6 points per decade, it appears that the world might reach a net reproduction rate of 1.0 in about the year 2020. This would lead to a steady-state population of 11 billion some 70 years later.

If the date at which replacement-level fertility is reached could be advanced from 2020 to 2000 (by following, for example, the suggestions made later in this paper), the ultimate population would be approximately 3 billion less, a number equivalent to 75 percent of today's world total. This reveals in startling terms the hidden penalties of failing to act, and act immediately to reduce fertility.

If global replacement levels of fertility were to be reached around the year 2000, with the world ultimately stabilizing at about 8 billion, 90 percent of the increase over today's levels would be in the developing countries. It would mean, if each country followed the same general pattern, an India of 1.4 billion; a Brazil of 275 million; a Bangladesh of 245 million; a Nigeria of 200 million; and a Mexico of 175 million.

But as I have pointed out, given today's level of complacency in some quarters, and discouragement in others, the more likely scenario is a world stabilized at about 11 billion. Populations in the developing countries would be 40 to 60 percent greater than indicated above because of two decades of delay in reaching replacement levels of fertility.

We have to try to comprehend what such a world would really be. We call it stabilized, but what kind of stability would be possible? Can we assume that the levels of poverty, hunger, stress, crowding, and frustration that such a situation could cause in the developing nations—which by then would contain 9 out of every 10 human beings on earth—would be likely to assure social stability? Or political stability? Or, for that matter, military stability? It is not a world that anyone wants.

Even in our present world of 4 billion,

excessive population growth severely penalizes many of the developing nations.[2]

It drains away resources, dilutes per capita income, and widens inequalities. At the national level, the government must devote more and more investment simply to provide minimal services to an ever-increasing number of children. At the family level, the same needs press in on the parents of large families.

During their early years, most children are primarily consumers rather than producers. For both the government and the family, more children means more expenditure on food, on shelter, on clothing, on health, on education, on every essential social service. And it means correspondingly less expenditure on investment to achieve the very economic growth required to finance these services.

As children reach adulthood, the problem is compounded by mounting unemployment. There are not enough jobs to go round because the government—grappling with the daily demands of the increasing numbers—has been unable to invest enough in job-

[2]I should stress that in choosing to write on population, I do not mean to imply that it is the sole or predominant cause of social injustice and poverty. On several previous occasions, most recently in Manila last October, I have discussed the policy measures that governments of developing countries need to take to tackle poverty in both rural and urban areas. I have also reviewed the role that the developed nations must play through additional stimulus to international trade and higher levels of foreign assistance. To my mind, as later sections of this paper will demonstrate, policies to solve the poverty problem and to reduce the rate of population growth are complementary to each other: an effective attack on poverty is essential if population problems are going to be fully solved; and effective population policies are essential elements in the attack on poverty.

producing enterprises. Thus the cycle of poverty and overpopulation tightens—each reinforcing the other—and the entire social and economic framework weakens under the weight of too great a dependency ratio.[3]

The sudden global surge in population over the past quarter-century has, of course, been a function of two opposite trends: the gradual slowing down of the growth rate in the developed nations, and the rapid acceleration of the growth rate in the developing countries. The experience of the developed countries gave rise to the theory of the demographic transition.

The Demographic Transition

The theory holds that societies tend to move through three distinct demographic stages:

1. High birth rates, and high death rates, resulting in near stationary populations;
2. High birth rates, but declining death rates, producing growing populations;
3. And finally, low birth rates and low death rates, reestablishing near stationary populations.

If one examines the history of the developed nations, the facts support the theory. Preindustrial societies grew very slowly. Birth rates and death rates generally were both high, and very nearly in balance. But with the advent of industrialization, more adequate nutrition, and improved public health measures, death rates gradually began to fall and growth rates to increase. The process continued in the industrializing

societies into our own century until birth rates in turn began to diminish, and growth level off.[4] Today in all but two or three developed countries fertility rates are near, or at—and in some cases even below—replacement levels. As a consequence, in 1975, the total fertility rate for the developed countries as a group was 2.1, exactly at replacement level.

It has taken the developed world as a whole about 150 years to pass through the demographic transition. But most of the developing countries remain today in the second stage of the transition. Their birth rates range between 30 and 50 per thousand, and their death rates between 10 and 25 per thousand. The result is that as a group their population is growing at about 2.3 percent a year and at that pace it will double in about 30 years.

Now, if the developing countries were to require 150 years to complete the transition, the world's population would grow from its present 4 billion not to 8 or 11, but to 15 or 16 billion. No one believes it will actually reach that magnitude. But no one is very certain what precisely is going to avert it, short of a major catastrophe brought on by human folly, or by nature's revenge. The fundamental question is: what, if anything, can rationally and humanely be done to accelerate the demographic transition in the developing world? Some serious observers say nothing can be done. I do not share that view. And to explain why I do not, I want to turn now to a more detailed examination of the current demographic situation in the developing countries.

---

[3]A typical example is the case of Algeria, as contrasted with Sweden. In Algeria, with its high birth rate, every 100 persons of working age in 1970 had to support 98 children under the age of 15. In Sweden, with its low birth rate, every 100 persons of working age had to support only 32 children under 15.

[4]Recent research indicates there were some exceptions to the typical pattern of demographic transition. In some cases, the decline in fertility preceded the fall in mortality.

RECENT DEMOGRAPHIC TRENDS

One, as always, must begin with the most recent data. And one, as always, must begin with cautions about the data. They are preliminary, they are not very precise, and they are best only suggestive of trends. But the trend they suggest is cautiously encouraging. What appears to have happened in the developing world over the six-year period, 1969-1975 is that the crude birth rate (CBR)—the number of births per thousand of population—has declined 3.9 points. The crude death rate (CDR)—the number of deaths per thousand—during the same period has declined 1.9 points. The result is that the rate of natural increase (NI) declined slightly.

It we expand the six-year period to a two-decade period, 1955-1974 the birth rates appear to have declined an average of about 5.6 points in 20 years, or nearly 13 percent. By major region, the decline has been 6.5 points in Asia; 5.4 points in Latin America; and 2.3 points in Africa. Further, this decline of the CBR was general and widespread. It occurred in 77 of the 88 developing countries for which estimates are available. Significantly, the decline appears to be gathering momentum: in the developing countries it is less for the earlier years, and greater for the more recent years.

But even if the higher rates of decline were to continue into the future, it would mean only 6 points off the CBR in a decade. And that is only about half of the generally accepted target of 1 point a year. Thus, though the trend in birth rates is encouraging, its pace is still far too slow. Moreover, the overall CBR decline obscures wide variations among individual countries as shown in Table 2.

Among those nations with populations of more than 50 million, India achieved the greatest CBR reduction, possibly as much as 17 percent; and Indonesia the second best, possibly 13 percent. Bangladesh, on the other hand, and Nigeria, registered no decline at all. In countries with populations of 20 to 50 million, several demonstrated very large reductions: Korea, 30 percent; and Thailand, Turkey, Colombia, and Egypt, 25 percent each. But the Philippines, Iran, Burma, Zaire, and Ethiopia—all countries with very high birth rates—showed only slight declines of less than 5 percent. Finally, among the smaller developing countries, the CBR went down by more than 40 percent in two, and by more than 20 percent in all the others listed in Table 2. Most of the larger declines occurred in the last decade, again suggesting the existence of a genuine trend, rather than merely an insignificant statistical aberration.

But, to repeat: statistics in this field are fragmentary, and the situation they describe varies widely from country to country. It is, then, too soon to be fully certain, but the indications do suggest that crude birth rates in the developing world—outside sub-Saharan Africa—have at least begun to turn downward. If this conclusion is confirmed by the various censuses scheduled for 1980, then what we are witnessing here is a historic change of immense moment. Its importance lies in this. Experience illustrates that once fertility turns definitely downward from high levels, it generally does not reverse direction until it has fallen quite low. Further the higher the level at which it starts down, the more rapid is its descent.

All of this is obviously a welcome development—if it is in fact taking place. And a reasonable interpretation of the admittedly incomplete data indicates that it is. It is welcome particularly because it is far easier to expedite a declining fertility trend once it has really begun, that it is to initiate it in the first place. But it is essential that we remain

Country	1975 Pop. (in millions)	% Decrease in CBR	CBR in 1974
Group 1 (over 50 million)			
India	598	17	36
Indonesia	132	13	42
Mexico	60	11	40
Brazil	108	7	39
Pakistan	70	5	47
Bangladesh	79	0	47
Nigeria	63	0	50
Group II (20 to 50 million)			
South Korea	35	30	28
Thailand	42	25	37
Turkey	39	25	33
Columbia	25	25	32
Egypt	37	25	35
Burma	31	5	40
Philippines	42	5	36
Iran	34	5	43
Zaire	25	5	45
Ethiopia	28	5	48
Group III (under 20 million)			
Africa—Mauritius	0.9	37	25
Tunisia	5.6	21	36
Americas—Costa Rica	2.0	42	30
Barbados	0.2	35	21
Chile	10.3	33	23
Trinidad & Tobago	1.1	30	24
Panama	1.7	24	31
Asia—Singapore	2.3	55	18
Taiwan	16.0	47	23
Hong Kong	4.4	44	18
Fiji	0.6	37	28
Sri Lanka	13.6	27	27
Malaysia	10.5	27	30

SOURCE: The Population Council, *Population and Family Planning Programs: A Factbook, 1976.*
UN data on birth rates revised by Parker Mauldin of the Population Council.

realistic. The truth is that at best the current rate of decline in fertility in the developing countries is neither large enough, nor rapid enough, to avoid their ultimately arriving at steady-state populations far in excess of more desirable—and attainable—levels. And I repeat: for every decade of delay in achieving a net reproduction rate of 1.0—replacement-level fertility—the world's ultimate steady-state population will be approximately 15 percent greater.

Current trends, as I have noted, point to

a finally stabilized global population of about 11 billion. If we accelerate those trends sufficiently to save two decades of time, it would reduce that dangerous pressure on the planet by approximately 3 billion: 75 percent of the world's current total. Is that acceleration realistically possible? It is. How, then, can we achieve it? Let me turn to that subject now, and begin by examining the causes and determinants of fertility decline. . . .

Compared to the last century, the means of controlling birth are far more numerous, more effective, and more easily available. Modern mass communications are both more pervasive, and more influential. The elite in the developing countries, and increasingly the mass of the people as well, are becoming more aware of living standards in the developed world, including smaller family size and less traditional life styles. Exposure to alternate possibilities stirs their imaginations, and affects their aspirations. Governments have much greater ability now to reach across subnational barriers of linguistic, ethnic, and cultural differences, and can stay in touch with villagers, if they choose to do so. Debate about education policy continues, but most developing countries regard basic literacy for both males and females as essential for development goals, and greater national unity.

Finally, there are an increasing number of governments in the developing world committed to lowering fertility, and an even larger number supporting family planning programs. In 1969, when as President of the World Bank I spoke on population, at the University of Notre Dame, only about 40 developing countries officially supported family planning, and only 20 of those had specific policies to reduce fertility. By 1975 there were 63 countries with official family planning programs, and 34 with explicit policies to reduce the growth rate.

The correlation in developing countries between certain social changes and fertility reductions is persuasive, and is supported by the trends from 1960 to 1970. During that decade, literacy and education advanced; infant mortality declined; life expectancy increased; and the crude birth rate fell. Assuming that the social indicators continue to change at the rate of that decade, and that their relation to fertility patterns remains the same, the crude birth rate in the developing countries as a whole would drop approximately half a point per year.

What this means is that without additional intervention, the current population in the developing world is going to continue to grow at rates very substantially in excess of those that would facilitate far more economic and social progress. It is these rates which would lead to an ultimate steady-state population in the world of 11 billion. That is clearly undesirable. Governments, then, must intervene. But how precisely? Let us examine the choices available.

POSSIBLE INTERVENTIONS TO REDUCE FERTILITY

The range of possible interventions divides into two broad categories:

—Those designed to encourage couples to desire smaller families;
—And those designed to provide parents with the means to implement that desire.

Both approaches are, of course, necessary. The first sets out to alter the social and economic environment that tends to promote high fertility, and by altering it to create among parents a new and smaller norm of family size, and therefore a demand for birth control. And the second supplies the requisite means that will make that new norm attainable. Thus family planning services are essential, but in the end can succeed only to the extent that a demand for lower fertility exists.

That demand apparently does not now exist in sufficient strength in most of the developing countries. There are a number of policy actions that governments can take to help stimulate the demand. None of them is easy to implement. All of them require some reallocation of scarce resources. And some of them are politically sensitive. But governments must measure those costs against the immeasurably greater costs in store for societies that procrastinate while dangerous population pressures mount. What, then, are those specific social and economic actions most likely to promote the desire for reduced fertility?

Governments should try to:

—Reduce current infant and child mortality rates sharply.
—Expand basic education and increase the proportion of girls in school.
—Increase the productivity of smallholders in the rural areas, and expand earning opportunities in the cities for low-income groups.
—Put greater stress on more equitable distribution of income and services in the drive for greater economic growth.
—And above all else raise the status of women socially, economically, and politically. . . .

Promoting a Social Consensus

Governments have considerable capacity, as well, to help create a generalized atmosphere of social consensus in an anti-natalist direction. Villages and local communities, just as individual families, can be rewarded by government policies for good performance in fertility restraint. Alloca-tions of central government funds for community improvements—roads, electrification, public works—can be conditioned on evidence of community commitment to new-style family norms. India, for example, recently adopted a measure which provides that both the political representation of local areas, and their allocation of national financial resources, will no longer increase simply as a function of their population growth. In the future, additional numbers will not automatically mean additional votes or additional claims on tax revenues.

But it is not only the central government in a society that can apply disincentives to high fertility. Community authorities can do the same. In preindustrial Japan, for example, a strong tradition of social cooperation and consensus at the village level maintained severe constraints on the number of households in the village, often permitting no increase at all. These social pressures were transmitted to heads of households, who in turn exerted authority over individual household members in matters of marriage, divorce, and adoption. This tradition appears to have been a significant influence in holding population increase during the last 150 years of Tokugawa Japan to less than 0.2 percent a year.

It is obvious that the interest of a local community in the fertility of its membership will be proportional to the social costs of population increase that it is called upon to bear. If schools and other public services are in part locally financed; if pressures on the land lead to local deforestation and erosion; and if local unemployment becomes serious, then communities may well become conscious of the adverse social effects of excessive population growth.

It is clear that there are many different approaches to the task of promoting a new social consensus on population problems within a society, and the choice of one over another—or any particular mix of actions—must, of course, be guided by the cultural context of the society in question. But the truth is that most of the approaches, and all of the actions, are difficult to implement. And we must face the reality that if these approaches fail, and population pressures become too great, nations will be driven to more coercive methods.

Coercion

A number of governments are moving in the direction of coercion already. Some have introduced legal sanctions to raise the age of marriage. A few are considering direct legal limitations on family size, and sanctions to enforce them. No government really wants to resort to coercion in this matter. But neither can any government afford to let population pressures grow so dangerously large that social frustrations finally erupt into irrational violence and civil disintegration. That would be coercion of a very different order. In effect, it would be nature's response to our own indifference.

Let me underscore what we have been analyzing here. We have been discussing those kinds of interventions that governments can make to help stimulate the desire among parents for a small family size. But those efforts must, of course, be accompanied by corresponding interventions that provide parents with readily available means to do so.

Family Planning Services

Governments must improve the access to the modern means of fertility control both qualitatively and quantitatively: more and better services to greater numbers of people. In practice, that requires:

—Providing a broad selection of the current contraceptives: pills, condoms, IUDs; as well as sterilization, and—where the society desires it—abortion.

—Establishing a broad spectrum of delivery services and informational activities utilizing: physicians in private practice; paramedical workers; professional field workers; community-based local agents; the commercial sector; widespread distribution of contraceptives; sterilization centers; mobile clinics; postpartum arrangements; and the integration of contraceptive services into the maternal and child-health system, the general health system, and the community development system.

—And, finally, improving the acceptability, continuity, and effectiveness of the means of fertility control by accelerating research on such possibilities as: a contraceptive vaccine; a better implant; an IUD free of side effects; a safer and more convenient pill (a once-a-month pill or a once-a-year pill); a nonsurgical means to terminate pregnancy; or a currently unknown "ideal" contraceptive.

To put the matter succinctly, governments need to provide a broad choice of present contraceptive techniques and services to parents; they need to improve the delivery system by which parents can get the services they wish; and they need to support continuing research for better techniques and services. The majority of the world's population lives in countries with family planning programs that now have as their explicit objective the reduction of fertility. And yet the programs themselves often do not reflect much political conviction that they can and must succeed.

Many of these programs are small, and rely on foreign sources for much of their finance. All governments, of course, have resource constraints. But fertility reduction, as a priority, seldom commands even 1 percent of national budgets. Further, governments have often failed to give the programs the status and national attention that would attract top managerial talent. For these, and related reasons, the world's total family planning acceptors did not measurably increase in the period 1972–1975, despite the increase in the number of national programs.

I listed above a number of actions that governments—both developed and developing—can take to strengthen family planning programs. One of the most urgent needs is a much greater effort in reproductive biological research and contraceptive technology.

The investment in reproductive research is immensely worthwhile. And there is simply no question that more of it is needed. This expanded research will require years of effort before it can be translated into radically different methods of contraception. Governments cannot afford simply to wait for that. Rather, they must in the meantime take action to improve present family planning programs and make broader use of current contraceptive technology. Such programs are necessary in all countries with rapidly expanding populations, regardless of the particular stage of economic and social development.

Family Planning in Relation to the Stages of Development

In some countries, widespread use of contraception precedes a change in desired family size, and may help it occur. In others, contraception becomes popular only after other factors have reduced family norms. But in either pattern, family planning is important, and indeed ultimately essential to meet the demand of parents for reduced family size.

In the lower-income developing countries, where absolute poverty is endemic, family planning programs should be shaped to service those parents who already desire to reduce their fertility; to urge others to consider that option; to increase local awareness of the damaging consequences of rampant population growth; and to recognize that by improving the health of the local community—and particularly of mothers and children—the program is in fact laying the foundation for a change in fertility norms. Such an approach ensures that as the demand for family planning service increases, the supply is there to meet it. In the absence of more fundamental social and economic improvements, one cannot, of course, expect such a program to "solve" the population problem. But it would be equally naive to assume that it can have no effect on fertility whatever. Indonesia, for example, is a particularly interesting case of a country with strong political commitment to fertility decline, and a vigorous family planning program, that appears to be off to a good start in spite of immense development problems.

In any event, the view that development in and by itself can take care of the fertility problem in the developing world is an unfortunate oversimplification as applied to most of the countries and a dangerous error as applied to others. Even for the better-off developing countries such a "development-only" strategy would be wasteful. The fall in fertility without a strong family planning program, is likely to come later in the development process than it need to: per capita income would grow more slowly and the ultimate size of the population would be larger.

But for the lower-income countries a "development-only" strategy would be disastrous. In these countries it would take a much longer time to reach the socio-economic levels that normally correspond with significantly lower birth rates. Indeed in some of them, it is the very magnitude of the population pressures themselves that is retarding that progress. Were the fertility problem not dealt with directly, the progress would simply be too slow. At the rate at which literacy has been increased and infant mortality and fertility reduced during the last decade, it would take India, for example, until the year 2010 to reach the literacy levels that normally correspond with crude birth rates of 30; and it would take until the year 2059 to reach the infant mortality levels that correspond with a CBR of 30. If Nepal were to do nothing about its fertility directly, it would take it 170 years to reach the literacy level associated with a CBR of 30. India and Nepal—and many other countries—simply do not have that kind of time to experiment with a "development-only" strategy. And, happily, they have no intention of attempting it.

Whatever the rhetoric at Bucharest in 1974, no country has abandoned the anti-natalist policies it held then, and several have strengthened them. Competent observers do argue about the relative importance of social development and family planning efforts in reducing fertility rates. Some say the former is too indirect. Others say the latter is too inefficient. But the truth is that the latest reviews of the experience of individual countries—reviews completed within the past twelve months—clearly support the conclusion that significant reduction of birth rates depends on both social development and family planning.

The reviews suggest that family planning programs have a clear substantial and independent effect on country performance. Virtually all of the countries with reductions of 20 percent or more in their crude birth rates during the decade 1965—1974 had strong family planning programs. But the research also confirms what common sense itself would suggest: that the effect of family planning programs is greatest when they are joined to efforts designed to promote related social goals.

Raising Population Consciousness

The real problem—for all of us—is to try to grasp the complexity of the population issue. Population problems are not simple; they are not straight-forward; and they are certainly not very clear. They are like man himself: complicated. If we are to get down to solutions that really work, we have to try to see the problem in all its ramifications, and in all of its tangled interrelationships.

I recently asked a panel of distinguished experts to review our activities in the population field within the World Bank. They took a hard look at everything we have been doing since 1969, and they rightly reproached us for a tendency to treat population too much in isolation from our other activities. They pointed out that we have been prepared to lend for population projects, and were ready to bring specialized analysis to population issues when they were of obvious immediate importance. But too many of us in the Bank had proceeded as if population issues could be left to specialists, rather than considered automatically in all aspects of our investment and development programs. In short, they asked us to think about the problem in a more comprehensive way—and deal with it accordingly. They were right. And that is exactly what we plan to do.

SUMMARY AND CONCLUSIONS

It now appears that a significant decline in fertility may have at least begun in the developing countries. The data are not yet fully conclusive, but the indications are that the crude birth rates have fallen over the past two decades by an average of about 6 points, or nearly 13 percent.

By major region, the decline has been 6.5 points in Asia; 5.4 points in Latin America; and 2.3 points in Africa. Further, the decline appears to have been general and widespread. It has occurred in 77 of the 88 countries for which estimates are available. If these indications are confirmed by the censuses scheduled for 1980, then what we are seeing here is something of historic importance. It would mean that the period of rapid acceleration in the rate of growth of the world's population has finally reached its peak and is now definitely moving downward towards stabilization. But as welcome as this is, the fact remains that the current rate of decline in fertility in the developing countries is too slow to avoid their ultimately arriving at stationary populations far in excess of acceptable levels.

Unless governments, through appropriate policy action, can accelerate reduction in fertility, the global population may not stabilize below 11 billion. That would be a world none of us would want to live in. But governments can take action, and can accelerate the process, given the resolve and determination to do so. The critical point is this: for every decade of delay in achieving a net reproduction rate of 1.0—replacement-level fertility—the ultimate steady-state world population will be approximately 15 percent greater.

Governments, then, must avoid the severe penalties of procrastination, and try to hasten the process forward. But how? The causes and determinants of fertility reduction are extremely complex, but it appears likely that there are a number of key linkages between that reduction and certain specific elements of socio-economic development. The factors that appear to be the most important are: health, education, broadly dis-

tributed economic growth, urbanization and the enhanced status of women. These factors are at work in the developing world today, but their progress is too slow to be fully effective. Without additional intervention on the part of governments, the current population in the developing world is going to continue to grow at rates very substantially in excess of those that would permit far more economic and social progress.

There are two broad categories of interventions that governments must undertake: those designed to encourage couples to desire small families; and those designed to provide parents with the means to implement that desire. The first set of interventions sets out to alter the social and economic environment that tends to promote fertility, and by altering it to create a demand among parents for a new and small family norm. And the second set of interventions supplies the requisite means that will make that new norm attainable.

To create the demand for a change in family norm, governments should try to:

—Reduce current infant and child mortality rates sharply.

—Expand basic education and substantially increase the proportion of girls in school.

—Increase the productivity of smallholders in the rural areas, and expand earning opportunities in the cities for low-income groups.

—Put greater stress on more equitable distribution of income and services in the drive for greater economic growth.

—And above all else raise the status of women socially, economically and politically.

To satisfy the demand for a change in family norms, governments and the international community should:

—Provide a broad choice of the present contraceptive techniques and services to parents.

—Improve the delivery systems by which parents can get the services they wish.

—And expand present levels of research seeking better techniques and services.

Both categories of interventions are necessary. Recent studies confirm that the effect of family planning programs is greatest when they are joined to efforts designed to promote related social goals.

We know that eventually the world's population will have to stop growing. That is certain. What is uncertain is how. And when. At what level. And with what result. We who are alive today can determine the answers to those questions. By our action—or inaction—we will shape the world for all generations to come. We can avoid a world of 11 billion, and all the misery that such an impoverished and crowded planet would

imply. But we cannot avoid it by continuing into the next quarter century the ineffective approach to the problem of population that has characterized the past twenty-five years.

Man is still young in cosmic terms. He has been on earth for a million years or so. And our modern ancestor, *Homo sapiens*, for a hundred thousand years. But the universe of which he is a part is some twenty billion years old. And if we represent the history of the universe by a line a mile long, then modern man has appeared on that line for only a fraction of an inch. In that time perspective, he is recent, and tentative, and perhaps even experimental. He makes mistakes. And yet, if he is truly *sapiens*—thinking and wise—then surely there is promise for him. Problems, yes. But very great promise—if we will but act.

28   Let's Sink the Lifeboat Ethics

James W. Howe and John W. Sewell

James W. Howe is a Senior Fellow and John W. Sewell is Vice President of the Overseas Development Council.

. . . each rich nation can be seen as a lifeboat full of comparatively rich people. In the ocean outside each lifeboat swim the poor of the world, who would like to get in, or at least share some of the wealth.

—Garrett Hardin, "The Case Against Helping the Poor" (*Psychology Today*, September, 1974)

From WORLDVIEW, Col. 18, No. 10 (October, 1975) pp. 13–18. Reprinted with permission.

. . . the moment of truth will come the morning when the President must make a choice whether to save India or to save Latin America. . . .

—William and Paul Paddock, *Famine 1975!* (1967)

. . . American intellectual circles have spawned a new series of challenges to the morality and efficacy of responding to the needs of the poor countries. One of the surprising aspects of these arguments—one which has given considerable satisfaction to the devoted opponents of such aid and even raised eyebrows among the usually uninvolved—is the fact that these challenges have been spawned *within* the development community, by some who have spent a lifetime advocating help for the poor countries. Unlike earlier challenges which pointed out that much of American aid was used for overt political and military purposes, these new challenges hold that the provision of assistance is in and of itself immoral. Appearing under the rubric of "lifeboat ethics" and advocating the practice of "triage," these challenges take two distinct forms. The first maintains that some of the poorest countries are beyond saving, that nothing the rich countries do, no matter how generous or wise, can rescue them. Therefore, wasting resources on these countries deprives others that can better utilize them. The second revives Thomas Malthus's predictions of two centuries ago and holds that any help to the developing countries inexorably leads to higher birth rates. By so doing, any amount of aid merely postpones the inevitable famine, which, when it comes, will be even more disastrous because so many more will die. From this perspective aid is immoral because, if it continues, the sum total of deaths and, therefore, of human suffering, will increase.

It is ironic that these challenges have arisen precisely at the time when the developing countries are becoming increasingly important to the United States, just when the rich countries are facing a growing challenge from the developing countries to their dominant position in the international economic system. The most obvious examples of this shift are the actions of the oil-producing countries, which have both raised prices and used their dominance of the world's energy supply to increase their political power. But in many other arenas the developing countries are beginning to press for more equitable access to the world's wealth and for a greater voice in the governance of international economic institutions. The dramatic cohesion of the OPEC countries has tended to obscure a more basic long-term development—a major change in psychology on the part of *all* developing countries. These previously powerless countries will no longer tolerate being taken for granted and are demanding a voice in decisions that directly affect their future. As a result the Americans will find that, whether they like it or not, they are going to have to pay increasing attention to these countries. And most of the low-income countries have as the primary goal their own economic and social development. Thus, American foreign policy is going to have to consider what role should be given to development cooperation in our increasingly interdependent world.

The first group of challengers hold that some countries can never create viable economies and that any resources provided them, whether through aid or other means, are wasted. In fact, if we assist these countries, other countries that have a better chance of survival and that can better utilize scarce resources will be jeopardized. Some who hold this viewpoint invoke the battlefield medical principle of "triage," whereby the wounded are divided into three groups: those who will survive with little or no treatment, those who will die even if treated, and those who are likely to live only if they receive intensive care. In this situation it makes sense to concentrate the available resources on the last group, because doing so will insure that the maximum number survive. Other critics in this group use the analogy of the "lifeboat"—they claim that the rich countries can be likened to survivors in a lifeboat of limited capacity surrounded by others in the water waiting to be saved.

If too many of those in the water are rescued, the boat will be swamped and all will perish.

Implicit in the argument of those who advocated "lifeboat ethics" are three premises. The first is that certain nations can never be saved; second, that the world's resources are not adequate and can never be adequate to meet the needs of all; and third, that if sacrificed, certain nations will disappear and will no longer cause other countries problems. Strikingly enough, experience since World War II bears out none of these premises. The developing countries as a whole managed to maintain an average economic growth rate of about 6 percent per year in the decade of the 1960's, a record never equalled by any of the industrialized nations during comparable periods of their development. While there are problems with equating development and economic growth, particularly as it neglects the questions of the distribution of the benefits of growth within countries, the record does not indicate that any nations are beyond being saved. Indeed, it is useful to recall that in 1945 Europe, Japan, China, and virtually *all* of the underdeveloped areas of Asia, Africa, and Latin America were either devastated by war or economically stagnant. Today only 42 of 135 nations that are members of the United Nations are in comparably serious condition. Another score of countries are making measurable progress but are still in a somewhat precarious condition. All other countries are either making self-sustaining progress toward solving their problems or have the financial resources to do so. From another perspective, the population in countries that received aid or were stagnating economically twenty-five years ago constituted perhaps 90 percent of the world's people. Today such countries make up less than half the population, and the "Fourth World" of the poorest countries in greatest need of outside help constitutes only about 25 percent of the world's population.

Many of those who advocate a form of international "triage" use India as their best example of a very poor prospect for development. But in the mid-1960's, when India suffered a large food deficit, its government undertook a massive program designed to increase agricultural production. By 1971 India had essentially closed its food deficit and was able to provide food aid for refugees from war-torn Bangladesh. The reversal of this positive trend in food production in the past two years was the result of adverse weather in 1972 and 1974, a shortage of fertilizer during 1974, and a shortage of fuel to operate irrigation pumps in the same year. As a result, India has had to import more than six million tons of grain this year, most of it paid for with hard cash. (India this year has spent nearly $1 billion on food imports, most of it from the United States.) Barring these three unusual circumstances, India today could be producing all the cereals required to meet the current demands of its people. Thus there is reason to doubt that even those countries considered to be the "worst cases" are beyond saving.

The second premise of those who pose this challenge is based largely on the analysis of the Club of Rome, which holds that the earth's supply of resources is finite and that we will begin shortly to see real shortages. These estimates, particularly those concerning vital raw materials, are much in dispute. But even in the case most cited—the earth's capacity to produce more food—the future is not at all bleak. The opportunity to increase the production of food, particularly in the developing countries, is great. But the Food and Agriculture Organization of the United Nations estimates that unless agricultural production in the developing countries is increased, their grain deficit by 1985 could total nearly 85 million tons, a little more than half the total amount of grain traded in the world last year. However, if the proper measures are taken to increase production—particularly in the developing countries—that deficit could be as low as 10 to 15 million tons of grain. Clearly it is feasible to increase global food production levels if we go about it the right way.

Even if the ceiling on world food production actually had been reached, there still would be much that could be done to alleviate hunger by some modicum of redistribution. Currently each person in North America consumes each year nearly one ton of grain, mainly indirectly in the form of milk, meat, and eggs. In contrast, individuals in developing countries on the average consume less than four hundred pounds of grain a year, mostly in direct form. Thus it takes more than five times as many agricultural resources to feed an average American as it does to feed the average Indian, Nigerian, or Colombian. And the disproportionate consumption of energy and raw materials by the developed countries follows an even more exaggerated pattern.

Apart from the flaws of the first two assumptions underlying the "lifeboat" and "triage" analyses, these arguments have a still more serious weakness. Their proponents assume that nations—like persons drowning or bleeding to death—simply "die" and therefore cease to be "problems" for the rest of the world. Abandoning such countries does not get rid of them; it merely postpones the time when the problems must be dealt with. National boundaries are inadequate to quarantine permanently the tensions that build up when whole nations begin to disintegrate. Moreover, to solve them at

that stage is often more costly than if they had been dealt with earlier. (The dissolution of East and West Pakistan is a recent example of such cost.)

Finally, the proponents of the "lifeboat" analogy do not accurately describe the current global crisis. The rich are clearly not in possession of a secure lifeboat they *alone* command. Instead, the rich and poor "share" the same lifeboat—although the rich, despite their lesser numbers, take up much more space in the boat than the poor and command a far greater share of the supplies necessary for survival. Confronted with the fact that there is a hole in the boat and that the boat is slowly sinking, the rich seem quite sanguine; since the hole is not in their side, they insist, its existence is not their responsibility. Actually, all the evidence of recent history supports a rather different version of the lifeboat analogy, one virtually identical with the "spaceship earth" analogy, in that it recognizes and emphasizes the interdependence of all nations and peoples.

The second set of recent challenges is to the wisdom of helping the poor countries, and is similar to that originally propounded by Malthus many generations ago. The advocates of this view hold that supporting the development of the poor countries by providing food and medicine prevents people from dying, causing populations to continue to grow until they are finally held in check by starvation and disease. These neo-Malthusians feel there would be less human suffering if the rich countries did not directly provide food or medicine, thereby allowing the restraints on population growth to come into play earlier when population levels are lower. Like those who propound the triage and lifeboat arguments, these critics assume the countries being assisted will never be able to lower their birth rates, and consequently that they must "inevitably" experience a massive famine and a consequential increase in death rates at some point in the future. But this central premise ignores a crucial fact—there is no clear evidence that birth rates cannot be brought down in the developing countries, and there are already clear indications that outside support can help to bring down birth rates if it is used to support certain innovative domestic policies.

There is now a growing consensus, underlined by the U.S. World Population Conference held in Bucharest in the summer of 1974, that the problem of population growth cannot be addressed by the provision of contraceptive techniques alone. Rather, the root of the population problem lies in the factors that motivate parents to have large families; its solution depends on changing the reasons for wanting many children.

At least three factors underlie the urge for large families in the developing countries. In many of these countries the worth, as well as the social acceptability, of an individual is still closely linked to the number of children the parents produce. A second factor is that in many societies children are economically *useful* to parents, not only as laborers but also as providers of old-age security. And finally, for many people living at the survival margin—especially if they are women, barred by varying traditions from participation in other personally satisfying activities—a large family continues to be a major emotional counterweight to the tedium of a bleak struggle to keep alive. . . .

The final irony is that the debate in the United States over the efficacy and morality of providing aid comes precisely at the moment when the challenge from the developing countries encompasses a much broader set of issues. The demands put forth by the developing countries under the heading of the "New International Economic Order" range far beyond aid to cover issues of trade, commodity policy, investment, technology transfer, and decision-making in international organizations. Aid per se is becoming less important than other resource transfers, and Americans may find themselves in the position of arguing about a particular type of response to the needs of the developing countries.

In sum, Americans have already demonstrated that they can affect governmental policy. Private leaders and indeed the public in general have an obligation to reject proposals that nations be written off as unsalvageable and to make clear their response to the argument of the neo-Malthusians. The real choice and challenge before governments and the public in both rich and poor countries is whether or not they will address themselves to the basic causes of uncontrolled population growth. And in this effort development progress—and outside help—have an important role to play.

What will be the response of the U.S. Government and the American people to this historic challenge? It may well be that now is the time for Americans to make it good politics for their leaders to be good statesmen.

XII

Energy and Resources

The biggest shock to the international system in this decade has been not war but the OPEC decisions to increase oil prices from approximately $2.50 a barrel to $13.50 or $14.00 a barrel since 1973. The United States consumes approximately 20 million barrels of oil a day, of which an increasing proportion (now 9 million) comes from the Middle East and other OPEC nations. Translated into monetary terms, this has meant an increase of $42 billion a year (as of 1977) in what the United States must pay to foreign producers to meet its oil needs. The price hikes have put an even greater financial burden on Europe and Japan, and have dealt the Third and especially the Fourth Worlds' economies a devastating setback. The immediate consequence of the price hike was to bring economic growth throughout the world to a virtual halt and to pitch the world into a state of recession from which it has still not recovered. The immediate American response was to decry what the Arabs had done and to take a posture of studied determination to reduce the country's dependence on Arab oil.

Unfortunately, the United States and its partners are not really in a position to do much about the OPEC action. Oil, like many other minerals upon which we depend, is in finite supply. The U.S. oil supply is dwindling each year such that we will effectively run out of oil some time in the 1980s and be largely dependent on foreign imports.[1] While it costs less than $1.00 to produce Arab oil, the actual demand for oil permits the OPEC producers to charge much more.

There are many other minerals for which the United States, Europe, and Japan are almost totally dependent upon foreign imports; bauxite (aluminum), copper, zinc, and iron are among them. Several other producers of raw materials have banded together in emulation of OPEC to try to raise prices by forming a cartel. So far only one has succeeded—that of the bauxite producers—because American and European industries are so dependent upon this supply from two or three countries (principally Jamaica, in the American case).

Due to cheap and plentiful resources in this century we have overlooked the vital importance of raw materials in the production process. The 1970s have reminded us that resources do indeed constitute a vital element in the production equation along with capital and labor.[2] The stake which the United States government and other developed countries feel in securing access to strategic minerals already exercises a great and constant influence upon foreign policy. In Latin America, in southern Africa, in Indonesia and the Philippines, U.S. policy of disregard for human rights and support for the ruling elites or juntas has been justified by the importance to U.S. security of access to minerals; by this is meant, of course, access by American companies (or, as the case may be, European companies). How much greater is this concern likely to become as the mineral situation becomes more desperate, unless the advanced industrial countries, the American people in particular, can discipline themselves to reduce their enormous consumption habits?

The level of waste is almost entirely an American problem. The Swedes and Swiss enjoy high standards of living, and the per capita income of West Germany, Denmark, and Norway is not much below that of the United States; yet they consume less than half the oil we use. The profligate consumption by Americans of all forms of natural resources—in the form of

---

[1]The CIA report which follows may somewhat overstate the danger. There is ample Middle East oil and ample production capacity available, and there is no reason to assume that as the price rises Saudi Arabia and other producers will not meet the increased demand. See Robert S. Pindyck. "OPEC's Threat to the West" *Foreign Policy,* No. 30 (Spring, 1978), pp. 42–43.

[2]See Burkhard Strumpel, "The Changing Face of Advanced Industrial Economies: A Post-Keynesian View," *Comparative Political Studies* (March, 1977).

large cars, the wintertime heating of large homes, many rooms of which are never entered in the course of the day, the air conditioning of high-rise buildings whose windows cannot be opened and the refusal to adjust to mass transit and other forms of economy—give other nations, especially the poor and underdeveloped, strong grounds for criticism. We Americans must also consider whether our foreign policy is not being unduly influenced by the greed that we manifest in our consumption habits, which makes our dependence on foreign resources so great, especially as resources are soon to be in even scarcer supply.

An almost overlooked dimension of the raw material problem is that of assuring the sea routes upon which the West would be dependent for its supplies in time of war. However unlikely it may be that a major war would endure beyond a few days or weeks, the United States must plan policy for the security of trade routes. Threats to the security of sea transport can occur (1) along the shores of states close to the sea lanes, (2) at narrow passages, and (3) from hostile air and naval threats in open waters. The United States is currently developing a naval base at Diego Garcia, an island in the Indian Ocean, as assurance against disruption of our oil supply by Soviet forces.

As increased oil prices have meant a recession for the advanced industrial countries, they have dealt a devastating blow to the economies of all but a few of the less developed countries. Between 1973 and 1974 the cost of oil imports to the developing countries increased by $9.4 billion, to $13.1 billion in 1974. Oil takes an increasing percentage of their export earnings so that there is that much less available for food, machinery, and development purposes. Here we are talking about some eighty-five countries and two billion people with per-capita incomes of less than $500 per year.[3] Although efforts have been made by international loan agencies, the Arab oil states, the U.S., and Europe to help meet these countries' increased oil bills, these efforts have come nowhere near to covering the actual costs.

The other consequence of OPEC price hikes has been to drive a wedge between America and its European and Japanese allies. Because their dependency on Arab oil is much greater than ours, they have been less willing to support Israel at the price of risking an Arab boycott. Secondly, they have been far less keen than the U.S. at trying to form a consumers cartel with which to oppose Arab price hikes. Thirdly, at a time when the fall in the value of the dollar is playing havoc with the money market, Europeans resent the American failure to establish a realistic and comprehensive oil-conservation program. The Europeans and Japanese have been more conservation-conscious because of their almost total dependence on foreign

[3]Shams B. Feraidoon, "Oil-Poor Developing Countries," *Current History,* Vol. 74, No. 435 (March, 1978), pp. 109–112.

imports; until 1973 the United States did not feel any dependence (in part because five U.S. oil companies controlled 80 percent of Middle East oil), and it has been slow to accept the implications of its altered status.

Finally, the economic and oil crisis exacerbates other issues between the U.S. and its allies. Up until recently, nuclear energy has been produced from enriched uranium. Unfortunately, the supply of uranium is limited and much of the ore, in the hands of a few countries, is contracted for sale to the United States. A new type of reactor using plutonium, called a breeder reactor because it can reconstitute or replenish itself indefinitely, has been developed by the French and Germans. Naturally they are anxious to market it abroad. But since plutonium can be readily converted into nuclear weapons, Washington has tried to dissuade and even oppose the proliferation of such reactors abroad until a system of guarantees has been established against diversion of plutonium to weapons use. This too has driven a wedge between the U.S. and its principal allies.[4] Thus we see that our growing dependence on foreign supplies of critical minerals has both primary and secondary effects.

As the CIA analysis in this chapter indicates, the Soviet Union, although better off than the U.S., may soon run up against limits to readily available oil and gas. Unless it can discover and open up new reserves in Siberia, which has so far proven costly and beyond the capacity of Soviet technology, Russia's ability to meet its needs domestically will end by the 1980s and it too will become a competitor for OPEC oil. Unless the developed world, the U.S. in particular, begins scaling down its consumption of minerals which are in increasingly short supply and can only be gotten from abroad, there is a danger of some future crisis leading us into a new era of imperialism. Already, many of our troubles in foreign policy have occurred because of the desire on the part of the American government and companies for access to and security of access to valuable minerals. This puts us at a disadvantage in the competition with the Soviets for the hearts and minds of people, and even at odds with the people themselves in many of the underdeveloped parts of the world.

⁴Karl Kaiser, "The Great Nuclear Debate" *Foreign Policy* No. 30. (Spring, 1978), pp. 83–110.

29 International Considerations
of the President's Proposed Energy Policy

Cyrus R. Vance

Secretary of State

The facts of the energy crisis are stark and the implications profound. The year 1970 was a water-shed year. In 1970 the United States became a net oil importer. Our growing demand for oil, combined with that of Europe and Japan, caused a rapid and fundamental shift in the global supply-demand balance for energy. The Organization of Petroleum Exporting Countries [OPEC] moved to exercise more and more control over the production and disposition of 85 percent of the oil moving in world trade.

Our vulnerability was amply demonstrated by the embargo and sudden five-fold increase in the price of oil in 1973-1974. Yet since the end of the embargo more than three years ago, our demand for imported oil and hence our vulnerability to another supply interruption have increased further. In the winter months of this year, oil imports for the first time reached 50 percent of our national oil consumption. Moreover the OPEC producers have continued to increase the price of oil. We have little influence on their policies so long as our requirement for their oil continues to grow.

The CIA's recent analysis and independent

Statement by Secretary of State Cyrus R. Vance before the House Ad Hoc Committee on Energy, May 4, 1977, Washington, D.C.

studies undertaken in the OECD [Organization for Economic Cooperation and Development] and the International Energy Agency all indicate that by 1985 a gap will develop between world demand for oil and installed capacity to produce oil. Should we allow this to happen, we will face rapid price escalations, severe economic dislocations, and heightened global tensions.

The experience of the past few years and the forecasts for the years not far ahead require us to regard security of energy supply as a major national imperative. We cannot be in a position where we must accept a continuing vulnerability to arbitrary supply disruptions and price changes. We must resolve to regain control of our energy destiny.

To do this we must meet the following objectives:. . .

In the short term to reduce dependence on foreign oil and to limit supply disruptions;

In the medium term to prepare for the eventual decline in the availability of world oil supplies caused by capacity limitations; and

In the long term to develop new, reliable, and hopefully inexhaustible sources of energy for sustained economic growth.

Over the short and medium terms, we can best protect ourselves from uncertain supplies by reducing our demand for foreign oil, making the most of more abundant resources, notably coal and uranium for carefully safeguarded nuclear reactors. We are also developing a strategic petroleum reserve. The cornerstone of the President's plan is to conserve the fuels that are scarcest and use those that are most plentiful. It is a principle of the plan that prices should generally reflect the replacement cost of energy.

With respect to oil I wish to make clear that this does not mean that we consider the price imposed by OPEC producers as right or proper or that further OPEC price increases are justified. We are only recognizing the hard reality that the replacement cost to our country of each barrel of oil added to our consumption since 1970 has been at the OPEC price.

At the same time we should not consider the energy problem solely in national terms. It is a global problem, affecting all nations.

We cannot afford to lose sight of the energy problems of other nations, including our allies which are even more dependent on imported oil than we are. We share a collective vulnerability with them. In fact energy has become a central element in our political, economic, and security ties with our key trading partners. We must cooperate for our mutual benefit. Otherwise, as in the days following the 1973 embargo, energy will become a divisive issue that weakens our overall relationship.

We are joined with 18 other industrialized countries in the International Energy Agency to facilitate close cooperation in energy. The IEA has in operational readiness an emergency program to mitigate the impact of a sudden supply interruption through use of reserves, demand restraint, and allocation of available oil under agreed guidelines.

The IEA is also undertaking a program of long-term energy cooperation to reduce our collective dependence on imports through joint efforts in conservation, accelerated development of alternative energy sources, and research and development.

While progress has been significant, other member countries have looked to the United States to take the lead in adopting a strong and comprehensive national energy program. Frankly, unless we do, it is unrealistic to expect other consuming nations, for whom reduced import dependence is even more difficult and expensive, to do so.

The President's proposed program will permit the United States to play a leading role in joining with other consuming nations in coping with the global energy problem. It corresponds closely to findings and recommendations arising from the recent work of the IEA. Elements of the program will require detailed international consultation and negotiations—for example, nuclear fuel cycle issues and auto rebates. However, the reaction of the other major consuming countries represented in the IEA is very positive to the President's program as a whole.

The oil-producing countries have acquired special role as a result of the energy problem. They have acquired wealth, power, and influence in a brief period. They are becoming integrated step-by-step into the world economic and financial systems. But they too are concerned about the finite limits of their oil reserves. Their representatives have urged us to conserve oil and to moderate demand for their oil. In turn we have strongly urged them to pursue responsible price and production policies. Adoption of the President's energy program can provide an improved basis for our dialogue as well as a more balanced relationship of interests.

In reality the oil-producing countries share common long-term interests with the oil-consuming countries. They too need a growing, stable global economy and a liberal trading system that will insure the availability of future markets for their products, both energy and nonenergy related goods. Otherwise their efforts to develop and diversify their economies cannot succeed.

To insure global growth and prosperity, the oil-producing countries should recognize a responsibility for supplying adequate quantities of oil at reasonable prices. Special attention must be given to assisting the developing countries to overcome their energy burdens. These low-income nations cannot significantly reduce their energy consumption. They are not profligate energy users. Furthermore there is a high correlation between energy use and economic growth. But as increasing amounts of scarce foreign exchange are expended for energy imports, their other development needs suffer.

The OPEC countries should recognize the need to provide generous assistance to help deveoping nations overcome the direct and indirect costs of the post-1973 oil prices. We also have a responsibility to devise means to share our technology and other forms of assistance even as we are dealing with our own pressing energy concerns.

Finally the oil-producing nations, as well as the oil-importing nations, are joint participants in a new energy transition period. The world has entered a period in which its energy use will gradually shift from primary reliance on oil and gas for energy to increased use of other fossil fuels and synthetics and ultimately to expanded use of non-depletable energies, such as solar. All nations, including the oil producers, will some day have to meet their energy needs largely with supplies other than oil and gas.

There have been other energy transition periods, but this one will be the shortest in history. Because of the rapid depletion of oil and gas supplies, we do not have decades to complete the process. It is in the interests of all nations to manage this transition period so that it is not economically disruptive and politically destabilizing. To achieve this goal oil-consuming countries must conserve their energy use, accelerate development of conventional and new energy supplies, and speed up the pace of energy research and development. Adoption of the President's program will demonstrate that the United States has accepted its responsibility in this process and is ready to contribute.

The implications of the energy crisis for all nations and the global economy are profound. The President's program is a call to leadership. The United States and other industrial nations must eliminate their vulnerability to energy supply disruptions and arbitrary oil price decisions. Together with the OPEC countries, we must focus on our common long-term interests and insure cooperation for global growth, international financial stability, and a smooth energy transition period. We must help the oil-importing developing countries overcome their energy burdens and accelerate their economic development.

30 The International Energy Situation: Outlook to 1985

Central Intelligence Agency

SUMMARY

In the absence of greatly increased energy conservation, projected world demand for oil will approach productive capacity by the early 1980s and substantially exceed capacity by 1985. In these circumstances, prices will rise sharply to ration available supplies no matter what Saudi Arabia does. Although our forecast of oil demand broadly resembles other official and private forecasts, we are more pessimistic about the implication. This pessimism is largely based on (a) our estimate that the USSR will change from an exporter to a substantial importer of oil, and (b) our examination of the supply capabilities of Organization of Petroleum Exporting Countries (OPEC) and non-OPEC countries.

The underlying supply problem will be masked during the next few years because of greatly increased oil production from the North Sea and Alaska. Given this new production, demand for OPEC oil should stabilize at near current levels through 1979. Saudi excess capacity will be increasing during this period, allowing Riyadh to hold down oil prices in spite of upward pressure from other OPEC states. Since this will be a political decision on the part of the Saudis, they could reverse it at any time for political reasons.

Between 1979 and 1985, increasing world demand and stagnating oil production in the major consuming countries will result in increased reliance on OPEC oil. By 1985 we estimate that demand for OPEC oil will reach 47 to 51 million b/d. Even if all other OPEC states produce at capacity, Saudi Arabia will be required to produce between 19 and 23 million b/d if demand is to be met. This is well above present Saudi capacity of 10 to 11 million b/d, and projected 1985 capacity of at most 18 million b/d. With the present expansion plans of the Saudis, their excess productive capacity will be exhausted by 1983, and with it their ability to act as a price moderator in OPEC.

INTRODUCTION

This report examines the pattern of world oil demand and supply between now and 1985. For major consuming countries we have estimated total energy demand basically drawing on two factors (a) rates of economic growth and (b) the effect of con-

This Document No. ER10240V was published by the CIA in April 1977. (Some footnotes omitted.)

servation measures now in place. We do not, however, attempt to estimate the impact on demand of future policy changes regarding conservation. Demand for oil in other consuming areas was determined on the basis of projected economic growth rates. For each region total demand for oil was then determined by estimating the size of non-oil energy supplies. Separate estimates of non-OPEC oil supplies were made to determine demand for OPEC oil. Our supply estimates are based on a detailed analyses of such factors as government exploration and development policy, adequacy of the energy reserve base, existing contracts, and the lead time necessary to bring projects on line.

OECD DEMAND FOR ENERGY

Economic Growth and Conservation

Between now and 1985 economic growth is likely to be slower than during the decade prior to 1973. In part, this reflects balance-of-payments constraints and the lingering effects on demand of the sharp rise in oil prices during 1973-1974. Slow growth has brought about major social and political problems for Free World countries. As unemployment is very high by recent standards, the political leadership of most countries is under pressure to stimulate economic growth and employment. The growth rates chosen through 1985 take into consideration both external pressures retarding growth and political forces urging more rapid economic expansion (Table 1).

These growth rates are slower than the long-term projections employed by the OECD—a 4- to 5-percent rate for the United States, a 3- to 3.5-percent rate for OECD Europe, and a 6-percent rate for Japan.

The growth pattern of Canada is consistent with that of the United States, reflecting the close economic links between the two.

Before 1973 the relationship between energy demand and real GNP was very stable, reflecting the close connection between energy consumption and the stock of energy-consuming capital. Given this relationship, we found that the best predictor of energy demand prior to 1973 was a 4-year weighted moving average of GNP. The relationship— derived separately for each of the major energy-consuming areas (the United States, OECD Europe, Japan, and Canada)—was used to determine a baseline of energy demand through 1985. This base demand was then reduced to take account of projected energy savings from higher prices and conservation measures already introduced.

Determining savings from conservation is extremely difficult; since 1973, energy economists have attempted with little success to quantify these savings. Early estimates tended to overestimate the impact of price-induced conservation, in part because of difficulty in separating that portion of the drop in energy demand resulting from recession from the portion attributable to conservation. More recent estimates may have erred in the opposite direction, understating energy savings from conservation. We assume that, during the next 15 years, energy savings relative to the baseline forecast will range from 10 to 15 percent in the United States and from 5 to 10 percent in Japan and Western Europe. These estimates are appreciably higher than those implied in demand estimates prepared by the IEA Secretariat.

The Demand Forecast

Our calculations indicate that total OECD energy demand will approach 85 million b/d

TABLE 1
ECONOMIC GROWTH RATES
MAJOR DEVELOPED COUNTRIES
PERCENT

	Actual	Projected				
	1976	1977	1978	1979	1980	1981-85
United States	6.1	5.0	5.0	4.5	4.5	4.0
OECD Europe	4.1	3.0	3.0	3.0	3.0	3.5
Japan	6.0	6.5	6.0	6.0	6.0	6.0
Canada	4.8	4.0	4.0	4.5	4.5	4.5

oil equivalent in 1980, rising to about 100 million b/d in 1985. The 1985 demand is about 40 million b/d lower than what it would have been had the oil crisis of 1973-74 not happened. About 30 million b/d of this reduction is due to the slower economic growth now envisioned; the remaining 10 million is due to price effects and conservation. Even with these shifts, total OECD energy demand would be about 15 percent higher in 1980 than last year; by 1985 it would be nearly 40 percent higher (Figure 1).

The United States accounts for about 45 percent of the growth in OECD demand between now and 1985. This occurs despite the relatively large energy savings—5 to 7 million b/d oil equivalent by 1985—we have incorporated into the US estimate. (See Table 2 on page 278.) As much as 2.5 million b/d of this savings reflects the impact of higher gasoline mileage standards already mandated. The remainder would have to come from modifications in lifestyle and changes in capital stock (either retrofit or new). Achieving these savings would require a sharp increase in the energy efficiency of new capital. Rough calculations suggest that new capital installed during 1977-85 must be 15 to 20 percent more energy efficient than the existing capital stock.

West European energy consumption is projected to reach 27 to 28 million b/d oil equivalent by 1980 and at least 32 million b/d by 1985. This estimate incorporates savings of 3 million b/d by 1985. To accomplish this, however, the efficiency of new capital must increase even faster than in the United States. This reflects the fact that the turnover of energy using capital stock will be tempered by the slower rate of economic growth and capital investment we envision for Western Europe between now and 1985. Japanese energy consumption should reach 12 to 13 million b/d oil equivalent by 1985, up from 7.2 million b/d last year. Canadian 1985 demand is put in the range of 6 million b/d.

OECD ENERGY SUPPLIES

Between 1970 and 1976, OECD domestic energy production[1] grew only 1 percent annually. In the United States output actually fell as declines in oil and gas more than offset increases in nuclear, hydroelectric, and coal production. Gains in the other OECD countries were small. Nuclear energy output expanded in all regions. Natural gas and oil increased in Canada and Western

[1]For the purposes of this analysis, *domestic energy production* is defined as domestic production of all energy sources plus net imports of natural gas, coal, and electricity.

FIGURE 1 OECD Energy Demand[1]

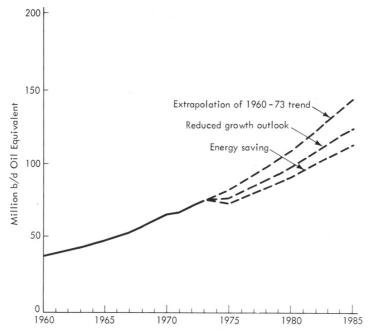

[1]Excluding Australia and NewZealand.

Europe, due mainly to the initiation of North Sea production. Coal output fell substantially in Western Europe.

Between now and 1980, OECD energy production will expand 4 percent annually (Figure 2). This reflects a sharp expansion in North Sea oil production and the opening of the Alaskan pipeline. Nuclear power will also be important, although the amount of new capacity is in doubt because of increasing delays due to environmental objections. Total energy production in the United States, OECD Europe, Japan, and Canada is projected to reach 56 million to 57 million b/d oil equivalent by 1980, up from an estimated 47.5 million b/d last year. North Sea and Alaskan oil output account for one-half of the gain and nuclear production for much of the remainder.

Beginning in 1980, growth in OECD energy production will slow dramatically. Output growth could be as low as 1 percent a year, and at best 4 percent a year until 1985, when it will reach 63 million to 66 million b/d oil equivalent. A key uncertainty is the pace at which nuclear power capacity will become available. Our high-side nuclear energy supply estimates count all plants for which orders have been placed or construction begun. Given the experience of the past few years, actual on-line capacity in 1985 could be much lower. For example, only about one-half of the plants expected in 1970 to be on line last year were actually operating. Our low-side estimates of 1985 nuclear capacity roughly assume that this record continues.

Another area of uncertainty is OECD coal

277

TABLE 2
ENERGY DEMAND PROJECTIONS
OECD COUNTRIES

Million b/d Oil Equivalent

	1976	1977	1978	1979	1980	1985
Total						
1960-73 trend	86.0	90.7	95.8	101.1	106.9	142.0
Adjusted for reduced growth	76.9	80.1	83.5	87.1	90.7	111.1
Adjusted for conservation	72.8	75.7-76.2	78.1-78.9	80.8-81.8	83.5-84.9	99.3-102.1
United States						
1960-73 trend	42.5	44.3	46.2	48.2	50.3	61.9
Adjusted for reduced growth	38.6	40.3	42.1	44.0	45.8	55.2
Adjusted for conservation	37.2	38.5-38.9	39.6-40.3	40.7-41.6	42.0-43.1	48.2-50.4
OECD Europe						
1960-73 trend	28.8	30.3	31.9	33.6	35.4	46.0
Adjusted for reduced growth	26.0	26.8	27.6	28.5	29.4	35.1
Adjusted for conservation	24.0	25.0-25.3	25.6-26.0	26.3-26.9	27.0-27.8	31.8-33.2
Japan						
1960-73 trend	9.7	10.8	12.0	13.3	14.8	25.3
Adjusted for reduced growth	7.7	8.2	8.7	9.3	9.9	13.5
Adjusted for conservation	7.2	7.5-7.6	7.9-8.1	8.5-8.7	9.0-9.3	12.1-12.7
Canada						
1960-73 trend	5.0	5.3	5.7	6.0	6.4	8.8
Adjusted for reduced growth	4.6	4.8	5.1	5.3	5.6	7.3
Adjusted for conservation	4.4	4.5-4.6	4.7-4.8	4.9-5.0	5.0-5.2	6.3-6.7

production, and our estimates may be too optimistic. For example, we have projected a small increase in West European coal consumption even though coal usage in major West European countries has fallen slightly since 1973. In the United States environmental concerns are slowing both production and consumption. Only a few of the 76 powerplants that the FEA ordered to shift from oil to coal have complied. If this pattern of resistance persists, our estimates of a 40- to 60-percent increase in US coal production and use between now and 1985 will be high. Coal will account for as much as 70 percent of the projected rise in US energy production between 1976 and 1985.

OECD oil production should increase only slightly between 1980 and 1985, at best reaching 17 million b/d by 1985. US production will stabilize at around 10 to 11 million b/d, if tertiary recovery techniques and increased drilling stem the production decline in the lower 48 states. Canadian production should also stabilize, at 1.5 million b/d. The only increase we foresee is about a 1 million b/d gain in OECD Europe's oil-production, reflecting North Sea output.

LDC DEMAND FOR OIL

As a group, the other industrial countries (such as Australia and New Zealand) and the non-OPEC LDCs will require substantial amounts of imported oil for the foreseeable future. The projected net oil deficit for non-OPEC LDCs is 2.4 million b/d in 1980,

FIGURE 2 OECD Domestic Energy Production[1]

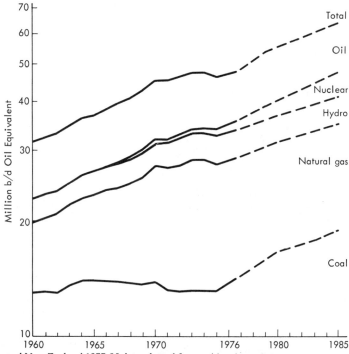

[1]Excluding Australia and New Zealand 1977-85 data plotted from mid-points of ranges.

rising to 3 to 4 million b/d by 1985 (Figure 3). This estimate assumes that the non-OPEC LDCs as a group achieve real GNP growth of 4.5 percent annually, appreciably below their long-term rate of 5.6 percent.

Domestic oil production in the non-OPEC LDCs is projected to increase from 3.7 million b/d last year to 6.1 million b/d in 1980 and 8 to 9 million b/d in 1985. The largest gains will be in Mexico and Egypt, with smaller increases in Brazil, Tunisia, Oman, Syria, India, and Burma. Production of oil and natural gas liquids in Mexico should rise from 900,000 b/d last year to about 2.2 million b/d in 1980. In 1985 production will range between 3.0 and 4.5 million b/d, depending on development policies. At most, Mexico could produce 5 to 6 million b/d by 1985. Egyptian oil output could reach 700,000

b/d in 1980 and possibly 1 million b/d by 1985.

The prospects for production in the other Free World countries—Australia, Israel, New Zealand, and South Africa—are dim (table 4). Australia, the only major producer among this group, will probably see its oil and natural gas liquids output decline to about 400,000 b/d or less by 1985.

Role of Communist Countries in the Oil Market

The Communist countries have been net exporters of about 1 million b/d of oil to the West. But the Soviet oil industry is in trouble. Soviet oil production will soon peak, possibly as early as next year and certainly not later

279

FIGURE 3   Non-OPEC LDCs: Oil Production and Consumption

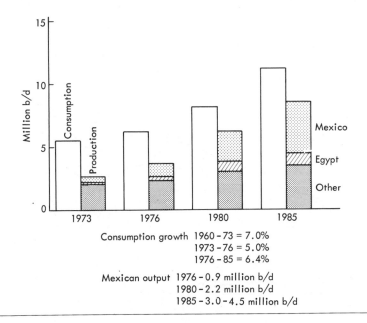

Consumption growth 1960 – 73 = 7.0%
1973 – 76 = 5.0%
1976 – 85 = 6.4%

Mexican output 1976 – 0.9 million b/d
1980 – 2.2 million b/d
1985 – 3.0 – 4.5 million b/d

TABLE 3
DOMESTIC ENERGY PRODUCTION[1]
OECD COUNTRIES[2]

Million b/d Oil Equivalent

	1970	1976	1980	1985		1970	1976	1980	1985
Total	45.2	47.5	56.0-57.0	63.2-66.1	Coal	5.6	4.9	5.1	5.3
Oil[3]	13.3	12.2	15.2	15.8-17.2	Hydro/geothermal	1.7	1.6	2.1	2.4
Natural gas	13.6	14.8	15.2-15.6	15.9-16.9	Nuclear	0.2	0.6	1.2-1.6	1.8-3
Coal	13.8	14.0	16.5-17.2	18.1-19.6	Japan				
Hydro/geothermal	4.2	4.6	5.4	6.5	Oil	0	0	0	0.1
Nuclear	0.3	1.9	3.4-3.8	5.4-7.2	Natural gas	0.1	0.2	0.5	1.0
United States	30.8	30.2	32.1-33.0	34.7-37.1	Coal	1.2	1.2	1.5	1.8
Oil[3]	11.3	9.7	10.0	10.0-11.0	Hydro/geothermal	0.4	0.4	0.4	0.6
Natural gas	11.4	10.3	9.0-9.6	8.5-9.5	Nuclear	0	0.2	0.3-0.4	0.4-6
Coal	6.7	7.6	9.5-10.2	10.5-12.0	Canada	3.3	4.0	4.2-4.4	4.5-4
Hydro/geothermal	1.3	1.6	1.7	2.0	Oil[3]	1.5	1.6	1.5	1.3-8
Nuclear	0.1	1.0	1.6-1.8	2.5 3.8	Natural gas	0.7	1.0	1.0-1.1	1.0-8
OECD Europe	9.4	11.3	16.7-17.1	19.2-20.8	Coal	0.3	0.3	0.4	0.5
Oil[3]	0.5	0.9	3.7	4.0-5.0	Hydro	0.8	1.0	1.2	1.5
Natural gas	1.4	3.3	4.6	5.4	Nuclear	0	0.1	0.1-0.2	0.1-6

[1] Defined as domestic production of oil and total domestic consumption of all other fuels

[2] Excluding Australia and New Zealand.

[3] Including natural gas liquids.

than the early 1980s. The maximum level of output is likely to be between 11 and 12 million b/d—up from the 1976 level of 10 million b/d—but it is not likely to be long maintained, and the decline, when it comes, will be sharp (Figure 4).

Before 1985, the USSR probably will find itself not only unable to supply oil to Eastern Europe and the West on the present scale but also having to compete for OPEC oil for its own use. Although there will be some substitution of coal and gas for oil in domestic use, the scale of such substitution will be small before 1985. Neither hydro-electric power transmission from the east nor the construction of nuclear powerplants can afford much relief until well past 1985.

We estimate that the Soviet Union and Eastern Europe will require a minimum of 3.5 million b/d of imported oil by 1985. At worst, slumping production could lead to import requirements as large as 4.5 million b/d.

In China, the reserve and production outlook is much less favorable than it appeared a few years ago. We anticipate that growing domestic oil needs, resulting from economic growth and trouble with coal production, will reduce oil exports to a negligible level by 1985. In 1980 exports will total no more than 500,000 b/d.

DEMAND FOR OPEC OIL

Because of slow development of alternative energy supplies during the past 3 years and a rebound in energy consumption, production of OPEC oil hit a new record last year—34 million b/d by yearend. This topped the previous peak of 33.4 million b/d reached in September 1973. All signs point to OPEC output in 1977 exceeding the 1976 yearly average of 31 million b/d. Rising US import demand (5.8 million b/d in 1975, 7.0 million

TABLE 4
OIL IMPORT PROJECTIONS FOR NON-OPEC
FREE WORLD COUNTRIES
(EXCLUDING OECD COUNTRIES)

						Million b/d
	1976	1977	1978	1979	1980	1985
Oil Demand	7.9	8.3	8.8	9.1	10.0	13.9
Australia/New Zealand	0.7	0.7	0.8	0.8	0.9	1.2
Other developed countries[1]	0.5	0.5	0.5	0.5	0.6	0.7
Non-OPEC LDCs	6.7	7.1	7.5	7.8	8.5	12.0
Oil Supply[2]	4.2	4.6	5.1	5.8	6.6	8.4-9.4
Australia/New Zealand	0.5	0.5	0.5	0.5	0.5	0.4
Non-OPEC LDCs	3.7	4.1	4.6	5.3	6.1	8.0-9.0
Oil Imports	3.7	3.7	3.7	3.3	3.4	4.5-5.5
Australia/New Zealand	0.2	0.2	0.3	0.3	0.4	0.8
Other developed countries[1]	0.5	0.5	0.5	0.5	0.6	0.7
Non-OPEC LDCs	3.0	3.0	2.9	2.5	2.4	3.0-4.0

[1] Israel and South Africa.
[2] Including natural gas liquids.

FIGURE 4   Soviet Crude Oil Production

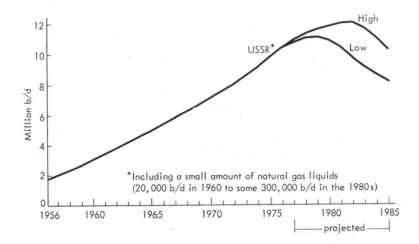

b/d in 1976, and about 8.5 million b/d in 1977) accounted for about one-half the rise in OPEC output last year and will acount for the entire rise in 1977.

THE NEXT SEVERAL YEARS

Because of large-scale production from Alaska and the North Sea, demand for OPEC oil will rise only gradually during the next few years. Under these conditions and assuming continued Saudi restraint on oil pricing, the real price of oil probably will not rise substantially and could even decline.

Demand for OPEC oil could total about 32 million b/d this year and will remain at about that level in 1978 and 1979. In 1980 it will jump by another 2 million b/d, beginning a strong upward trend. Alaskan output will have stabilized and growth in North Sea production will be slowing. At about the same time, the Soviet Union probably will be withdrawing as a net supplier of 1 million b/d to the West.

We estimate the 1980 demand for OPEC oil will be about 34 million b/d—2 million b/d more than in 1977. OPEC capacity should be more than adequate. Although the Saudis apparently hope to hold production below possible levels for conservation reasons, they are going ahead with a capacity expansion program which should allow them to produce 15 to 16 million b/d in the early 1980s. Other OPEC countries will be able to produce at or near capacity, and Saudi Arabia, as the residual supplier, can produce within its preferred range. Riyadh, meanwhile, will be in a position to use its excess capacity to encourage price moderation.

Beyond 1980

After 1980 demand for OPEC oil will rise rapidly, repeating the pre-1973 pattern. By 1985, we project demand for OPEC oil at a minimum of 47 b/d and a maximum of 51 million b/d. Increased US oil demand will account for a major portion of this rise (Table 5). US imports will run some 10 mil-

TABLE 5
OIL DEMAND AND SUPPLY PROJECTIONS
FREE WORLD

Million b/d

	1976	1977	1978	1979	1980	1985
Free World Oil Demand	48.4	49.8-50.5	51.2-52.2	52.5-54.1	54.9-56.7	68.3-72.6
United States	16.7	17.8-18.3	18.2-19.0	18.4-19.7	19.3-20.7	22.2-25.6
OECD Europe	13.6	13.9-14.3	13.8-14.2	13.7-14.4	13.7-14.7	15.8-18.2
Japan	5.2	5.3-5.4	5.5-5.8	5.9-6.2	6.2-6.6	8.1-8.8
Canada	2.0	2.0-2.1	2.1-2.2	2.2-2.3	2.2-2.4	2.9-3.5
Other developed countries[1]	1.2	1.2	1.3	1.3	1.4	1.9
Non-OPEC LDCs	6.7	7.1	7.5	7.8	8.5	12.0
OPEC countries	2.1	2.3	2.5	2.8	3.0	4.0
Other Demand[2]	0.9	0	0	0	0	0
Non-OPEC supply[3]	17.5	18.5	20.1	21.2	22.0	20.4-22.4
United States	9.7	9.6	10.2	10.2	10.0	10.0-11.0
OECD Europe	0.9	1.8	2.5	3.1	3.7	4.0-5.0
Japan	0	0	0	0	0	0.1
Canada	1.6	1.6	1.5	1.5	1.5	1.3-1.5
Other developed countries[1]	0.5	0.5	0.5	0.5	0.5	0.4
Non-OPEC LDCs	3.7	4.1	4.6	5.3	6.1	8.0-9.0
Net Communist trade						
USSR-Eastern Europe	0.9	0.7	0.5	0.2	—0.3	—3.5 —4.5
China	0.2	0.2	0.3	0.4	0.5	0
Required OPEC production	30.9	31.3-32.0	31.1-32.1	31.3-32.9	32.9-34.7	46.7-51.2

[1] Australia, Israel, New Zealand, and South Africa.

[2] Including stock changes and statistical discrepancy.

[3] Including natural gas liquids.

lion b/d in 1980 and could reach 12 to 15 million b/d in 1985. West European import demand will remain relatively stable, going up from about 10.5 million b/d in 1980 to 11 to 14 million b/d in 1985. The increase in net import demand by Communist countries between 1980 and 1985 is on the order of 4 million b/d.

The ability and willingness of OPEC countries to meet this demand is far from certain. As things now stand, we estimate that the productive capacity of OPEC countries other than Saudi Arabia will increase little, if at all, between 1980 and 1985 (Table 6). On the basis of the current pattern of

reverse depletion and development, we estimate their combined oil production capacity will approximate 28 million b/d in 1980, 28.2 million b/d by 1982, and at most 29.4 million b/d in 1985. Our 1985 calculations include capacity estimates for Iraq and Nigeria of 6 million b/d and 3 million b/d, respectively—the highest capacity figures mentioned by industry and government spokesmen. In the case of Kuwait, our 1985 estimate of capacity is consistent with strongly stated government policy.

We expect productive capacity of several of the other OPEC countries to fall after 1980 because of reserve depletion. In the

FIGURE 5 OPEC Oil: The Supply/Demand Gap

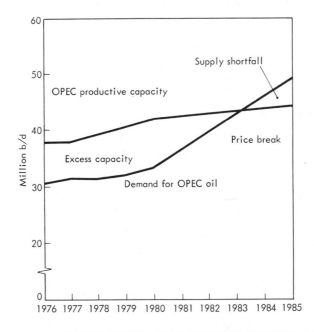

TABLE 6
PRODUCTION CAPACITY PROJECTIONS
OPEC COUNTRIES (EXCLUDING SAUDI ARABIA)

Million b/d

	March 1977	1980	1985
Total	26.8	27.6-28.3	27.5-29.4
Algeria	1.0	1.0	0.9-1.1
Ecuador	0.2	0.2	0.2
Gabon	0.2	0.2	0.2
Indonesia	1.7	1.9-2.1	1.6-2.1
Iran	6.7	6.5	5.5-6.5
Iraq	3.0	4.5	5.0-6.0
Kuwait	3.5	3.0	3.0
Libya	2.5	2.5	2.0-2.5
Nigeria	2.3	2.3	2.0-3.0
Qatar	0.7	0.6	0.5
United Arab Emirates	2.4	2.5-3.2	3.0-3.5
Venezuela	2.6	2.2-2.4	2.2

case of Iran, productive capacity is expected to peak in the early to mid-1980s. The best we expect from Iran at this juncture is output of 6.5 million b/d in 1985. We expect Venezuelan output to stagnate near 2.2 million b/d through the mid-1980s, and it may decline. Indonesia and Libya are unlikely to achieve any appreciable gain in productive capacity after 1980.

The Saudi Role

Given our capacity estimates for these OPEC suppliers, Saudi Arabia would have to increase production rapidly beginning in the early 1980s to meet growth in demand. Our projections indicate that demand for Saudi oil could be 7 million b/d in 1980, rising to 12 million b/d in 1982, and to some 13 to 16 million b/d in 1983. Unless demand is somehow curtailed, Saudi Arabia would have to supply 19 to 23 million b/d by 1985. This is roughly double current capacity.

Although the Saudis have the reserves needed to support production at this level, we doubt that an expansion program of this magnitude could be completed by 1985 without a major shift in Saudi priorities. Riyadh is committed to ambitious industrialization programs which are stretching management and logistical capabilities extremely thin. As it is, plans to expand capacity to 16 million b/d by 1980 are at least 2 years behind schedule; if this pattern continues, maximum capacity by 1985 at most would be 18 million b/d.

Even with adequate capacity, the Saudis might well be reluctant to produce at the rates required. Should they stay with present capacity expansion plans (16 million b/d by the early 1980s) and produce at that rate, the supply shortfall—as much as 7 million b/d by 1985—could only be postponed until 1984 at the latest.

How the Saudis will ultimately deal with the problem is difficult to assess. The rates of production needed to satisfy demand would not only generate enormous surpluses —at present prices Saudi Arabia's oil export earnings would approximate $125 billion annually—but would also risk rapid reserve depletion. Should Saudi Arabia allow production to reach 20 million b/d by the mid-1980s, output would begin to decline in the mid-1990s because of reserve depletion. Raising production to that level, moreover, could not be accomplished without flaring large quantities of gas, which the Saudis are determined to avoid.

The rising pressure of oil demand on capacity in the early 1980s is bound to cause oil prices to rise well in advance of any actual shortage. Saudi Arabia's ability to moderate OPEC price decisions will be weakened as Saudi excess capacity is used up. Even before this, market perceptions of supply and demand trends will tend to put upward pressure on prices. By 1982 or 1983, sizable price increases are inevitable unless large-scale conservation measures cut demand sharply. . . .

TABLE 1
DOMESTIC PRODUCTION AND IMPORT OF SELECTED
METALLIC ORES AND CONCENTRATES, 1968

	Production	West Germany Imports	Percent of Imports in Total Supply
Bauxite	. . .	1,978	100
Copper (copper content)	1.32	382	97
Lead (lead content)	52.44	135.5	72
Zinc (zinc content)	117.48	100.7	46
Iron Ore	6,444	39,644	86
		United Kingdom	
Bauxite	. . .	442	100
Copper (copper content)	. . .	484	100
Lead (lead content)	3.7	49	93
Zinc (zinc content)	. . .	166.7	100
Iron Ore	13,944	17,534	56
		France	
Bauxite	2,712	335	11
Copper (copper content)	. . .	269	100
Lead (lead content)	26.4	80.4	75
Zinc (zinc content)	21.8	189.6	90
Iron Ore	55,236	5,017	8

From monograph entitled "Raw Materials in a Multipolar World," published by the National Strategy Information Center and used with the permission of that organization. The last Table is from the Interna-tional Report of the President *(1974).*

	Production	Japan Imports	Percent of Imports in Total Supply
Bauxite	. . .	2,450	100
Cooper (copper content)	119.9	236	66
Lead (lead content)	62.9	78	55
Zinc (zinc content)	264	409.2	61
Iron Ore	5,430	68,143	93
		United States	
Bauxite	1,692	12,618	88
Copper (copper content)	1,093.2	507	32
Lead (lead content)	326.4	78.4	19
Zinc (zinc content)	480	495.7	51
Iron Ore	86,508	44,646	34

SOURCES: United Nations, *Monthly Bulletin of Statistics* (January 1973). Charles L. Kimbell, "Minerals in the World Economy," in Bureau of Mines, US Department of Interior, *Minerals Yearbook 1969*, vol. 4.

TABLE 2
THE ENERGY BALANCE OF SELECTED MAJOR POWERS
1970
(MILLION METRIC TONS OF COAL EQUIVALENT)

	West Germany	United Kingdom	France		Japan	United States	USSR
				NATO			
All Energy Sources				All Energy Sources			
Domestic Production	174.3	163.7	59.3	Domestic Production	54.8	2,053.8	1,210.6
Consumption	317.0	299.1	193.0	Consumption	332.4	2,279.0	1,076.9
Deficit (−) or				Deficit (−) or			
Surplus (+)	− 142.7	− 135.4	− 133.7	Surplus (+)	− 277.6	− 225.2	+ 133.7
Import	187.0	160.9	161.8	Import	314.2	272.9	17.0
Export	35.7	30.7	15.4	Export	0.7	77.8	162.9
Net Import (−)	− 151.3	−130.2	− 146.4	Net Import (−)	− 313.5	− 195.1	+ 145.9
Solid Fuels				Solid Fuels			
Consumption	130.6	152.3	55.7	Consumption	89.4	470.7	452.1
Domestic Production	144.2	144.6	39.0	Domestic Production	39.8	543.3	472.6
Net Import (−)	+ 13.6	− 7.7	− 16.7	Net Import (−)	− 49.6	+ 72.6	+ 20.5
Liquid Fuels				Liquid Fuels			
Consumption	160.3	126.8	115.6	Consumption	227.3	933.7	345.5
Domestic Production	9.8	0.2	3.4	Domestic Production	1.0	649.5	458.3
Net Import (−)	− 150.5	− 126.6	− 112.2	Net Import (−)	− 226.3	− 284.2	+ 112.8

(+) = Export surplus

SOURCE *World Energy Supplies, 1961-1970*, UN Statistical Papers, Series J, No. 15 (New York: United Nations, 1972), Table 2.

TABLE 3
REGIONS SUPPLYING U.S. IMPORTS OF SELECTED
INDUSTRIAL RAW MATERIALS
1973
(IMPORTS AS A PERCENT OF CONSUMPTION)

	Developed Countries				Developing Countries			
	Canada	Australia New Zealand	South Africa Rhodesia	Other	Africa	Latin America	Other	Communist
Aluminum	3.1	19.4		9.1	0.3	65.9	0.2	1.9
Chromium			40.4	10.0		1.0	30.2	18.4
Cobalt	2.1				96.9		1.0	
Columbium	.1		.1	.8	35.0	53.0	11.0	
Copper	40.6	.7	8.3		2.3	47.4	.7	
Flourspar				22.0	3.4	74.5		
Iron Ore	43.5			22.3	5.6	28.5		
Lead	16.9	16.6	1.5	40.2		25.1		1.1
Manganese			12.9	18.2	24.2	33.1	10.4	.2
Mercury	36.1			31.0	24.5	6.9	1.3	1.9
Natural Rubber					12.0		88.0	50.1
Nickel	64.3	7.7	3.9	14.9		7.2		2.9
Platinum	.7		14.1	33.1[1]		2.0		.9
Tin		3.4			.2	9.4	84.0	.7
Titanium		75.1		10.1		.	13.9	.2
Tungsten	30.4	3.1	0.7	4.4	2.9	39.9	17.8	
Vanadium			57.2			42.8		
Zinc	45.0	4.6	.2	38.9	2.9	8.3		

[1] U.K. refined base on raw materials from South Africa, Canada, and U.S.S.R.

SOURCE: *International Report of the President* (1974).

XIII

The North-South Confrontation

By the North-South confrontation we mean the conflict between the poor two-thirds of the world—generally located along or south of the equator—and the economically developed states of the temperate zone, chiefly the United States, Europe, and Japan.[1] The South, or Third World, is not a uniform bloc. The less developed countries vary greatly in relative wealth, in ethnic composition and political history, and in their capacity both culturally and socially to move toward modernization and development. What they have in common is a pervasive poverty and a shared goal of catching up with the developed world. To achieve some idea of the discrepancy between the developed and less developed, it is pertinent to point out that "all the countries of Latin America, Africa, the Middle East, and Asia together produce less than a third of what the United States produces alone."[2] And the gap between the rich and most of the poor nations is

[1]The Communist states were taken to form a third division, but since the Sino-Soviet split, China has sought to identify itself with the aspirations of the Third World while lumping the Soviet Union with the U.S. as an imperialist state.

[2]Steven Rosen and Walter Jones, *The Logic of International Relations*, 2nd ed. (Cambridge, Mass.: Winthrop, 1977) p. 128.

widening, not narrowing. The poorer nations increased their productivity between 1963 and 1973; but their rate of population growth exceeded their rate of economic growth, and they have been sliding back ever since.

As the hope of economic development has dwindled, the Third World countries have begun increasingly to insist that the disparity of wealth and development between North and South is the root cause of their poverty and that the system must be changed. They argue that because they are too weak and dependent upon foreign capital to protect themselves, they are being exploited. Secondly, their export trade is at the mercy of fluctuating demand for the products in the industrial countries. Changes in consumption pattern or a recession in the United States and Europe may mean a catastrophic fall in prices for their raw materials. Third, the terms of trade for the exchange of industrial goods for raw materials is unfair. The price fluctuation and unit value of primary commodities do not average out over time to a rate of increase comparable to the incessant inflation of industrial goods. Because the advanced industrial countries are not as dependent on raw materials as the Third World is dependent on finished goods, the latter pay more and receive less. Billions are taken from the poor and given to the rich through the impersonal mechanism of freely negotiated international trade pricing. Fourth, they argue that the multinationals do not contribute as much as they should to development. They only develop the sectors that are most profitable to the companies and do not contribute to the overall development of the country's needs. Finally, the Third World argues that it cannot sell enough to the developed world to pay off its debts. Here we come to one of the most critical problems facing not only the Third World countries but the United States as well. For years, public loans from the U.S. and Europe and from the World Bank (financed directly by the same governments) helped the countries of the Third World to meet their investment needs and to cover their foreign debts. Today nearly 30 percent of all external debts owed by non-oil-producing Third World countries are financed by the World Bank and UN loan agencies, as compared to less than 10 percent in 1968. In the meantime, private banks such as Chase Manhattan and Citibank of N.Y. began loaning and investing heavily in Third World countries—especially in Brazil, Peru, South Korea, the Philippines, Indonesia, and Nigeria. As a result, the prosperity of these banks which have loaned $52 billion has become dependent on the capacity of these countries to repay the loans. Many of these loans and investments were made at a time when it seemed possible that large profits could be made from the boom that was occurring in these countries. These loans were *not* made as part of any comprehensive, sensible program of development. Suddenly, the increase in oil prices and the worldwide recession of 1974 and 1975 cut demand for Third World imports and revealed the precarious basis of much of this Third World financing. Many of these countries are now obliged to spend 30 percent to 40 percent of their export earnings just to repay their enormous debt overload. This means that much less money is available to spend on imports, including imports necessary for their development. The role of the private banks, too, has changed dramatically. They find themselves financing balance-of-payments deficits on an unprecedented scale—a new function quite different from their original task of supplying credit to private investors. As a condition for their help, they, together with the World Bank and International Monetary Fund, insist that the debtor governments must cut back on welfare and reform programs and impose lower wages and harsher working conditions on the poor people.

As a result of this crisis, the Third World countries, banded together in the "Group of 77" (actually it numbers over 100), are demanding a moratorium on debt repayments and a new international economic order (NIEO) that would: mandate the transfer of technology and investment capital free of charge; mandate lower tariffs and a minimum price for their goods (a price that would rise automatically as the price of manufactured goods rose); and that would exert greater control over the multinationals. The developed countries, led by the United States, have so far refused to accept these terms.

Beside the unrelenting criticism that the Third World and so-called Fourth World nations have mounted in the United Nations and elsewhere against the great disparity in wealth, there are real dangers that the economic recovery of the North cannot be separated from the economic recovery of the South. Meanwhile, the poverty and desperation of the situation facing the South breeds repression and the destruction of human values.

One of the most powerful arguments against a greater sharing of wealth between rich and poor nations is that there is no guarantee that the Third World people as individuals would really benefit from such a redistribution. The case for redistribution is often made on the grounds that the world is becoming more interdependent, and therefore extremes of wealth must be reduced. But all too often the Third World leaders who demand a greater sharing of the wealth in the name of their people are precisely those who maintain the most extreme form of inequality within their own society. They are not the apostles of a new and more integrated international system, but the most ardent exponents of the supremacy of the principle of national sovereignty. Far from providing any assurance that a redistribution of wealth would go to their own people, there is much evidence that it would continue to go to the rich and to strengthening the military and repressive power of Third World governments. Furthermore, the Third World governments are demanding equality, not in the name of some new and more humanistic world order, but so that they can reinforce their own national sovereignty. In other words, their goal of sharing is not to advance to some higher form of world order but to retain the existing state-centric order while reinforcing their country's position within it. This is a very important consideration because, as Robert Tucker observes, "There is no way of insuring internal equity without setting political conditions for the recipient government that will almost certainly prove unacceptable because these conditions touch the nerve root of its domestic order [meaning the power and privileges of the rich]. In doing so [such conditions] must also strike at the equality of state doctrine."[3] In other words, just as there is presently no way to achieve reforms that touch at the existing 'patron-client' relationship without a revolution, there is no way that the ruling elites could be made to abandon their wealth and privileges in return for a fairer distribution of wealth between the North and South. Tucker concludes that however good the intentions of those who want to share a greater portion of our wealth to help the impoverished masses of the Third World, "the rights of the 'needy' will, in practice, remain first and foremost the rights of states and not of individuals."[4]

The fact of the matter is that there are likely to be less, not more, resources available to help the Third World in the years to come. Not only are we bumping up against the limits to our energy and mineral resources, but the capitalist economies themselves are in deep trouble.

> Whereas in the past foreign aid programs were largely profitable to the developed nations, the combination of defense spending, aid, commitments to loan programs, failures of recipient nations to repay loans, higher costs for raw materials, and competition for markets, make them less so for the future. Multinational corporations are increasingly earning and retaining their profits outside the developed nations, and inflation makes it difficult to cater even to domestic priorities without deficit spending imbalances. Fuel imports are shifting capital into hands of oil exporting nations . . . [Europe and America] do not have regular balance-of-payment surpluses . . . as a result of all these forces, their currencies become less stable. In the face of this, heavy imports and expenditures to maintain markets and supply bases abroad may seem less attractive to them than in the past.[5]

In other words, the present economic stringencies that face the capitalist nations may be driving them toward protectionism and toward less, not more, aid and investment in the Third World. Developed countries are hardly going to be in a position to do more for the Third World when their own economies are floundering. Instead of greater interdependence and integration of Third World economies with the world capitalist system, they may be thrown back even more upon their own resources. This could weaken the present orientation of the capitalist sector of those economies which are heavily dependent for their markets and capital upon the developed states. To weather the storm, they would have to turn inward and try to achieve a viable social and political system based upon self-help and slow rates of

[3]Robert W. Tucker, "Inequality Among Nations and the Future of International Order" *The Colorado College Studies* No. 14 (May, 1977) p. 25.

[4]*Ibid.*, pp. 25–26.

[5]Robert E. Gamer, *The Developing Nations* (Boston: Allyn & Bacon, 1976), pp. 336–337.

economic growth [as in China and Cuba] rather than upon rapid industrialization. Already the United States is beginning to make its compromise with the forces of Third World nationalism (in Panama, in southern Africa, and in the Middle East) and is reducing its efforts to prop up by overt and covert intervention its control and influence over the status quo. Instead, the Carter Administration, by espousing black majority rule and human rights, is trying to get out in front of a situation which it can no longer control by economic and military means.

While economic interdependence will continue to develop between North and South, and Third World demands are not likely to disappear; it seems more likely than ever that people will have to depend upon self-help efforts within their own national boundaries if anarchy is to be avoided.

32   Counterrevolutionary America

Robert L. Heilbroner

Robert L. Heilbroner is the author of **The Making of Economic Society, The Great Ascent,** and, **The Limits of American Capitalism.**

Is the United States fundamentally opposed to economic development? The question is outrageous. Did we not coin the phrase, "the revolution of rising expectations"? Have we not supported the cause of development more generously than any nation on earth, spent our intellectual energy on the problems of development, offered our expertise freely to the backward nations of the world? How can it possibly be suggested that the United States might be opposed to economic development?

The answer is that we are not at all opposed to what we conceive economic development to be. The process depicted by the "revolution of rising expectations" is a deeply attractive one. It conjures up the image of a peasant in some primitive land, leaning on his crude plow and looking to the horizon, where he sees dimly, but for the *first time* (and that is what is so revolutionary about it), the vision of a better life. From this electrifying vision comes the necessary catalysis to change an old and stagnant way of life. The pace of work quickens. Innovations, formerly feared and resisted, are now

From Commentary, *43, no. 4 (April 1967), 31–38. This article was adapted from a paper given by Mr. Heilbroner at a conference on American foreign policy held at Colorado State University.*

eagerly accepted. The obstacles are admittedly very great—whence the need for foreign assistance—but under the impetus of new hopes the economic mechanism begins to turn faster, to gain traction against the environment. Slowly, but surely, the Great Ascent begins.

There is much that is admirable about this well-intentioned popular view of "the revolution of rising expectations." Unfortunately, there is more that is delusive about it. For the buoyant appeal of its rhetoric conceals or passes in silence over by far the larger part of the spectrum of realities of the development process. One of these is the certainty that the revolutionary aspect of development will not be limited to the realm of ideas, but will vent its fury on institutions, social classes, and innocent men and women. Another is the great likelihood that the ideas needed to guide the revolution will not only be affirmative and reasonable, but also destructive and fanatic. A third is the realization that revolutionary efforts cannot be made, and certainly cannot be sustained, by voluntary effort alone, but require an iron hand, in the spheres both of economic direction and political control. And the fourth and most difficult of these realities to face is the probability that the political force most likely to succeed in carrying through the gigantic historical transformation of development is some form of extreme national collectivism or Communism.

In a word, what our rhetoric fails to bring to our attention is the likelihood that development will require policies and programs repugnant to our "way of life," that it will bring to the fore governments hostile to our international objectives, and that its regnant ideology will bitterly oppose capitalism as a system of world economic power. If that is the case, we would have to think twice before denying that the United States was fundamentally opposed to economic development.

But is it the case? Must development lead in directions that go counter to the present American political philosophy? Let me try to indicate, albeit much too briefly and summarily, the reasons that lead me to answer that question as I do.

I begin with the cardinal point, often noted but still insufficiently appreciated, that the process called "economic development" is not primarily economic at all. We think of development as a campaign of production to be fought with budgets and monetary policies and measured with indices of output and income. But the development process is much wider and deeper than can be indicated by such statistics. To be sure, in the end what is hoped for is a tremendous rise in output. But this will not come to pass until a series of tasks, at once cruder and more delicate, simpler and infinitely more difficult, has been commenced and carried along a certain distance. . . .

. . . Development is much more than a matter of encouraging economic growth within a given social structure. It is rather the *modernization* of that structure, a process of ideational, social, economic, and political change that requires the remaking of

society in its most intimate as well as its most public attributes.[1] When we speak of the revolutionary nature of economic development, it is this kind of deeply penetrative change that we mean—change that reorganizes "normal" ways of thought, established patterns of family life, and structures of village authority as well as class and caste privilege.

What is so egregiously lacking in the great majority of the societies that are now attempting to make the Great Ascent is precisely this pervasive modernization. The trouble is not merely that economic growth lags, or proceeds at some pitiable pace. This is only a symptom of deeper-lying ills. The trouble is that the social physiology of these nations remains so depressingly unchanged despite the flurry of economic planning on top. The all-encompassing ignorance and poverty of the rural regions, the unbridgeable gulf between the peasant and the urban elites, the resistive conservatism of the village elders, the unyielding traditionalism of family life—all these remain obdurately, maddeningly, disastrously unchanged. In the cities, a few modern buildings, sometimes brilliantly executed, give a deceptive patina of modernity, but once one journeys into the immense countryside, the terrible stasis overwhelms all.

To this vast landscape of apathy and ignorance one must now make an exception of the very greatest importance. It is the fact that a very few nations, all of them Communist, have succeeded in reaching into the lives and stirring the minds of precisely that body of the peasantry which constitutes the insuperable problem elsewhere. In our concentration on the politics, the betrayals, the

[1]See C. E. Black, *The Dynamics of Modernization.* (New York: Harper and Row, 1966).

successes and failures of the Russian, Chinese, and Cuban revolutions, we forget that their central motivation has been just such a war *a l'outrance* against the arch-enemy of backwardness—not alone the backwardness of outmoded social superstructures but even more critically that of private inertia and traditionalism. . . .

It is this herculean effort to reach and rally the great anonymous mass of the population that is *the* great accomplishment of Communism—even though it is an accomplishment that is still only partially accomplished. For if the areas of the world afflicted with the self-perpetuating disease of backwardness are ever to rid themselves of its debilitating effects, I think it is likely to be not merely because antiquated social structures have been dismantled (although this is an essential precondition), but because some shock treatment like that of Communism has been administered to them.

By way of contrast to this all-out effort, however short it may have fallen of its goal, we must place the timidity of the effort to bring modernization to the peoples of the non-Communist world. Here again I do not merely speak of lagging rates of growth. I refer to the fact that illiteracy in the non-Communist countries of Asia and Central America is increasing (by some 200 million in the last decade) because it has been "impossible" to mount an educational effort that will keep pace with population growth. I refer to the absence of substantial land reform in Latin America, despite how many years of promises. I refer to the indifference or incompetence or corruption of governing elites: the incredible sheiks with their oil-doms; the vague, well-meaning leaders of India unable to break the caste system, kill the cows, control the birthrate, reach the villages, house or employ the labor rotting on the streets; the cynical governments of

South America, not one of which, according to Lleras Camargo, former president of Colombia, has ever prosecuted a single politician or industrialist for evasion of taxes. And not least, I refer to the fact that every movement that arises to correct these conditions is instantly identified as "Communist" and put down with every means at hand, while the United States clucks or nods approval.

To be sure, even in the most petrified societies, the modernization process is at work. If there were time, the solvent acids of the 20th century would work their way on the ideas and institutions of the most inert or resistant countries. But what lacks in the 20th century is time. The multitudes of the underdeveloped world have only in the past two decades been summoned to their reveille. The one thing that is certain about the revolution of rising expectations is that it is only in its inception, and that its pressures for justice and action will steadily mount as the voice of the 20th century penetrates to villages and slums where it is still almost inaudible. It is not surprising that Princeton historian C. E. Black, surveying this labile world, estimates that we must anticipate "ten to fifteen revolutions a year for the foreseeable future in the less developed societies."

In itself, this prospect of mounting political restiveness enjoins the speediest possible time schedule for development. But this political urgency is many times compounded by that of the population problem. Like an immense river in flood, the number of human beings rises each year to wash away the levees of the preceding year's labors and to pose future requirements of monstrous proportions. To provide shelter for the three billion human beings who will arrive on earth in the next forty years will require as many dwellings as have been constructed since recorded history began. To feed them will take double the world's present output of food. To cope with the mass exodus from the overcrowded country-side will necessitate cities of grotesque size —Calcutta, now a cesspool of three to five millions, threatens us by the year 2000 with a prospective population of from thirty to sixty millions.

These horrific figures spell one importunate message: haste. That is the *mene mene, tekel upharsin* written on the walls of government planning offices around the world. Even if the miracle of the loop is realized— the new contraceptive device that promises the first real breakthrough in population control—we must set ourselves for at least another generation of rampant increase.

But how to achieve haste? How to convince the silent and disbelieving men, how to break through the distrustful glances of women in black shawls, how to overcome the overt hostility of landlords, the opposition of the Church, the petty bickerings of military cliques, the black-marketeering of commercial dealers? I suspect there is only one way. The conditions of backwardness must be attacked with the passion, the ruthlessness, and the messianic fury of a jehad, a Holy War. Only a campaign of an intensity and single-mindedness that must approach the ludicrous and the unbearable offers the chance to ride roughshod over the resistance of the rich and the poor alike and to open the way for the forcible implantation of those modern attitudes and techniques without which there will be no escape from the misery of underdevelopment.

I need hardly add that the cost of this modernization process has been and will be horrendous. If Communism is the great modernizer, it is certainly not a benign agent of change. Stalin may well have exceeded Hitler as a mass executioner. Free inquiry in China has been supplanted by dogma and catechism; even in Russia nothing like freedom of criticism or of personal expression is allowed. Furthermore, the economic cost of industrialization in both countries has been at least as severe as that imposed by primitive capitalism.

Yet one must count the gains as well as the losses. Hundreds of millions who would have been confined to the narrow cells of changeless lives have been liberated from prisons they did not even know existed. Class structures that elevated the flighty or irresponsible have been supplanted by others that have promoted the ambitious and the dedicated. Economic systems that gave rise to luxury and poverty have given way to systems that provide a rough distributional justice. Above all, the prospect of a new future has been opened. It is this that lifts the current ordeal in China above the level of pure horror. The number of human beings in that country who have perished over the past centuries from hunger or neglect, is beyond computation. The present revolution may add its dreadful increment to this number. But it also holds out the hope that China may finally have been galvanized into social, political, and economic attitudes that for the first time make its modernization a possibility.

Two questions must be answered when we dare to risk so favorable a verdict on Communism as a modernizing agency. The first is whether the result is worth the cost, whether the possible—by no means assured —escape from underdevelopment is worth the lives that will be squandered to achieve it.

I do not know how one measures the moral price of historical victories or how one can ever decide that a diffuse gain is worth a sharp and particular loss. I only know that the way in which we ordinarily keep the books of history is wrong. No one is now toting up the balance of the wretches who starve in India, or the peasants of Northeastern Brazil who live in the swamps on crabs, or the undernourished and permanently stunted children of Hong Kong or Honduras. Their sufferings go unrecorded, and are not present to counterbalance the scales when the furies of revolution strike down their victims. Barrington Moore has made a nice calculation that bears on this problem. Taking as the weight in one pan the 35,000 to 40,000 persons who lost their lives—mainly for no fault of theirs—as a result of the Terror during the French Revolution, he asks what would have been the death rate from preventable starvation and injustice under the *ancien regime* to balance the scales. "Offhand," he writes, "it seems unlikely that this would be very much below the proportion of .0010 which [the] figure of 40,000 yields when set against an estimated population of 24 million."[2]

Is it unjust to charge the *ancien regime* in Russia with ten million preventable deaths? I think it not unreasonable. To charge the authorities in pre-revolutionary China with equally vast and preventable degradations? Theodore White, writing in 1946, had this to say: . . . "some scholars think that China is perhaps the only country in the world where the people eat less, live more bitterly, and are clothed worse than they were five hundred years ago."[3]

I do not recommend such a calculus of corpses—indeed, I am aware of the license it gives to the unscrupulous—but I raise it to show the onesidedness of our protestations against the brutality and violence of revolutions. In this regard, it is chastening to recall

[2]*Social Origins of Dictatorship and Democracy*, p. 104.
[3]*Thunder Out of China*, p. 32.

the multitudes who have been killed or mutilated by the Church which is now the first to protest against the excesses of Communism.

But there is an even more terrible second question to be asked. It is clear beyond doubt, however awkward it may be for our moralizing propensities, that historians excuse horror that succeeds; and that we write our comfortable books of moral philosophy, seated atop a mound of victims—slaves, serfs, laboring men and women, heretics, dissenters—who were crushed in the course of preparing the way for our triumphal entry into existence. But at least we are here to vindicate the carnage. What if we were not? What if the revolutions grind flesh and blood and produce nothing, if the end of the convulsion is not exhilaration but exhaustion, not triumph but defeat?

Before this possibility—which has been realized more than once in history—one stands mute. Mute, but not paralyzed. For there is the necessity of calculating what is likely to happen in the absence of the revolution whose prospective excesses hold us back. Here one must weigh what has been done to remedy underdevelopment— and what has not been done—in the past twenty years; how much time there remains before the population flood enforces its own ultimate solution; what is the likelihood of bringing modernization without the frenzied assault that Communism seems most capable of mounting. As I make this mental calculation I arrive at an answer which is even more painful than that of revolution. I see the alternative as the continuation, without substantial relief—and indeed with a substantial chance of deterioration—of the misery and meanness of life as it is now lived in the sinkhole of the world's backward regions. . . .

The great arena of desperation to which

the revolutionizing impetus of Communism seems most applicable is primarily the crowded land masses and archipelagoes of Southeast Asia and the impoverished areas of Central and South America. But even here, there is the possibility that the task of modernization may be undertaken by non-Communist elites. There is always the example of indigenous, independent leaders who rise up out of nowhere to overturn the established framework and to galvanize the masses—a Gandhi, a Marti, a pre-1958 Castro. Or there is that fertile ground for the breeding of national leaders—the army, as witness Ataturk or Nasser, among many.[4]

Thus there is certainly no inherent necessity that the revolutions of modernization be led by Communists. But it is well to bear two thoughts in mind when we consider the likely course of non-Communist revolutionary sweeps. The first is the nature of the mobilizing appeal of any successful revolutionary elite. Is it the austere banner of saving and investment that waves over the heads of the shouting marchers in Jakarta and Bombay, Cairo and Havana? It most certainly is not. The banner of economic development is that of nationalism, with its promise of personal immortality and collective majesty. It seems beyond question that a feverish nationalism will charge the

atmosphere of any nation, Communist or not, that tries to make the Great Ascent—and as a result we must expect the symptoms of nationalism along with the disease: exaggerated xenophobia, thin-skinned national sensitivity, a search for enemies as well as a glorification of the state.

These symptoms, which we have already seen in every quarter of the globe, make it impossible to expect easy and amicable relations between the developing states and the colossi of the developed world. No conceivable response on the part of America or Europe or, for that matter, Russia, will be able to play up to the vanities or salve the irritations of the emerging nations, much less satisfy their demands for help. Thus, we must anticipate an anti-American, or anti-Western, possibly even anti-white animus from any nation in the throes of modernization, even if it is not parroting Communist dogma.

Then there is a second caution as to the prospects for non-Communist revolutions. This is the question of what ideas and policies will guide their revolutionary efforts. Revolutions, especially if their whole orientation is to the future, require philosophy equally as much as force. It is here, of course, that Communism finds its special strength. The vocabulary in which it speaks —a vocabulary of class domination, of domestic and international exploitation—is rich in meaning to the backward nations. The view of history it espouses provides the support of historical inevitability to the fallible efforts of struggling leaders. Not least, the very dogmatic certitude and ritualistic repetition that stick in the craw of the Western observer offer the psychological assurances on which an unquestioning faith can be maintained.

If a non-Communist elite is to persevere in tasks that will prove Sisyphean in

[4]What are the chances for modernizing revolutions of the Right, such as those of the Meiji Restoration or of Germany under Bismarck? I think they are small. The changes to be wrought in the areas of greatest backwardness are much more socially subversive than those of the 19th century, and the timespan allotted to the revolutionists is much smaller. Bourgeois revolutions are not apt to go far enough, particularly in changing property ownership. Still, one could imagine such revolutions with armed support and no doubt Fascistic ideologies. I doubt that they would be any less of a threat than revolutions of the Left.

difficulty, it will also have to offer a philosophical interpretation of its role as convincing and elevating, and a diagnosis of social and economic requirements as sharp and simplistic, as that of Communism. Further, its will to succeed at whatever cost must be as firm as that of the Marxists. It is not impossible that such a philosophy can be developed, more or less independent of formal Marxian conceptions. It is likely, however, to resemble the creed of Communism far more than that of the West. Political liberty, economic freedom, and constitutional law may be the great achievements and the great issues of the most advanced nations, but to the least developed lands they are only dim abstractions, or worse, rationalizations behind which the great powers play their imperialist tricks or protect the privileges of their monied classes.

Thus, even if for many reasons we should prefer the advent of non-Communist modernizing elites, we must realize that they too will present the United States with programs and policies antipathetic to much that America "believes in" and hostile to America as a world power. The leadership needed to mount a jehad against backwardness—and it is my main premise that only a Holy War will begin modernization in our time—will be forced to expound a philosophy that approves authoritarian and collectivist measures at home and that utilizes as the target for its national resentment abroad the towering villains of the world, of which the United States is now Number One.

All this confronts American policymakers and public opinion with a dilemma of a totally unforeseen kind. On the one hand we are eager to assist in the rescue of the great majority of mankind from conditions that we recognize as dreadful and ultimately dangerous. On the other hand, we seem to be committed, especially in the underdeveloped areas, to a policy of defeating Communism wherever it is within our military capacity to do so, and of repressing movements that might become Communist if they were allowed to follow their internal dynamics. Thus, we have on the one side the record of Point Four, the Peace Corps, and foreign aid generally; and on the other, Guatemala, Cuba, the Dominican Republic, and now Vietnam.

That these two policies might be in any way mutually incompatible, that economic development might contain revolutionary implications infinitely more far-reaching than those we have so blandly endorsed in the name of rising expectations, that Communism or a radical national collectivism might be the only vehicles for modernization in many key areas of the world—these are dilemmas we have never faced. Now I suggest that we do face them, and that we begin to examine in a serious way ideas that have hitherto been considered blasphemous, if not near-traitorous. . . .

A world in which Communist governments were engaged in the enormous task of trying to modernize the worst areas of Asia, Latin America, and Africa would be a world in which sharp differences of national interest were certain to arise within these continental areas. The outlook would be for frictions and conflicts to develop among Communist nations with equal frequency as they developed between those nations and their non-Communist neighbors. A long period of jockeying for power and command over resources, rather than anything like a unified sharing of power and resources, seems unavoidable in the developing continents. This would not preclude a continuous barrage of anti-American propaganda, but it would certainly impede a movement to exert a coordinated Communist influence over these areas.

Second, it seems essential to distinguish

among the causes of dangerous national and international behavior those that can be traced to the tenets of Communism and those that must be located elsewhere. "Do not talk to me about Communism and capitalism," said a Hungarian economist with whom I had lunch this winter. "Talk to me about rich nations and poor ones."

I think it *is* wealth and poverty, and not Communism or capitalism, that establishes much of the tone and tension of international relations. For that reason I would expect Communism in the backward nations (or national collectivism, if that emerges in the place of Communism) to be strident, belligerent, and insecure. If these regimes fail—as they may—their rhetoric may become hysterical and their behavior uncontrolled, although of small consequence. But if they succeed, which I believe they can, many of these traits should recede. Russia, Yugoslavia, or Poland are simply not to be compared, either by way of internal pronouncement or external behavior, with China, or, on a smaller scale, Cuba. Modernization brings, among other things, a waning of the stereotypes, commandments, and flagellations so characteristic of (and so necessary to) a nation engaged in the effort to alter itself from top to bottom. The idiom of ceaseless revolution becomes less relevant—even faintly embarrassing—to a nation that begins to be pleased with itself. Then, too, it seems reasonable to suppose that the vituperative quality of Communist invective would show some signs of abating were the United States to modify its own dogmatic attitude and to forego its own wearisome cliches about the nature of Communism.

I doubt there are many who will find these arguments wholly reassuring. They are not. It would be folly to imagine that the next generation or two, when Communism or national collectivism in the underdeveloped areas passes through its jehad stage, will be a time of international safety. But as always in these matters, it is only by a comparison with the alternatives that one can choose the preferable course. The prospect that I have offered as a plausible scenario of the future must be placed against that which results from a pursuit of our present course. And here I see two dangers of even greater magnitude: (1) the prospect of many more Vietnams, as radical movements assert themselves in other areas of the world; and (2) a continuation of the present inability of the most impoverished areas to modernize, with the prospect of an eventual human catastrophe on an unimaginable scale.

Nevertheless, there *is* a threat in the specter of a Communist or near-Communist supremacy in the underdeveloped world. It is that the rise of Communism would signal the end of capitalism as the dominant world order, and would force the acknowledgement that America no longer constituted the model on which the future of world civilization would be mainly based. In this way, as I have written before, the existence of Communism frightens American capitalism as the rise of Protestantism frightened the Catholic Church, or the French Revolution the English aristocracy.

It is, I think, the fear of losing our place in the sun, of finding ourselves at bay, that motivates a great deal of the anti-Communism on which so much of American foreign policy seems to be founded. . . .

33 New International Order May Not Be Mainly Economic

Paris Arnopoulos

Professor Arnopoulos teaches international politics at Concordia University in Montreal.

The seventh special session of the General Assembly of the United Nations in 1974 marked a milestone in contemporary world affairs when it called for the establishment of a "new international economic order" (NIEO) and proposed a program of action to lead towards this goal.

Since then, scholars have been studying the implications of this new order and diplomats have been negotiating the implementation of its programs. . . .

The demands for an NIEO arose from a widespread perception that there was something fundamentally wrong with the present state of world affairs. The storm of crises that has been lashing the world lately has built up to global proportions and, if left to continue unabated, would result in irreversible damage to, and even the collapse of, the present international system.

Here we shall consider these problems, and the issues they produce, from the functional, geographic and strategic points of view. . . .

SOCIAL COMPLEXITY

One of the most significant developments in the modern world is the increasing complexity of social systems. This functional sophistication of human instruments and

International Perspectives, Sept./Oct. 1977.

institutions makes societies much more problem-prone than previously, at the same time as it makes these problems much more difficult to solve. It seems that the intricacy and magnitude of world affairs move events beyond human control and surpass our ability to deal with them.

The difficulty of understanding social problems and controlling their effects is evident in many areas of public affairs. Here we shall look at the most important forces in the economic, social and political arenas, out of whose interaction arise the complex issues in the present international system the NIEO is proposing to correct.

The problem of relative underdevelopment in some parts of the world and overdevelopment in others appears to be at the basis of international economic issues. All countries want to engage in the process of economic growth—not only in order to provide their people with their basic needs but also to increase the production and consumption of manufactured goods. Accordingly, increasing the gross national product has become the sole measure of progress and the ultimate criterion of success.

This process, however, has met with certain complications, both natural and artificial. To begin with, the uneven distribution of natural resources in the world has endowed some countries with an abundance of energy and materials, and has left others with a scarcity. This natural maldistribution creates unequal development potentials, which in time widen into economic gaps between the rich and poor nations.

Natural inequalities are further exacerbated by different cultural tendencies, technological capabilities and historical precedents. Thus, industrially-advanced countries have acquired a decided advantage over agrarian societies because they can harness large amounts of energy. This capability is readily translated into power, whereby the strong can dominate the weak nations.

For this reason, although international trade is supposed to maximize the comparative advantage of complementary capabilities, it actually favours the rich and strong systems. Thus, unequal terms of trade compound the inherent discrepancies among nations, enriching the strong and impoverishing the weak even more.

So far, all attempts to reverse this tendency through international aid have failed. Both the first and second UN Development Decades have not only fallen short of their targets but have witnessed deterioration in the condition of most countries. The aid given is too little and too late to compensate for the discriminative terms of trade and alleviate the increasing indebtedness of the poor to the rich.

The NIEO proposes to cure this endemic condition of the present international system by major changes in the economic relations among nations. Through large transfers of technology, resources and capital, as well as improved terms of trade and increased aid, the NIEO aims to spread economic development all over the world and thus effect a more equitable distribution of the common wealth.

In aiming for economic development, the NIEO expects to solve the major social problems caused by overpopulation, poverty,

unemployment and oppression. However, even though economic and social factors interact, it is not easy to determine cause-effect relations between them, especially in complex matters of population growth, cultural change and class structures. . . .

DANGEROUS ROAD

This road, however, is very dangerous because it involves great social changes. Industrialization destroys traditional cultures and breaks historical continuities, thus disorienting people and distorting their values. Its accompanying urbanization unbalances the social groups of both town and countryside, thereby creating more problems than it solves.

Moreover, it is now accepted that economic development does not necessarily alleviate social injustice. On the contrary, it may promote greater disparities if the benefits of growth are not equitably distributed. In societies where there exist rigid class differences and hierarchical structures, distribution cannot but be unequal, thus increasing the inequalities. This situation, along with the rising expectations of all people, create frustration, alienation and conflict, which eventually lead either to suppression or to revolution.

If the earth had sufficient resources to maintain a good rate of economic growth indefinitely, the problematic social by-products could be submerged in the euphoria of material improvement. This is, in fact, what has happened so far in the advanced industrial systems. But, as we are approaching the limits of economic growth, these social problems are now coming to the fore. When production can no longer increase the total wealth, distribution becomes the most critical issue of society. This, in effect, is looming ahead on a global scale, and the NIEO has no way of preventing it.

Although power politics are supposed to be kept out of the NIEO, they do come in whenever the issue of redistribution is raised. If the NIEO means anything, it signifies real shifts of power in the world. These shifts are bound to affect matters of national security, international law and intergovernmental organization. . . .

Because of its economic, social and political inadequacies, the present international system has become unacceptable to many people. And thus its legitimacy is questioned and its laws are in dispute. This is particularly so in the areas most affected by technology, where new methods and institutions are evolving rapidly. In these areas, traditional national jurisdictions overlap and conflict with modern transnational activities, making it necessary to develop new codes of conduct and dispute-settlement procedures to handle novel situations.

The complexity of the problems and the intransigence of the interests involved, however, make this legislating process very tortuous. After a few years of protracted wrangling in the United Nations Conference on the Law of the Sea and UNCTAD, to mention only two arenas, the nation states of the world have still a long way to go before reaching any consensus on the new rules of the international game.

Yet the pressures are rising for a new international order. The many disadvantaged nations are challenging the supremacy of the few satisfied ones and demanding a greater say in the management of the world. Many intergovernmental organizations, for a long time dominated by the great powers, are now under pressure from their dissatisfied majorities. . . .

The deep roots of these problems and the complex interactions among them compound our inability to grasp and resolve them. The traditional attitude of pragmatic or "agnostic" crisis-management and *ad hoc* tinkering has produced more problems than it has solved because it has coped with immediate and proximate issues at the expense of the ultimate and universal ones.

The NIEO tries to avoid this weakness by considering global problems in the longer run. Its program, however, assumes the continuation of things past, both in values and in structures. Thus it embraces industrialization, modernization, integration and the technological "fix" as the path to the future. And so it is an optimistic economic solution to problems that are beyond economics.

In order to tackle these broader social problems, nation states would have to go considerably further than the NIEO and change their internal systems. A truly new international order would arise only with the development of new national orders based on the principles of resource conservation and steady-state economics in the MDCs, balanced growth and equitable distribution in the LDCs, and self-reliance and independence on the part of all social systems.

Accordingly, "development" should be redefined by each culture to fit the particular values and capacities of its society, so that its goals may be attained by self-directed and self-generated means. To do so, social systems must respect natural limits to growth and optimize their quality of life within these limits in their own way. In any case, whether we like it or not, either by social planning or natural catastrophe, this will be the eventual development of the NIO.

CONFLICTING SYSTEMS

In spite, or perhaps because, of its growing interdependence, the world is still deeply divided between conflicting economic, political and cultural systems. The widest fissures run East-West and North-South. Recent events have shown that the older ideo-political cleavage has entered a period of attenuation, whereas the more recent socio-economic gap is growing into a confrontation, thus replacing the Cold War as the most critical issue of the day.

At the heart of the North-South conflict is the 13:1 ratio indicating the wealth gap between the rich and the poor nations of the world. Worse still, this gap has been growing steadily from 10:1 in 1960, and is likely to reach 14:1 by 1980. This means that two-thirds of humanity subsist in abject poverty, while one-third enjoys unprecedented wealth. Obviously this situation cannot continue without increasing suppression of the resulting dissatisfaction of the masses.

The NIEO proposes to close this widening gap, at least by half (6:1), within this century. This is indeed a formidable goal, given the present power configuration in the world. As we have already mentioned, the economic problems of increasing production and the political problems of improving distribution appear to rule out the possibility of any such evolution taking place peacefully.

However one may deplore world inequalities, it would be economically impossible to raise the material standard of living of everyone to the levels of the Northwest, and politically unrealistic to expect the rich to lower their standards by distributing their wealth among the poor. As long as materialistic values prevail in the North and the "catching-up" syndrome motivates the South, protracted conflict will be the outcome.

In order to avoid this eventuality, the nations of the world must redefine "development" in social rather than economic terms. The so-called "North-South gap" is as much semantic as it is real because it focuses on material production as the measure of all things. A better-balanced social index may, however, show that the gap between the "qualities of life" in the North and South is not so great after all. . . .

REALIZING POTENTIAL

If economic development means realizing the potential of a community to provide for the basic needs of its members, the economic viability of a nation should be measured by the extent to which it fulfills this function. Once basic human needs (nutrition, sanitation, shelter, training, work and leisure) are met, further development should depend on particular cultural and natural constraints.

The best that an NIEO could do is help societies become economically viable as an absolute priority. Beyond that, every nation should determine for itself how far its resources allow it to go and what its values permit it to attain—always provided that it does not interfere with the same determination by others. It is unreasonable to expect much more from the international system, without engaging in economic domination, political interference or cultural imperialism.

Our analysis so far indicates that the various crises that have come upon us are not merely incidental but are symptoms of deep and persistent trends in world history. Because of this, it seems that the "muddling through" approach of the present international system is less and less effective in handling its problems. Unfortunately, many key proposals of the NIEO will do nothing to change this situation; on the contrary, they might exacerbate it. What is needed to apply to such historical forces is a more fundamental restructuring of national and international systems.

Perhaps the prime mover of modern developments is the dramatic transformation of nature by technology. This change has led to artificial economic growth that consumes inordinate quantities of energy and resources, thus degrading the environment and increasing the rate of its entropy.

Moreover, the technological innovations of science have institutionalized rapid change in social systems. This historical acceleration of change and movement in human affairs has created great instability and transitoriness both in individual psychologies and in group relations.

These trends have had certain significant repercussions in the international system. The uneven rates of change have produced great gaps between socio-economic systems. The main cleavage between the more- and less-developed countries (MDCs and LDCs) had grown from an estimated ratio of 3:1 in 1800 to 6:1 in 1900, and is not likely to be less than 12:1 in the year 2000.

THREE POSSIBILITIES

As things are evolving, we can envisage three possibilities for the foreseeable future: the rich will continue to get richer, though at a reduced rate, and the poor will get poorer; the limits to growth will catch up to and impoverish everyone; there will be a basic change of values and structures from which everyone will benefit.

Of these alternative directions the world could conceivably take, the first is the most probable in the short run and the second the most likely by the next century, if things continue as before. A few people can exploit the many for a long time, and the many can exploit nature for a short time, but they cannot all keep up this pace indefinitely.

Recent events make it increasingly clear that we cannot maintain concurrent economic growth of the whole system. Either a few can grow at the expense of the many or everyone will have to accept a general, steady-state condition of material production and consumption at a lower level. It is up to us to make the best out of this inevitability by sufficient socio-cultural change.

Such change will require a shifting of our aspirations away from demands for more manufactured products toward more intangible and more permanent goods, more equitably distributed. To do otherwise would increase the frustration of unfulfilled promises for most of the world's people. Disillusion of this kind is dangerous because it often leads to desperate actions and nihilistic behaviour.

The NIEO reflects the rising demands of the LDC's for greater material prosperity, which the MDCs must help them attain. These demands are backed by strong economic, social and political arguments. The LDCs appeal to the self-interest and moral responsibility of the MDCs, as well as to the legitimacy of their expectations of compensation. At the same time, they hint at reprisals and warn of impending social instability if they do not get their fair share of the world's common wealth. . . .

POLICY PROSPECTS

The most likely cause of an NIO would be natural pressures rather than LDC demands. Our dynamic, complex and interdependent system requires great amounts of energy to keep it in operation. It is thus easy to predict that, as the energy resources of the world are becoming scarcer and costlier, we are bound to reach a critical point of inflection where recent trends will be reversed sufficiently to restore the natural balance between the supply and demand of power.

For any society to escape the catastrophic effects of such a reversal of its way of life it must plan a gradual disengagement from this escalating power spiral. This means it has to try to live within its own means by increasing its self-reliance and decreasing its dependence on the resources and good-will of others to keep it afloat. So unpopular a policy, of course, can only succeed in communities of strong cohesion, responsible citizenship and collective self-discipline.

These requirements indicate that the real power of a nation to survive such traumatic shocks depends not only on its natural resources and economic strength but also on its social organization and political ideology. The role of good government in this difficult situation is to provide realistic goals and credible leadership that will inspire people to make sacrifices in order to attain them.

Unfortunately, it is very difficult to combine all these conditions in the same place at the right time. Where there is enough political will, there is no economic way, and *vice versa*. As environmental and economic trends move in one direction, social and political forces keep going in another. Meanwhile, governments are caught in the momentum of past policies because they were once successful and are still lucrative for some. Thus, although the old international order is breaking down, the remaining vested interests, coupled with social inertia, prevent the development of an NIO.

The common thread running through the demands for a new international economic order is that all countries, rich and poor alike, have urgent and inseparable problems that are rapidly getting out of control. More specifically, the present international system suffers from: energy and resource scarcities attributable to the accelerated growth of the MDCs; gross inequalities and widespread proverty owing to unbalanced growth in the LDCs; and international frictions and conflicts owing to the perceived inequities of the interdependent relations between MDCs and LDCs.

The deep roots of these problems and the complex interactions among them compound our inability to grasp and resolve them. The traditional attitude of pragmatic or "agnostic" crisis-management and *ad hoc* tinkering has produced more problems than it has solved because it has coped with immediate and proximate issues at the expense of the ultimate and universal ones.

The NIEO tries to avoid this weakness by considering global problems in the longer run. Its program, however, assumes the continuation of things past, both in values and in structures. Thus it embraces industrialization, modernization, integration, and the technological "fix" as the path to the future. And so it is an optimistic economic solution to problems that are beyond economics.

In order to tackle these broader social problems, nation-states would have to go considerably further than the NIEO and change their internal systems. A truly new international order would arise only with the development of new national orders based on the principles of resource conservation and steady-state economics in the MDCs, balance growth and equitable distribution in the LDCs, and self-reliance and independence on the part of all social systems.

Accordingly, "development" should be redefined by each culture to fit the particular values and capacities of its society, so that its goals may be attained by self-directed and self-generated means. To do so, social systems must respect natural limits to growth and optimize their quality of life within these limits in their own way. In any case, whether we like it or not, either by social planning or natural catastrophe, this will be the eventual development of the NIO.

XIV

Detente and Arms Control

Detente is a French word meaning relaxation of tensions. It was introduced under Nixon and Kissinger to denote the gradual easing of the Soviet-American cold-war relationship toward a more relaxed and less hostile relationship. Its development rested upon two changes in the world situation. First and foremost, as Simon Serfaty explains in the first article in this chapter, Kissinger and Nixon managed to reorient United States foreign policy away from an obsession with anti-communism toward a more pragmatic and realistic assessment of American national interest. Detente represented a greater willingness to define American foreign policy in terms of the balance of power (which was discussed in Chapter 5) and in terms of strategic rather than ideological goals and objectives. Containment would continue to be the basis of U.S. foreign policy, but Washington would be more willing to negotiate issues, whereas before we had not.

Secondly, detente on the Soviet side probably represented a response to the strategic pressures caused by America's normalization of its relations with China and by the Chinese deployment toward the Soviet frontier in

Inner Asia. It also rested on an apparent Soviet need for investment and technology from the West if Russia was to make up deficiencies in its economy. The high points of detente came in June 1972 when Nixon and Brezhnev signed agreements limiting nuclear weapons systems (SALT 1) and in the following year when each side signed an agreement to avoid engaging in conflicts that might involve the danger of confrontation and nuclear war.[1]

Kissinger may have gone too far in arousing expectations about detente that were not in the cards, given the logic of the Soviet ideology and situation. The Kremlin views detente from the perspective of ongoing competition between two opposed systems, the communist and the capitalist, not as some form of entente by which the two superpowers would bury their differences. Current Soviet policy modernizes the long-established "two-track" conceptualization of peaceful coexistence: "that is, peaceful diplomacy and a policy of getting along with the capitalist West combined with a dialectical militancy in the areas of ideology and class struggle, with material support for revolutionary movements."[2] Brezhnev underscored this dialectical fusion of opposites for the 25th Soviet Party Congress in 1976.

> We will come forward wherever our consciences and our convictions may lead us. . . . Detente in no way replaces, nor can it replace, the laws of class struggle. . . . Detente creates favorable conditions for the broadest dissemination of the ideology of Socialism. . . . The ideological battle between the two systems [capitalist and socialist] becomes more intense.

The Kremlin does not see detente as ending the adversary relationship, but as a condition forced upon a still imperialist America by changes in the international system. Soviet analysts attributed the shift in U.S. foreign policy to the failure of its Vietnam War policy and to the attendant loss of U.S. global superiority. Viewed through the prism of Soviet perceptions, America has been thrown onto the defensive, the "correlation of forces" has turned unfavorable to the United States, and detente has been adopted to compensate for this loss of power. The question in the Kremlin for a time seems to have been whether American adversity favored a more relentless pursuit of the "cold war" or a more complete adherence to peaceful competition.

In this debate Brezhnev seems to have succeeded in convincing his opponents that the Soviet Union can exploit detente to avoid the dangers of unrestrained conflicts which might result in nuclear war while maintaining its ideological vigilance and quest for an eventual Socialist "victory." Beyond expectations of beneficial trade and technology acquisitions from the West, the Kremlin underscores the notion that the capitalist-imperialists

---

[1]Agreement on the Prevention of Nuclear War, June 22, 1973.

[2]Louis L. Ortmayer, "The Several Faces of Detente," BOOK FORUM, Vol. III, Nov. 4, 1978. p. 489.

have no other alternative, given the Soviet gains and the shift in the world correlation of forces, but to accept detente on Soviet terms. Of course this optimistic assessment may be no more than a rationalization by Brezhnev to justify the needs of the Soviet state.

In line with their ideological formulations and with their spirit of opportunism, the Kremlin draws a sharp distinction between detente as a basis for reducing the chances of nuclear conflict and acquiring Western investment and technology and detente as a harmonization of U.S. and Soviet values and interests. It is based on the proposition that the Soviet Union need not and must not deny itself the possibility of asserting itself globally wherever the political situation—as in Africa or the Middle East— favors Soviet intervention. Whether the Kremlin can harmonize its paramount search for security (against nuclear war) with the risky and provocative support for revolution and defeat of the capitalist order is dubious.

The U.S. in turn has not viewed detente as ending its struggle for security and stability either. While Kissinger admonished Americans that they "must outgrow the notion that any setback is a Soviet gain," the Nixon Administration continued to act in the non-communist sphere on that very premise, viewing a defeat in Vietnam, Chile, or Angola as a blow at the credibility of America's global position. Nor has detente meant an end to the American strategy of containment. In Europe, in the Persian Gulf, and in the Far East, the U.S. still maintains a structure of alliances and military power designed to limit the risk of Soviet expansion. Kissinger was and continues to be vehemently outspoken in his conviction that any form of communist participation in the governments of Italy or France would be disastrous for the military and moral unity of the West. The Carter administration has adopted a similar view since coming to power.

According to Simon Serfaty in this chapter, detente merely added a strategy of inducement (principally economic) to the former strategy of military warning and threat. And it is certainly true that one of the biggest gains to Russia from detente has been the opportunity to acquire necessary investment capital, credits, technology, and foodstuffs from the West. In addition to some $4 or $5 billion in purchases of U.S. wheat, the West,- principally Europe and Japan, has loaned and invested $46 to $50 billion in the Soviet Union and Eastern Europe. In their anxiety to find new outlets for their money and goods, Western capitalist and banking interests have let the countries of eastern Europe have long-term credit on very favorable terms. Whether they will ever export enough to pay back the loans is another matter.

Because the U.S. Senate insisted that Russia would have to permit 30,000 Jews to emigrate each year as a condition for ratifying the treaty extending to Russia all the benefits of U.S. credit and trade, the Soviet Union rejected the treaty and American capitalists have had far less business than their European and Japanese competitors. This is a good example of the uneasiness with which many Americans view detente. President Carter's subsequent emphasis upon human rights, and his insistence that making the Soviet treatment of dissidents an issue does not represent interference in Soviet internal affairs, drew a violent reaction from Moscow. Secretary Brezhnev declared: "Washington's claims to teach others how to live cannot be accepted by any sovereign state. . . . We will not tolerate interference in our internal affairs by anyone and under any pretext." For awhile after Carter wrote his letter to Soviet physicist and dissident Andre Sakharov, Soviet-American relations were under severe strain, and Carter has certainly given the Kremlin reason to wonder if detente is as "irreversible" as they once assumed.

It is a measure of the limitations of detente that neither side is willing to refrain from attacking the other's domestic system. The sensitivity is most acute on the Soviet side, which cannot portray detente internally as ending the need for vigilance and sacrifice. "Without an external enemy the Kremlin would be hard put to explain to its own people the rigid political controls, the absence of the most elementary democratic freedoms, and the constant shortage of consumer goods."[3]

As to the question of whether detente has favored the Soviet Union more than it has the West, there are clearly two different schools of thought. There are those like the members of the Committee on the Present Danger, the American Security Council, and the editors of the prestigious Jewish journal COMMENTARY who feel that detente has been a snare and delusion leading America to minimize the Soviet threat and to let down its guard.

But there are also those scholars as well as the members of the government who believe that the military power of the U.S.S.R., while enormous, is not without its weaknesses, that Russia has not succeeded in neutralizing the forces of containment on its eastern and western borders, and that its foreign and military policies have served to compound its many domestic problems. Certainly it has lost ground in the Middle East. Detente has not permitted the French or Italian Communists to slip into power. And unless it really anticipates risking a war to achieve some political end, much of Russia's concentration on military power seems a costly and bootless waste of money at the cost of deforming the Soviet economy.

By contrast, detente has permitted Americans and their government to take a fresh look at foreign policy and to make many adjustments which might otherwise not have been possible: to relax our obsessive globalism and interventionism; to adjust to the forces of nationalism in Africa and the Middle East while endeavoring to make an effective contribution to the long-term settlement of the Arab-Israeli and black majority—white

---

[3]Dimitri Simes, *Detente and Conflict: Soviet Foreign Policy 1972-1977* (Beverly Hills: Sage, 1971). Of course, it is for this reason that Solzhenitsyn and even Sakharov deplore the percent terms of detente. If rapproachment were to proceed totally, without qualification, on Soviet terms, it would pose a serious threat to the world as a whole. There cannot be genuine detente so long as the Soviet domestic system remains unaffected.

minority problems; to relinquish our control of the Panama Canal; and to free our economy to cope with the monetary crisis that began in the early 1960s. Whatever gains the Kremlin has made with its forays into Africa are likely to be transient, and they have certainly weakened support for detente among Americans. The real threat to the West is not from detente but from our failure to solve the economic crisis facing the capitalist world before it divides us irretrievably from our allies, and to hold out some hope to the Third World based upon a realistic acceptance of the revolutionary potential in that part of the world and our willingness to accommodate our foreign policy to it.

ARMS CONTROL

One of the most hopeful aspects of detente has been the effort to achieve some control over the nuclear-arms race. Although an important Soviet-American agreement—the Nuclear Test Ban Treaty—was signed as early as the summer of 1963, the two governments did not actually eliminate a weapons system (the anti-Ballistic Missile, or ABM) or set numerical limits on the numbers of offensive weapons until June 1972 when SALT I was agreed to. The latter agreement was only an interim five-year agreement that was to be followed by a comprehensive, long-term treaty. Such a treaty is presently under negotiation, but it is proving exceedingly difficult to arrive at an agreement.

As Dr. Panovsky observes in the selection that follows, "progress in the direction of arms control has been so slow that evolution of military technology continues to outpace the rate at which diplomacy can lead to agreements constraining the character and number of weapons." This is precisely what has happened since 1972. Each side has upgraded the destructive capacity of its existing nuclear delivery vehicles and has added new, more accurate and more powerful weapons to its nuclear arsenal. The Soviet Union has MIRVed 1,320 of its missiles (MIRVing means that two or more independently retargetable nuclear warheads have been installed in each missile) to match the U.S. program. (As of 1977, the U.S. had 7,093 MIRVed warheads and, like the Soviet Union, was planning for a new missile (MX) that will carry as many as ten or twelve warheads!)

The Soviet Union has deployed new and more powerful rockets (the SS-18 and SS-19), while the U.S. has developed the cruise missile. The cruise missile has a nuclear warhead and is capable of being launched from an airplane, a sub, or a surface vessel. It has the advantage of being so small (only 26 feet long) that upwards of ten can be carried in the bomb bays of a B-52. Launched from 1,500 miles outside of Russia, it can fly along the contours of the earth's surface and thereby evade the Soviet radar screen. Conversely, the Soviets have reportedly developed a killer satellite that can knock out U.S. satellites designed to guide U.S. missiles to their targets. Both sides are working on lasers with which to intercept and disable the other's incoming missiles. Here we see one of the great obstacles to nuclear arms control: each side continues to upgrade and develop new weapons faster than they can be controlled. The weapons engineers and military on both sides are engaged in a relentless search for ever newer and more sophisticated weapons. As a consequence of these changes, each side now accuses the other of seeking a numerical and qualitative advantage such that it could strike first and destroy the other's retaliatory capability.

This brings us to the second obstacle to reaching an arms control agreement. For the decade between 1962 and 1972 deterrence was thought to rest upon the possession by each side of an invulnerable nuclear retaliatory capacity. By this is meant that whoever attacked first could not hope to knock out all of the enemy's missiles deployed in underground silos, on submarines, or in the bomb-bays of B-52s kept on constant airborne alert. Each side, knowing that the other retained sufficient undamaged missiles to destroy the other several times over, would hesitate to risk an attack. However, as both sides MIRVed, as the Soviets increased the throw weight (the weight its rockets can launch into orbit), and as the Americans increased the accuracy of their missiles, the argument has arisen that one side might be able to knock out all of the other's land-based missiles with silo-busting warheads. This would still leave intact the submarine-launched retaliatory capacity of each side, which in the American case amounts to some 5,443 MIRVed warheads capable of destroying 30 to 40 percent of the Russian people.

Nevertheless, each side argues that the other may be intent upon gaining a first-strike, knockout capacity, and this has seemed to undermine the basis for stable deterrence and for further arms limitation. Each side's deployment of more powerful and more accurate weapons has given rise to charges by the other side that in effect it is striving for a first-strike capability. The danger is that even if it is not true but the other side believes it is, the results are the same—distrust and instability ensue. Furthermore, each side adheres to strategic doctrines which also complicate the attainment of arms control. In addition to having their strategic thought dominated by standard military biases and "worst possible case" predilections, one writer notes that "the Soviets may operate (1) with a deep obsession that the capitalist enemy is unremittingly hostile and out to get Russia if an opportunity to attack opens up, and (2) with a deep-seated historical sense of vulnerability."[4]

Richard Head, a military man, writes that Soviet military doctrine "extends from fundamentally different cultural and political roots from that in the United States" and that it does not draw the same distinction

---

[4]Dennis Ross. *Rethinking Soviet Strategic Policy: Inputs and Implications* for the Center for Arms Control and International Security, UCLA, p.11.

between a nuclear force maintained for deterrence and a nuclear force designed to fight and win should nuclear war occur. "Whereas the weapons requirements for assured destruction are *relatively* [author's emphasis] quantifiable given certain assumptions, the requirements for security through buying a convincing war fighting capability are much more open-ended."[5] The emphasis in Soviet doctrine on possessing the capacity to fight and win a nuclear war should it occur [by minimizing damage at home], together with the deployment of rockets with enormous throw weight has given rise to the charge that Russia is intent upon achieving a first-strike capability (the capacity to destroy as much as possible of the U.S. land-based ICBMs before the U.S. can retaliate) and limiting the damage to its society as much as possible so that the Soviet Union would not only survive a nuclear war but would emerge victorious. In advancing this proposition, Richard Pipes writes that "unless we are so blinded by arrogance as simply to preclude *a priori* the possibility of ever forfeiting the ability to defend ourselves, the very striving of the Soviet Union for strategic superiority . . . should give us cause for concern."[6] Pipes "cause for concern" has taken the form of a strenuous campaign by the Committee on the Present Danger and by Senate critics of detente to put pressure on President Carter to force the Soviets to cut back on their deployments of the SS-18.

Somewhat in contrast to Soviet strategic doctrine which adheres to a counterforce—damage limitation strategy, the American posture is in principle still committed to the concept of an invulnerable retaliatory and assured destruction capacity to deter the Soviet Union; that is, the ability, to quote Robert McNamara when he served as Kennedy's Secretary of Defense, to "retaliate against a surprise attack and kill about twenty percent of the Soviet population—regardless of Soviet capabilities." Nixon appeared to give support to a similar posture with his enunciation of the principle of "essential equivalence." Nevertheless, the principle of "essential equivalence" has not meant that the U.S. has let its nuclear lead disappear. There has been a constantly expressed determination on the part of the American government, including the Carter Administration, not to allow Russia to build up "disproportionate" strength or to permit a situation to emerge in which America "possessed no more than the theoretical minimum needed to destroy some predetermined percentage of Soviet society." In fact, under Nixon the Pentagon adopted a flexible response-counterforce strategy that could be viewed as an American move toward the development of a first-strike capability. Counterforce means targeting on Soviet missile sites and military bases instead of on cities. The justification for this was that it would help reduce the political and strategic impact of the

[5]Richard G. Head. "Technology and the Military Balance," *Foreign Affairs* (April 1978), p. 549.

[6]Richard Pipes, "In Nuclear Competition, Numbers Are Not All," *The New York Times*, February 6, *Op Ed* page.

Soviet achievement of relative parity and would provide Washington with a declared option of launching selective nuclear strikes against Soviet targets as a warning to the Soviet Union against a conventional attack in Western Europe or a blackmail threat in the Middle East. This new flexible response-counterforce doctrine was accompanied by the deployment of the improved Mark 12-A warhead and low-cost accuracy improvements which give the United States an 85 percent probability of destroying a Soviet missile silo, targeting only two weapons per silo. Technologically, the United States thereby acquired an effective ability to knock out much of the Soviet land-based ICBM force without actually announcing that it had adopted a counterforce strategy. This strategy could also be interpreted to mean that the U.S. was moving to acquire a first-strike capability! Like the Soviet deployment of rockets with a heavy throw weight and megatonnage, these U.S. moves have been a destabilizing factor. Both sides adopted strategic postures that make negotiation of a new arms-limitation agreement extremely difficult. Critics on each side use the moves by the other to arouse concern and alarm which they hope will justify new weapons (in the American case the B-1 bomber, the cruise missile and a new mobile missile, MX) and which make negotiation of a mutually acceptable strategic arms limitation treaty extremely difficult. As the Soviet strategist Trofimenko writes, "by, say, 1985 both arsenals will probably exhibit the full panoply of destabilizing qualities: a high ratio of warheads to launchers, ultra high accuracy, high yield-weight ratio, and greater throw weight."[7]

Arms negotiation, like nuclear deterrence, depends upon each side being manifestly confident of the credibility of its nuclear retaliatory capability. To the extent that alarmists stress our potential weaknesses but not our existent strength, they undermine the basis for negotiation. No administration can negotiate an acceptable arms-limitation agreement if the American people believe that we are leaving ourselves open to blackmail and devastation. "In general," writes David C. Gompert in a recent study, "in the coming decade we may find Americans less and less satisfied with the country's strategic strength, even in the absence of any rational basis for such dissatisfaction."[8]

In the absence of a will on the part of each side to negotiate a comprehensive nuclear-disarmament treaty, partial and limited agreements in which neither side gets all it wants are bound to be open to criticism on the grounds that they are one-sided. Should these criticisms be allowed to frustrate the ability of the two governments to negotiate agreements acceptable to both sides, we stand in danger that not only will we not be able to contain technology, but political solution will be that much harder to achieve.

[7]Henry Trofimenko, "The 'Theology' of Strategy," *Orbis*, vol. 21 (Fall, 1977), pp. 497–517.

[8]In Gompert et al. *Nuclear Weapons and World Politics: Alternatives for the Future* (New York: McGraw-Hill, 1977), p. 280.

The chief U.S. negotiator, Paul Warnke, observes that "arms control is not a reward for good Soviet behavior. It's not a favor we do for the Soviet Union. Its not something in which we're being kind to them because they are behaving the way we want them to behave elsewhere. It's something that must be pursued on its own merits."[9] This goes at least some way in the direction of meeting Dr. Panovsky's belief that we must eschew escapism and recognize that the nuclear arms race is the single most dangerous threat to civilization.

In the final analysis, SALT II depends on each side's ability to provide the other with incentives for restraint. And this becomes increasingly difficult as each deploys new weapons whose numbers, disposition (mobile or underground), and warhead content are not susceptible to verification by satellite, upon which security against cheating depends.

The same Soviet obsession with the buildup of overwhelming military power also seems to be operating in the European theater. The article by Richard Burt depicts the disturbing effect that Soviet deployments of all types of weapons have had upon the strategic balance in Europe. So far, the efforts to negotiate a scaling down of Warsaw Pact and NATO forces has come to naught.

[9]"The SALT Process," January 19, 1978. State Department News Release.

34 The Kissinger Legacy: Old Obsessions and New Look

Simon Serfaty

The author is in the Department of International Relations at the Johns Hopkins University's Washington branch.

. . . . It appears, in retrospect, that during his eight years as the key foreign policy-maker in the United States, Kissinger actually conceptualized a New Look which might be regarded as the first significant and sustained departure from American diplomacy after the Second World War. To be sure, we have seen numerous New Looks over the past 31 years, but new looks behind which was hidden a striking continuity in terms of both the global conceptualization and the specific implementation of American foreign policy. For nearly three decades, America essentially spoke the same Wilsonian language, fought the same elusive enemy, aimed at the same military superiority, and sought the same hegemony within a world whose bipolar distribution was thought to be irreversible.

Thus, the American New Look rests first of all on the end of a rhetoric. "It is part of American folklore," complained Kissinger in 1966, "that while other nations have interests, we have responsibilities; while other nations are concerned with equilibrium, we are concerned with the legal requirements of peace. We have a tendency to offer our altruism as a guarantee of our reliability."[1] Accordingly, Kissinger discarded the old folklore and rediscovered the basic themes of the early period of the Republic's foreign policy—national interest, balance of power, self-preservation and self-expansion. Expressed in a succession of well-timed major foreign policy pronouncements, America under Kissinger first recognized the ideological diversity of the international system, second, the limitation of American resources and, third, the dominance of national interests as the guidelines to diplomatic action. In 1973, Nixon pledged that the new "structure of peace" to which his administration was committed, would and could be devised "despite profound differences between systems of government," and that "the time has passed when America will make every other nation's conflict her own, or make every other nation's future our responsibility, or presume to tell the people of other nations how to manage their own affairs."[2] And Kissinger to add subsequently: "We are one nation among many. . . . We must give up the illusion that foreign policy can choose

From The World Today, *March 1977, monthly journal of the Royal Institute of International Affairs, London, pp. 81–89. Reprinted with permission.*

[1]*American Foreign Policy,* Three essays by Henry Kissinger (New York: W. W. Norton, 1969), pp. 91–2.

[2]Second inaugural address, January 1973.

between morality and pragmatism. . . . No nation has a monopoly of justice and virtue. In the nuclear age especially, diplomacy involves the compromise of clashing principles."[3]

In a narrow perspective, such aspirations must be compared to the rhetoric of the Truman Doctrine which, from 1947 on, shaped American diplomacy: the inflexible analysis of a frozen international system within which America was endowed with a rigid national interest. Unapplied at first, the Truman rhetoric was given global significance following the outbreak of the Korean conflict as Secretaries Acheson and Dulles extended the scope of American commitments to every part of the globe. In a larger perspective, however, this new rhetoric must also be compared to the traditional manner in which America, throughout this century, has sought to present its policies and its objectives. Speaking shortly before he became the Special Advisor to President Nixon on foreign affairs, Henry Kissinger had clearly stated "Vietnam is more than a failure of policy, it is really a very critical failure of the American philosophy of international relations. . . . We have to assess the whole procedure and concepts that got us involved there . . . if we are not going to have another disaster that may have quite a different look but will have the same essential flaws."[4] There is no need to dwell once again on the intellectual mistakes of the former rhetoric. Suffice it to say that, devised to justify a given policy, such a rhetoric ultimately became the policy itself within a framework which offered little resemblance to prior international and domestic conditions. By sub-

[3]Address to the American Society of Newspaper Editors in Washington, 17 April 1975.

[4]See Richard M. Pfeffer (ed.), *No More Vietnams? The War and the Future of American Foreign Policy* (New York: Harper & Row, 1968), p. 13.

mitting America to a seminar in international relations, by providing the realist terminology with a new public legitimacy, by implicitly endorsing much of what the critics of the late 1960s had themselves concluded, Henry Kissinger helped transform this philosophy. In truth, he took the nation away from the Wilsonian syndrome, emptied the old utopias of their popular credibility, and in the process, as Irving Kristol suggested, he "Europeanized" the American philosophy of international relations. Indeed, it is only on the basis of such a new rhetoric that any one Secretary of State can ever attempt to achieve the balance of means, objectives and purposes which was, after all, the ultimate demand of most of the critics of the 1960s. To be sure, with the new rhetoric also came renewed secrecy. But is there any true alternative to secrecy when engaged in diplomatic bargaining? Mediation more particularly requires the dissimulation of differences between adversaries, as well as between the adversaries and the mediator. Without the latter, mediation becomes a variation on intervention.

IDEOLOGICAL OBSESSION

In terms of substance, the New Look entails the reassessment of three major obsessions which shaped, from the American viewpoint, the years of the Cold War. First among these is an ideological obsession which found its expression in the belief in a Communist monolith, inspired and led by the Soviet leadership. Such a belief implied an inability on the part of American policymakers to draw a valid distinction between ideology as an end in itself and ideology as a means towards other national ends.

It is this ideological obsession which gave

American policy in the 1950s and 1960s a *raison d'etre* that pre-empted progressively the need for any further more rational justification, and provided the complex web of international relations with a simplicity which it did not, and could not, have. The enemy was everywhere, and his success anywhere was democracy's defeat regardless of the specifics of the situation. What was wrong with such a vision of the world was not so much that Russia should not be trusted, or that the Communists should not be acknowledged as legitimate partners in Western democratic governments. What was wrong, of course, was the global assumption that the only motivating force behind Moscow's foreign policy was its ideology, that the foreign policy of any and all Communist states was directed by and from Moscow, and that any force in favour of change was Communist, and, conversely, any force or group opposed to Communism was democratic. As empires crumbled, America failed to make the necessary distinction between Communism and nationalism, and unwittingly led many to seek in Moscow what could not be obtained from Washington. As a new social consciousness developed everywhere, America failed to make a distinction between revolution and evolution, and naturally emerged as the main pillar of a status quo which was being eroded by irreversible forces of change. Our own changes, whenever they did take place, came less out of wisdom than out of the evidence of failure.

Examples of such failures are many, and explanations even more numerous. This is not the place to list them. Suffice it to say what has by now become obvious: that Vietnam was the logical outcome of a policy so defined and that by the late 1960s, therefore, the time had come to draw the boundaries of our possible behaviour—not only what we could do but, even more importantly, for and against whom.

Thus, the American New Look implied several adjustments in the nation's response to Communist ideology. First, while Communism remained abhorrent to the American way of life, it was progressively agreed that America's relationship with Communist states was not to be denied on the basis of this ideological incompatibility alone; second, that Soviet influence over other Communist states varied widely from region to region, if not from country to country, thereby opening important opportunities which the US could explore selectively and cautiously; and, third, that any change anywhere was not always anti-American, nor was it always the result of Soviet diabolical influence. The rapprochement with China and detente with the Soviet Union are, of course, the most obvious expressions of this new attitude.

Needless to say, such a decline of America's ideological obsession is neither final nor has it proceeded thus far on a straight line. With regard to China, the Sino-American relationship finds its limits in the disparity between what each side can do for the other. Or, to put it more explicitly, while there is much that the United States can do for the Chinese, there is still very little the Chinese can concede to the United States—with the possible exception of time: a slowdown of their nuclear efforts (assuming that they ever meant to go any faster than they now are) and a slowdown in their effort to regain Taiwan (assuming that they could do more than they now do).

More complex, however, are the limits of the detente between the United States and the Soviet Union which does remain the dominant adversary relationship of the 1970s. For one, while detente is based on the recognition by both Washington and Moscow of the status quo in Europe, such acceptance is highly asymmetrical as Moscow's control of events in Eastern Europe is far in excess of Washington's control of events in Western Europe. Indeed, the whole triangular relationship between the United States on the one hand, and the Soviet Union and China on the other, is characterized by the conflicting and contradictory opportunities and expectations which it has produced. Thus, the Chinese criticism of American policy has not been so much that America has not done enough for China—but, indeed, that it has not done enough against the Soviet Union. In other words, the limits of Washington's rapprochement with China reflect Washington's need to preserve detente with the Soviet Union as well—and, up to a point, the reverse is true too.

In sum, while adversary relationships no longer respond to ideological divergencies alone, they remain relationships among adversaries nevertheless. It follows that America's response to ideology now takes three different forms depending on its power and influence. Where Communism is firmly entrenched in power—as it is in Russia, China and Eastern Europe—America recognizes it and deals with it in spite of its misgivings over the lack of freedom which generally characterizes such governments. With Communist-leaning governments still facing substantial opposition from a disgruntled middle class—as in the case of Chile, for instance—the United States has followed a policy of opposition ("destabilization") providing relatively modest direct support to the opposition parties while refusing to assist such governments economically or politically. (Such opposition, it should be noted, has not been based so much on a systematic perception of a Soviet involvement in the growing leftism of the area involved as on a fundamental appraisal of America's economic and strategic interests as well as an assessment of America's political preferences.) "We must outgrow the notion," pledged Kissinger in May 1975,

"that every setback is a Soviet gain or every problem is caused by Soviet actions."[5] Finally, in those cases where Communism remains in opposition, Washington has continued to oppose it, openly and, at times, unnecessarily loudly, as is the case in Italy.

MILITARY OBSESSION

The second obsession which has been reassessed by the New Look is of a military nature. Throughout the Cold War years such an obsession was reflected in a continuous and vain search for the preservation of a nuclear hegemony which, on the basis of the most optimistic estimates, could not have lasted more than seven to ten years; and, once hegemony had been ended, the preservation of a nuclear supremacy which would help fulfill James Forrestal's early pledge that there was nothing which the Truman Administration or any subsequent administration in Washington could accept short of 100 percent security for the American people. Granted such a framework, America's military security would be assured only to the extent that Soviet military insecurity could be maximized. America would negotiate but only from a position of strength. In repeated instances, disarmament conferences faced the problem of neither side willing to make valid concessions until the other side had accepted a position of intrinsic inferiority.

As such, then, Washington went through two phases of military exuberance. First, following the outbreak of the Korean War when the initial atomic build-up took place between 1950 and 1955; and, second, during the Kennedy Administration when, on the basis of fallacious interpretations of Soviet

[5]Speech to the St. Louis World Affairs Council, 12 May 1975.

intentions, America undertook a build-up of its missile capabilities which saw its forces grow to over 800 ICBMs by 1964, while Soviet resources during the same period remained inferior to 200.

Robert McNamara described the rationale of such military obsession. "Security", he wrote in his *The Essence of Security*, "depends upon assuming a worst plausible case, and having the ability to cope with it. . . . Since we could not be certain of Soviet intentions, we had to ensure against [it] . . . by undertaking . . . a major build-up of our own . . . forces."[6] The problem with such reasoning is that it leads repeatedly to a self-fulfilling prophecy whereby the adversary actually does what he did not intend to do because of what the other protagonist does on the basis of his own perception of the adversary's action. Thus, the Soviet build-up discovered in Washington in 1960 took place during the second half of the 1960s. In this light, the search for security led to still more insecurity, and the Forrestal pledge of 1946 was paralleled by President Nixon's 1970 acknowledgement of 100 percent insecurity for the American people.

By accepting such principles as nuclear sufficiency and nuclear parity—however one might want to define these—the Kissinger New Look has given diplomacy a new legitimacy. Undoubtedly, negotiations were held during the Cold War years too. But the seeming objective of all sides engaged in those negotiations remained a maximization of satisfaction which made any agreement unlikely. When taken at face value, such terms as apppeasement, Munich, credibility, or domino theory, basic to an analysis of Cold War policies, ultimately ended the search for a balancing of dissatisfaction even before the search could be initiated. If nego-

tiations were to imply concessions, the Munich-minded policymakers thought, then they would clearly imply appeasement, thus reducing one's credibility, and in the process, opening the gate to either further concession or to war. Writing in the mid-1960s, Kissinger disputed the relevance of debates in which "more attention is paid to whether to get to the conference room than to what to do once we arrive there."[7] At least whether or not the United States should sit in the conference room at all, and whether or not it should sit there now, is no longer a point of contention as it remained for too long a time. Indeed, those in America who have criticized detente, and (or) have criticized the outcome of the various negotiations entered into by the United States over the past years, have been rather timid in their presentation of options. Is roll-back the alternative to detente? Is a further escalation of military expenditures the alternative to SALT? Is confrontation the alternative to co-operation?

Au fond, detente means neither the end nor the continuation of containment. If containment implied the nation's commitment to stopping Russian expansionism, detente merely added a strategy of inducement (primarily economic inducement) to the former strategy of discouragement (primarily military discouragement). If it implied the nation's commitment to halting the spread of Communism, detente certainly abandoned any pretence of roll-back (as symbolized, for instance, at Helsinki), probably reduced the national interest in the ideology of a given government outside America's areas of direct influence (in Asia and in Africa) and, as indicated above, clearly reasserted America's unwillingness to tolerate ideologically hostile governments within areas of direct influence, namely,

[6]Robert S. McNamara, *The Essence of Security, Reflections in Office* (New York: Harper & Row, 1968), pp. 53–8.

[7]*American Foreign Policy, op. cit.,* p. 87.

Latin America and Western Europe. Detente is containment without doctrine (i.e. the Truman Doctrine) and one need not be a warm partisan of Henry Kissinger to appreciate the delicate balance between confrontation and conciliation which has been maintained with the Soviet Union—in admittedly favourable circumstances evolving from the perceived decline of American leadership abroad (in the aftermath of Vietnam) and at home (in the aftermath of Watergate).

THE END OF BIPOLARITY

Finally, the last component of the New Look relates to the end of an obsession with an international system which, it was widely believed, would never end. Instead, over the past few years America has been told that bipolarity is now a thing of the past, and that the Cold War system, as it was known between 1945 and 1970, no longer exists. From an academic perspective, this is not much of a novelty; the end of bipolarity had been announced long before Kissinger went to the White House. But from the viewpoint of American policy-makers, as well as from the viewpoint of the American public at large, this is indeed a novelty. Similarly, it is now being widely accepted that such a system was both an accident and an aberration. It was an accident because it implied the coincidental occurrence at a given time in history of two events—on the one hand, the dominant emergence of two nations, the United States and Russia, which had been ascending ever since the 19th century, and, on the other hand, the collapse of the traditional European sources of power, which had been declining for an even longer period of time. Furthermore, the old system was an aberration because of the very manner in which such an inevitable confrontation between the two remaining great powers took place. Seen in retrospect, and freed of the myths which the American and the Soviet ideologies gave birth to, the Cold War was nothing more than a struggle for the hegemony of Europe which extended progressively to the rest of the world. In terms of the objectives sought by the great powers, such a conflict was very much comparable to the other three major conflicts which had taken place over the previous 200 years for the control of the European continent, during the Napoleonic Wars, the First World War and the Second World War. Like such previous conflicts, then, this one too was bound to come to an end. Like such other conflicts, with the end of the Cold War came the need for a restructuring of the international system. Now, as then, the questions faced in building a new structure of peace are questions of membership, objectives and procedures. If nothing else, the precedents of 1815, 1919 and 1945 show that there is more stability in a system which aims at the balancing of dissatisfaction between allies and former enemies alike (as it was sought in Vienna in 1815), than in a system which aims at the maximization of satisfaction for the former allies (as it was sought in Versailles in 1919), or a maximization of dissatisfaction for some of the allies (as it was sought in 1945).

The Nixon-Kissinger-Ford Administration did not create the conditions which are causing such transformations in the international structure. Nor could it, in truth, invent a new structure. But it was in the historical position to reassert the global dominance of two power centres while acknowledging the regional ascendancy of other sources of power and influence, and, accordingly, recognize the emergence of new international issues different from the traditional security issues of the past. This is a role that has been fulfilled rather well especially considering the heavy inheritance of the Vietnam war and the devastating burden of Watergate.

This new international system calls neither for a balance of power politics as such, nor for the so-called world order politics. The balance between the poles of power needs to be maintained both globally and regionally. At the same time, however, the dispersion of enmity within the system stimulates further the need for diplomatic intervention to preserve a modicum of order around the world either through the preemption or through the containment of such conflicts. From this perspective, the attention granted by the American New Look to the Third World and its related non-physical security issues is highly encouraging. That such interest would have been around at a time when the mood of the public favoured retrenchment makes it also quite surprising. Intervention has not been replaced by isolationism, as many foresaw it by the end of the Vietnam war—and shuttle diplomacy has to be seen as a marked improvement over the gunboat diplomacy of previous years.

Most criticism of Kissinger's New Look can be reduced to one common denominator: impatience with the pace of change. Political units have spent a large part of their history negotiating the end to conflict and subversion, the end to economic exploitation and international inequality, the end to arms races of all types. At one's optimistic best, it will still take several decades to transform detente into entente, ideological confrontation into democratic convergence, and limited arms control into disarmament. For foreign policy does not lend itself to instant reversals—yesterday we were bipolar, today we are multipolar; yesterday we intervened to oppose Communist or coalition governments, today we accept, if not encourage, them; yesterday we had troops in a non-nuclear Western Europe, today we no longer have any in a nuclear Western Europe. Those observers who promoted withdrawals of all kinds yesteryear may next promote a renewed wave of interventionism, if only because of an obvious but forgotten lesson of academic history in this field, which teaches that today's perception of failure may well become tomorrow's acknowledgement of success. In sum, in foreign policy less than in any other field there is no room for heroes—but there is indeed much room for a compassion which Secretaries of State seem to find difficult to receive when the time for retirement comes. As observers continue to add up the mistakes and missed opportunites, should not such compassion be shown towards a Secretary of State who, at the very least, was able to conceptualize some of the adjustments which America needed to make to changed international and domestic circumstances, even if his administrative methods and personal perspectives did not permit him to implement specifically what was envisaged globally? The true challenge of the new foreign policy administration in Washington will be to practice effectively what the previous administration preached convincingly—and let history alone praise and condemn the past.

35 The SS-20 and the Eurostrategic Balance

Richard Burt

The author is correspondent for the **New York Times**, having previously worked with the International Institute for Strategic Studies in London.

In a period characterized by political uncertainty and rapidly changing military technology, it is not unusual for governments to place great significance on the weapons deployment decisions of potential adversaries. Thus, growing scepticism in the West over the motives of the Soviet Union in what used to be called the detente process has naturally coincided with indications that Moscow and its allies are engaged in a fairly extensive programme of modernizing and, in some cases, expanding Warsaw Pact military capabilities. These improvements range from the deployment of new tanks in Eastern Europe to the development of a new family of intercontinental-range ballistic missiles (ICBM). But, one facet of this modernization programme has curiously managed to escape close scrutiny in the West. This is the Soviet Union's large-scale effort to bolster existing capabilities for delivering nuclear weapons against targets on its periphery, especially in Western Europe. During 1975-6, Russia deployed a new generation of nuclear-capable deep strike aircraft in Eastern Europe as well as a new swing-wing, medium bomber, the *Backfire*. However, the most important (and intriguing) component of this buildup of Soviet regional nuclear capabilities is a

From The World Today, *March 1977, monthly journal of the Royal Institute of International Affairs, London, pp. 43–51. Reprinted by permission.*

new intermediate-range ballistic missile (IRBM), known by Nato as the SS-20. The missile, which will probably begin to replace older systems this year in Western regions of the Soviet Union, has only recently stimulated comment in the West.[1] Yet its significance for the East-West nuclear relationship, superpower arms-control efforts and the continued stability of the Western Alliance cannot be underestimated.

EUROSTRATEGIC FORCES

To appreciate the importance of the SS-20 decision, it is first necessary to distinguish between different categories of delivery systems within the context of the overall East-West nuclear balance. Based on their range and the size of their payloads, nuclear delivery systems have traditionally been divided into two categories: those possessing shorter ranges and smaller warheads for use

[1] While references to the existence of the SS-20 programme first emerged in official Western statements during 1975, the missile did not receive widespread attention from the press until September 1976, when Fred Ikle, then the Director of US Arms Control and Disarmament Agency, argued in a speech that its deployment was 'unwarranted' and that it could jeopardize East-West arms control efforts. See *The New York Times,* 1 September 1976.

on or near the battlefield have been termed "tactical" nuclear weapons, while longer-range, more destructive systems targeted against important centres in the homeland of the adversary have borne the familiar designation of "strategic" weapons. The boundary between these two classes of nuclear weapons has never been precisely defined and, in fact, a new generation of multi-role missile systems threatens to obliterate it altogether.[2] But if the distinction between "strategic" and "tactical" weapons is becoming less meaningful, another distinction is taking on a new importance. This is the distinction between super-power and regional strategic weapons. The former possess inter-continental ranges and are based in the homeland of the super-powers. These include ICBM, long-range bombers and, for all practical purposes, submarine-launched ballistic missiles (SLBM). Regional strategic weapons, on the other hand, do not possess the range for intercontinental strikes and these systems are therefore either deployed in, or targeted against, Western Europe. This category of "Eurostrategic" nuclear forces is composed of a far more disparate group of systems: Nato and Warsaw Pact nuclear-capable strike aircraft, Soviet medium-range bombers, Soviet and French IRBM and the British and French submarine-borne missile systems.[3] These weapons receive little of the attention accorded to super-power strategic forces and despite the fact that an IRBM attack on London or Paris would be difficult to distinguish from an ICBM attack on New York,

the general tendency is to lump them together with "tactical" nuclear weapons.[4]

It is difficult, then to compare Eastern and Western regional capabilities and, for this reason, it is also dangerous to attempt to determine the precise character of the Eurostrategic balance. In quantitative terms, however, it is hard to resist the conclusion that the Soviet Union presently enjoys a clear advantage in Eurostrategic capabilities. As shown in the table, the Soviet Union presently deploys over 2,900 systems capable of, and perhaps dedicated to, undertaking strategic missions against Western Europe. Nato (including France), on the other hand, appears to possess far fewer Eurostrategic weapons; that is, delivery vehicles based in Europe that could deliver nuclear strikes against the Soviet Union. This comparison is given added significance by the fact that the majority of Nato's strategic-capable, regional delivery systems are strike aircraft, in most cases assigned tactical missions. Many of the Soviet combat aircraft are also probably deployed for tactical use (or in the case of medium bombers, for maritime missions), but the Soviet force of approximately 600 IRBM can only be understood to possess strategic utility and, as such, their deployment constitutes one of the most striking asymmetries in the East-West military balance.

It is the existence of this asymmetry that makes the Soviet SS-20 programme seem so peculiar. Already possessing a substantial edge in IRBM capabilities (and Eurostrategic forces generally), why has the Soviet Union apparently chosen to replace its existing IRBM force with what appears to be a much more destructive missile? There are several possible explanations:

[2] See Richard Burt, 'The Cruise Missile and Arms Control,' *Survival*, January/February 1976.

[3] The Eurostrategic category does not include shorter-range, nuclear systems for use in the European theatre in tactical roles, such as nuclear artillery or surface-to-surface tactical missiles like the US *Lance*, the French *Pluton* or the Soviet *SCUD*.

[4] Nuclear-capable aircraft especially present definitional problems because, while many possess the capability to carry out strategic missions in Europe or the Soviet Union, most are assigned tactical roles.

TABLE 1

THE EUROSTRATEGIC BALANCE, 1977

	Warsaw Pact	Nato
Intermediate-Range Ballistic Missiles	600	146*
Medium-Range Bombers†	600	60
Combat Aircraft‡	1,000	400
Naval Aircraft	400§	200¶
Nuclear Armed Cruise Missiles	300‖	0

* These include 64 French SLBM (4 submarines) and 64 British SLBM (4 submarines) as well as the 18 land-based French IRBM. The ten American Polaris submarines assigned to Nato are not included here.

† This category includes *Badger, Blinder* and *Backfire* bombers for the Warsaw Pact and FB-III aircraft for Nato.

‡ This only includes US and Soviet nuclear-capable aircraft based in Central Europe. Both sides could substantially augment these numbers with allied aircraft and aircraft now deployed in the United States or the Soviet Union.

§ These are land-based aircraft.

¶ This assumes 5 American carriers deployed at any given time.

‖ Soviet submarine-borne cruise missiles (the SS-N-3) could also be used against targets in the United States.

SOURCES: Estimates derived from *The Military Balance 1976–1977* (London: IISS) and *Arms Control Report* (US Arms Control and Disarmament Agency), July 1976.

First, the SS-20 may simply represent the answer to a number of technical problems that plague the existing Soviet IRBM. The two IRBM that presently make up the force —the SS-4 and SS-5—are both over 15 years old and reflect Soviet missile technology of an earlier period. Both are obsolescent by Western standards: they possess unwieldy, liquid-fuel propulsion systems, inaccurate guidance devices and require extensive logistical support. Thus, their replacement could probably be justified on grounds of cost-effectiveness alone.

Second, there is also a strong military incentive attached to the replacement of the SS-4/5 force. While the Soviet ICBM force (most of which was procured over the last decade) is housed in hardened, underground silos, most of the existing IRBM are deployed above ground, in "soft" sites, and they are thus vulnerable to pre-emptive attack by the West. The SS-20, on the other hand, is a solid-fuel missile which can be easily transported and launched; deployed aboard a mobile launcher, it will greatly enhance the ability of Soviet Eurostrategic forces to survive attack from the West. The missile, moreover, represents a qualitative jump in destructive capability. Fitted with multiple, independently targeted re-entry vehicles (MIRV) and possessing improved accuracy, the SS-20 will not only make existing targets in Western Europe more vulnerable to attack; a larger number of smaller, more accurate warheads will enable the Soviet Union to place a larger range of Western European assets at risk and with greater discrimination.

Third, there is also an organizational explanation for the replacement decision. Although the SS-20 is a substantial improvement over earlier IRBM designs, it does not represent a dramatic departure from the Soviet missile programme as a whole. In fact, the SS-20 seems to reflect a certain amount of "bureaucratic opportunism" on the part of the Soviet military. The missile is a direct spin-off from ICBM research and is actually thought to be a two-stage version of a land-mobile ICBM, the SS-16, under development since the early 1970s. Thus, there is good reason to believe that the SS-20 merely represents the determination of a powerful military service—the Strategic Rocket Corps—to get maximum mileage (and budget money) from new weapons designs.

Taken together, these three explanations provide a convincing rationale for the SS-20 replacement decision. But they offer little insight into the wider questions of why Russia originally sought to achieve a position of Eurostrategic dominance with the deployment of IRBM and why, with the deployment of the far more lethal SS-20, she seems bent on enhancing it. The answers to these questions do not lie with technical or bureaucratic considerations, but with overriding Soviet strategic priorities.

HOSTAGE EUROPE?

The Soviet Union's bid in the early 1960s to achieve a position of regional nuclear hegemony in Europe came as a surprise to many in the West, particularly in the United States. Intelligence projections of Soviet missile deployment during the Eisenhower-Kennedy era were based on the belief that, like the United States, the Soviet Union's primary strategic goal was to achieve a credible retaliatory capability against the opposing super-power. Thus, it was widely assumed that the Soviet Union would not invest heavily in IRBM technology but, following the US pattern, would move quickly to deploy a new generation of intercontinental-range rockets. To the chagrin of some and the relief of others, the fabled US-Soviet "missile gap", of course, never appeared. Instead, the Soviet leadership seemed more preoccupied with the strategic equation in Europe and with the rapid deployment of the SS-4/5 force between 1959–63; it was in this area that a real "missile gap" did develop.

Why the Soviet Union chose to concentrate on Eurostrategic, rather than super-power strategic forces during this period is unclear. In part, the answer may be that IRBM were less technically demanding than longer-range missiles. Perhaps the Soviet Union simply lacked the skills to compete with the United States in ICBM procurement in the early 1960s (a situation that dramatically changed in the latter half of the decade). But other considerations may have also been at work. As some writers have suggested, the early Soviet emphasis on regional nuclear forces could have reflected a long-standing desire to establish a privileged nuclear relationship with Western Europe where Soviet Eurostrategic superiority would keep Western Europe politically and militarily "hostage", while in time of war the Soviet Union would remain a sanctuary free from European nuclear retaliation.[5] The rapid expansion of US strategic power during the mid-1960s and the slower but steady growth of British and French strategic capabilities undermined the political and military impact of Soviet IRBM deployment and thus shattered any hope that the Soviet leadership might have possessed of becoming a "sanctuary" from nuclear attack. At the

[5] See Johan Jorgen Holst's remarks in 'SALT in the Process of East-West Relations in Europe,' NUPI/N-90 (Oslo: Norsk Utenrikspolitisk-Institutt), April 1975.

same time, the deployment by France and Britain of relatively invulnerable sea-based missile forces frustrated the Soviet objective of making a nuclear "hostage" out of Western Europe. By the mid-1960s, the East-West nuclear relationship had evolved into a complex series of balances, which gave the Soviet Union an edge in regional nuclear forces, but provided the United States with superiority in intercontinental-range systems and Western Europe with a limited degree of nuclear autonomy.

In the following decade, the situation fundamentally changed. The most significant development was the Soviet Union's attainment of "parity" in intercontinental-range strategic forces with the United States in the early 1970s. While this action reflected a general Soviet desire to match US capabilities, in particular, it served to diminish the capacity of US intercontinental strategic forces to offset Soviet Eurostrategic systems. Thus, super-power strategic equality provided the Soviet Union with the opportunity of exploiting its advantage in regional nuclear capabilities in relations with Western Europe. With the decision to deploy the SS-20, it now seems to be seizing this opportunity—a course of action that is given added significance by the slow growth and, in Britain's case, the uncertain future of Western European nuclear capabilities.

SALT AND THE ALLIANCE

Ironically, arms control efforts have only reinforced the incentives for Soviet IRBM modernization. At the US-Soviet Strategic Arms Limitation Talks (SALT), negotiators have only sought to limit the deployment of systems with direct strategic relevance to the two super-powers. In the 1972 SALT Interim Agreement on offensive missiles, for example, both sides agreed to limit land-based missiles with ranges exceeding 5,500 km (ICBM) and ballistic missiles deployed aboard "modern" (nuclear-powered) submarines. For all practical purposes, this left Eurostrategic forces out of the 1972 SALT accords altogether. The Soviet Union did attempt in the early rounds of the talks to include US European-based aircraft in the Interim Agreement, but this was firmly resisted by US negotiators who maintained that these weapons were not relevant to the super-power strategic relationship, but were assigned missions in and around the European theatre.

More recently, the task of keeping Eurostrategic weapons from intruding into the super-power strategic sphere at SALT has become immeasurably more difficult. Despite an understanding reached in 1974 at the US-Soviet summit at Vladivostok[6] to include super-power strategic forces (ICBM, SLBM and intercontinental-range bombers) under an aggregate ceiling for delivery vehicles, the two governments have conspicuously failed to iron out the terms of a ten-year accord to replace the Interim Agreement. Several technical issues have impeded progress at the talks, but the primary problem is more fundamental: both sides are reluctant to limit new weapons that might possess military value outside the super-power strategic relationship. The Soviet Union, for instance, has resisted US efforts to place the *Backfire* under SALT controls because the bomber is said to have been designed for regional, rather than intercontinental, nuclear missions. As a Eurostrategic weapon, Soviet negotiators insist that the bomber has no business being discussed in the context of the super-power strategic balance. For its part, the US Government has resisted Soviet ef-

[6]See Richard Burt, 'SALT after Vladivostok,' *The World Today,* February 1975.

forts to limit a new family of revolutionary new cruise missiles whose deployment, like the *Backfire*, will have an impact on both the regional and the super-power nuclear balance.

The deployment of the SS-20 will further complicate the task of isolating super-power and Eurostrategic military concerns. The missile has reportedly been tested with different warhead configurations which affect its range characteristics. Fitted with MIRV, the missile does not appear to possess the necessary range to threaten targets in the United States and thus, like the older IRBM it will replace, it can be considered a regional weapon. But the SS-20 has apparently also been tested with a single, lightweight warhead at ranges exceeding 7,000 km.[7] Deployed in northern latitudes of the Soviet Union, this version would possess all the attributes of a super-power strategic weapon.[8]

Yet from the perspective of Western Europe, anxiety at SALT over whether the SS-20 (like the *Backfire*) is a "strategic" weapon in the super-power context seems strangely irrelevant. For whether it can or cannot threaten targets in the United States does not alter the fact that its deployment will further distort the already lop-sided Eurostrategic balance. This has disturbing implications for both the future East-West regional nuclear arms control and the stability of the Western Alliance. For a start, if Soviet modernization continues unabated, Western Europeans could put pressure on the United States to take the Eurostrategic balance into account in framing negotiating

[7] See *Aviation Week and Space Technology*, 31 May 1976, p. 12.

[8] The fact that the SS-20 is comprised of the two upper stages of an ICBM now under development also raises the possibility that, in time of crisis, even the MIRV version of the missile could be converted to ICBM status by adding an additional rocket stage.

positions at SALT. This would require negotiators to insist that weapons like the *Backfire* and the SS-20 be limited in a new SALT accord, a position that is likely to find little favour in a new Administration in Washington intent on consolidating its relations with the Soviet leadership. At best, an attempt by the Carter Administration to press the Soviet Union on the inclusion of the SS-20 in a new SALT agreement would delay negotiations as well as souring US-Soviet relations generally. At worst, it could lead to a breakdown in negotiations altogether. The worsening of the Eurostrategic balance thus confronts the United States with a painful dilemma: on the one hand, it can give priority to reaching agreement with its super-power partner at SALT and, by ignoring the IRBM threat to Europe, accept the strains this might place on Alliance cohesion. On the other hand, it can take pains to minimize opportunities for Alliance disruption in its negotiations with the Soviet Union, but at the expense of a new SALT agreement.

If the United States is unwilling, or unable, to use SALT as a mechanism for limiting Soviet Eurostrategic programmes, then the United States could feel pressure from allies to directly respond to developments like the SS-20 by augmenting its own Eurostrategic capabilities. In fact, this pressure already exists: the transfer of 84 nuclear-capable F-III aircraft from the United States to Britain in September was clearly designed to demonstrate US concern over the maintenance of regional nuclear deterrence in Europe. But there are limits to the extent that US deployments can offset Soviet regional nuclear power. The Soviet Union has already attempted to introduce US European-based aircraft into the SALT negotiations and a dramatic increase in US airpower in Europe would surely prompt Moscow to resurrect this demand. More importantly, the most interesting military option available to the West for countering the expansion of Soviet Eurostrategic capabilities is already under discussion at SALT—the long-range, precision-guided cruise missile. In deciding whether to exploit cruise missile technology in this manner, the United States must therefore once again choose between placing priority on strengthening Alliance ties and quickly obtaining a new SALT agreement.

But the choice confronting the United States is not as simple as it first appears. In the short term, the Europeans will remain dependent on the US nuclear protection no matter how distorted the Eurostrategic balance becomes, so that the United States could probably afford to down-peddle developments like the Soviet SS-20 in order to reach agreement at SALT. However, in the longer term, Western Europe does not have to solely depend on US goodwill in order to cope with the Soviet Eurostrategic buildup. Like Soviet IRBM, the French and British nuclear forces are also conspicuously absent from discussion at SALT and there is nothing to prevent Britain and France from responding themselves to the growth of Soviet regional nuclear capabilities. Thus, the Soviet deployment of the SS-20, coupled with tacit decisions at SALT to either ignore it or to withhold the means of responding to it, could ultimately spur efforts on the part of Western Europe to achieve larger and more independent strategic capabilities. The consequences of this for both Alliance cohesion and super-power arms control would be unsettling to say the least.

A NEW FRAMEWORK

Yet there seems little way of forestalling the disruption that could result from the widespread Soviet deployment of a new IRBM. Moreover, the SS-20 is only one of several categories of weapons that have been effectively excluded from East-West arms control discussions. As the categories of weapons grow in size and military importance, it will become increasingly more difficult to ignore their presence. But the problems of systematically dealing with them at SALT is enormous; as a bilateral channel of communication between the super-powers, SALT is inherently unsuited to dealing with the multilateral, Alliance-wide consequences of controlling the deployment of Eurostrategic forces. So too are the Mutual and Balanced Force Reduction (MBFR) talks now under way in Vienna; although multilateral in character, the MBFR boundaries are too narrow to encompass the whole range of Eurostrategic forces; stopping short of Soviet territory, the MBFR "reduction area" only highlights the anomalous position of Soviet IRBM in East-West arms control.

Does this mean that a new Eurostrategic arms control framework is necessary? In theory, this is an interesting proposal. A Nato-Warsaw Pact forum for the limitation of regional nuclear arms would not only provide the Alliance, for the first time, with a mechanism for limiting Soviet Eurostrategic power, but it would also minimize the intrusion of Eurostrategic issues into the super-power strategic dialogue. But, in practice, a forum for Eurostrategic arms control seems neither politically feasible nor militarily realistic. Aside from the suspicion with which some Western nations, particularly France, would view such talks, there are few incentives for the Soviet Union to take the concept seriously: already possessing a regional nuclear advantage, Moscow would only be interested in formalizing this position in agreements that would be unacceptable to the West. In the final analysis, then, the solution to the SS-20 problem is unlikely to come from restructuring existing institutions of East-West arms control, despite their ineffectiveness in coping with Eurostrategic forces. The real answer must stem from the willingness of Western governments to absorb the meaning of the SS-20 and their ability to convince the Soviet Union of its significance. If Soviet Russia comes to grasp that her current efforts to achieve a position of nuclear hegemony in Europe are not only illegitimate, but, more importantly, could jeopardize her relationship with the United States at SALT as well as trigger off new Western European nuclear programmes, she too could come to recognize the full implications of the SS-20 decision.

36 Arms Control: Disappointments and Hopes

Wolfgang K. H. Panofsky

The Author is Director of the Stanford Linear Accelerator Center.

Introductory statement by editors: Professor Panofsky has asked us to point out to readers that the article was delivered as a lecture on February 21, 1976, and that at that time the Vladivostok Agreements had been reached but the subsequent moves to convert those agreements into a possible SALT II Treaty had not yet begun. Accordingly, although the general considerations of the article are still valid, there are some matters of detail which have been changed by more recent events. Specifically, the total absence of any qualitative constraints, which was a characteristic of the Vladivostok Agreement, is no longer quite correct as applied to the ongoing SALT II negotiations, in which attempts are being made to incorporate limits of "modernization" of subsequent generation of missiles.

From Johns Hopkins Magazine (September, 1976), pp. 12-16, 33-34. Reprinted with permission of Wolfgang K. H. Panovsky.

. . . I maintain that the risks inherent in peaceful nuclear power—so long as it stays peaceful—are greatly overshadowed by the dangers inherent in the growing stockpiles of nuclear weapons. At worst an accident involving the current generation of reactors would lead to reactor core meltdown and subsequent dispersal of radioactivity. The chance for such an accident is agreed to be low—although there is little conviction as to how low—and the consequence would be an increase in the risk of cancer to perhaps thousands of individuals out of a population of 1 million over the course of tens of years. In contrast, a single atomic bomb over Hiroshima and Nagasaki killed on the order of 100,000 persons, and currently the world's nuclear arsenal—mainly in the hands of the United States and the Soviet Union—exceeds 20,000 bombs, each of which is much more powerful than those which destroyed Hiroshima and Nagasaki. No one would care to estimate the probability that one or more of these bombs might be used in deliberate warfare or by accident in the balance of the century but few would dare to maintain that the risk is negligible. Words such as those of Secretary Schlesinger in September 1974, spoken before the Congress— "The likelihood of limited nuclear attacks cannot be challenged on the assumption that massive fatalities and injuries would result" —give little comfort in this regard. I therefore consider the ongoing efforts to bring the spread, improvement and accumulation of nuclear weapons under control through negotiated treaties to be singularly important; I wish that much more public concern were directed to this area.

Currently six nations have detonated nuclear explosions, and the world's nuclear weapons stockpile has grown to an extent which exceeds rational comprehension. To say that "The world's nuclear arsenals now contain an equivalent in excess of ten tons of TNT available for each man, woman and child on the globe" is technically correct, but does not do justice to the actual problem. The captain of a single Poseidon boat is in effect a nuclear power, for he has under his command on the order of 150 nuclear warheads, each more potentially destructive than the weapon which destroyed Hiroshima and Nagasaki. . . .

This is the frightening side of the nuclear weapons story. On the positive side, the long period of non-belligerency between the two super powers since World War II is probably due to the existence of nuclear weapons and the deterrent effect they have exerted against engaging in all-out warfare. Therefore the problem which must be solved by the world's peoples is how to limit the irrational evolution of nuclear weaponry, while maintaining some deterrent effect until a new international order might evolve.

I cannot describe here in any detail the course of the world's past efforts toward controlling nuclear arms. There have been some successes and many failures. Over all, progress has been so slow that evolution of military technology continues to outpace the rate at which diplomacy can lead to agreements constraining the character and number of weapons capable of delivering nuclear warheads.

Superficially, the world has seen many impressive achievements in arms control during the last two decades. There has been a ban on nuclear weapons orbiting in outer space and emplaced on the seabed. There has been a prohibition signed by about 100 signatories against nuclear testing in the atmosphere, in outer space and under water; this has drastically reduced the polluting effect of nuclear weapons testing, but has hardly retarded the evolution of nuclear military technology. There has been a ban on biological weapons and severe restrictions on chemical warfare. The Nuclear Non-Proliferation Treaty (NPT) constrains the diffusion of nuclear military devices and military technology, while at the same time attempting to spread the benefits of peaceful nuclear energy. Yet with the exception of this agreement and the SALT I treaty, on which I will comment later, these treaties have by and large prohibited activities which the signatories, acting in their own self-interest, would have considered of minimal military use. The really hard issues remain to be faced.

Weapons which can be launched by forces of one country and can hit the homeland of the other are called *strategic*. The Strategic Arms Limitation Talks (SALT) are intended to bring competition in such weapons under control. While SALT I, signed in 1972, indeed represents progress in this respect, it has not sufficed to reverse the escalation of strategic arms competition. The SALT I *treaty* deals only with *defensive* armaments (ABM); it is supplemented by an *interim* five-year agreement for the control of *offensive* missile launchers. This interim agreement has drawn a great deal of criticism;. efforts to supersede this interim measure by a satisfactory SALT II treaty have been slow, erratic, and haunted by critics.

In 1974 President Ford and Secretary Brezhnev agreed to principles at Vladivostok which established ceilings on aggregates of vehicles delivering nuclear weapons, and a separate sub-limit on multiple-warhead missile launchers. These numerical ceilings are so high, however, that they do not significantly limit those nuclear weapons contained in plans now conceived unilaterally by the two nations. The most tangible arms control benefit is likely to be that the *worst case projections* which both nations tend to use in evaluating future threats against their country will be limited.

For this and other reasons, one can argue persuasively that the nuclear buildup would be even worse without the prospective SALT II agreement. This assertion might well be correct—a depressing conclusion in itself. Yet the numbers of nuclear weapons under the agreed ceiling remain so enormous that no substantial fraction could possibly be detonated against enemy targets without the most dire consequences for civilization. Most disappointing is the fact that it is not anticipated that the SALT II treaty, should it indeed become a reality . . . [will do much to] constrain the evolution of military technology. To say it in other words, the SALT process will have shifted the quantitative arms race more into qualitative competition.

The Soviet Union and the United States are different strategically in many fundamental respects: there are geographic asymmetries, and negotiation between an open pluralistic society and a more controlled nation poses many difficulties. Moreover, the strategic arms race in itself has not been

symmetrical. The Soviet Union has tended to concentrate on the deployment of a large number of weapons of substantial size and weight; the United States, in contrast, has emphasized advances in high technology leading to sophisticated weapons systems which deliver warheads with high accuracy and high multiplicity for each carrier. Of course this pattern need not persist: the Soviets have developed accurate multiple warhead missiles and have begun to deploy them; the US could convert its missiles to much heavier models. Within this asymmetric pattern it is futile to seek a simple measure of relative strategic standing of the two nations.

In the past the every essence of arms control agreements (such as SALT) has been to arrive at negotiated accords which limit an agreed, carefully circumscribed subset of weapons. To do so, it is essential to define in legally binding language such items as strategic delivery vehicles, sea-launched ballistic strategic missiles, heavy strategic bombers, etc., etc. Many of the contested items in the negotiation of the SALT II treaty which have leaked into the public press stem from ambiguities in defining different categories of weapons. When is a bomber strategic and when is it tactical? How do you know when anti-submarine weapons protect against strategic attack and when they are to protect commercial shipping lanes? How do you know whether interceptor missiles are intended to shoot down incoming *ballistic missiles* or to protect against attacking *aircraft?* Etc., etc. The more we add to the complexity of the aresenal of destruction the harder it becomes for the arms control negotiation to define separable categories.

The debate regarding long range strategic cruise missiles which has recently become public illustrates this problem. These weapons, in the words of Dr. Malcolm Currie,

Director of Defense Research and Engineering, constitute a "fourth arm" of the US deterrent, to supplement the already formidable strategic "triad" of aircraft, sea-launched ballistic missiles, and land-based Minuteman ICBM forces. Yet the goal for SALT II as agreed to at Vladivostok was to limit the aggregate number of missile launchers and bombers in the "triad" of both nations; permitting a fourth member of strategic weapons which can grow in numbers without restraint would destroy most of the value of a hoped for SALT II agreement.

Cruise missiles are in essence pilotless aircraft which can be steered while in flight to a variety of targets and then deliver nuclear or (non-nuclear) explosives. Such missiles can be launched from many platforms, can have a variety of ranges, and can serve a large spectrum of military missions—tactical and strategic. Their range is controlled by their fuel load, which can easily be raised within the confines of the vessel and its weight-carrying capacity. Thus the precise range attainable by a cruise missile is hard to police.

It is generally agreed, even by the most conservative military leaders, that the present US "triad" is safe against destructive attack for at least another decade, and probably very much longer. Is it then in the US interest to keep the door open for the addition of large numbers of cruise missiles of intercontinental range? The US currently leads in this technology. But if history is a guide, once the US has initially developed a new weapon, then we will, after a fraction of a decade, face that same weapon deployed against us by the Soviet Union. Thus the evolution of long-range cruise missiles would not only drastically diminish the value of SALT II, but would also add another dimension of complexity to the arms competition in the future. In the long run, our national

security would be diminished at a higher level of armament—an all too familiar pattern.

We have seen from the foregoing that as the complexity of weapons increases we find it progressively harder to cope with policing any type of arms control agreement that tends to ban or limit a separate category of weapons. Moreover, as technology evolves it tends to destroy the existing strategic stability, which is based on retaliatory forces secure from destruction. As the accuracy of missiles is upgraded, as the multiplicity of highly accurate warheads carried by a single missile is increased, and as anti-submarine warfare becomes more proficient, the certainty that retaliatory forces will survive a first preemptive strike tends to diminish—although I hasten to add that in my view the possibility of such a strike is still highly remote.

Although the SALT I agreement can be considered to be a useful step, and the prospective SALT II treaty ought to be a useful, albeit very limited, measure, there have been a substantial number of undesirable byproducts concomitant to the strategic arms limitation process. Let me enumerate some of these.

1. "Bargaining Chips"

As we are negotiating with the Soviet Union, many US participants have emphasized the thesis that we must negotiate from "a position of strength." In consequence, several new military programs have been introduced into the Congress as "bargaining chips" in support of that strength. In other words, development and deployment of new strategic systems have been justified as giving bargaining leverage at the SALT table—with the expectation that they will be given up, provided the Soviets make corresponding concessions. A problem with this approach is, of course, the real risk that such a trade-off will not be accepted. Should this happen, a new program will have been added to our military budget which would have been difficult to justify on its own merit. . . .

2. Political Nuclear Numerology

The very process of SALT negotiation, followed by public discussion of the numbers of permitted nuclear weapons systems, has given undue emphasis to the strategic importance of specific numbers of nuclear weapons. For instance, Senator Jackson accused the administration of accepting an apparent inequity in favor of the Soviets in the missile systems permitted under the SALT I Interim Agreement, while ignoring the inequality then in existence which *favored* the US on those weapons systems not yet brought under control. Similarly, the proposed enshrinement in the Vladivostok agreement of a number of 2400 permitted aggregate strategic weapons systems and of 1320 permitted numbers of MIRV'd launchers, and the reputed downward revision by 10 percent of the aggregate numbers as a result of Secretary Kissinger's [later] visit, has given these numbers a significance which their military potential does not deserve. No one knows what a nuclear war actually employing these enormous arsenals would forebode for mankind, and no one can paint any rational scenario which actually employs strategic weapons in such numbers. Yet ascribing diplomatic and political leverage to such numbers becomes a self-fulfilling prophecy: If statesmen say that they are either "ahead" or "behind" in terms of numerical strategic deployments, then such statements, if repeated often enough, give them political weight. This perversion of militarily meaningless collections of weapons into political reality makes it considerably more difficult to climb down from these high numbers. Once the numbers of nuclear weapons become political rather than strategic tools, then nations lose the ability to answer this question: *How much potential destruction is enough?*

A most unhappy consequence of the undue public emphasis on the political leverage of nuclear weapons is further acceleration of the global spread of nuclear weapons.

3. Getting in Under the Wire

As the deadline for conclusion of an arms control agreement approaches, there is a tendency for an acceleration of military research and development before a particular direction is foreclosed. Such programs are frequently ill-conceived, at best wasteful and at worst escalatory.

4. Mistrust

A notable achievement of the SALT I agreement was the establishment of a Standing Consultative Commission (SCC). This is a forum before which suspicious occurrences are to be brought which might be considered violations of the SALT II agreement. Privacy is essential to the success of such an arrangement. Yet the highly political climate in the United States around SALT resulted in a situation in which the suspicious events being discussed before the SCC were also being touted in military journals and by military spokesmen as demonstrated Soviet violations of the SALT agreements. Thus the constructive role of the SCC has become distorted to become a new seed of mistrust among the nations, notwithstanding the fact that none of the alleged events has yet been demonstrated to be a violation, and in spite of the fact that under any agreement ambiguous events are apt to occur on both sides. . . .

And what of the future?

Most. notable among the events concomitant to the SALT negotiations has been a lack of self-restraint in the acquisition of strategic military armaments on both sides. The Soviets have proceeded to test new strategic missiles at an unprecedented rate, and have developed four new missile weapons systems, some of them MIRV'd, during the last few years—all of this in full compliance with existing agreements. The motivation for proceeding this rapidly may well have been a desire to catch up technologically with the US before future arms control agreements might impose a freeze on further development. On the US side, a whole gamut of new research and development programs in the nuclear strategic area has been initiated, at least some under the "bargaining chip" rationale. The Defense Department budget submitted to Congress for the year starting October 1, 1976 proposes a further jump in Strategic Arms Expenditures, accompanied by warnings that more money will be needed if SALT II doesn't succeed. We thus are seeing no respite, and in fact possibly an acceleration in the strategic arms race, each nation proceeding in its own technological style: the Soviet Union using large numbers and heavy weapons and the Americans pursuing further advances in military technology.

It is clear that this pattern will have to stop if disaster is to be prevented, and stop soon. A halt could be produced by internal forces on each side, once the total futility and dangers of further evolution of nuclear strategic weapons is recognized. Let us hope so.

On the negotiation front our hopes rest mainly on rapid progress on reaching accords on qualitative, rather than quantitative limitations. However, proposals for such measures have not yet been agreed to in either capital, let alone broached at the bargaining table. *There is extreme urgency to carry arms control negotiations beyond the numerical limits now in view for SALT II. Even if future reductions decrease these numbers, we must add qualitative constraints that reduce the pace of evolution of military technology; we must give diplomacy a chance to catch up.*

We can visualize agreements to limit the pace of military technology which should prove negotiable. For instance, agreements could and should be reached to severely limit the annual number of experimental test firings of long-range missiles. Such a restraint could be easily policed, and the evolution of new generations of long-range missiles would be slowed. Moreover, each side's confidence that its existing long-range missiles would function with high reliability and precision would be impaired. Far from being a disadvantage, this lack of confidence would put a brake on possible plans to use such missiles first in a nuclear attack. If a decision maker had little confidence that he could completely destroy the opponent's nuclear forces in a first strike, he would not dare to contemplate such an attack.

Restriction on missile flight testing or similar measures, such as the establishment of numerical limits on the number of new generations of military systems that may be deployed in any decade, would be real arms control—much more significant than those measures now on the books. It is for this reason that such measures will surely be opposed vigorously by some parties on both sides of the Iron Curtain, and even from other parts of the world. However, it is my belief that without such accords we will very soon lose our ability to deal with the arms race by negotiated means leading to controls on distinct classes of weapons; we would then be reduced to the contemplation of unilateral measures.

There are some hopeful aspects of arms control. The SALT I treaty, for one, could be a truly significant brake on the arms race. This agreement was signed by President Nixon and Secretary Brezhnev in 1972 and was later amended in 1974; the revised treaty restricts the deployment of anti-ballistic missile systems to a level which is militarily totally negligible. As a result, each missile in our arsenal and that of our European allies is assured penetration. Thus SALT I *could* form a basis for reductions in present stockpiles, since the deterrent value of each missile launcher is increased.

SALT I provides explicitly that "Each party undertakes not to deploy ABM systems for the defense of the territory of its country and not to provide a base for such a defense. . . ." Thus this treaty documents agreement between the US and the Soviet Union that in the nuclear age the populations of each side are unavoidably hostage to one another. Little would be gained, and more would be lost, if a widespread anti-ballistic missile (ABM) defense of the population were installed by one or both of the two countries. This conclusion is indeed an important one. It acknowledges that, irrespective of continually vacillating doctrines enunciated by US Secretaries of Defense or Soviet Ministers, the mutual hostage relationship now existing remains a reality. No credible promise can be made by anyone that a limited nuclear war will remain limited; recent analyses corroborated in Congressional testimony have

amply demonstrated that effective purely *anti-military* attacks against, for instance, all our hardened silos, would cause *civilian* casualties in the tens of millions.

Let me draw your attention to another important provision in the SALT I treaty. The treaty states that "Each party agrees not to interfere with the national means of verification of the other party. . . ." In other words, the treaty provides that such spy devices as intelligence satellites circling the globe must not be interfered with. Or, to state it simply, the SALT I treaty acknowledges that technology has made this a more open world, irrespective of the communications barriers each nation might impose in the form of censorship, and however stringent the limitations on the freedom of movement of individuals. Thus we have here an example of the threat posed by one technology being limited by another.

These fundamental achievements of SALT I and the expected but more limited impact of SALT II *could* form a basis for a more secure strategic future. . . .

In no field of human endeavor is it more important for mankind to evolve decision and control methods, to select beneficial developments and reject destructive applications, than for nuclear technology. Simplistic "pro-nuclear" or "anti-nuclear" national decisions with respect to civilian nuclear power won't do. The problem is global, and the risks associated with real or potential military use outweigh those inherent in civilian application. Only a complex sequence of national and international decisions, combined with enlightened self-restraint, can prevent eventual disaster. Whether humans are capable of such decisions will determine whether technology will be master or servant.

XV

Human Rights

The issue of human rights is not new to international relations. To go no further back than the nineteenth century, a number of incidents testify to the importance which human rights assumed in the relations of states. When the British abolished slave trade in the early nineteenth century, they compelled other states to end it also. Slavery within the British colonies was not completely ended until 1833 and in America not until 1863, but it was the subject of intense agitation all through the first half of the nineteenth century. In 1876 the Turks, in putting down a rebellion of their Bulgarian subjects, massacred some twelve thousand persons including women and children. The British Prime Minister, Disraeli, tried to minimize the atrocities, arguing that anti-Turk agitation had been got up for political purposes, to justify the aggressions and advances of Russian power into the Balkans. Nevertheless, the Liberal Party, led by Gladstone, inflamed the country against Turkey and forced the Tory government to make joint demands with Russia against Turkey—which, when they were rejected, led to a Russian invasion to liberate their Slavic brethren in Bulgaria.

The effort of minorities within the Austro-Hungarian empire to assert their rights was an important cause of World War I, and under the Treaty of St. Germain following the war, Czechoslovakia, Yugoslavia, Poland, and Hungary were given their independence, subject to the condition that they respect the political and human rights of the German and other minorities that were ceded to them as part of the territorial settlement. In all these cases, it was recognized that guarantees of human rights were indispensable to the peace of Europe.

The subject of human rights was much discussed but little acted upon in the 1930s with respect to the Jews in Germany. Had the view prevailed that the plight of the Jews was an international, and not just a domestic, matter, an outcry might have been raised before the war broke out, and before six million had been killed and hundreds of thousands driven from their homes and made refugees.

It was in response to these horrors as well as to the conviction that the violation of human rights was a responsibility of the international community that the United Nations Charter made specific reference to the protection of human rights (both in the preamble and in Articles 1 and 2) and that a Commission on Human Rights was created which drew up a Universal Declaration of Human Rights, adopted by the General Assembly in 1948. The Declaration represents the first attempt to set common standards of achievement in human rights for all people of all nations. As a Declaration, it has only moral, but not legal force.

The relationship of human rights to international relations is a complex subject. There are at least two aspects of the relationship that need to be clarified. In principle, every state that belongs to the United Nations and signed the Declaration on Human Rights undertook to respect human rights, political as well as personal. However, many of these societies do not share the Western tradition from which these rights have emerged. The notion of the individual as a self-directing person or as a citizen endowed with civil rights is unknown to many non-Western cultures. "Questions whether a given human grouping has a demonstrable will and capacity to approximate the model of the democratic nation state; whether its traditional life-style favors the principle of individuation; or whether its customary norms of law and administration allow for the liberty of speech or religion," are questions that must be examined by anyone making human rights as we know them in the West an objective of international politics.[1] In many societies the idea of individual rights is unknown and subordination of the individual to the group, even at the price of rights as we know them, is the cultural norm. It follows that different cultures have brought about different evaluations of the individual's status in society, and different conceptions of right and justice. How can one respect differing cultures and at the same time attempt to reform them in the image of American culture—especially when the material and psychological prerequisites of democracy are non-existent?

[1]Adda B. Bozeman, "How to Think about Human Rights" Proceedings of the National Security Affairs Conference, Washington, D.C. (July 18-20, 1977), p. 3.

Secondly, in Third World countries suffering from poverty, widespread illiteracy, and a yawning gap in domestic distribution of income and wealth, a constitutionally guaranteed freedom of opposition and dissent may not be as significant as freedom from disease and economic deprivation. Third World governments contend that it is only after a minimum of economic well-being has been achieved that political rights and freedom can be instituted. To believe that the latter can come before the former is an ethnocentric American idea born of unique wealth and economic opportunity afforded Americans over three centuries. This of course does not excuse the illegal incarceration of people for years on end or the practice of torture and other unspeakable acts of barbarity and genocide about which the present concern for human rights has sprung up.

It would not do for Americans to dismiss violations of human rights by African, Latin-American, and Communist governments simply on the grounds that their societies do not place the same emphasis upon the individual as does Western culture. Latin America is, after all, part of Western civilization, and several countries (Argentina, Uruguay, Chile, even Brazil) had achieved a high level of democratic rule before the present violations of legality and torture began. The Soviet Union is an example of a society in which Marxism-Leninism rejects both in theory and practice the proposition that the individual has rights apart from society. The situation is somewhat different when it comes to economic and social rights, if only because the Soviet Union is ideologically committed to raising the material standards of the people. Yet it would not justify ignoring the lack of political rights or the suppression of dissent within the Soviet Union.

A second dilemma with which the issue of human rights confronts international relations is the inhibition that sovereignty places upon intervention by an outside power into the domestic affairs of another country. Ernest Lefever, whose article is included in this chapter, argues against making human rights a goal of foreign policy, on the following grounds: "There is and should be a profound moral constraint on efforts designed to alter domestic practices, institutions, and policies within our states." To do so is to set ourselves up as the judge of other societies which may not share the same values as we do, and "to confuse domestic and foreign policy." Exponents of the human rights campaign, Lefever continues, "do not take seriously the distinctions in authority and responsibility that flow from the concept of sovereignty." A government must limit its foreign policy to maintaining its own interests in its relations with other countries without trying to change their domestic behavior; "we cannot export human rights or respect for the rule of law."

These are all powerful arguments against letting foreign policy become involved with human rights. For example, it was immediately apparent when President Carter espoused human rights as a goal of American foreign policy, that the Soviet Union among other countries regarded it as an attempt to interfere in its domestic affairs. The Soviet Union has the advantage in these matters, in that it can justify repression of dissent and political rights in the name of a higher form of society—communism. At the same time, Communists exploit the freedom of expression and assembly that exists within a democracy as a justifiable part of the class struggle for power —a struggle which, when the communists have won, comes to an end. On the other hand, it can be seen that the Soviet hostility to Carter's human rights campaign is an expression of the Kremlin's insecurity and fear that opposition might well get out of hand and put the legitimacy of the regime itself in doubt. The Soviet reaction to Carter's human rights campaign was to warn that detente and other goals of American foreign policy would be lost if Washington persisted. This is the dilemma with human rights: those regimes which cannot exist without the denial and supression of human rights will resort to hostility toward whoever challenges them. The challenge is especially acute when the Soviet Union knows that the American government's intent is to change the status quo within the existing communist states in order to "transform established power relationships and enhance the security not only of individual rights but also of the societies that share the European space" by reducing Soviet power and influence in Eastern Europe.[2] So the campaign for human rights in Soviet eyes is not just a matter of challenging the principles of Soviet rule, but also of altering external power relationships, with, in Soviet eyes, an attendant threat to Soviet security. Of course, Soviet support for revolution and the conquest of power by Communist parties in Western Europe represents a similar challenge to American security. Thus human rights become inextricably intertwined with issues of regime survival and national security; and any effort to uphold human rights must be carefully balanced against the damage to peace and detente.[3] Thus Carter has had to reduce his criticism of Soviet violations of human rights in order to assure progress on strategic-arms limitation.

Much of the criticism that has attended Carter's human rights campaign has come from those who do not object to making Soviet or Cuban treatment of dissidents an issue, but who oppose making Brazilian, Chilean, Philippine, South Korean, or South African violations of human rights an issue. They do not have the same intensity of feeling about the suppression of human rights in non-communist countries, either because the latter are our allies or because they believe that repression of dissent is not done out of totalitarian motives and that improvements can be realized without U.S. interference. It was chiefly when Carter attempted to make *universal* respect for human rights a goal of American policy and threatened to cut off economic and military aid to non-communist countries that a hue and cry

[2]*Ibid.*, p. 5.

[3]Of course, both leading Soviet Dissidents Solzenitzen and Sakharov argue that no normalization of relations with the Kremlin is possible unless the regime abandons repression; otherwise detente merely permits it to tighten its grip and augment its power with the full intention of overthrowing the West.

arose: "we must not intervene in the domestic affairs of our allies and thereby undermine our security to the advantage of the Communists." The critics of the President forget that intervention can take many forms: it can take the form of multinationals that exploit the economic resources of another country without benefit to the majority of the populace; it can take the form of transfers of military equipment designed to keep the poor down; and it can take the form of just enough public and private aid to keep the incumbent elites in power at the expense of social and economic reform. As one observer remarks, "there is no natural affinity among capitalist [or communist] growth, political freedom, and social justice. In the contemporary underdeveloped world, repression and poverty have become integral and essential parts of the dominant growth strategies."[4] It was precisely because the Johnson and Nixon administrations had gone so far in the direction of unstinting support—including military and economic aid—for many regimes that were guilty of violating human rights that Americans felt a moral revulsion. Under the guise of national security, Washington had buttressed a number of regimes guilty of violations of human rights. In many of these countries, particularly in Latin America, there was in reality no threat to national security, and American policy represented a form of intervention on behalf of military juntas and against radical regimes such as that of Castro in Cuba and that of Allende in Chile.

The present policy represents as much a swing of the pendulum as it does an expression of American moralism and messianism. It certainly would not do for Washington to embark on a human-rights crusade. But even in those countries which have had no great experience with democracy or human rights, lip service is paid to human dignity—sometimes expressed through the Catholic Church as in Latin America, sometimes through dissidents and intellectuals, and sometimes through the leaders themselves, even though they may not honor their ideals. At a time in history when revolutionary needs and aspirations are important factors in both national and international politics, and when the Communist regimes are not loath to exploit them, would it not be a mistake for American foreign policy to downplay its contribution to the ideal of human progress? While America ought to concentrate on improving its own society and not make every instance of inequity or injustice a target of foreign policy, still it should be possible to combine realism and sobriety with a decent respect for the opinions of mankind by speaking up for human rights. Too often, Americans have let their foreign policy become the vehicle for purely material interests and unworthy ends, with very little objection from those who today declaim against Carter's emphasis on human rights. As we explained in the chapter on "The Framing and Implementing of Foreign Policy Goals," a careful weighing of human rights along with other interests and values is not incompatible with international politics in an age of revolution and change.

[4]Sylvia Ann Hewlett, "The Rights of Cogs," *The New Times*.

37 Excerpts from Relevant Documents

THE U.N. CHARTER (1945)

We the Peoples of the United Nations Determined
. . . .
to reaffirm faith in fundamental human rights, in the dignity and worth of the human person, in the equal rights of men and women and of nations, large and small. . . .

Have Resolved to Combine our Efforts to Accomplish these Aims. . . .

Article 1

The purposes of the United Nations are:
. . . To achieve international cooperation in solving international problems of an economic, social, cultural, or humanitarian character, and in promoting and encouraging respect for human rights and for fundamental freedoms for all without distinction as to race, sex, language, or religion. . . .

Article 55

With a view to the creation of conditions of stability and well-being which are necessary for peaceful and friendly relations among nations based on respect for the principle of equal rights and self-determination of peoples, the United Nations shall promote:

a. higher standards of living, full employment, and conditions of economic and social progress and development;
b. solutions of international economic, social, health, and related problems; and international cultural and educational cooperation; and
c. universal respect for, and observance of, human rights and fundamental freedoms for all without distinction as to race, sex, language, or religion.

2. UNIVERSAL DECLARATION OF HUMAN RIGHTS

Pursuant to the Charter provisions, a Commission on Human Rights was created which drew up a Universal Declaration of Human Rights, adopted by the General Assembly in 1948. Mrs. Eleanor Roosevelt, the widow of the former American President, was the chairperson of this Commission. The statement was the first effort to set common standards of achievement in human rights for all peoples of all nations. As a statement, it has no legal force, but has moral impact.

Among the thirty specific goals enunciated in this Statement, the following deserve brief mention:

1. All human beings are born free and equal in dignity and rights. They are endowed with reason and conscience and should act towards one another in a spirit of brotherhood.
2. Everyone is entitled to all the rights and freedoms set forth in this Declaration,

without distinction of any kind, such as race, colour, sex, language, religion, political or other opinion, national or social origin, property, birth or other status. . . .

3. Everyone has the right to life, liberty and the security of person;

4. No one shall be held in slavery or servitude;

5. No one shall be subjected to torture or to cruel, inhuman or degrading treatments or punishment;

6. Everyone has the right to recognition everywhere as a person before the law;

7. All are equal before the law and are entitled without any discrimination to equal protection of the law;

8. Everyone has the right to an effective remedy by the competent national tribunals for acts violating the fundamental rights granted him by the constitution or by law. [Note: The tribunals here are national, not international.]

9. No one shall be subjected to arbitrary arrest, detention or exile;

10. Everyone is entitled in full equality to a fair and public hearing by an independent and impartial tribunal, in the determination of his rights and obligations and of any criminal charge against him

11. Everyone charged with a penal offence has the right to be presumed innocent until proved guilty. . . . No one shall be held guilty of any penal offence on account of any act or omission which did not constitute a penal offence . . . when it was committed;

12. No one shall be subjected to arbitrary interference with his privacy, family, home or correspondence, nor to attacks upon his honour and reputation. . . .

13. Everyone has the right to freedom and movement and residence within the borders of each State. Everyone has the right to leave any country, including his own, and to return to his country.

14. Everyone has the right to seek and to enjoy in other countries asylum from persecution;

15. Everyone has the right to a nationality. No one shall be arbitrarily deprived of

his nationality nor denied the right to change his nationality.

16. Men and women of full age . . . have the right to marry and to found a family. They are entitled to equal rights as to marriage, during marriage and at its dissolution; marriage shall be entered into only with the free and full consent of intending spouses;

17. Everyone has the right to own property. No one shall be arbitrarily deprived of his property;

18. Everyone has the right to freedom of thought, conscience, and religion. . . .;

19. Everyone has the right to freedom of opinion. . . .;

20. Everyone has the right to freedom of peaceful assembly and association. No one may be compelled to belong to an association;

21. Everyone has the right to take part in the government of his country, directly or through freely chosen representatives;

22. Everyone has the right to social security in accordance with the organization and resources of each State;

23. Everyone has the right to work, to free choice of employment, to equal pay for equal work. . . . Everyone has the right to form and to join trade unions. . . .

24. Everyone has the right to rest and leisure. . . .

25. Everyone has the right to a standard of living adequate for the health and well-being of himself and of his family, including food, clothing, housing and medical care. . . .

26. Everyone has the right to education Education shall be free, at least in the elementary and fundamental stages. Elementary education shall be compulsory. . . .

27. Everyone has the right freely to participate in the cultural life of the community, to enjoy the arts and to share in scientific advancement and its benefits.

28. Everyone is entitled to a social and international order in which the rights and freedoms set forth in this Declaration can be fully realized. . . .

3. UN CONVENTION ON PREVENTION AND PUNISHMENT OF GENOCIDE

In 1948, the UN General Assembly adopted a "Convention of the Prevention and Punishment of the Crime of Genocide." As of 1976, eighty-two nations (not including the United States) had ratified this convention. Genocide is defined as

> any . . . acts committed with intent to destroy, in whole or in part, a national, ethnical, racial or religious group, as such.

4. INTERNATIONAL CONVENTION ON THE ELIMINATION OF RACIAL DISCRIMINATION

In 1965 the UN General Assembly adopted an "International Convention on the Elimination of all Forms of Racial Discrimination." The U.S. has signed this convention, but it has not yet been sent to the Senate for approval and ratification. 94 nations have adhered to the Convention.

Racial discrimination is defined as

> any distinction, exclusion, restriction or preference based on race, colour, descent, or national or ethnic origin which has the purpose or effect of nullifying or impairing the recognition, enjoyment or exercise, on an equal footing, of human rights and fundamental freedoms in the political, economic, social, cultural or any other field of public life.

Note: Parts of this Convention present certain difficulties for the United States, especially in light of the first ten Amendment guarantees. These include condemnation of "all propaganda and all organizations which are based on ideas or theories of superiority of one race or group of persons of one colour or ethnic origin"; there is also a provision that States "shall declare illegal and prohibit organizations . . . which promote and incite racial discrimination."

5. COVENANT ON ECONOMIC, SOCIAL, AND CULTURAL RIGHTS

In 1966, the UN General Assembly adopted a Covenant on Economic, Social, and Cultural Rights. Among its major terms are the following:

1. All peoples have the right of self-determination. . . .;
2. All peoples may, for their own ends, freely dispose of their natural wealth and resources without prejudice to any obligation arising out of international economic cooperation based upon the principle of mutual benefit, and international law. . . .;
5. The rights of men and women are equal,
6. The States Parties to the present Covenant recognize the right to work;
7. The States Parties to the present Covenant recognize the right of everyone to the enjoyment of just and favourable conditions of work (including fair remuneration, fair wages and equal remuneration, decent living, healthy working conditions, rest, leisure and reasonable limitation of working hours);
8. The right to form trade unions is guaranteed. So is the right to strike;
9. The right of everyone to social security including social insurance;

10. Widest possible protection and assistance to the family; special protection to be accorded to mothers during a reasonable period before and after childbirth. Special measures of protection and assistance on behalf of all children and young persons;

11. Adequate standard of living for himself and his family, including adequate food, clothing, and housing, and to the continuous improvement of living conditions. Freedom from hunger. Improved methods of production, conservation, and distribution of food;

12. Rights of everyone to the enjoyment of the highest attainable standard of physical and mental health;
Reduction of the still-birth rate and of infant mortality; improvement of all aspects of industrial hygiene; prevention, treatment and control of epidemic, occupational and other diseases; creation of conditions which would assure to all medical services and medical attention in the event of sickness;

13. Right of everyone to education. Primary education shall be compulsory and available free to all;
Secondary education shall be made generally available and accessible to all by every appropriate means, and in particular by the progressive introduction of free education;
Higher education shall be made equally accessible to all, on the basis of capa-city, by every appropriate means and in particular by the progressive introduction of free education;

14. The right of every one to take part in cultural life, to enjoy the benefits of scientific and material interests resulting from any scientific, literary or artistic production of which he is the author.

6. INTERNATIONAL COVENANT ON CIVIL AND POLITICAL RIGHTS

In 1966, the UN General Assembly adopted an "International Covenant on Civil and Political Rights." This is the most similar in conception to the U.S. Constitution and Bill of Rights. It consists primarily of limitation upon the power of the State to impose its will on the people under its jurisdiction and, in large measure, guarantees those civil and political rights with which the United States and the Western democratic tradition have always been associated. The U.S. has not signed it nor sent it to the Senate. While there are some sticky points in it (e.g., Aticle 20, Sec. 1: "Any propaganda for war shall be prohibited by law.") These could clearly be struck out as a condition of U.S. ratification.

38   Human Rights: Principles and Realism

Warren Christopher

Warren Christopher is Deputy Secretary of State. The following is a speech delivered by him before the American Bar Association, Chicago, August 9, 1977.

Throughout the United States there is a new awareness of the vitality and value of our founding principles. Now, after 200 years, they continue to bind us together and to define our national identity. We have come through a difficult period of self-doubts and self-criticism, but once again we are less conscious of what divides us and more committed to the principles and values we hold in common.

We believe our underlying principles and values must be reflected in American foreign policy if that policy is to have the support of our people and if it is to be effective. Reflecting this conviction, the promotion of human rights has become a fundamental tenet of the foreign policy of the Carter Administration.

In our efforts to promote human rights we must carefully define the principles we seek to apply, for glittering generalities can lead to unworkable policies. We must also serve our principles with an abiding realism, since rigidity in the pursuit of principle, especially in foreign policy, is likely to lead us astray.

In defining what we mean by human rights, we believe that we should direct our efforts to the most fundamental and important

Published by the Department of State, Bureau of Public Affairs, August 9, 1977.

human rights, all of which are internationally recognized in the Universal Declaration of Human Rights which the United Nations approved in 1948. Thus, we emphasize three categories of human rights:

First, the right to be free from governmental violation of the integrity of the person. Such violations include torture; cruel, inhuman, or degrading treatment or punishment; arbitrary arrest or imprisonment; denial of fair public trial; and invasion of the home. When human beings are forcibly abducted from their homes, interrogated incessantly at the pleasure of their captors, and prodded with electrodes or held under water to the point of drowning—when such things are happening in the world in which we live—and they are—all who truly value human rights must speak out.

Second, the right to the fulfillment of such vital needs as food, shelter, health care, and education. The stage of a nation's economic development will obviously affect the fulfillment of this right. But we must remember that this right can be violated by a government's action or inaction—for example, when a government diverts vast proportions of its country's limited resources to corrupt officials or to the creation of luxuries for an elite, while millions endure hunger and privation.

Third, the right to enjoy civil and political liberties: freedom of thought, of religion, of assembly; of speech; of the press; freedom of movement both within and outside one's own country; freedom to take part in government. These liberties that we Americans enjoy so fully, and too often take for granted, are under assault in many places. That authoritarian regimes are premised on a denial of these rights is well known. It is all the more distressing, however, when regimes in countries with democratic traditions violate these precious rights; for example, when they shut down newspapers and imprison journalists who have done nothing more than print ideas which are out of step with official policy.

It is our goal to promote greater observance by governments of all three groups of the fundamental human rights I have described. It is, after all, these rights that make life worth living. . . .

UNIVERSAL IDEAS

Having defined the three categories of rights that are the subject of our policy, it is only fair for me to acknowledge that there are those who suggest that it is unwise for us to be promoting abroad the human rights principles that gave the nation its birth. Such critics argue that we cannot expect non-Western societies to find much relevance in what are sometimes disparagingly referred to as 18th century Western ideas.

But there is nothing parochial about the principles we seek to promote. They respond to universal yearnings of mankind. They have been formally adopted by virtually all governments both in their own constitutions and through international commitments. What we are urging is that more than lip-service be accorded to these principles.

Those who say we should not seek to impose our particular form of democracy on the world have set up a straw man. It is not a matter of form we are talking about; it is the substance of human freedom.

Even though people are very poor, they are still profoundly interested in being free to go where they want, to say what they want, to practice the religion of their choice, and to have a voice in determining the rules under which they live. Do the critics really mean to suggest that those struggling to break the bonds of mass misery are content permanently to trade in their freedoms for material advancement? My own view is that those who make such suggestions have failed to recognize the deepest aspirations of human beings.

I see no necessary inconsistency between economic development on the one hand and political and civil rights on the other. And I think people will eventually reject leaders who unnecessarily impose such a choice. In the short run, some people may have tempered their desire for freedom, but in the long run I believe that desire is irrepressible.

POSITIVE MEASURES PREFERRED

We have no illusions that the process of encouraging greater respect for human rights around the world will yield early or easy successes. We realize that there are compelling reasons why we must season our idealism with realism.

There is no blinking at the fact that our ability to change human rights practices in other societies is limited, even where we use all the mechanisms and approaches at our disposal. We must not proceed as if we had unlimited power.

Just as our power is limited, so is our wisdom. We must avoid certitude and its unattractive partner, self-righteousness. We recognize the variety of human experience. Differing histories and circumstances will necessarily mean that there will be a great diversity in political systems and economic conditions throughout the world.

In addition, we must recognize that our actions may provoke retaliation against our short-term interests or even sometimes against the victims of repression we seek to assist. We would much prefer to find positive and creative ways to encourage governments to respect human rights, rather than to penalize poor performance. But where such positive measures are not possible, the risks of imposing sanctions must be faced and carefully assessed.

It is also realistic to recognize that unless our domestic actions reflect a firm commitment to human rights, the message we are sending to others will ring hollow. We are taking important steps to improve our own human rights record. We have removed all restrictions on the right of our citizens to travel abroad. With our support, Congress has just passed a relaxation of our visa requirements, so that foreigners wishing to visit our country will not be excluded because of political affiliation except in the rarest instances. In addition, we are seeking expansion of our refugee and asylum policies, the most current example being the plans to admit an additional 15,000 Indochinese refugees. The efforts we are making to prevent a recurrence of abuses by the intelligence community and to overhaul our outmoded and unfair welfare sysem are also important contributions to the cause of human rights.

DIPLOMATIC APPROACHES

When we find it necessary to address ourselves to the human rights conditions in other countries, our first approach is to express our views in private to the government involved. There are a variety of ways in which this can be done. We can therefore choose between a rather wide range of signals. It can be done, for example, by a State Department desk officer talking to a minister in a foreign embassy. It can be done by having the Secretary of State call in a foreign ambassador. It can be done by our ambassador in a foreign country going in to see the foreign minister. Or it can be done by a letter from our President to the leader of a foreign government, and so forth. The point is that diplomacy is a rich resource that can be fully mined only by a calibrated, sequential approach.

We have made scores of diplomatic approaches with respect to human rights, and by and large we are achieving good results: Governments all over the world, even where they disagree with us, are beginning to understand our policy better and to gauge accurately the depth of our commitment.

Diplomatic approaches enable other governments to respond privately to our concerns. This is appropriate since our objective is improvement of human rights conditions, not embarrassment of others or publication of our successes.

Other governments must be aware, of course, that when private discussions fail to convey our message, public comment may at times be necessary. And we shall never apologize for expressing our commitment to our principles.

Our bilateral economic assistance programs also must reflect our commitment to human rights. For our part, we are committed to providing substantial and increasing economic assistance to the Third World. . . .

Of course, we are eager to use our economic assistance affirmatively to promote the cause of human rights. For example, we helped arrange an international loan to

Portugal to aid that country in its difficult transformation into a democratic society.

As for military assistance, our military assistance programs are reviewed in light of the human rights practices of the recipient governments. In some cases we may decide to limit or withdraw security assistance. In other cases where the human rights performance of the recipient is unsatisfactory, we may decide to continue to provide aid because of overriding U.S. national security interests—but not without expressing our concern.

We are also taking important initiatives in multilateral bodies. For example, we are using our voice and vote in the World Bank and other international financial institutions to promote the cause of human rights. We do this by opposing or seeking reconsideration of loans to governments that are flagrant human rights violators, again with special consideration being given to loans that would clearly help meet the needs of the poor.

At the United Nations, we are working closely with other governments to give new strength and validity to that organization's efforts on behalf of human rights. It is especially important that the United Nations take the difficult but crucial step of making its investigations of human rights violations evenhanded and comprehensive. We are therefore enthusiastically supporting an initiative of Costa Rica to establish a U.N. high commission for human rights. And we have urged the General Assembly to establish a special panel to give new impetus to the campaign against torture.

In the Organization of American States, we supported a successful initiative by Venezuela to increase the resources and effectiveness of the Inter-American Human Rights Commission. We believe that the commission can play a critical role in investigating allegations of human rights violations in this hemisphere and in suggesting improvements. . . .

These are some of the tools at our disposal. I want to stress that in deciding whether and how to use them in particular cases, we will not be distracted by token improvements that other governments may make. Rather, our attention will be fixed on the long-term trend.

I also want to underscore that as we use these approaches and mechanisms, it will always be our desire to expand our cooperation with other governments and peoples. For we know that in the long run we will fail unless we make the promotion of human rights an international movement.

ENCOURAGING DEVELOPMENTS

Is our policy working? It is certainly too early to say. In a sense, it will probably always be too early to say. The quest to secure human rights is never ending, like the search for peace. We may hope and pray for the day when the world will seem more civilized, when governments will uniformly treat their citizens with decency and humanity, but we will not be discouraged by the shortcomings we see. Indeed, the failures we observe will only cause us to redouble our efforts.

We take encouragement, but do not take credit, for favorable signs which we observe around the world on the human rights front, signs which indicate that the issue of human rights has touched a responsive chord in a growing number of countries.

With respect to violations of integrity of the person, some governments, we hope with a real intent to halt repression, have begun to release large numbers of political prisoners as well as to curtail the indiscriminate arrest of alleged subversives. And some governments have punished those responsible for torture and ordered that such practices cease.

With respect to economic rights, many governments are showing a renewed determination to promote the economic rights of their citizens. They are turning away from grandiose schemes and showcase improvements to apply their energies to economic projects that provide the broadest benefits. The governments of several African countries, recognizing the vast disparities between rich and poor, are beginning long-range and difficult development programs to provide a better standard of life for their people. In addition, in some Latin American countries land reform is again being pursued as a way to give people a stake in their own country and provide them an opportunity for economic advancement. I would also note that in Portugal the new democratic government is moving ahead in the areas of housing and health care, social security and welfare benefits, and new schools. Further, the international financial institutions are gradually redirecting much of their resources toward rural development and agricultural projects that help the largest number of people.

With respect to political and civil rights, one can perceive a resurgence of democracy. Recent developments in India and Spain, as well as Portugal, are proving that democracy can stage a comeback. In some of the military regimes in Latin America, there are hesitant but hopeful signs of "retorno" —a return to elected civilian government. In addition, some East European countries have permitted the reunification of divided families and otherwise eased their emigration rules.

I think all of these positive developments are clear and convincing evidence of the power of an idea. When all is said and done, the idea of human rights has a life and force of its own which governments can nurture or oppose, but never extinguish. I can see this so vividly as I review cables from all over the world. The human rights initiative echoes in official circles; even more, it has a resonance in the homes and hearts of people around the world.

If we have moved human rights to the front page, it is not because of us, but because of the power of the ideas we are espousing. I see now more clearly than ever before why it has been said that the cause of human freedom is the world's only great revolutionary cause. As Walter Lippmann once put it:

> The deepest issue of our time is whether the civilized people can maintain and develop a free society or whether they are to fall back into the ancient order of things, when the whole of men's existence, their consciences, their science, their arts, their labor, and their integrity as individuals were at the disposal of the State.

Let me conclude by saying that, as in any new undertaking, our human rights policy will not be free from mistakes and miscalculations. But with the understanding and support of our citizens—as well as of our leading private organizations, such as the American Bar Association—and with practical and persistent effort, I believe that over time this new policy will achieve historic results. The time is propitious. The challenge is enormous. But our principles are sound and vital, and when applied with realism, they can and will provide a harvest of freedom for us and for people everywhere.

39   The Trivialization of Human Rights

Ernest W. Lefever

The author is a Senior Staff member of the Brookings Institution in Washington, D.C.

Fifteen centuries ago Saint Augustine said that were it not for government, men would devour one another as fishes. But when governments often become corrupt, cruel, or tyrannical, they are the most monstrous fish of all. Depending on its character, government can be the most effective protector of human rights or the most vicious violator of them. Hence, the struggle for viable and humane government is the heart of politics.

It is important to distinguish between two frequently confused concepts of human rights.[1] One has more immediate universal application because it is rooted in the religion and ethics of virtually all cultures and calls for sanctions against political authorities and others guilty of genocide, brutalizing innocent people and similar atrocities. The second and more precise concept of human rights is the fruit of the recent Western democratic experience and embraces a variety of substantive and procedural rights and safeguards that are enforced in perhaps fewer than a score of states. These rights include freedom of speech, assembly, press, and religion; equality before the law; periodic elections; the concept of being innocent until proved guilty; a judicial system independent from executive authority; and a range of

From Policy Review *(Winter, 1978). Reprinted by permission. (Some footnotes omitted.)*

[1]This distinction is elaborated in Peter L. Berger's "Are Human Rights Universal?", *Commentary,* September, 1977.

safeguards for accused persons. Many of these Western democratic rights are unknown and unattainable in large parts of the world where both history and culture preclude the development of full-fledged democratic institutions. Nevertheless, there are significant differences in the extent to which human rights, more generally defined, are honored in undemocratic states. And some of these states have introduced a few of the specific Western safeguards.

The never-ending battle to maintain and enlarge the areas of proximate liberty and justice must be fought against external and internal forces which seek to impose authority without freedom, often by brutal means. Human rights as we know them in the United States and other democratic countries can be eroded or even obliterated from within by acquiescing to willful men who seek to capture the reins of power for their own narrow ends or from without by totalitarian regimes determined to extend their dominion.

Our Founding Fathers wrestled with the problem of creating a free and independent country ruled by a government with sufficient authority to overcome domestic and alien threats and with sufficient openness to respond to the will of the people. Their formula was the judicious balance between authority and freedom embraced in the Declaration of Independence and elaborated in the Constitution. The former asserted that "governments are instituted among men, deriving their just powers from the consent of the governed" to secure certain fundamental rights, among them "life, liberty, and the pursuit of happiness." The Constitution was promulgated to "establish justice, insure domestic tranquility, provide for the common defense, promote the general welfare, and secure the blessings of liberty."

This audacious experiment prospered in an inauspicious world. In the face of new challenges, the American system provided for increasingly broader political participation and other specific rights spelled out or implied in the Constitution and its amendments. Our history is not without blemish, but compared to other political communities past and present, the American record is a beacon of freedom and justice in a world bedeviled by chaos, authoritarian rule, and messianic tyranny.

THE CURRENT HUMAN RIGHTS CAMPAIGN

The current wave of concern for human rights around the world was foreshadowed by several developments, notably Woodrow Wilson's crusade for "self-determination" and the Universal Declaration of Human Rights adopted by the United Nations in 1948. The U.S. campaign to make the advancement of human rights abroad an objective of foreign policy is more recent, but it did not start with President Jimmy Carter. He simply built on the lively interest developed in Congress during the past several years which has been expressed largely in foreign aid legislation designed to prohibit or restrict economic or military assistance to any government "which engages in a consis-

tent pattern of gross violations of internationally recognized human rights, including torture or cruel, inhumane, or degrading treatment or punishment, prolonged detention without charges, or other flagrant denial of the right to life, liberty, and the security of person" (Foreign Assistance Act, Section 502B, adopted in 1974). Most of the congressional human rights activists have limited their advocacy of punitive measures to Chile, South Korea, and Iran. In practice, the restrictions have had little effect on limiting aid, loans, or military sales, even to these countries.

Human rights was a natural cause for President Carter. As a born-again Baptist and a latter-day Wilsonian, he repeatedly stated his intention to restore integrity and compassion to American domestic and foreign policy. In his address at Notre Dame University on March 22, 1977, Mr. Carter looked back to the immediate past and deplored our "intellectual and moral poverty," illustrated by our Vietnam policy, and our "inordinate fear of Communism which once led us to embrace any dictator who joined us in that fear." He called for a "new" American foreign policy, "based on constant decency in its values and an optimism in its historical vision." The most conspicuous manifestation of his new policy is the effort to promote human rights in other countries by means of U.S. statecraft, including private diplomacy, public preaching, and measures to deny or threaten to deny economic, military or nuclear assistance. Mr. Carter's campaign has been given bureaucratic visibility by establishing a new post, Assistant Secretary of State for Human Rights and Humanitarian Affairs. . . .

The human rights campaign has received mixed reviews at home and abroad. Last

July in a *New Yorker* article friendly to the effort, Elizabeth Drew reported that Mr. Carter's people "are pleased, and some even a bit awestruck, at the impact that the human-rights campaign has had thus far. 'I think' says one, 'that the mulish world has noticed the two-by-four.' "

There is no doubt that the threatening plank has been noticed, and probably in isolated cases it has accomplished some good. But it should be recorded that some un-mulish elements in the world, including friendly and allied governments, have also seen the two-by-four and are not convinced that its whack, however well-intended, has always been redemptive. There is no doubt that it has harmed relations with some allies and has both irritated and comforted adversaries.

It is by no means clear that the campaign has resulted in any significant relaxation of Soviet restrictions against emigration or political dissent. There is evidence that the opposite may be the case. On December 30, 1977, a *New York Times* page-one story reported: "The small Soviet human rights movement . . . is at its lowest point in years after a campaign of arrests, threats, and forced exile."

It is clear, however, that a score of allies has been unhappy with a policy they regard as arrogant and unfairly applied. Brazil, Argentina, Uruguay, and Guatemala have been alienated to the point where they have refused military assistance from Washington. And Brazil has served notice that it wishes to withdraw from its Security Assistance Agreement of 25 years standing. This alienation of allies gives aid and comfort to Moscow which more than offsets the minor embarrassment it suffers from Mr. Carter's conspicuous "intervention" on behalf of Soviet dissidents.

SIX FLAWS IN THE HUMAN RIGHTS POLICY

Far more serious, however, the Carter campaign has confused our foreign policy goals and trivialized the concept of human rights. It both reflects and reinforces serious conceptual flaws in the world view of its most articulate spokesmen. These flaws, if permitted to instruct foreign policy, or even influence it unduly, could have catastrophic consequences for the security of the United States and the cause of freedom in the world. Six interrelated flaws deserve brief mention:

1. Underestimating the Totalitarian Threat

Human dignity and freedom are under siege around the world. It has been ever so. The islands of community protected by humane law have been contracting ever since postwar decolonization began. The citizens of most of the newly independent states in Asia and Africa now experience less freedom and fewer guaranteed rights than they did under Western colonial rule.

But the greatest threat to human rights comes from messianic totalitarian regimes whose brutal grip brooks no opposition. Their self-anointed and self-perpetuating elites have become the arbiters of orthodoxy in every sphere—politics, economics, education, the arts, and family life. The ruling party even usurps the place of God. In totalitarian states like the U.S.S.R., Cuba, Cambodia, and Vietnam, there are no countervailing forces to challenge the power, will, or policies of the entrenched elite.

In spite of notable exceptions, the general

political situation in the Third World is characterized by chaos and authoritarian regimes. Democratic and anti-democratic ideas and institutions are competing for acceptance. In this struggle, we should not underestimate the attraction of the totalitarian temptation to leaders who are grappling with the perplexing problems of moving traditional societies into modern, welfare states.

The human rights activists tend to underestimate the totalitarian threat to the West and the totalitarian temptation in the Third World. Hence, they neglect or trivialize the fundamental political and moral struggle of our time—the protracted conflict between forces of total government based on coercion and the proponents of limited government based on popular consent and humane law. In their preoccupation with the minor abridgment of certain rights in authoritarian states, they often overlook the massive threat to the liberty of millions. They attack the limitation of civil rights in South Korea and at the same time call for the United States to withdraw its ground forces, an act that may invite aggression from North Korea. It would be a great irony if Washington in the name of human rights were to adopt a policy that would deliver 35,000,000 largely free South Koreans into virtual slavery.

2. Confusing Totalitarianism with Authoritarianism

In terms of political rights, moral freedom, and cultural vitality, there is a profound difference between authoritarian and totalitarian regimes. Most Asian, African, and Latin American countries are ruled by small elites supported by varying degrees of popular consent. Some are run by brutal tyrants like General Idi Amin of Uganda, others by one-party cliques, military juntas, or civilian-military committees. Almost all authoritarian regimes permit a significantly greater degree of freedom and diversity than the totalitarian ones in all spheres—political, cultural, economic, and religious. Authoritarian rulers often allow opposition parties to operate and a restrained press to publish. Foreign correspondents usually can move about freely and send out uncensored dispatches. They often permit and sometimes encourage relatively free economic activity and freedom of movement for their citizens. The quality of life possible under such rule, of course, depends not only on the character of central control, but on the cultural and economic level of the population as well.

There is, for example, far more freedom of choice, diversity of opinion and activity, and respect for human rights in authoritarian South Korea than in totalitarian North Korea. There is also far more freedom and cultural vitality in Chile—even under its present state of siege—than in Cuba. There have been political prisoners in Chile and there may be a handful now, but there are an estimated 15,000 to 60,000 political detainees in Cuba. These facts are noted, not to praise Chile or condemn Cuba, but to emphasize the consequential difference of human rights in the two kinds of regimes.

Another crucial difference is the capacity of authoritarian rule to evolve into democratic rule. This has happened recently in Spain, Portugal, Greece, and India. In sharp contrast, a Communist dictatorship has never made a peaceful transition to more representative and responsive rule.

3. Overestimating America's Influence Abroad

If the human rights zealots do not indulge in what Denis Brogan once called "the illusion of American omnipotence," they tend to overestimate our capacity, or the capacity of our government, to influence the external world, particularly domestic developments in other countries. America is powerful, but it is not all-powerful. Our considerable leverage of the 1950s and even our diminished leverage of the 1960s has been seriously eroded by OPEC, the great leap forward in Soviet military might, and our abandonment of Vietnam.

Quite apart from our limited capacity to influence intractable realities abroad, there is and should be a profound moral constraint on efforts designed to alter domestic practices, institutions, and policies within other states. Neo-Wilsonian attempts to make the world safe for human rights seem to be rooted in what Professor Ronald Berman has called "a planned confusion between domestic and foreign policy. The rest of the world is depicted as if it were an American constituency, driven by our own motives, vulnerable to our own rhetoric." To be sure, the extravagant rhetoric of a Carter or a Wilson, with its crusading and paternalistic overtones, draws upon a persistent idealistic stream in the American character. But there is another and quieter stream equally honorable, but less pushy and perhaps more persuasive—symbolized by the Biblical parable of a candle upon a candlestick or a city set upon a hill, an example to the "lesser breeds without the law," as it was put in a more candid era.

John Quincy Adams expressed this more modest understanding of America's external responsibility: "We are the friends of liberty everywhere, but the custodians only of our own." Thirty years later, Abraham Lincoln spoke of "liberty as the heritage of all men, in all lands everywhere," but he did not claim that the United States was the chosen instrument for fulfilling this heritage.

4. Confusing Domestic and Foreign Policy

Elaborating on Professor Berman's point, many human rights crusaders confuse the fundamental distinctions between domestic and foreign policy which are rooted in age-old practice, international law, the U.N. Charter, and common sense. They do not take seriously the distinctions in authority and responsibility that flow from the concept of sovereignty which underlies the modern state system. Our President and all other heads of state have authority to act only in their own states, within the territory of their legal jurisdiction. They are responsible only for the security and welfare of their own people, including their citizens living or traveling abroad.

There are, of course, multiple modes of interaction and cooperation between states based on mutual interest, ranging from trade, investment, and cultural exchange to military assistance and alliance ties. These activities are consistent with the concept of sovereign equality and non-interference in internal affairs. But short of a victorious war, no government has a right to impose its preference on another sovereign state. The mode and quality of life, the character and structure of institutions within a state should be determined by its own people, not by outsiders, however well-intentioned. The same is true for the pace and direction of social, political or economic change.

U.S. foreign policy toward another state should be determined largely by the foreign policy of that state. Domestic factors and forces are significant determinants only if they bear on external realities. Washington is allied with Iran, Taiwan, Thailand, and South Korea, not because their governments are authoritarian, but because they are regarded as vital in the struggle against the expansion of Soviet or Chinese power. It is therefore appropriate to provide economic or military assistance to them, even if they do not hold regular elections. In sum, U.S. aid can properly be given to encourage a friend or ally to pursue constructive external policies, but not to promote internal reforms opposed by the assisted government. This leads to the next point.

5.   Ignoring the Perils of Reform Intervention

The impulse to impose our standards or practices on other societies, supported by policies of reward and punishment, leads inevitably to a kind of reform intervention. We Americans have no moral mandate to transform other societies, and we rightly resent such efforts on the part of the totalitarians. There is more than a touch of arrogance in our efforts to alter the domestic behavior of allies, or even of adversaries.

As noted above, the Foreign Assistance Act states that a principal goal of U.S. policy is to promote internationally recognized human rights abroad. Further, Title IX of the Act says that U.S. aid should be used to encourage "democratic private and local government institutions" within the recipient states. The implications of this seemingly innocent phrase are disquieting. Should U.S. assistance be used to alter domestic institutions? Should we insist on an ideological or reform test before providing economic or military aid? Is this not a form of uninvited interference in domestic matters? If we take sovereign equality seriously, we will recognize that the people of every state should determine their own system of justice and how they want to defend themselves against domestic or foreign dangers.

Other states may request assistance from friendly governments on mutually agreed terms. But external forces, however nobly motivated, cannot impose justice, human rights, or freedom on other states without resorting to conquest. It may be possible to "export revolution"—as the phrase goes—but we cannot export human rights or respect for the rule of law. Freedom and justice are the fruit of long organic growth nurtured by religious values, personal courage, social restraint, and respect for law. The majesty of law is little understood in traditional societies where ethnic identity tends to supersede all other claims on loyalty and obedience.

6.   Distorting Foreign Policy Objectives

A consistent and single-minded invocation of a human rights standard in making U.S. foreign policy decisions would subordinate, blur, or distort other essential considerations. After all, our foreign policy has vital but limited goals—national security and international peace—both of which have a great impact on human rights. Aggressive war and tyranny are the two chief enemies of freedom and justice. Our efforts to deter nuclear war and nuclear blackmail are calculated to protect the culture and free institutions of Western Europe and North America. In the Third World we seek to maintain a regional stability conducive to responsible political development and mutually beneficial economic intercourse among states. Economic productivity alleviates stark poverty and thus broadens the range of cultural and political choice.

Therefore, our policies of nuclear deterrence should be determined by our understanding of the Soviet nuclear threat and our trade policies toward Moscow should be determined by our economic and security interests. Neither should be influenced, much less determined, by the extent of human rights violations in the Soviet Union. Likewise, in dealing with Third World countries, their foreign policy behavior should be the determining factor, not their domestic practices. Even though South Korea has an authoritarian government, we should continue our security support because it is a faithful ally under siege from a totalitarian neighbor and because its independence is vital to the defense of Japan and Japan's independence is vital to the U.S. position in the Western Pacific and the world.

THE PITFALLS OF SELECTIVE APPLICATION

These six conceptual flaws which underlie the human rights crusade have already led to unwise policies and if carried to their logical conclusion, could end in disaster. Perhaps the most widely criticized and resented aspect of the campaign thus far has been its capricious and selective application to both Communist states and American allies.

During his visit to Poland last December, President Carter raised the human rights issue several times in public. On the one hand, he criticized his hosts for not permitting a handful of dissident journalists to attend his press conference. On the other, he praised Poland's rights record (compared to that of other Eastern European states) and said: "Our concept of human rights is preserved in Poland," to which a Polish writer replied "The words are the same," but they "mean different things in the United States." The impropriety, not to say irony, of raising the sensitive rights issue in a Communist state whose fragile and problematic autonomy is precariously maintained at the sufferance of

a totalitarian superpower, did not seem to concern Mr. Carter. Nor did the fact that Poland is forced to imitate many of the repressive measures of its master. By focusing on the absence of a handful of dissenting journalists at his press conference when the entire Polish people are held in bondage by the Soviet Union, President Carter distorted and trivialized the real meaning of human rights.

The policy of the Administration and the Congress toward the Soviet Union has also been vacillating and confused, seemingly more intent on scoring merchandisable victories than on grappling with the fundamental problem. Were it not for the Jewish emigration issue, Moscow would probably be receiving less critical attention than it is. How else can one explain the almost complete neglect of the massive violation of civil and political rights in Communist China, North Korea, Vietnam, and Cambodia?

Cambodia provides a particularly poignant example of this double standard toward totalitarian countries. Since the Communists took over on April 17, 1975, reliable studies estimate that 800,000 to 1.5 million Cambodians have died by execution or from starvation and disease caused by the forced evacuations from cities. This means that one in every six or seven has perished in the ruthless Communist bloodbath. Yet, where is the outcry from the advocates of human rights? Why this strange silence about what may well be the most brutal atrocity of our century? Measured by relative population, the Communist purge in Cambodia has destroyed more lives than Hitler's concentration camps or Stalin's Gulag Archipelago.

The great silence can be explained in part by racial and ideological factors. To certain rights advocates it somehow seems more reprehensible if violations or brutality are directed toward members of a different race.

A white South African regime denying blacks the vote seems more morally repugnant than black regimes denying all citizens the vote (which is the case in most other African states). Filtered through a racist lens, it does not seem as bad for Cambodian Communists to murder thousands of innocent Cambodians—men, women, and children—as for a much smaller number of Cambodian soldiers to die in a war in which the United States was involved.

This suggests that an ideological factor is also present. A recent *Wall Street Journal* editorial pointed to the frequent alliance between liberal moral outrage and revolutionary causes: the "crimes of the Khmer Rouge, even though they dwarf some other state crimes of our times . . . have attracted less attention because they are inflicted in the name of revolution." One can only wonder what the reaction would be if the new government had employed "conservative" rhetoric and announced that it was going to cleanse the country of all socialist or Marxist influences.

Turning to American allies, some of the most articulate rights advocates concentrate their outrage on the very regimes that are under the most severe pressure from the totalitarians—South Korea, Taiwan, Iran, and Chile. The first three are geographically and militarily exposed to Communist power. Chile under Allende was the target of a massive internal and external assault by Marxist forces seeking to transform it into a Cuban-style dictatorship. All four of these states have authoritarian regimes, primarily in response to their present or recently endangered position, but in each the range of rights permitted or guaranteed by the regime is far greater than that of the Communist governments that seek to subvert or replace them. This suggests that the human rights standard is sometimes used, not to advance freedom, but as a cloak to attack anti-totalitarian allies.

Some rights advocates have simultaneously urged punitive policies against Chile and measures to normalize relations with Cuba. This is a double irony. Human rights are more honored in Chile than in Cuba and Chile is pursuing a more peaceful foreign policy than Cuba. Havana is a mischief maker on a grand scale, acting as a cat's-paw for Moscow. Castro, in addition to shoring up a minority regime in Angola with 19,000 Cuban troops, has sent Cuban soldiers to support the Marxist military junta in Ethiopia and to assist "revolutionary" regimes and other groups in a dozen other African states. . . .

This double standard is often promoted by the media. According to a tabulation of news stories, editorials, and signed opinion for 1976, the prestige media's big five—*New York Times, Washington Post,* and the TV evening news shows of ABC, CBS, and NBC—carried 227 items about rights violations in two allied countries, Chile and South Korea, in contrast to only 24 stories about violations in three Communist countries, North Korea, Cuba, and Cambodia. The tabulation drawn up by Accuracy in Media follows: (See Table I on page 361.)

The content of the items was not examined, but the bias was clearly revealed by the inordinate attention given the small human rights sins of two loyal allies compared to the massive sins of three totalitarian adversaries—a ratio of almost ten to one.

Admittedly, it is far easier to get reliable information about the imperfections of authoritarian societies than those of closed, totalitarian states, but this is hardly an excuse for the media which pride themselves on vigorous investigative reporting. certainly a little effort could have yielded considerably more data on violations in Cambodia, North

TABLE I

	Chile	South Korea	North Korea	Cuba	Cambodia
New York Times	66	61	0	3	4
Washington Post	58	24	1	4	9
ABC-TV	5	2	0	0	1
CBS-TV	5	3	0	0	2
NBC-TV	3	0	0	0	0
Totals:	137	90	1	7	16

Korea, and Cuba, to say nothing of China where both blunt and subtle forms of repression have been developed into an exquisite craft.

The lopsided application of human rights criteria is justified by White House and State Department spokesmen on pragmatic grounds. They frankly admit that they give more critical attention to allies than to adversaries because they have more leverage over the former—we can withhold or threaten to withhold aid from our friends, so why not strike a blow for freedom where we can, or, if one prefers, why not administer the two-by-four to a mulish friend?

WHAT IS AMERICA'S RESPONSIBILITY?

In a formal and legal sense, the U.S. Government has no responsibility—and certainly no authority—to promote human rights in other sovereign states. But this is hardly the whole story. Because of our heritage, our dedication to humane government, our power, and our wealth, we Americans have a moral responsibility, albeit ill-defined, in the larger world consistent with our primary obligations at home and commensurate with our capacity to influence external events. We are almost universally regarded as a humanitarian power and as the champion of freedom and decency. We should be proud of our humane occupation policies in Germany and Japan. But we enjoy no occupation rights now, and the role of our government abroad is less clear. Saying this, the American people and their government can make two major contributions to the cause of human rights in other countries.

First, in the spirit of John Quincy Adams and Lincoln, we can be worthy custodians of the freedom bequeathed us by the Founding Fathers and thus continue to give heart to the aspirations of peoples everywhere. We can give hope to those in bondage by illustrating what the late Reinhold Niebuhr has called "the relevance of the impossible ideal." We can never fully realize our own ideals. And in most other cultural settings, full respect for human rights cannot be expected in the foreseeable future. A quick change in government will not enshrine liberty or justice. The message of our example is subdued, but not without hope—the struggle for a bit more freedom of choice or a better chance for justice is a never-ending one and after small gains have been made, eternal vigilance is vital to avoid sliding back into bondage. Serving as an example of decency, then, is our most effective way to nudge forward the cause of human dignity.

Second, our government can advance human rights by strengthening our resolve and our resources to defend our allies who are threatened by totalitarian aggression or subversion. This requires security guarantees, military assistance, and in some cases the presence of U.S. troops on foreign soil. Our combined effort to maintain a favorable balance of power has succeeded in preserving the independence of Western Europe, Japan, and South Korea. But because of our half-hearted commitment, we failed in Vietnam, Cambodia, and Laos, and in a different sense, in Angola. . . .

Beyond serving as a good example and maintaining our security commitments, there is little the U.S. Government can or should do to advance human rights, other than using quiet diplomatic channels at appropriate times and places. Moscow and other governments should be reminded of their pledges in the United Nations Charter and the Helsinki Agreement. Public preaching to friend or foes has limited utility. As we have already seen, it is both embarrassing and counter productive to threaten punitive measures against friendly, but less than democratic, regimes which are attempting to achieve a reasonable balance between authority and freedom at home, often under severely trying circumstances, and are pursuing constructive policies abroad.

THE IRONY OF VIRTUE

The Carter Administration is not of one mind on the significance, purpose, or effects of the human rights crusade. The administration is even less united in the implementation of the program in specific cases. During his visit to Iran last December, President Carter gave his final approval for the sale of six to eight nuclear reactors to that country whose government has been the target of human rights activists as well as of Marxist groups. Alleged rights violations

by the Shah's government have apparently had little effect on U.S. arms sales there. The same appears to be true of South Korea. In fact, some observers believe that the entire campaign so far has been more rhetoric than reality, and some suggest that it was launched more to satisfy the impulses of U.S. domestic groups than to effect real changes in the external world.

In any event, there appears to be a growing recognition of the moral and political limitations of a foreign policy crusade which, to repeat Mr. Carter, is based on "constant decency" and "optimism." While defending the campaign in principle, Secretary of State Cyrus Vance notes some of the reservations and flaws developed above. In a Law Day address, April 30, 1977, Mr. Vance warned against a "self-righteous and strident" posture and said "we must always keep in mind the limits of our power and of our wisdom." He added that "a doctrinaire plan of action" to advance human rights "would be as damaging as indifference. . . ."

The canons of prudence, statesmanship, and accountability all suggest that the President tone down his rhetoric. He should quietly recognize the political and moral limits of promoting particular reforms in other societies. He should recognize that a policy rooted in a presumption of American righteousness and in our capacity to sponsor virtue in other states often leads to the opposite effect. In some circumstances, the invocation of a rigid standard could undercut our security ties and invite a disaster in which millions of persons would move from partial freedom to tyranny.

Mr. Carter's policy is full of irony, precisely because his good intentions may lead to dire consequences. Irony is not the result of evil intention or malice, but rather of a hidden defect in virtue. In Mr. Carter's case, at least in rhetoric, the defect is a kind of vague, romantic optimism with an excessive confidence in the power of reason and good-will. This comforting view of human nature, the child of the Enlightenment and Social Darwinism, differs sharply with the more sober Biblical understanding of the nature and destiny of man. Be that as it may, the President should not be judged on his philo-sophical consistency, but rather by the actual policies he pursues. Since there is some re-lation between how one thinks and feels and what one does, it is not inappropriate to recall the words of columnist Michael Novak: "One of the best ways to create an immoral foreign policy is to try too hard for a moral one."

Part Five

PROSPECTS FOR WORLD ORDER IN THE 1980s

XVI

Prospects For World Order in the 1980s

We come in this last chapter to an examination of the nature of the problems that presently confront the nations of the world and alternative models for their resolution. It is probably clear by now that this is a distinctive age —the culmination of processes that had their origins in the political, scientific and industrial revolutions of the eighteenth and nineteenth centuries. Although we are still compartmentalized into national states and expect our government to guarantee us security, economic well-being, and an orderly life, the conditions of that life are increasingly dependent upon economic developments beyond our control, and order is at the mercy of forces and weapons that may destroy us all.

Moreover, as Daniel Bell explains in the selection that follows, the affluence that for the last twenty-five years has softened greed and class inequities within our society (and in the developed world generally), and the economic and military power that permitted Washington to manage the international system, have suddenly dwindled. There are those who argue that America is only suffering a loss of nerve and an abdication of will to act as a great power in the aftermath of Vietnam, which will have devastating consequences if not overcome.[1] This is not a demonstrable proposition, and in any case it would require a mobilization of will and material resources in the U.S. and among our allies that is just not forthcoming. Had our government not squandered so much of our national wealth and confidence in Vietnam, it is conceivable that we would have had the will to break the Arab oil "heist," but since we put so much stress on the sanctity of private property, it is hard to see how we could justify interfering with the right of the OPEC countries to do with their property as they wish.

Instead, we may yet take cognizance that most of our problems depend on working out cooperative relations with others and on overcoming impasses to action within our own society and between ourselves and our allies.

Bell points out that many of the problems that confront the capitalist world today are the same ones that brought on the 1929 depression and the rise of Fascism and Nazism. The principal difference is that in the 1930s the national state still had the means to pull the economy and society together again. "But the national state [today] is an ineffective instrument for dealing with the scale of major economic problems and decisions which will be necessary in the new world economy that has grown up."

There are generally two alternatives presented for achieving a manageable world order. One with which the U.S. has been operating for the past decade is the balance-of-power model. This model was taken up and popularized by Nixon and Kissinger as a replacement for the global-leadership model that had broken down so badly in Vietnam. The balance-of-power model postulates that each state by acting to preserve and enhance its security and national capability will maintain a stable system. This does not mean that there will not be international violence and the danger of war. But the balance of power model postulates that, despite increasing scarcity, technological uncertainties (new nuclear powers, new weapons, etc.), and interdependence, there is sufficient adaptiveness and innovativeness in the sovereign state system so that order can be preserved. Under the balance-of-power model no change will be required in the values by which we presently live and manage our affairs; each state will be the judge of its own best interest, and no motivation for questioning the present distribution of wealth and values within and between societies will be needed, because any disruptive tendencies will be handled by the efficacious workings of the balance of power.

Of course, this model does not ask what the consequences will be for the several billion people who have to accept their fate as a result of their inferior power, nor does it really guarantee against non-rational behavior. As Walter Burrows points out, at most the balance-of-power system operates in such a way that competitive actors pursuing their self-interest are likely

[1]Good examples of this viewpoint are to be found in COMMENTARY, in conservative quarters generally, and in the writings of Paul Seabury, Michael Curtis, Richard Pipes, and others.

"to shun or minimize war as a rational course of action."[2] But what if the Soviet side cannot refrain from taking advantage of the disorder and chaos that exists in parts of the Third World—disorder and chaos for which the balance of power offers no solution? How much assurance do we have against an accidental or escalatory war? "Implicit has been the assumption that *all* the great powers however rational, can to a high degree tolerate ambiguity, process communications, handle uncertainty, impose self-control, and maneuver flexibility."[3] But we already know that this is not characteristic of behavior under crisis conditions. The danger of war exists precisely because there is no guarantee—that under conditions of stress and crisis, statesmen will manifest these qualities. Instead of requiring a change of values, the balance-of-power model depends upon technique to avoid the worst disaster.

The balance-of-power approach does not ask us to adopt a different set of values toward our fellow men. Instead it relies upon technique to avoid disaster. "Indeed," writes Burrows, "it is probably correct to say that more resources will be invested in techniques for dealing with the environment in a balance of power system than in one where a less competitive set of norms prevails."[4] Bell proffers a similar nostrum. On the one hand, he warns that "the existing of political structures no longer match the underlying economic and social realities, and just as disparities of status and power may be a cause for revolution, so the mismatch of scales [political states—global economics] may be the source of disintegration." Yet, Bell still hopes that by giving freer play to the market mechanism breakdown can be avoided.

An alternative model for behavior is one which, while not doing away with the nation-state—with which people identify too strongly for it to be abolished—calls for a modification of the values which up until now have governed the conduct of states. The traditional state system assumes that domestic politics stops at the water's edge and that the framing of national goals and policy is made exclusively with an eye to security and other so-called national interests of the state, as distinct from the individuals who live within it. But the view of the state as an autonomous actor is anachronistic, because international relations now involve as many economic, ethical, ideological, and moral determinations affecting both individuals and domestic interests as do domestic politics; and, vice versa, the content and style of domestic policy making is having an increasing impact upon international politics. Secondly, the political and economic values can no longer be separated; just as order at home has required that the weak and poor be included in the national community, so they cannot be ignored if order is to prevail in the world community. The domestic tensions of all industrial

[2]Walter Burrows, "Can the State Centric Model Survive until 1984?" Paper 1973.
[3]*Ibid.*
[4]*Ibid.*

and industrializing societies are increasingly spilling over onto the international scene. And, "more perturbing to national politics and thus more threatening, are the direct effects of the international [dis]order on the tug-of-war between privilege and equality that is the stock-in-trade of all domestic politics."[5]

Under these circumstances, acting out of exclusive self-interest is only likely to worsen the crisis for the weaker countries. Going abroad with "no acceptance of the mutuality of obligations, no felt need to compromise, and no desire to establish a community of interests involving the happiness of living and sharing together [conversely, acting multilaterally] . . . is much the same as one seeks to create a national community within one's own borders."[6]

Such an approach cannot rely exclusively upon technique to achieve international order. As the late Kalman Silvert, a noted Latin-Americanist observes,

> The notion that techniques alone can solve our problems remains with us in both international and domestic affairs. The pretense is made that politics can be understood and administered in an essentially value-free way, as a play of effective desires and pressures among participants in the "game." In this construction balance of power politics abroad are the same as interest group politics at home. One must simply accept the rules of play, and let power plus perceived interest work themselves out—all the while making certain that one's own power and explicit recognition of interest are maintained at as high a pitch as possible.[7]

The value-free pragmatism and neutrality of such an approach is not possible when the nature of the world system is itself in contention.

> Fundamental choice is unavoidable and thus amorality is impossible when the survival of societies and their systems of behavior and beliefs are at stake. . . . There are no *technical* solutions to basic *policy* problems, only political ones; and *all* political solutions are seated in ideologies—in systems of belief that interpret the past, justify present behavior, and seek to control the future in derived ways. . . . To continue a pretense of "pragmatic" amorality associated with the balance of power is only to invite self-delusion, unreason, hence, failure.[8]

Does this mean that we should cast our foreign policy in terms of ideological crusade? Not at all. It means that we should be aware that, in their essence, international problems are political problems requiring the promise of justice and equity as well as the application of power if that power is to have the appearance of being exercised legitimately.

[5]Kalman Silvert, ESSAYS IN UNDERSTANDING LATIN AMERICA (Philadelphia: Institute for the Study of Human Issues, 1977) p. 149.

[6]*Ibid.*

[7]*Ibid*, p. 150

[8]*Ibid*, pp. 151–52

Increasingly in the 1950s and 1960s, the balance of power meant that the United States made common cause with ruling elites and military juntas in defense of security and privilege, but at the cost of enormous stress and a crippling inability to deal flexibly and equitably with problems surging from rapidly changing economic, technical, and demographic factors. A pursuit of too exclusive a national interest in a world in which problems can only be mastered on a multilateral basis, and therefore in terms of the real needs and problems of people everywhere, is likely to be counterproductive in the long run, as we have already discovered in Vietnam and elsewhere.

> In a time of increasing entanglement of domestic with international affairs, we have no sound choice but to want for others what we want for ourselves. What we should expect is not any instant equalization of physical [and material] conditions. . . . What we can rationally desire in common has to do with a process—the procedures by which societies can satisfy material wants for their populations and find ways to organize themselves so that they can [survive in order and] constantly expand their ability to reduce alienation and master their national life.[9]

The balance of power will provide the touchstone for American strategy in dealing with the Soviet Union. Despite detente, our relations are still those of adversaries. But relations with our allies and with the Third World are of a different order; there, we depend upon a spirit of cooperation and community if we are not to make them into adversary relations. You do not build community by adhering to the balance of power. If we are to fend off the Soviet Union, we must achieve the work for the stability and integration of the non-communist world; building cooperation and community, without which anarchy threatens, is a political task quite different from manipulating the balance of power. Technique is not enough; there must also be a concern for others and a sense of what is right and just. This can only come about if we, as the richest and still strongest nation in the free world, can provide the example and leadership by subordinating self interest to the collective interest. This does not require a change in human nature or the abandonment of our national self-identity. We have already shown that living in a national community is possible; why not a world community? And we have already shown imaginativeness and generosity in cooperating with others. Why not ask what it would take in changes within our own selves, and in the way in which our economy and government presently function, to make good the still lacking ingredient in our relations with others.

The final selection, "The Search for Peace" by John Lovell, provides an example of the kind of thinking—in this case, about the eradication of war—that is needed to see clearly how we may advance out of the jungle (or state of nature) into a more civilized system of international relations.

[9]*Ibid.*

40 The Future World Disorder: The Structural Context of Crises

Daniel Bell

The, author is Professor of Sociology at Harvard University.

. . . What follows is . . . not a forecast of the next decade . . . but an effort to sketch the broad socio-economic context which, at its loosest, will constrain policy makers and pose, in direct form, as yet unresolved dilemmas.

From 1948 to 1973, there was a 25-year boom in the world economy which was greater than that of any previous period in economic history. Gross Domestic Product, in real terms, increased by more than three and a half times, a world rate of over 5 percent a year. Japan's growth was almost double that rate; Britain's was half. This real per capita growth was shared almost equally by about half the world (the middle-income countries—e.g., Brazil and Mexico—being slightly the largest gainers). The very poor countries grew at an annual rate of 1.8 percent, small in comparison with the others, respectable on the basis of their own past.

The same period saw two extraordinary sociological and geopolitical transformations in the social structures of the world. Within the Western advanced industrial societies, there was the transition to a more open and egalitarian society. . . . that complex of new social rights which is summed up in the ideas of the Welfare State, what I have called

Reprinted with permission from FOREIGN POLICY magazine #27 (Summer 1977) Copyright 1977 by National Affairs, Inc. (Footnotes omitted.)

the "revolution of rising entitlements," and the greater freedom in culture and morals. . . .

The second transformation, which in historical perspective is of greater import for the future, was the end of the old international order with a rapidity that had been almost entirely unforeseen, and the emergence of a bewilderingly large number of new states of vastly diverse size, heterogeneity, and unevenly distributed resources. As a result of this development, the problem of international stability in the next 20 years will be the most difficult challenge for those responsible for the world polity. Some of the consequences of this transformation have been conceptualized as new North-South divisions, cutting across the East-West divisions which have been the axis of Great Power conflicts for almost all of modern times. . . . The fact remains that, just as within the advanced industrial societies of the West, so in the world at large, there has been a vast multiplication of new actors, new constituencies, new claimants in the political arenas of the world.

Underlying both these changes (though not determining them) have been two extraordinary technological revolutions: the revolution which has tied the world together in almost real time and the rise of the new science-based industries of what I have called the postindustrial society. The revolutions have given the Western countries an extraordinary advantage in high technology, and paved the way (if one can handle the huge problems of economic dislocation and displacement) for the transfer of a large part of the routinized manufacturing activities of the world to the less-developed countries.

III

These structural changes, which have been taking place within each advanced industrial society and in the world economy, have created a new kind of "class struggle," with a greater potential for social instability and difficulties of governance than those characteristic of the old industrial order. . . .

In this situation, the salient social struggles in the advanced . . . industrial societies are less between employer and worker, . . . than between organized social groups—syndicalist (such as trade unions), professional (such as academic, medical, scientific research complexes), corporate (business and even nonprofit economic enterprises), and intergovernmental units (states, cities, and counties)—for the allocation of the state budget. And as state tax policy and direct state disbursements become central to the economic well-being of these groups, and as political decision-making rather than the market becomes decisive for a whole slew of economic questions (energy policy, land use, communications policy, product regulation and the like), the control and direction of the political system, not market power, becomes the central question for the society.*

*Editors' note: Many economists and political scientists would challenge Bell on this point, contending that the scale and power of business and banking conglomerates acting independently of the market are still as powerful as ever. See Charles Lindblom, *Politics and Markets* (New Haven: Yale U. Press, 1977).

The corollary fact, that economic dealings between nations become more subject to national political controls, means that the international political arena becomes the cockpit for overt economic demands by the "external proletariat" (to use Tonybee's phrase) of the world against the richer industrial nations.

It is in this context that the worldwide recession which began in 1973 acquires such brutal significance. If the economic growth which has been the means of raising a large portion of the world into the middle class—and also a political solvent to meet the rising expectations of people and finance social welfare expenditures—cannot continue, then the tensions which are being generated will wrack every advanced industrial society and polarize the confrontation between the "south" (in all probability tied more and more to the "east") and the advanced industrialized, capitalist societies of the West. . . .

In a crucial sense, the modern era is defined as the shift in the character of economies—and in the nature of modern economic thinking—from supply to demand. For thousands of years, the level of supply (and its low technological foundation) dictated the standard of living. What has been singular about modern life is the emphasis on demand, and the fact that demand has become the engine of economic advance, moving entrepreneurs and inventors into the search for new modes of productivity, new combinations of materials and markets, new sources of supply, and new modes of innovation. The re-entry of a destroyed Germany and Japan into the world economy; the rapid industrialization of Brazil, Mexico, Taiwan, Korea, Algeria, South Africa, and similar countries; the expanding world trade of the Soviet-bloc countries—the revolution of rising expectations and the urge to get into the middle class—have all produced this extraordinary synchronization.

Yet, while we have the genuine foundations of a world economy, we evidently lack those cooperative mechanisms which can adjust these different pressures, create a necessary degree of stabilization in commodity prices, and smooth the transition to a new international division of labor that would benefit the world economy as a whole. . . .

If one looks ahead to the next decade, there are four structural problems that will confront the advanced industrial societies in the effort to maintain political stability and economic advance.

1.   The Double Bind of Advanced Economies

The facts that every society has become so interconnected and interdependent and that the political system has taken on the task of managing, if not directing, the economy mean that, increasingly, "someone" has to undertake the obligation of thinking about the system "as a whole." When the economic realm had greater autonomy, the shocks and dislocations generated through the market could be walled off, or even ignored—though the social consequences were often enormous. But now all major shocks are increasingly *systematic*, and the political controllers must make decisions not for or against particular interests, powerful as these may be, but for the consequences to the system itself. . . .

In practical fact, this major change has resulted in the sharp rise in government expenditures over the last 40 years and in social expenditures in the last decade and a half. Since 1950, the growth in public expenditure, per year, has been between 4.3 percent in Great Britain, at the low end of the scale, to 11.6 percent for Italy, at the high end. In these years, the growth in GNP has been

from 2.8 percent a year in Britain to 5.7 percent in Germany. (Italy was growing at 5.3 percent a year.) As a share of GNP, public expenditure varies from 30 percent of GNP in France to 64 percent in Sweden, which has experienced the highest growth in the 25-year period. (Italy's public expenditure is 58 percent of GNP, Britain's is 53 percent, and the United States' is 38 percent.)

These rates of growth of public expenditures over a quarter of a century, in countries such as Great Britain and Sweden—almost 50 to 75 percent greater than the growth of GNP—raise some complex economic and social questions. . . . Richard Rose calls it "overload"—the condition in which expectations are greater than the system can produce—and speculates whether nations can go bankrupt.

Jurgen Habermas calls it a "legitimation crisis," putting it into the larger philosophical context of political justifications. Under the prevailing tenets of the liberal theory of society, each individual is free to pursue his own interests and the rule of law is only formal and procedural, establishing the rules of the game without being interventionary. But the emerging system of state capitalism lacks the kind of philosophical legitimation that liberalism has provided. Samuel P. Huntington and Samuel Brittan have argued that democracies are becoming increasingly ungovernable, because the "democratization of political demands," in the Schumpeterian sense of the term, is subject to few constraints, or fewer than those represented by the limited credit available to individuals or firms that at some point would have to pay their debts, rather than "postpone" them by increasing the public debt.

I think these diagnoses are all accurate but partial. For the issue concerns not only the democracies but *any* society which seeks economic growth, yet has to balance the needs (if not the public demands) of its citizens for satisfactions and security. The Soviet Union could emphasize growth (a naked "primitive accumulation," in Marx's very sense of the term) by promises of a utopian tomorrow, the brutal repression of its peasants, and the direct and indirect coercion of its workers. But how long could this go on? It is evident that the next generation of Soviet rulers will face more and more demands, open or disguised, for the expansion of social claims, as well as for some influence (particularly among the managerial elites) over the allocation of state budgets.

The problem already exists in Poland, where Gierek—who in that sense faces the same problems as Denis Healey*—has to worry about capital formation for the renovation of Polish industry, yet maintains high prices for peasants as inducements to produce, and food subsidies for workers to keep *their* prices down. When he sought to realign the system by raising food prices, as economic logic compelled him to, he had almost a full-scale revolt by the workers on his hands. In fact, one can say that Poland is probably the only real Socialist government in Europe since it is the government most afraid of its working class.

If one searches for a solution, the double bind manifests itself in the fact that inflation or unemployment have become the virtual trade-offs of government policy, and governments are in the difficult position of constantly redefining what is an "acceptable" level of unemployment and an "acceptable" level of inflation. It is compounded by the fact that where there are deflationary pressures, particularly within declining economies, every group seeks to escape the necessary cut in its standard of living or its wealth, so that the pressures toward a greater corporate organization of society (and

*Gierek is the Prime Minister of Poland; Healey, the British Chancellor of the Exchequer, comparable to the U.S. Secretary of the Treasury.

the ability to use that corporate power for wage indexing or tax advantages) increase, and the heaviest burdens fall on the unorganized sections of the society, largely sections of the poor and the middle classes. The final irony is that with all the money being spent on social expenditures there is an evident sense that the quality of the services is poor, that the social-science knowledge to design a proper health system, or a housing environment, or a good educational curriculum, is inadequate, and that large portions of these moneys are increasingly spent on administrative and bureaucratic costs.

2. Debt and Protectionism

Almost every Western society, as a result of Keynesian thinking, has stimulated its economy in the last 40 years by means of deficit financing and pump priming . . . with the result that it has incurred ever deeper debts. . . .

The difficulty in most countries today is that not only has the "internal" debt level been mounting steadily, but there is also a rising "external" debt which presumably has to be repaid at some point. And it is the combination of the two which seems so threatening to the stability of the international monetary system.

The major problem is the growth of external debt. To meet its obligations, Great Britain has now borrowed about $20 billion dollars, quite a low figure compared to its internal debt. Yet that money has to be repaid. To obtain money from the International Monetary Fund (IMF), Britain (like Italy, which is in a similar situation) has had to comply with various stringencies imposed by the IMF as its "price" for the loan, one of these being even larger cuts in public expenditures than the Labour party had planned.

But the question of external debt is a minor one, as yet, for the advanced industrial societies. The heaviest burdens fall on the non-oil-producing less-developed countries, about a hundred in number. A conservative estimate by the Organization for Economic Cooperation and Development (OECD) in its Economic Outlook of December 1976 puts the figure at roughly $186 billion (some estimates go as high as $220 billion), most of this incurred in recent years as a result of the rise in oil prices. Projections of that debt in 1985 go from nearly $350 billion to $500 billion. For these countries, the ratio of *external* debt to GNP is about 25 percent; by 1985 it would rise to 45 percent.

If one takes the conservative figure of the aggregate external debt in 1976 as $190 billion, the deficit trade balance (imports over exports) is about $34 billion, and the debt service about $13 billion. This makes, for 1976, a total of $47 billion as the amount of *additional* external borrowing required. If one takes the scenario to 1985, and an external debt of $500 billion, the projected trade deficit would be $52 billion and the debt service $34 billion, or a requirement of $86 billion in that year from the "richer" countries.

How can this be done? In 1974 to 1976, two-thirds of the Third World's borrowing (of $78 billion) was financed by the recycling of petrodollars through the Western banks. But how long can this continue? Any new loans would have to come from international agencies such as the IMF. But one of the conditions that the IMF usually imposes is that debtor countries reduce or eliminate their payments deficits—and this can be done only by the sizable reduction of imports.

In effect, the very discipline that an IMF would impose could only lead to a heightened economic nationalism and protectionism.

The British Left is advocating a "siege economy." But the pressures for protectionism are evident in almost every country that is feeling the shock of dislocations under competitive pressures. Japan, as every country knows, has subtly kept many foreign products outside its home market, while allegedly "dumping" various products onto other markets. The United States has begun retaliating by raising the tariff on Japanese television sets. American trade unions, once largely for free trade, are now completely protectionist, and the maritime unions have often been successful in their demands that various subsidized exports be carried in American bottoms.

The 1929 world depression came when Britain decamped from international free trade and instituted "imperial preference"; actions soon followed by other countries, such as the United States, going off the gold standard and imposing export controls on capital. None of the present-day pressures exist on the same scale. But there is a great temptation for many countries, Britain included, to have a go at the game of protectionism. . . .

3. The Demographic Tidal Wave

The third structural problem derives from demographic change, particularly in Latin America and Asia. Most demographic discussions have focused on the problem of the size of the world's population by the year 2000—whether it would be six billion or seven billion, and whether the world could sustain those numbers. But in any immediate sense, the year 2000 is not the issue. A scrutiny of the accompanying table shows what *is* urgent: *the percentage of the age cohort now under 15 years of age.* This is a

TABLE I

Area or Country	Population 1975	Population Growth Rate	% Urban	Inflation Rate	Population under 15 (%)
Latin America	327.6	2.9	60.4		43
Mexico	59.3	2.4	63.2	22.5	48
Brazil	113.8	2.9	59.5	32.7	42
Colombia	24.7	3.2	61.8	31	47
Venezuela	12.0	2.9	82.4	11.9	45
Chile	10.7	1.9	83.0	365	40
Argentina	25	1.5	80		29
Asia	2,407.4	2.5			
India	636.2	2.6	21.5	31	42
Bangladesh	79.6	3.0	6.8	100	45
Pakistan	71.6	3.6	26.9	*	44
Indonesia	137.9	2.7	19.3	34.4	45
Philippines	44.7	3.2	36	30	43
Thailand	42.3	3.1	16.5	21.3	46
China	942	2.4	23.5	*	36
Japan	111.9	1.3	75.2		24
Africa	420.1	2.8	24.5		44
Nigeria	81.8	2.5	23.1	12	45
Ethiopia	28.8	2.6	11.2		45
Zaire	24.9	2.8	26.2	29.3	44
Egypt	37.2	2.2	47.7		42
Algeria	16.8	3.3	49.9		47
Europe (Excluding USSR)	474.2	0.8	67.2		26
United Kingdom	56.2	0.2	78.2		24
France	53	0.8	76.1		25
W. Germany	62.6	0.5	83.4		23
E. Germany	16.8	− 0.4	74.9		21
Poland	34.0	0.9	56.5		25
USSR	254.3	0.9	60.5		29
USA	219.7	1.0	76.3		27

* Not available.

group already alive, which within the next decade will flood the schools and labor markets of the less-developed countries.

If one looks ahead to the next decade, what is striking is the extraordinarily high proportion of young people in Latin America (with the exception of Argentina), Asia (except Japan), and Africa. In Europe, during the 1960s, the large number of "surplus" workers in Turkey, Yugoslavia, Greece, and southern Italy could be drawn "north" by the expanding economies of the Western European tier. . . .

But where will the "surplus" population of the developing world go in the coming years? The problem is compounded by the fact that there already exists in Latin America a high degree of urbanization, high inflation rates, and high unemployment or underemployment rates. Both Mexico and Brazil, whose industrial production have been growing at the astounding rates of between 12 and 15 percent a year,* are by now almost at the peak of their potential. Yet both face a doubling of the entry rates into schools and the labor force in the next decade.

Mexico, with its highly concentrated population in the Federal District of Mexico City—which contains about a fourth of the entire population of Mexico—is an especially sensitive case. In 1920, Mexico had a population of little more than 14 million persons. Fifty years later, it was more than 60 million (or more than almost every country in Western Europe), and by the end of the century it will probably have at least 100 million persons. The United States is belatedly waking up to the problem of millions of illegal aliens flowing across the border and finding sleazy jobs in small service and manufacturing establishments whose owners welcome the cheap, exploitable labor, since they need not pay large social fringe benefits, and the workers have to be docile lest they be deported. But what is the solution? Is one to string barbed wire across two thousand miles of border? Or engage in periodic dragnets in the major cities of the country? And can Mexico itself, facing these explosive problems of population, escape the risks of military dictatorship when its problems become "unmanageable"? What will foreign capital do under those circumstances? Can any of these questions be met without some form of international migration policy?

4. Rich and Poor Nations

The rich and the poor may always be with us, but in what proportions? One of the

*Editors' note: The lion's share of this increased wealth has accrued to the upper 10 percent of the population, while the lowest 40 percent of the population has suffered a relative and even an absolute reduction in living standards, health care and sanitation, and employment opportunities.

most striking facts about the period since World War II, in terms of its psychological impact, has been the growth in the world's middle class—using the term, crudely, to mean those who could purchase domestic electrical appliances, have a telephone, buy a car, use a stated amount of energy per capita, etc. According to the calculations of Nathan Keyfitz, between 1950 and 1970, the middle class grew from 200 million to 500 million persons—to about 12.5 percent of the world's population, or more than 40 percent if we assume that this growth was largely within the rich and middle income countries. If we were able, in the next 20 years, to maintain that rate—4.7 percent a year achieved in the best period we have seen in world economic history—about 15 million of the 75 million persons who are being added to the world's population each year would be added to the middle class. But the remaining 60 million would be poor.

Of the many important issues between the rich and the poor nations, perhaps the most sticky, and the real time bomb in international economic relations, is that of industrialization. The goal of the developing countries, stated in the UNIDO Declaration and Plan of Action on Industrial Development and Co-operation issues agreed in Lima in 1975, is that *by the year 2000, the developing countries should account for at least 25 percent of the world's industrial production. . . .*

To put that figure in meaningful perspective, the growth rates of manufacturing output in the developed "market-economy countries" from 1960 to 1972 was 5.6 percent and for the "Socialist countries" 9.0 percent a year. The prospect of reaching the UNCTAD target, even by radical restructuring of the composition of the manufacturing output (i.e., a shift from light to heavy industry), is clearly improbable. . . .

What, then, is the answer? The ILO report, echoed by the UNCTAD document, states that *"if substantial income redistribution policies were introduced,* most developing countries would appear to achieve the basic needs objective by growth at an annual rate of approximately 7 to 8 percent," and that "the proposed strategy implies quite high levels of investment, without which there would be neither growth nor meaningful redistribution." The rhetoric is not that of the *Communist Manifesto.* Given the platforms, those of United Nations' agencies, the language is stiff and bureaucratic. Given the proponents, however, the key terms "substantial income redistribution" and "high levels of investment" have a menacing ambiguity. The point, however, is clear. Here is the agenda of international politics for the rest of the century. Whether the proponents of the "new international economic order" have the political or economic strength to enforce these demands, is another question.

V

If one reviews the nature of the structural situations facing the advanced industrial societies in the 1970s, what is striking are the parallels to the 1920s and 1930s. If one looks at the period not in terms of the character of the extremist movements of the time, but to understand why the Center could not hold—from the vantage point of the governments, so to speak—there were four factors that, conjoined, served to reduce the authority of the governments, imperil their legitimacy, and facilitate the destruction of the regimes. These were:

The existence of an "insoluble" problem.

The presence of a parliamentary impasse, with no group being able to command a majority.

The growth of an unemployed educated intelligentsia.

The spread of private violence which the ruling regimes were unable to check.

In that period, the "insoluble" problem was unemployment. No government had an answer. . . .

The parliamentary impasse arose out of the polarization of parties and, in the Latin countries, the unwillingness of the Socialist parties to enter "bourgeois governments" lest they be co-opted. . . .

The unemployed intelligentsia consisted of lawyers without clients, doctors without patients, teachers without jobs, the group that Konrad Heiden, the first historian of National Socialism, was to call "the armed Bohemians." The entire first layer of the Nazi party leadership, Goebbels, Rosenberg, Strasser, were of this stripe.

The spread of private violence arose out of the private armies of the extremist groups —the Black Shirts, the Brown Shirts, the Communists. . . .

The result, of course, was the rise of authoritarian and Fascist regimes in Portugal, Italy, Germany, Austria, and Spain, and the menacing threat of Fascist movements in France . . . in Belgium . . . and in Great Britain. . . . In these instances, the decisive support came from the middle class, which feared being declassed, and the traditionalist elements, which feared the rising disorder. When Hans Fallada asked, in the famous title of his novel, "Little Man, What Now?" the answer was a right-wing reaction as preferable to left-wing Bolshevism. The Center no longer had a chance in most of these countries.

If one looks at the situation in the 1970s, there are some sinister parallels. The insoluble problem is inflation. . . .

The increase in the educated intelligentsia is an obvious fact in every Western country, a product of demographic idiosyncrasy and deflationary cuts in public expenditures, but an explosive force no less, as is being shown in Italy today.

The private violence of the 1920s and 1930s is replaced by urban terrorism, fitful and sporadic in most cases, yet sufficiently menacing in Northern Ireland to turn that country into a garrison state. . . .

Even with the growing anxieties of the middle class, as in Denmark and Sweden and England, and, less obviously, in France and Italy, it is highly unlikely that any of the European countries will go Fascist, or see a strong right-wing reaction. These movements are too discredited politically and would lack any historical legitimacy. What is more likely to happen in Europe, as well as in many other countries, is *fragmentation*—both in geographical terms and as a result of the unraveling of the society in functional terms.

There are two reasons for the greater possibility of fragmentation as the likely response in the coming decade, and they are clearly visible. One is that most societies have become more self-consciously *plural* societies (defined in ethnic terms) as well as *class* societies. The resurgence of minority-group consciousness in almost every section of the world—in national, linguistic, religious, and communal terms—shows that ethnicity has become a salient political mechanism for hitherto disadvantaged groups to assert themselves. The second reason is that in a world marked by greater economic interdependence, yet also by a growing desire of people to participate at a local level in the decisions that affect their lives, *the national state has become too small for the big problems in life, and too big for the small problems.* In economic terms, enterprises seek regional or transnational locations, moving their capital and often their plants where there is the greatest comparative advantage. In sociological terms, ethnic and other groups want more direct control over decisions and seek to reduce government to a size that is more manageable for them.

The threat of *geographical* fragmentation can be seen in the United Kingdom, with possible devolution for Scotland and Wales; in Northern Ireland, with the bitter religious fratricide; in Belgium, with the traditional enmity of the Flemish and the Walloons; in Canada, on the linguistic issue between the French in Quebec and the English-speaking groups in the other provinces; in France, where there are small separatist movements in Corsica and in Brittany; in Spain, with the traditional claims for Catalonian and Basque autonomy; in Yugoslavia, where there are the smoldering rivalries of the Serbs, Croats, Slovenes, and Montenegrins; in Lebanon, where the binational state has fallen apart and become a client of Syria. Pakistan split apart into West Pakistan and Bangladesh. Nigeria has just survived a civil war, overcoming the threat of Biafran succession. In various African countries, in the landlocked areas of the Sudan, and Rwanda-Burundi, whole tribes and peoples are being quietly slaughtered, almost unnoticed.

Nor is the Soviet bloc immune. Politically, there has been a very real fragmentation in the loss of the earlier Stalinist hegemony over the countries of Eastern Europe and the European Communist parties. The unrest is ever latent in Poland and in Czechoslovakia. Within the Soviet Union, there is the evident unease at the shifting demographic balances that, by the year 2000, will make the Great Russians a minority in the Soviet world, and will produce a piquant situation where three of every ten recruits for the Soviet army will be Muslim.

Functionally, fragmentation consists of the effort of organized corporate groups to exempt themselves from the incomes policies that regimes inevitably have to resort to, in one way or another—through an overt social contract or through the tax mechanism—in order to reduce inflation. There is the likelihood in many countries of the breakup of the party systems. Though such structures have a powerful life of their own, in many countries they evidently do not reflect underlying voter sentiment. In Britain, the majority of people are for the "center," yet the party machines fall into the hands of the more extreme right-wing, as in the Conservative party, or in the hands of the left-wing, as is almost the case in the Labour party. Where the party system does not break up, there is a greater likelihood of volatility, with individuals arising—as did Jimmy Carter—to present themselves as "protest" candidates, and, using the mechanisms of primaries, direct elections, and the visibility generated by the media, catapult themselves into office.

VI

Is there a way out? In principle, there is an answer. It is the principle of "appropriate scale." What is quite clear is that the existing political structures no longer match the underlying economic and social realities, and just as disparities of status and power may be a cause for revolution, so the mismatch of scales may be the source of disintegration.

What was evident in the 1930s, in a wide variety of political circumstances, was that the national state became the means to pull the economy and society together. If one looks back at the New Deal of Franklin D. Roosevelt, it was not "creeping socialism" or "shoring up capitalism" that characterized his reforms (though there were elements of both in his measures), but the effort to create national political institutions to manage the national economy that had arisen between 1910 and 1930. By shifting the locus of policy from the states to the federal government, Roosevelt was able to carry out macroeconomic measures which later became more self-conscious, particularly as the tools of macroeconomic analysis (the ideas of national income accounts and GNP, both of which were only invented in the 1940s and were introduced in the Roosevelt budget message of 1945) came to hand.

But the national state is an ineffective instrument for dealing with the scale of major economic problems and decisions which will be necessary in the new world economy that has grown up, though national interests will always remain. The problem, then, is to design effective international instruments—in the monetary, commodity, trade, and technological areas—to effect the necessary transitions to a new international division of labor that can provide for economic and, perhaps, political stability. (It would be foolish, these days, to assert that economics determines politics; but the economic context is the necessary arena for political decisions to be effective.) Such international agencies, whether they deal with commodity buffer stocks or technological aid, are necessarily "technical," though political considerations will always intrude. Yet the creation of such mechanisms is necessary for the play of politics to proceed more smoothly, so that when some coordinated decisions are taken for political reasons, there is an effective agency to carry them out.

At the other end of the scale, the problem of decentralization becomes ever more urgent. The multiplication of political decisions and their centralization at the national level only highlight more nakedly the inadequacies of the administrative structures of the society. The United States, as Samuel

P. Huntington once remarked, still resembles a Tudor polity in its multiplication of townships, counties, incorporated or unincorporated villages. With such overlapping jurisdictions and inefficiencies not only are costs —and taxes—multiplied, but services continue to decline. We have little sense of what is the appropriate size and scope of what unit of government to handle what level of problem. What is evident is that the overwhelming majority of people are increasingly weary of the large bureaucracies that now expand into all areas of social life—an expansion created, not so paradoxically, by the increased demand for social benefits. The double bind of democracy wreaks its contradictory havoc in the simultaneous desire for more spending (for one's own projects) and lower taxes and less interference in one's life.

Yet here, too, there is the possibility of a way out: the use of the market principle— the price mechanism—for social purposes. As against the ritualistic liberal, whose first reaction regarding any problem is to call for a new government agency or regulation, or the hoary conservative who argues that the private enterprise system can take care of the problems (it often cannot, for some coordinated action by a communal agency is necessary), one can use the market for social purposes—by giving people money and letting them buy the services they need in accordance with their diverse needs, rather than through some categorical program. . . .

[I]n a world where, at the large and small ends of the scale, social stability is threatened and governance becomes difficult, questions of domestic and foreign policy quickly intertwine. For if the national state is too small for the big problems of life and too big for the small problems, we have to begin to think—and, given the shortness of time and the specter in the streets, to concentrate the mind, as Dr. Johnson would have said— about what other political arrangements may be necessary to give us stability and freedom in this shrinking world.

41 The Search for Peace: an Appraisal of Alternative Approaches

John P. Lovell

The author is professor of Government at Indiana University.

(Following are excerpts from Professor Lovell's monograph, emphasizing some of his key points.)

This paper . . . provides a critical appraisal of the efforts of human beings to devise a remedy to the problem [of war] and to ensure continuing peace. A combination of approaches to peace that offer realistic hope of being attained is identified.

[Reviewing the history of the horror of war, especially as it pertained to the events of World War II, Professor Lovell concludes] It was widely believed that if another world war were to occur in the future, civilization literally might be threatened with extinction. This view became even more pronounced . . . when atomic weapons were introduced as an element of modern war at Hiroshima and Nagasaki. . . . The first words of the preamble to the Charter of the United Nations capture well the key concern of the signatory members: "We the people of the United Nations . . . (are) determined to save succeeding generations from the scourge of war, which twice in our lifetime has brought untold sorrow to mankind."

As we look back over the decades since the United Nations Charter was signed, we

Reprinted by permission of Professor Lovell and the International Studies Association.

must ask to what extent have the hopes of its founders been realized? The answer is tragically obvious. The number of nuclear powers continues to increase. Nuclear-tipped missiles continue to be poised in readiness to bring death to millions within minutes of launch. Furthermore, war in "conventional" form continues unabated. In *each* of the following wars since 1945 at least a million persons have been killed, wounded, or left homeless: the chronic Arab-Israeli dispute; the violent . . . encounters between Hindus and Moslems in India/Pakistan; the Korean War; the conflict in the Congo; the strife in Indonesia after 1965; the war in China in the waning years of its civil war (1948-1949); the war in Nigeria from 1967 to 1970, and the war in Indochina (Vietnam).

Some of the consequences of these wars have been that millions of persons have become refugees; that critical shortages of food, shelter, clothing, and medical supplies have occurred; that societies have experienced rampant inflation, black markets, hoarding, looting, and gross inequities in wealth; that there have come into being millions of individuals who will find it difficult, if not impossible, to adjust to the lives they face in the future; that tensions between various sectors in societies have been produced or aggravated; that the legitimacy of prevailing political institutions has been undermined; that the morale of many armies has likewise been undermined, producing disaffection; and that individuals as well as institutions have been corrupted by war.

One must ask some painful questions: Have the United Nations and other institutions committed to the preservation of peace been built on feet of clay? Have the principal approaches to peace, such as arms control, collective security, and mutual deterrence been totally misguided? Have explanations of the causes of war that have been advanced as diagnoses that would facilitate the search for cures been erroneous? Have peace movements typically been naive exercises in wishful thinking? Is war the inevitable consequence of man's aggressive tendencies?. . .

This paper answers no to all of these questions. A cautious optimism emerges from a careful assessment of the lessons of the past, a sifting and winnowing of the grains of truth from the chaff of error in the abortive earlier efforts to seek and maintain peace. The argument is advanced that the elements are present in the world now for combining short-range programs for the avoidance of nuclear holocaust with longer range programs for the development of both peaceful *and* just and humane societies—if energies and resources are properly mobilized and allocated.

[Professor Lovell next turns to the question of the eradicability of war. He cites evidence that war is not inevitable, that it is not based on an inherent aggressiveness or sinfulness in man.] In some groups, warfare is unknown. There is no evidence of pugnacious instincts. Human aggression is a secondary, or derived, impulse, not a primary one, like hunger or sex. However, he warns that once a social invention is made which proves congruent with human needs or social forms, it tends to persist. Hence,

measures for peace must include more than the design of "a better invention" than warfare for resolving conflict among and within nations. The other important component is that of devising institutions and structures that will meet human needs for challenge, commitment, and fulfillment while reducing the public willingness to engage in war.

The approaches to war prevention that especially have captured the attention and utilized the energies of the world's statesmen in recent decades have been: mutual deterrence; commitment to peaceful settlement of disputes; arms control and disarmament; an "all-for-one, one-for-all commitment to collective security; use of international peacekeeping forces to "encapsulate" conflicts and thereby keep them from escalating; developing of functional integration among nation-states; and promotion of a sense of world community. Efforts to devise a world government with authority that would transcend that of nation-states also should be mentioned. . . .

Each of these approaches has roots in the past. [Professor Lovell traces some of the roots of the various approaches, as well as the achievements and failures of each of them. His conclusion is as follows.]

Viewing each of several current approaches or proposals for the prevention or control of war in historical context cannot help but make one sensitive to the fact that none of the approaches offers a panacea in the search for peace. Yet it is erroneous to suppose that the failure of a particular effort to prevent war necessarily invalidates the concept or theory of war prevention upon which the effort was based. . . . Moreover, it is erroneous to suppose that because diverse approaches to peace rather than a single, unified approach characterized current efforts to prevent or control war, that advocates of the various approaches are oblivious to the complexity of the problem. . . .

Generalizations about the causes of war, and remedial procedures and institutions based upon such generalizations, must be modified and adjusted to fit the distinctive circumstances of particular wars. Failure of particular approaches in the past may reflect a failure to adapt the approach to distinctive existing circumstances. In short, the theories that underlie the various current approaches to war prevention and control . . . are not necessarily invalidated by the recurrence of war, nor by the inability of the theory to explain particular wars. . . .

The dynamics of conflict . . . have important implications for an appraisal of alternative approaches to preventing or ending wars. Conceptually one can picture four characteristic phases. A particular conflict may be resolved at any one level, and therefore not proceed to the next level. However, major conflicts (such as large-scale wars) typically have proceeded through all four levels prior to resolution.

The first phase, which might be described as a fermentation period, is one in which two parties become aware of conflicting interests, possessions, or goals. To the extent that grievances or demands of one party toward the other become expressed, it is characteristic of the first phase of conflict that they are confined to a few relatively specific issues. [Also] in the initial phase only a core leadership group on each side tends to be committed to a showdown. Thus conflict smolders below the level of confrontation.

In the fermentation phase, conditions tend to be favorable for peaceful resolution of the conflict if leaders can be found on both sides who are willing to seize the opportunity for a compromise solution. In many conflicts, however, events have moved from a fermentation stage to a confrontation between the parties. Key individuals on one side or another have acted in such a way as to bring smoldering disagreements to a head, and to provoke the other party to respond with increased militancy. Negotiation is still possible at the confrontation stage. But the militancy of demands that are made make peaceful resolution less probable than during the fermentation period.

Characteristically, once a conflict has become violent, the issues broaden and become blurred, with positions expressed in ideological rather than legalistic terms. Leadership often shifts at this stage from moderate to more militant hands.

Once a conflict has run the course from fermentation to confrontation to violence to escalation, a resolution may be achieved that greatly reduces the probability that confrontation and violence will erupt between them in the near future. For instance, the total defeat of Germany at the end of World War II made a recurrence of armed conflict between Germany and any of the Allied powers in the near future improbable. . . . In other disputes, however, even though a conflict has resulted in major loss of life, destruction and hardship to the parties involved, the manner in which violence is terminated has left fundamental issues between parties sufficiently unresolved and the capabilities of the parties to inflict injury on one another sufficiently intact as to pave the way for recurrent outbreaks of violence. . . . Sensitivity to the dynamic character of conflict situations alerts one to the fact that the effectiveness of measures and the durability of measures that can be applied to halt or brake a conflict will vary at different phases of the conflict. Resolution of a conflict is likely to be easiest in the earliest phases; yet, if initially effective, such measures are more likely to be durable than comparable measures applied later.

Although immediate concern about the prevention of nuclear war must remain paramount, there is no good reason why long-range concern with eradicating or reducing fundamentals, causes of war should be neglected. Indeed, myopic concern only with the most urgent, immediate problem might well mean that the underlying preconditions of war would thereby flourish, rather than diminish. Thus in the long run—and it might not be very long—an exclusively short-range approach to preventing war would prove self-defeating.

LONG-RANGE PROGRAMS FOR PEACE

The difficulties of designing effective long-range measures for improving the possibilities for world peace long have been recognized by many sophisticated observers of human affairs. Even if in a fundamental sense it is correct, as "tender-minded" proponents of long-range peace strategies characteristically maintain, that "wars begin in the minds of men," the problem of effecting significant changes in the values and beliefs—such as nationalism—that promote or condone war is immense.

The difficulties should not be minimized. Yet our modern-day sophistication is for naught if it only makes us aware of the complexity and inertia of existing institutions, and thus skeptical of visions of a radically better future. Sensitivity to the complexity and inertia of institutions ought to be a challenge, not an impediment. The long-range problem demands attention—and for reasons that go beyond the desirability of peace to include other values, such as those of justice and human development. In short, if "a better invention" than war is to be devised for the resolution of international conflicts, it needs to provide human

beings not only with order but also with fulfillment.

Some ideas that were discussed earlier . . . are included in Figure 1 as part of the long-range programs that are advocated here. Also needed, however, are measures designed to alter social, economic, and political institutions within societies, in ways that will improve the quality of life for individuals while posing challenges that will elicit from them commitment and a sense of purpose.

One might do worse than to revive and develop further William James' proposal for the development of a "moral equivalent to war." Writing prior to World War I, but at a time when the jingoistic spirit was prevalent in the United States, James described how a society might go beyond wishful speculation to detailed planning for the diversion of human energies and competitive impulses from destructive channels into peaceful ones.

Prevention of nuclear war must be of paramount concern to persons interested in peace. The problem is made more complex by the fact that wars may be triggered not only by deliberate acts of those centrally involved in a conflict but also in other ways. Profound miscalculation may lead nations into wars that neither their leaders nor their peoples wanted—and historical examples abound. A party peripheral to a dispute may, for its own reasons, aggravate the central parties in the conflict or engage in deception that makes one party believe that the other has committed an act that demands a warlike response (this is the so-called catalytic war, in which a third party acts as a catalyst to the conflict). Finally, especially in the missile age when delivery systems and nuclear devices are part of an intricate network of communications and control, war may start by accident.

FIGURE 1. Some Illustrative Distinctions between Short Range and Long Range Approaches to Peace.

	Range of Accomplishment Feasible or Anticipated	
	Short Range Control or elimination of war; or temporary reduction of incentives or capabilities for waging war	Long Range Elimination or reduction of preconditions of war
Possible requirements for successful accomplishment of objective	Mutual deterrence (balance of terror) Agreements for peaceful settlement of disputes Arms control and disarmament agreements UN peacekeeping; encapsulation of conflicts	Functional integration Cultivation of world community Fundamental change of domestic social, economic and political institutions

A thorough and adequate approach to the prevention of nuclear war must cope with all significant possibilities, and to do so implies a diversified approach. Measures are required, such as arms control, to keep tensions among the nuclear powers at controllable levels. The defenses of the nuclear powers must be maintained sufficiently to keep low the incentives for an adversary to launch a surprise attack: for the same reason, the rapid buildup by any one power of weapons and delivery systems must be prevented. Another important component of the diversified approach is that of maintaining direct communications among the nuclear powers (such as the so-called hot-line between Washington and Moscow). In time of crisis especially, such communications could prevent a tragic miscalculation. The approach requires also the cultivation of institutional channels (such as the United Nations) for negotiations, and the peaceful settlement of disputes not only between the superpowers, but also among the superpowers and other nations.

But prevention of nuclear war requires an approach directed not only at "harnessing" the nuclear powers, but also at keeping conflict among non-nuclear powers in check, because non-nuclear war could escalate into a nuclear exchange. The problem of keeping small wars limited is perhaps even more complex than that of keeping the nuclear powers from each other's throat. It is trite but true that the world is experiencing a time of revolutionary change. Especially in parts of Latin America, the Middle East, Africa, and Asia, we must expect important outbreaks of domestic violence and revolutionary insurrection for the foreseeable future. Can institutional means be devised that will encapsulate such conflicts and prevent them from fanning broader conflicts without serving to enforce the status quo and forward the forces of reaction at the expense of the oppressed? The question has not been answered satisfactorily in current world affairs, but remains an important challenge for persons concerned not only with peace but also with justice.

SHORT-RANGE AND LONG-RANGE GOALS

The ideas expressed [above] perhaps can be clarified further with reference to a hypothetical dialogue between persons who might be described as "tender-minded" advocates of peace and those who might describe themselves as "tough-minded" advocates of peace. Readers who have been attentive to policy discussions in the United States over the past two or three decades will recognize that the dialogue, although simplified for purposes of emphasis here, corresponds to genuine differences of viewpoint that have emerged in public debate. "Tender-minded" peace advocates are likely to express skepticism if not horror at the notion that nuclear deterrence can contribute to peace, and to contend that "lasting peace" can be attained only through the cultivation in mankind of a willingness to forego the use of violence to solve conflict. "tough-minded" persons, however (including many sincerely committed to world peace) are likely to scoff at the notion of effecting fundamental changes in human nature, and to argue that in any event, the urgent immediate problem is that of preventing nuclear war, thus deterrence and other measures, however expediential in nature, must be of paramount concern.

Although many readers will find themselves more in sympathy with one side than the other in such a dialogue, it is useful to recognize the extent to which both points of view can be accommodated once the ranges of accomplishment feasible or antici-

pated from the competing proposals are compared. We mentioned above phases of conflict, and introduced the notion that the efficacy and durability of various measures to prevent or control conflict will vary, depending on the phase at which they are introduced. Put in other words, we may speak on the one hand of approaches to peace that are directed toward immediate, or short-range goals (limiting a war that has already started, for instance) and on the other hand of approaches that are directed toward eliminating or ameliorating preconditions of war (as through measures recommended by the "tender-minded" for reducing popular inclination toward violence.) The relationship of current approaches to peace to these distinctions between short-range and long-range goals is suggested in Figure 1.

SOME IMMEDIATE NEEDS

"Tough-minded" persons who express skepticism about the importance of peace proposals aimed at effecting long-range changes of outlook among men are surely correct at least in the argument that a program for the long-range improvement of world harmony is of no avail if a nuclear war breaks out in the short run.

Like many fellow pacifists, William James had been alarmed at the war fever that had swept much of the country at the time of the Spanish-American War; he found especially repugnant the glorification of war and militarism rationalized in Darwinistic (survival of the fittest) terms by men such as Theodore Roosevelt or General Homer Lea. On the other hand, James believed that the "strenuous life" that Roosevelt extolled did indeed have something to commend it, if one were to regard its merits in less mystical and romantic terms than was characteristic of the militarists. By failing to recognize what was valid and potentially constructive in the arguments of the militarists and by offering instead only naive utopian formulas for peace, James felt that many of his fellow pacifists were pursuing a self-defeating course. As he put it, "the whole atmosphere of present-day utopian literature tastes mawkish and dishwatery to people who still keep a sense for life's bitter flavors. It suggests, in truth, ubiquitous inferiority." Thus, the way to peace that James recommended was not one that would reject the so-called martial virtues, such as discipline, courage, and dedication of the individual to service on behalf of his country; rather such virtues would be mobilized for peaceful ends rather than warlike ends.

Perhaps because James's proposal for developing a "moral equivalent of War" led to no immediate, tangible results, but instead was all but forgotten with the outbreak of World War I, many writers after James tended to scoff at his ideas as being woefully naive. . . . What [those] who have treated James as a simpleton ignore, however, is that James was describing not merely a means of reducing the probability of war through reducing its appeal, but also a means of attracting more societal energies and resources to programs for human improvement. The Civilian Conservation Corps of the 1930's, and more recent programs such as the Peace Corps, the Job Corps, and VISTA, all correspond closely to governmental activities that James recommended—activities justified for their own sake, but with the added feature that they provided a means other than military service for mobilizing and channeling the latent desire of many persons—especially young people—to find challenge and social commitment in their lives. The groups of young people working with Ralph Nader to illuminate and correct a variety of social ills—

"Nader's Raiders"—are non-governmental examples of what James had in mind.

One must not shy away from the political as well as the social and economic implications of programs designed to effect a long-range and enduring approach to peace. Neither a "moral equivalent of war" . . . nor "a better invention" for resolving international conflicts . . . will be implemented merely through proselytising on behalf of the cause of peace. Efforts to effect major transformation of social, economic, or political systems—which surely is implicit if the long-range objectives are to be realized—will be resisted by those whose positions of privilege or power are threatened by change. What is required, therefore, is the design of political strategies that will cope successfully with the resistance that must be anticipated.

To argue that success in the design and implementation of long-range approaches to peace can be attained only through political struggle is not to argue for turning to violence as a means of transforming existing systems. Romantic visions of utopian futures can become present nightmares if mindless violence is turned loose under the banner of eradicating evil or under any other banner. Too much nightmarish violence in the past has been perpetrated in the name of "peace" and "justice"—some of it by those who would overthrow a government believed to be evil or purge it of leaders believed to be corrupt or misguided. . . .; some of it by governments purporting to uphold the law and quell dangerous subversion. . . . Unless past calamities are to be repeated perhaps with even more disastrous effects—those who would build a better world must acknowledge not only the importance of the problem but also the possible consequences of poorly designed "solutions." Thoughtful and creative analysis as well as dedicated commitment to peace are needed.